Survival for a Small Planet

Survival for a Small Planet

The Sustainable Development Agenda

Edited by
Tom Bigg

International
Institute for
Environment and
Development

London • Sterling, VA

First published by Earthscan in the UK and USA in 2004

Copyright © The International Institute for Environment and Development, 2004

ISBN: 1-84407-077-8 paperback
      1-84407-076-X hardback

Typesetting by MapSet Ltd, Gateshead, UK
Printed and bound by Creative Print and Design (Wales), Ebbw Vale
Cover design by Declan Buckley

For a full list of publications please contact:

Earthscan
8–12 Camden High Street
London, NW1 0JH, UK
Tel: +44 (0)20 7387 8558
Fax: +44 (0)20 7387 8998
Email: earthinfo@earthscan.co.uk
Web: **www.earthscan.co.uk**

22883 Quicksilver Drive, Sterling, VA 20166-2012, USA

Earthscan publishes in association with WWF-UK and the International Institute for
Environment and Development

A catalogue record for this book is available from the British Library

Library of Congress Cataloging-in-Publication Data

Survival for a small planet : the sustainable development agenda / edited by Tom Bigg.
    p. cm.
Includes bibliographical references and index.
   ISBN 1-84407-077-8 (pbk.) – ISBN 1-84407-076-X (hardback)
  1. Sustainable development. I. Bigg, Tom.
   HD75.6.S856 2004
   338.9'27--dc22

                                               2003018295

This book is printed on elemental chlorine-free paper

Contents

Part 1: Global Governance

Part 2: National and Local Governance

Part 3: Equity and Sustainable Development – Towards New Ways of Working?

Part 4: Poverty Reduction and Natural Resource Management

Part 5: Markets and Sustainable Development

List of Tables, Figures and Boxes

Tables

Figures

Boxes

List of Contributors

Maria Adebowale is the founder and director of the new non-governmental organization (NGO) Capacity Global, working on community participation, poverty, environment and human rights issues at local, national and international levels. She is a commissioner of the UK Sustainable Development Commission. She is a trustee of One World Trust, and is also a research fellow at the University of Westminster, Centre for Sustainable Development.

Tariq Banuri is senior research director at the Stockholm Environment Institute (SEI), Boston. His work has focused on conceptual as well as practical issues in sustainable development – including the analysis of macroeconomic and trade policies, institutions, governance, legal systems, and community development. He is a leading member of two of the largest professional networks in this area: the Intergovernmental Panel on Climate Change (IPCC), in which he is a convening lead author; and IUCN – the World Conservation Union, where he is the elected chair of the Commission on Environmental, Economic and Social Policy (CEESP).

Stephen Bass was the International Institute of Environment and Development's (IIED) director of programmes until September 2003. He specializes in participatory environmental and forest policy, having started his career with IUCN as adviser to the ground-breaking national conservation strategy processes in Nepal and Zambia. He also has considerable experience in institutional development in forestry and environment in many countries, principally in southern Asia, the Caribbean and southern Africa. He was previously IIED's director of forestry and land use, and received the Queen's Award for outstanding achievement in forestry in 2001.

Keith Bezanson is director of the Institute of Development Studies at the University of Sussex, Brighton, UK. Previously, Dr Bezanson has been Canada's ambassador to Peru and Bolivia; manager of the administrative department at the Inter-American Development Bank in Washington; and president of the International Development Research Centre (IDRC) in Canada.

Tom Bigg is senior research associate for Global Governance at IIED. A particular focus for his work was the World Summit on Sustainable Development, held in Johannesburg in August–September 2002. Prior to this, he worked for over seven years with the United Nations Environment and Development UK Committee (UNED-UK). Tom recently completed a PhD in

Sociology at City University, London, and has written and edited a number of publications on sustainable development.

Roberto Bissio is the coordinator of Social Watch, a network with member NGO coalitions in over 50 countries that monitor implementation of the Copenhagen and Beijing commitments. Roberto is a member of the Third World Network's international committee and of the civil society advisory group to the UNDP administrator. He was the founder and first director of the Instituto del Tercer Mundo, a non-profit research, publishing and advocacy centre based in Montevideo (www.item.org.uy).

Nicola Borregaard is executive director at Recursos e Investigación para el Desarollo Sustenable, a Chilean research institute. She holds a PhD in land economy from Cambridge University, UK. She has worked as head of the Department for Environmental Economics at the Chilean National Commission on Environment, as executive director of the Center on Environmental Research and Planning, CIPMA, as a researcher and consultant for international and national agencies, and as a lecturer in Chile and in Germany.

Chris Church has been co-chair of the Northern Alliance for Sustainability (ANPED) for five years. He works in the UK as an adviser on sustainable development at the local and community level to the UK Community Development Foundation and to many other organizations. He is a co-founder of the UK Environmental Justice Network and works extensively on poverty, health and environment issues. He is also a member of the European EcoForum Coordinating Board and from 1998 to 2000 he was special NGO adviser to the TACIS Environmental Awareness Programme. He has worked on numerous projects in Eastern Europe. For more information see www.suscom.org.

Barry Dalal-Clayton has extensive experience in sustainable development planning and policy assessment, natural resource management, environmental assessment, soil survey, tropical rural development and agriculture. Dr Dalal-Clayton is currently director for strategies, planning and assessment at IIED, concentrating on broad issues of sustainable development. He has directed research on the environmental assessment of the development projects, programmes and policies of aid agencies and has been involved in a range of major project feasibility and appraisal studies. In addition, he has been deeply involved in analysing approaches to national sustainable development strategies and environmental action plans, and in assisting governments in the development and implementation of such strategies.

Luke Danielson was the project director of the Mining, Minerals and Sustainable Development project at IIED. Prior to this he was the director of the Mining Policy Research Initiative, a project of the International Development Research Centre in Montevideo, Uruguay. The Mining Policy Research Initiative exists to promote research into the role of mining in balances and sustainable development of Latin American and Caribbean communities.

Mr Danielson was with IDRC between September 1998 and March 2000. Prior to that, he was a faculty member at the University of Chile Faculty of Law. He has also served as Latin American programmes consultant to the Tulane Institute for Environmental Law and Policy at Tulane University Law School in New Orleans, Louisiana, US. Mr Danielson also has considerable experience in analysis of energy projects of various types, including hydroelectric, solar thermal, nuclear, wind, coal, and other types of projects.

Mark Halle is director for trade and investment for the International Institute for Sustainable Development. He was previously director for global policy at IUCN – The World Conservation Union, and has worked with the World Wildlife Fund and the United Nations Environment Programme. He founded the International Centre for Trade and Sustainable Development in 1996 and was the first chairman of the board. Mr Halle lives in Geneva, Switzerland.

Saleemul Huq founded the Bangladesh Centre for Advanced Studies, the major non-government research and policy institute working on environment- and development-related issues in Bangladesh. He was also awarded the Robert McNamara Fellowship from the World Bank (1986–1987) and Duggan Fellowship (1989) from the Natural Resources Defence Council (NRDC), US. As one of the leading environmental planners at the national and international level, he has worked for numerous international agencies and advised national government planners on global environmental issues. He currently runs IIED's Climate Change Programme and is an adviser to UNDP's Capacity 21 Programme where he has helped develop the Agenda 21 programmes in Mongolia, Bhutan, Gambia and Kazakhstan.

Nazneen Kanji joined IIED in May 2000 to develop a 'Participation and Livelihoods' research programme. She is currently involved in a research project on the policy influence of NGOs on land reform in sub-Saharan Africa. She has been involved in social development research, programming, consultancy, teaching and training for the past 20 years. Her research has focused on the impact of economic and social policy change at the household level and on policy-oriented participatory poverty research. She has worked as a social development consultant for the UK Department for International Development (DFID), the Swedish International Development Cooperation Agency (SIDA), NORAD, Swiss Development Corporation and for international NGOs. She has also been involved with gender training in a number of countries, particularly in east and southern Africa.

Paul Kapelus is a founding director of the African Institute of Corporate Citizenship. He has a masters degree in social anthropology (Sussex University, UK). He has 12 years' experience in the field of corporate citizenship and has worked throughout Southern Africa on corporate social responsibility projects and programmes. Paul is a member of the Global Reporting Initiative (GRI) Stakeholder Council, and on the AccountAbility Council.

Shaheen Rafi Khan, a research fellow at SDPI, earned his PhD in economics from Columbia University in the US. He joined SDPI in 1997 as consultant to the resident secretariat of the IUCN Commission on Environmental, Economic and Social Policy (CEESP). Dr Khan's research covers water resource management, deforestation, biodiversity conservation, climate change and trade and environment. A cross-sector focus of his work has been on the poverty and equity aspects of environmental management.

Damian Killeen is director of The Poverty Alliance in Scotland (www.povertyalliance.org) and chair of the UK Coalition Against Poverty. Damian represented Scottish 'social justice' organizations at the Johannesburg Summit and currently convenes the Future Scotland initiative of the Scottish Civic Forum that seeks to create opportunities for the general public to understand and activate their role in promoting sustainable development.

Marianne Kjellén is a researcher at SEI and a doctoral student at the Department of Human Geography, University of Stockholm. At SEI she has coordinated studies of urban environment and health in cities in developing countries, and overviews of health and environment linkages. Environment and health issues, as well as issues of urban water and sanitation have been studied particularly in the context of poverty. Her present research focuses on the privatization and informalization of water provisioning in Dar es Salaam, Tanzania.

Izabella Koziell is currently working as environment adviser for DFID Kenya, managing an environmental governance programme. She previously coordinated the Biodiversity and Livelihoods Group at IIED, during which time she conducted some innovative policy research on biodiversity and poverty.

James Mayers is director of the Forestry and Land Use Programme at IIED. He has worked on forestry, conservation and rural development issues for 15 years, with experience principally in west, south and east Africa, south Asia and Melanesia. This work has emphasized analysis of policy, institutions and planning, and participatory approaches for research and management. He is currently managing a number of IIED's projects focusing on forestry. He is the lead author of several books: *Policy That Works for Forests and People, Forestry Tactics* (Malawi), *Raising the Stakes* (South Africa) and *Company–Community Forestry Partnerships*; and co-author of the *Sustainable Forestry Handbook*.

Gordon McGranahan is currently director of the Human Settlements Programme at the IIED. Trained as an economist, he spent the 1990s at SEI, where he directed their Urban Environment Programme and coordinated an international study of local environment and health problems in low and middle income cities. He has published widely on urban environmental issues, and was the lead author of *The Citizens at Risk: From Urban Sanitation to Sustainable Cities* (Earthscan, 2001) and co-editor of *Air Pollution and Health in Rapidly Developing Countries* (Earthscan, 2003).

Jeffrey A McNeely is chief scientist at IUCN in Gland, Switzerland, where he has worked since 1980. Prior to joining IUCN, he worked in Asia for 12 years on a range of biodiversity-related topics. Author or editor of over 30 books, he sits on the editorial board of seven international journals. His latest book is *Ecoagriculture: Strategies to Feed the World and Save Wild Biodiversity* (with Sara J Scherr, Island Press, 2003).

Charles McNeill is the manager of the Environment Programme Team within the United Nations Development Programme and in that capacity he oversees the development, resource mobilization and implementation of UNDP's Environment Global Programme and its Thematic Trust Fund. Dr McNeill is also responsible for UNDP's programme on biodiversity conservation and poverty reduction, and UNDP's participation in the Convention on Biological Diversity. He oversees UNDP's work on the Equator Initiative, a multi-partner effort to identify and disseminate information about, and build capacity for, successful community initiatives in the equatorial belt to reduce poverty through the protection and wise use of biodiversity.

Kalyani Menon-Sen is a member of JAGORI, a Women's Resource Centre in Delhi, India. She has 20 years of experience as an activist, researcher and trainer on issues of women's rights and gender equality. She has been associated with UNDP India, where her work focuses on the gender impacts of macroeconomic policies.

Liliana Miranda is the national executive secretary for Foro Ciudades Para la Vida (Cities for Life), as well as the president of the Ecociudad Association. She is a visiting professor at three universities, where she lectures at masters level in urban environmental management, as well as an independent consultant with various international organizations. Miranda was also the official civic society (FCPV network) representative to the National Commission and Executive Commission for Rio +10.

Adil Najam is an associate professor of international negotiation and diplomacy at the Fletcher School of Law and Diplomacy, Tufts University, US. He also serves as a visiting fellow at the Sustainable Development Policy Institute (SDPI), Pakistan, and serves on the boards of the Pakistan Institute for Environment–Development Action Research (PIEDAR); the Center for Global Studies, University of Victoria, Canada; the Pardee Center for the Study of the Longer-Range Future, Boston University; and the Pakistan Center for Trade and Sustainable Development. He teaches and has published widely in the areas of sustainable development, global governance, environmental negotiation, and development politics. His recent books include a seven-volume book series on civic entrepreneurship (with Tariq Banuri, 2002) and an edited book *Environment, Development and Human Security* (2003).

Beatrice Nduta Kairie works with the Environment Liaison Centre International in Nairobi, Kenya.

Yelena Panina works with Eco-Pravo Kyiv, an independent environmental law NGO in Ukraine, which aims to protect the environment, not by means of public action and pressure on governmental authorities, but by means of environmental enforcement against violators of environmental legislation.

Jan Pronk was minister for development cooperation in the Den Uyl government of the Netherlands from 1973 to 1977. From 1980 to 1985 he was deputy secretary-general of UNCTAD and from 1985 to 1986 assistant secretary-general of the United Nations. He was first deputy chairman of the Labour Party from 1986 to 1989. Jan Pronk has been secretary to the Mansholt Committee, a member of the editorial boards of the *International Spectator, Wending* and *Socialisme en Democratie* and treasurer of the Brandt Commission.

Re-appointed as minister for development cooperation in the Lubbers government in 1989, Jan Pronk received the appointment for a third time in the first Kok government in 1994. In 1998 he was appointed minister of housing, spatial planning and the environment in the second Kok government. He was UN secretary-general Kofi Annan's special envoy for the 2002 World Summit on Sustainable Development. He is presently the chair of IIED.

Dilys Roe is a senior research associate at IIED where she works on tourism and on biodiversity. She is a member of the tri-partite 'Pro-Poor Tourism Partnership' with ODI and ICRT – a research group which launched the concept of pro-poor tourism in 1999 and continues work on this issue (see www.propoortourism.org.uk for more details).

David Satterthwaite is senior fellow of the IIED Human Settlements Programme and editor of the international journal *Environment and Urbanization*. He also teaches at the University of London and the London School of Economics (LSE). A development planner by training, he has been working at IIED on issues relating to housing and the urban environment since 1974. Recent publications include *Environmental Problems in an Urbanizing World* (with Jorge E Hardoy and Diana Mitlin) and the *Earthscan Reader on Sustainable Cities* (editor). He has advised various agencies on urban environmental issues, including the Brundtland Commission, the World Health Organization (WHO), UNICEF, the United Nations Human Settlements Programme (UN-Habitat), DFID and SIDA, and is currently serving as one of the lead authors in the chapter on human settlements for the Intergovernmental Panel on Climate Change.

Sara J Scherr currently focuses on policies to reduce poverty and restore ecosystems through markets for sustainably grown forest products and ecosystem services; policies to promote ecoagriculture; and development of local institutions for natural resource management. She is senior policy analyst at Forest Trends, an NGO that promotes forest conservation through improved markets for forest products and ecosystem services, and director of Ecoagriculture Partners, an international partnership to promote increased productivity jointly with enhanced natural biodiversity and ecosystem services in agricultural landscapes. She also serves as a member of the United Nations Millennium Project Task Force on Hunger. She received her MSc and PhD in international economics and development at Cornell University, New York. She has published numerous papers and ten books; her most recent being *Ecoagriculture: Strategies to Feed the World and Save Wild Biodiversity* (with Jeff McNeely, Island Press, 2003).

Charles Secrett was director of Friends of the Earth (FOE UK) from 1993 to 2003. He frequently appears on national TV and radio news and current affairs programmes, and has written extensively on a wide range of environmental topics. He was a member of the UK Round Table on Sustainable Development and chair of its transport sub-group, which was responsible for its influential report 'Defining a Sustainable Transport Sector' (1996). Charles sits on the advisory council of the Environmental Law Foundation, and on the advisory board of *The Ecologist* magazine. He has recently joined the board of the Carolina Environment Programme, at the University of North Carolina. He regularly speaks at public meetings organized by local environmental campaigners around the country, and enjoys working with community groups.

Youba Sokona is executive secretary for international relations and co-ordinator of the Energy Programme of the organization Environnement et Développement du Tiers Monde (ENDA-TM) based in Dakar in Sénégal. He has wide experience of energy, environment and development issues in Africa. Dr Sokona participated in many international negotiations and follow-ups from the Rio process and related conventions, including climate change, desertification, and biodiversity. He is often solicited by governments in Africa and organizations such as the World Bank and UNDP to serve as a steering committee member of their programmes, to conduct programme evaluation missions, to chair sessions at high-level conferences, and to contribute scientific papers. Throughout his career, he has also had the privilege of serving in various advisory capacities to many African governments and organizations. He has published many articles on energy, environment and development issues of interest in Africa.

Dr Cecilia Tacoli is responsible for IIED's rural–urban interactions and livelihoods strategies project jointly promoted by the Human Settlements and the Sustainable Agriculture programmes. The project involves collaborative research in Africa, Asia and Latin America on a series of issues related to this topic. Cecilia has advised international agencies (such as UN-Habitat and the World Bank) and bilateral donor agencies (such as DFID, DANIDA) on emerging issues in rural–urban interactions, and ways to incorporate them in their activities.

Simon Upton is chairman of the Round Table on Sustainable Development at the Organisation for Economic Co-operation and Development (OECD). Prior to that he was New Zealand's minister for the environment, in which capacity he chaired the seventh Session of the Commission on Sustainable Development. He is a board member of the International Research Institute for Climate

Prediction at Columbia University's Earth Institute and contributes to a wide range of public policy fora.

Penny Urquhart is an environmental consultant whose central focus is poverty eradication. Her work on community-based ecotourism and sustainable tourism has included grass-roots work with communities on the west coast of South Africa, co-ordinating IIED's Stimulating Sustainable Tourism Project in South Africa, and participatory multi-stakeholder work around South Africa's protected areas to ensure that tourism development benefits the poor. Penny was the lead researcher on South Africa's 2002 review of progress towards sustainable development. She has written guidelines for the planning of community ecotourism processes and is the author of books on sustainable development planning at the local level and environmental considerations of low-cost housing.

Boris Vasylkivsky works with Eco-Pravo Kyiv, an independent environmental law NGO in Ukraine, which aims to protect the environment, not by means of public actions and pressure on governmental authorities, but by means of environmental enforcement against violators of environmental legislation.

Luz Stella Velasquez is with the Institute of Environmental Studies (IDEA) which is part of the Faculty of Architecture, Universidad Nacional, Manizales, Colombia.

Sonja Vermeulen is a research associate in the Forestry and Land Use Programme at IIED. Her current areas of work include development of policy tools for marginalized managers of natural resources, practical approaches for equitable valuation of biodiversity, and action research towards sustainable land use and forest management in Southeast Asia.

Bill Vorley joined IIED's Sustainable Agriculture and Rural Livelihoods Programme in November 1999 to run the Policies that Work for Sustainable Agriculture and Regenerated Rural Economies Project. He previously worked at the Institute for Agriculture and Trade Policy in Minnesota, US. He has a wide experience of trade and agriculture issues, and an insider's knowledge of the agribusiness industry, about which he has written extensively. Bill also works on the SARL Programme's Marketing Sustainable Agriculture Project.

Halina Ward is director of IIED's Corporate Social Responsibility for Environment and Development Programme. She leads a programme of action-oriented research and capacity building that aims to bring developing country stakeholder perspectives into the international corporate responsibility agenda. Before joining IIED she was a senior research fellow in corporate responsibility with the Royal Institute of International Affairs. She has also practised commercial environment law as a solicitor and worked for the company ERM.

Foreword

Our generation will probably be among the last that will have the opportunity to make fundamental choices about the future of our people and our planet. And the World Summit on Sustainable Development (WSSD), which took place in Johannesburg in 2002, was one of those key decision-making moments.

But the work begun at WSSD is not over. We must continue to push for achievement of the central Millennium Development Goal – to halve levels of poverty by 2015. Poverty is more than lack of income – it is about access to health care, education, productive assets and secure livelihoods. Future generations will judge us on whether we were able to rise above our national and sectoral interests to work together to achieve these goals. If we fail, and continue on our current trajectory, a combination of ill health and disease, conflict over resources, migration, underdevelopment, environmental degradation and poverty will continue to undermine prospects for global prosperity and political and social stability.

This book provides an authoritative and extensive picture of the policy challenges that confront us, presenting the analysis and ideas of key sustainable development thinkers. In addition, many of the papers produced by civil society organizations for the Johannesburg Summit have been collected and made available here on CD-ROM. Thanks to the International Institute for Environment and Development (IIED), this anthology is as comprehensive as possible in recording the many, various and inspiring civil society contributions to WSSD.

Agenda 21 and the Rio Principles are, by common consent, as valid today as when we negotiated them in 1992. The Rio Summit changed the way we operate at global, regional, national and local levels by placing the concept of sustainable development firmly on the agenda. The Johannesburg Summit provided a renewed commitment to the implementation of the Rio agreements and set a series of targets towards which all nations of the world need to strive. As the title of this book suggests, the future of our planet is at stake.

Despite leaps forward in technological development and economic growth, the last decade has seen an extra 10 million people each year joining the ranks of the very poor. For some 1 billion people – in Africa, Asia, Latin America, and also in those expanding pockets of poverty in Northern countries – sustainable development remains a distant dream. The gap between the rich and poor, wherever they are, grows ever wider.

The Millennium Declaration has set targets for the eradication of poverty and other key development goals. The World Summit elaborated mechanisms and strategies for achieving these targets – particularly through partnerships involving different constituencies, skills and resources. South Africa acknowledges that governments alone cannot achieve the programmes and outputs called for at WSSD and described in this book. Sustainable development requires the mobilization of civil society, governments, inter-governmental bodies and the business sector to strengthen commitment and enhance delivery. WSSD was a major step forward in initiating both dialogue and joint action. Real partnerships for sustainable development will require a shift in power relations. We should work towards the establishment of an equitable, stable and balanced global economic system, with sustainable systems of production and consumption.

South Africa is advancing an economic platform for development that must include meaningful access for developing countries to markets of the North, including access for agricultural products, textiles and value-added natural products; increasing investment for developing economies; the deepening and extension of the debt relief programme to other developing countries; and technology development, transfer and knowledge sharing. Issues of access to markets, finance, investment, and technology should be seen as integral prerequisites for poverty alleviation that require concerted efforts at national and international levels.

What we need from global leaders and stakeholders in the years following WSSD is a genuine commitment to the implementation of agreed policies and programmes that can overcome the obstacle of non-delivery since Rio. The potential is there for us to realize the vision of an equitable and prosperous society in balance with the resources and ecosystems of our planet. I believe that this book can help us to make real progress towards that goal.

Mohammed Valli Moosa
Minister of Environmental Affairs and Tourism
South Africa

List of Acronyms and Abbreviations

ABTA	Association of British Travel Agents
AENP	Addo Elephant National Park (South Africa)
ANPED	Northern Alliance for Sustainability
APEC	Asia Pacific Economic Co-operation
ASM	artisanal and small-scale mining
BCAS	Bangladesh Centre for Advanced Studies
CAMMA	Mining Ministers of the Americas Conference
CAP	Common Agricultural Policy (EU)
CBD	Convention on Biological Diversity (UN)
CBNRM	community-based natural resource management
CCD	Convention to Combat Desertification (UN)
CDF	Comprehensive Development Framework
CDM	Clean Development Mechanism
CEDHA	Centro de Derechos Humanos y Medio Ambiente
CEO	chief executive officer
CGIAR	Consultative Group on International Agricultural Research
CICOL	Central Intercomunal Campesina del Oriente de Lomerio
CIPAF	Centro de Investigación para la Acción Feminina
CITES	Convention on International Trade in Endangered Species of Wild Fauna and Flora (UN)
CMH	Commission on Macroeconomics and Health
COP	Conferences of the Parties
CRT	Centre for Responsible Tourism
CSD	Commission on Sustainable Development (UN)
CSR	corporate social responsibility
CTD	Committee on Trade and Development (WTO)
CTE	Committee on Trade and Environment (WTO)
DAC	Development Assistance Committee (OECD)
DALYs	disability adjusted life years
DFID	Department for International Development (UK)
DSM	demand-side management
ECHR	European Convention on Human Rights
ECOSOC	Economic and Social Council (UN)
EIA	environmental impact assessment
ELCI	Environment Liaison Centre International
EMS	environmental management systems
ENDA-TM	Environnement et Développement du Tiers Monde
EPA	Environmental Protection Agency (US)

ESM	environmental space method
FAO	Food and Agriculture Organization (UN)
FCCC	Framework Convention on Climate Change (UN)
FDC	Forest Development Corporation (Pakistan)
FfD	United Nations International Conference on Financing for Development
FOEI	Friends of the Earth International
FSC	Forest Stewardship Council
G7	Group of 7 leading industrialized countries
G77	Group of 77 developing countries (now with 133 members)
GATS	General Agreement on Trade in Services
GATT	General Agreement on Tariffs and Trade
GDP	gross domestic product
GEF	Global Environment Facility
GEPA	Global Environmental Protection Agency
GEO	*Global Environment Outlook* (UNEP)
GMOs	genetically modified organisms
GNP	gross national product
GPF	Global People's Forum
GPGs	global public goods
GRI	Global Reporting Initiative
GWP	Global Water Partnership
HDR	*Human Development Report* (UNDP)
HIPC	heavily indebted poor countries
ICEM	International Federation of Chemical, Energy, Mine and General Workers' Unions
ICLEI	International Council for Local Environmental Initiatives
ICMM	International Council on Mining and Metals
ICRAF	International Centre for Research in Agroforestry
ICTSD	International Centre for Trade and Sustainable Development
IDRC	International Development Research Centre
IDTs	international development targets
IFIs	international financial institutions
IFPRI	International Food Policy Research Institute
IHEI	International Hotels Environment Initiative
IIED	International Institute for Environment and Development
IISD	International Institute for Sustainable Development
ILO	International Labour Organization (UN)
IMF	International Monetary Fund
IOM	International Organization for Migration
IPCC	Intergovernmental Panel on Climate Change
IPF	Inter-governmental Panel on Forests
IPRs	intellectual property rights
ITTO	International Tropical Timber Organization
IUFRO	International Union of Forest Research Organizations
IUCN	World Conservation Union
IWRM	integrated water resource management

JPOI	Johannesburg Plan of Implementation
KYWS	Kalkot Youth Welfare Society (Pakistan)
LA21	Local Agenda 21
LDCs	least developed countries
MAFF	Ministry of Agriculture, Fisheries and Food (UK)
MAI	Multilateral Agreement on Investment
MDBs	multilateral development banks
MDGs	Millennium Development Goals
MEAs	multilateral environmental agreements
MES	markets for environmental services
MMSD	Mining, Minerals and Sustainable Development project
MRE	monitoring, recording and evaluation
MSC	Marine Stewardship Council
NAFTA	North American Free Trade Agreement
NCS	National Conservation Strategy
NEAP	national environmental action plan
NEPAD	New Partnership for Africa's Development
NFP	National Forest Programme
NGO	non-governmental organization
NSDS	national sustainable development strategy
NWFP	North West Frontier Province (Pakistan)
ODA	Official Development Assistance
ODI	Overseas Development Institute
OECD	Organisation for Economic Co-operation and Development
PC&I	principles, criteria and indicators
PPP	public–private partnership
PPT	pro-poor tourism
PrepCom	Preparatory Committee meeting
PRSP	Poverty Reduction Strategy Paper
PSP	private sector participation
RIDES	Recursos e Investigación para el Desarollo Sustenable (Chile)
Ring	Regional and International Networking Group
SANP	South African National Parks Board
SARL	sustainable agriculture and rural livelihoods
SD	sustainable development
SDIN	Sustainable Development Issues Network
SDPI	Sustainable Development Policy Institute (Pakistan)
SEI	Stockholm Environment Institute
SERI	Socio-Economic and Environmental Research Institute
SEWA	Self-Employed Women's Association
SFM	sustainable forest management
SHD	sustainable human development
SIDS	small island developing states
SMEs	small and medium-sized enterprises
TFAP	Tropical Forest Action Plan
TNC	transnational corporation
TRIPs	Trade-Related Intellectual Property Rights Agreement

TVE	Television Trust for the Environment
UN	United Nations
UNCED	United Nations Conference on Environment and Development (Rio de Janeiro, 1992)
UNCHE	United Nations Conference on the Human Environment (Stockholm, 1972)
UNCHR	United Nations Commission on Human Rights
UNCTAD	United Nations Centre for Trade and Development
UNDESA	United Nations Department for Economic and Social Affairs
UNDP	United Nations Development Programme
UNECE	United Nations Economic Commission for Europe
UNEP	United Nations Environment Programme
UNESCO	United Nations Educational, Scientific and Cultural Organization
UNF	United Nations Foundation
UNFF	United Nations Forum on Forests
UNFPA	United Nations Population Fund
UNGA	United Nations General Assembly
UNHCHR	United Nations High Commissioner for Human Rights
UNICEF	United Nations Children's Fund
USCR	United States Committee for Refugees
USDA	United States Department of Agriculture
VISTA	Vision for Industry in Sustainable Tourism Action
WBCSD	World Business Council for Sustainable Development
WCD	World Commission on Dams
WEF	World Economic Forum
WEHAB	water, energy, health, agriculture, biodiversity (priorities for the Summit proposed by Secretary-General Kofi Annan)
WFP	World Food Programme (UN)
WHO	World Health Organization (UN)
WRI	World Resources Institute
WSF	World Social Forum
WSSD	World Summit on Sustainable Development (Johannesburg, 2002)
WTO	World Trade Organization
WTTC	World Travel and Tourism Council
WuI	Wuppertal Institute
WWC	World Water Council
WWF	World Wide Fund for Nature

Acknowledgements

Earlier versions of a number of the chapters in this volume were prepared for the World Summit on Sustainable Development (WSSD). Thanks to all of the authors for sharing their ideas and expertise at the various stages of this process. Work by IIED and the Ring in preparation for WSSD was made possible by support from the Swedish International Development Co-operation Agency (Sida), the Royal Danish Ministry of Foreign Affairs (Danida), and the Norwegian Agency for Development Co-operation (NORAD).

Nigel Cross, Steve Bass and Lilian Chatterjee were all heavily involved in IIED's WSSD work and in getting this material together. The Ring network has also been central to this exercise, and we are very grateful to all Ring members and to the network coordinator Viv Davies for their help. Trine Nielsen did a great job chasing up authors and keeping on top of a complex project. And finally Olivia, Remus and Holden were always there when it all got too much.

Tom Bigg

About IIED

The International Institute for Environment and Development (IIED) is an independent, non-profit research institute working in the field of sustainable development. IIED aims to provide expertise and leadership in researching and achieving sustainable development at local, national, regional and global levels. In alliance with others we seek to help shape a future that ends global poverty and delivers and sustains efficient and equitable management of the world's natural resources.

About the Ring

The Regional and International Networking Group (Ring) is a global alliance of predominantly Southern independent research and policy organizations. It was formed in 1991 to stimulate preparations for the 1992 Rio Summit. There are now 15 Ring member organizations based in five continents. See www.ring-alliance.org

Part 1

Global Governance

Chapter 1

The World Summit on Sustainable Development: Was it Worthwhile?

Tom Bigg, IIED

When the progress from Johannesburg is reviewed in 2012, it will be critical to demonstrate that the people who live in poverty currently have significantly improved quality of life and economic opportunities, and that the next generation will live in a safer and more healthy environment (South African Government, 2002).

The World Summit on Sustainable Development (WSSD) took place from late August to early September in 2002 in Johannesburg. The events held during this period went far beyond the official inter-governmental negotiations at the Sandton Convention Centre. Events included: a ten-day International Science Forum; the People's Earth Summit; a full calendar of meetings at the World Conservation Union (IUCN) Environment Centre; a gathering of landless peoples from Africa and the world; the Global People's Forum at the NASREC venue; events and displays in the specially created Ubuntu Village; the Water Dome exhibition centre; major conferences organized by business, local government, legislators and parliamentarians; and a wealth of other activities. And beyond this, elsewhere in South Africa, an international conference on responsible tourism was held in Cape Town; the Children's Earth Summit took place in Soweto; and in Kimberley there was the Summit of Indigenous Peoples.

Each of these was a significant international event in its own right and generated numerous new commitments, ideas, alliances and activities. The events also allowed organizations to learn more about each other's work and take stock of what has happened in different parts of the world and at different levels of governance in the ten years since the UN Conference on Environment and Development (UNCED) in Rio.

What was the Significance of Johannesburg?

Compared to WSSD, UNCED was the soul of generosity. The ability of governments to work together to find solutions for global problems seems to be deteriorating at an alarming rate, even as the need for them to work together increases with increased globalization (Sharma et al, 2002).

[WSSD] put sustainable development at the centre of the international agenda. The world leaders representing governments, major groups, civil society and other stakeholders recommitted themselves to achieving the goal of sustainable development. Governments agreed to an impressive range of concrete commitments to action for promoting implementation of Agenda 21 and the Programme for the Further Implementation of Agenda 21. The summit also generated a variety of other outcomes, including partnerships for sustainable development. There is now a solid repertoire of commitments and ideas to turn the Rio vision into reality (UN Secretary-General, 2003).

In trying to make sense of the Johannesburg Summit, it is important first to acknowledge the diversity of activities and ways in which the significance of the event can be understood. Tariq Banuri has likened the 1992 Rio Summit experience to an evening at a multiplex cinema – you may have turned up at the same time as someone else, and been in the same building, but seen very different films. And the Johannesburg multiplex was showing a lot more movies than its predecessor.

Assessing what came out of WSSD therefore depends critically on your understanding of what the summit was about. If your focus is on the inter-governmental negotiations, then it is relatively easy to gauge its impact. A cursory glance first at the UN General Assembly terms of reference for WSSD from late 2000 and then at the summit outcomes reveals the chasm between expectations and results, even on the part of governments – and the gulf is still wider as far as many other commentators and activists are concerned. If your evaluation encompasses the diversity, dynamism, creativity, expertise and interaction of the broader web of activities listed above (as well, to be fair, as their occasional predictability, partiality and intransigence) then it is rather harder to reach a judgement.

This overlap is in itself significant. WSSD may well come to be seen as the last of the UN mega-summits, where success is measured by the number of participating heads of state and the conference is preceded by years of negotiation to arrive at a consensus text which reflects the common purpose of the international community. As we will explore in more detail below, the opportunity costs of this approach are becoming unacceptably high, while the returns from WSSD are overwhelmingly seen as unacceptably low. A further critical flaw of the Johannesburg process is that, while these exercises are intended to cement common purpose and set out the means for collaboration to achieve shared goals, two years of preparation merely served to emphasize the gaps between key countries and blocs and entrench their positions. And finally, the emphasis from governments and the UN on 'implementation of existing commitments' merely drew attention to the mismatch between the process behind a global summit and the action required to make a difference.

At the same time, WSSD may increasingly be seen as the coming of age of new ways of addressing sustainable development at the global level. Governments meeting in negotiation mode may have difficulty getting to grips with the challenges of 'implementation' but the same is not true of many of the civil society organizations meeting elsewhere in Johannesburg. The activities of non-governmental organizations (NGOs) at the Rio Summit in 1992 had focused predominantly on the official negotiations. While this was still true of many in the WSSD process, the locus seems to have shifted significantly towards a more decentralized understanding of where change comes from and the best use of such international gatherings.

Straddling this divide between the official process and concurrent civil society activities were the much-vaunted – and criticized – 'Type 2' partnerships, of which more is said below. Although contentious in the build-up to the summit and (undoubtedly) controversial in the aftermath, Johannesburg was almost like the eye of the storm – when attention moved to other, more immediately problematic, issues.

In part this was because, although the notion of collaboration (potentially) involving the private sector in delivery of sustainable development raised the spectre of 'greenwash' – by which multinationals could gain credibility while continuing their rapacious practices – in practice, hardly any of the officially recognized partnerships involved businesses. It was also in part because the atmosphere in Johannesburg was rather different from the hothouse climate of the preparatory meetings, and there were many more people present with a more pragmatic attitude towards alliances so long as they achieved desirable goals. Finally, it was in part because, in the positions taken by the US government (and its few supporters, such as the Australian government) on the summit agenda, most summit participants found a ready rallying point which made their differences with others seem less significant. Greenpeace and the World Business Council for Sustainable Development (WBCSD) made common cause in opposing US positions on climate change – which is a measure of the extent to which the US was beyond the pale for a large proportion of summit participants (Greenpeace/WBCSD, 2002).

What Did Governments Sign Up to in Johannesburg?

Heads of state go from summit to summit, while many of their people go from abyss to abyss (Venezuelan president Hugo Chavez).

The main official outcomes of the summit were a political statement and the WSSD Plan of Implementation. The former was prepared in President Mbeki's office, and was released halfway through the summit. It was not opened for negotiation, and was endorsed more out of courtesy to the hosts than because it contained significant text. Unlike the Rio Declaration, the Johannesburg Statement did not set out international principles which could be invoked in legal or political contexts, but served rather as a general philosophical contextualization of the more detailed commitments in the Plan of Implementation.

Plan of Implementation

The Plan of Implementation went through a tortuous process of negotiation, including near-collapse at the final preparatory meeting in Bali. It arrived at Johannesburg with many key issues still unresolved, and with a text well short of the initial intention to agree targets and timetables to help shape action to realize sustainable development (UNGA, 2000). It would be churlish to imply that the Plan of Implementation is worthless, as some have done. Although not much progress has been made in most key areas, there are significant new commitments which should be recognized. There are over 30 targets in the agreed text, though many of these are restatements of existing Millennium Development Goals (MDGs) or other previous agreements.

New targets and commitments

Significant new targets and commitments include:

- to halve the number of people without access to basic sanitation by 2015 (now incorporated in the system-wide UN range of activities on the MDGs);
- new measures to regulate toxic chemicals by 2008;
- a cautious commitment to restore fish stocks 'where possible' by 2015, together with new marine protected areas by 2012;
- an aim to achieve a 'significant reduction' in the current rate of species loss by 2010;
- moves to improve developing country access to alternatives to ozone-depleting substances; and
- some progress in establishing a stronger benefit-sharing regime under the Convention on Biological Diversity (CBD), which would give Southern countries stronger rights to a share of profits from 'bioprospecting' and 'biopatenting'.

While the time targets noted above are new, most of the goals stated are not. And the Johannesburg text says very little about how these aims will be realized or who will be responsible for their achievement. Without new funding commitments and clarity on responsibilities it is difficult to see how they will be acted upon effectively.

Corporate accountability

Many NGOs focused attention on the negative roles played by the private sector, and particularly by multinational companies. This included a broad coalition in support of what Friends of the Earth termed 'a binding framework to secure the accountability of corporations to citizens and communities'. Elements of this campaign included 'establishing effective international and national law on corporate accountability, liability and reporting' and 'effective sanctions and citizen and community rights to consultation, legal challenge and redress over environmentally and socially damaging corporate activities' (FOEI, 2002).

Perhaps spurred by corporate scandals involving Arthur Andersen, WorldCom and Enron, a broad coalition of governments from the EU and many G77 countries were willing to push for new mandatory standards for corporate accountability. The US and others resisted this as far as possible, but the final text agreed does call for 'active promotion' of corporate accountability – although the US insisted that this should apply only to existing agreements rather than to new ones, in an effort to limit its legal significance. Even so, this does represent a significant new basis on which to build stronger, binding standards for global companies.

Social and economic aspects

It was evident at WSSD that the social and economic aspects of sustainable development are much better integrated with environmental goals than was the case at the Rio Summit – though this did not translate into significant new agreements. The eradication of poverty is now seen as an underlying theme in all work on sustainable development. This must in part be credited to the UN Commission on Sustainable Development (CSD), which from 1998 to 2001 addressed ways in which this policy integration could be achieved. Although commitments to specific measures to tackle poverty were not agreed at Johannesburg, at least the groundwork has been done so that future global attention to sustainable development will have to address issues of poverty – and perhaps even lead to real change if the political circumstances are right.

Globalization

The Johannesburg Summit also showed that globalization has emerged as a priority in its own right, increasingly understood as distinct from the duties and aspirations of states. There were various indications that a consensus is emerging. This will see countries collaborating to address problems of globalization that require collective action and stepping up the regulation that could fetter global capitalism if democratically agreed and applied. Predictably, the US was out of step with these developments and (largely as a result) they are not clearly reflected in the agreed text. Two WSSD debates illustrate the divisions which exist on issues of global governance and globalization:

Trade

It was hoped by many that WSSD would be able to agree a framework for sustainable development governance which would encompass global trade. Given the participation of all countries in the negotiations and the more equitable ways of working of the UN, this might really come to influence the World Trade Organization (WTO) in the ongoing Doha negotiations. However, the US was persistent in arguing that multilateral environmental agreements (MEAs) should conform to WTO rules. There was a real danger that the message coming from Johannesburg would be that environmental policy should be subservient to economic policy. Indeed, the EU was prepared to go along with this position and it was only avoided when an impromptu coalition of countries – notably Ethiopia, Norway and Switzerland – raised eleventh-hour objections. Although this dramatic resistance was widely celebrated (not least by the relieved countries of the EU) the text did no more than maintain the existing lack of clarity on the issue, which was hardly a cause for major rejoicing.

The Precautionary Principle

Principle 15 of the Rio Declaration states that:

> *Where there are threats of serious or irreversible damage, lack of full scientific certainty shall not be used as a reason for postponing cost-effective measures to prevent environmental degradation.*

The principle has been invoked in a number of trade disputes, most notably over genetically modified organisms. In the WSSD process the US consistently argued for scientific certainty as one of the principal goals of sustainable development policy (at one point even citing the Intergovernmental Panel on Climate Change – IPCC – as a positive example, despite the history of run-ins between the US government and the IPCC). The US and Japan wanted a weaker reference to 'the precautionary approach', while the EU pushed for endorsement of the Rio terminology. Not surprisingly, the principle was not restated – although there was a more general reference to the continued relevance of the Rio Principles as a whole.

Renewable energy

There were concerted efforts, notably by the EU and others including Brazil, to agree targets for a proportional increase in the use of renewable energy. However, the combined efforts of the US, Australia, Canada, Japan and the major oil producing countries of the G77 proved too much to overcome. The same opposition halted agreement on steps to phase out export credit and other subsidies for fossil fuels. The final text includes a vague reference to the need for 'a sense of urgency' on the issue of renewable energy. In response to this setback, Brazil and the countries of the EU announced the creation of a 'coalition of the willing' involving over 30 countries interested in making progress on the renewables issues.

Human rights

Division also flared up over issues of human rights, including the tension between universal commitments to gender equality and practices common in certain traditional societies. The final text, however, does represent a welcome restatement of the importance of universal rights in this context. In addition, attempts were made through the summit process by a range of NGOs and some European countries to agree a stronger framework of procedural and substantive environmental rights (building on Principle 10 of the Rio Declaration). However, these were resisted by a number of governments which were not happy with the implications for domestic policy of these proposals (see Chapter 11 of this volume).

Sustainable development governance

One area in which WSSD really failed to grasp the nettle was sustainable development governance. Despite a two-year programme of work on international environmental governance initiated by the UN Environment Programme (UNEP) culminating in a ministerial meeting in Colombia in February 2002, and negotiations through the three WSSD PrepComs of 2002, the final text agreed does not go very far in addressing the inadequacies of the current institutional framework. The CSD has had some impact over its ten years of existence, but where it has really fallen short is in its inability to engage and call to account organizations responsible for economic policy and governance. It is now a truism of sustainable development that it requires shifts in established economic systems of incentives (economic subsidies, terms of trade, etc) and penalties (tariff barriers, technology costs, etc) if we are to improve the contexts in which progress towards social and environmental goals can be made. The decisions taken in Johannesburg fail to give any significant new impetus to this objective and put back the date when the international governance system comes to recognize sustainable development as central to their collaborative efforts in all policy spheres. For the time being at least, it remains subservient and peripheral.

The following two frameworks for action in follow-up to WSSD were advanced during the summit process.

Millennium Development Goals

The Millennium Development Goals (MDGs) were endorsed as the overarching objectives which should guide efforts to implement existing commitments and (as noted above) were augmented with one notable new target for provision of sanitation, and a number of subsidiary undertakings. The MDGs seem quickly to have become central to the approach of many donor agencies, along with the Poverty Reduction Strategy Paper approach championed by the World Bank. However, misgivings about the value of global targets driving policy and practice at national levels were also evident in Johannesburg.

WEHAB Agenda

The WEHAB Agenda (water, energy, health, agriculture, biodiversity) put forward shortly before the summit by UN Secretary-General Kofi Annan was widely seen as a useful way to concentrate on key policy areas in the final negotiations for Johannesburg. The degree to which WEHAB will survive after the summit is less clear; the US has proposed that these issues be the basis for the annual programme of work of the CSD, but a number of G77 countries have reservations and have noted that this framework was never negotiated by governments and so is a pretty tenuous basis for future action.

All in all, even though there are some significant steps forward in the Johannesburg Plan of Implementation, there is not enough evidence of real progress to add up to much – and certainly not enough to meet the criteria set out by the UN General Assembly when it agreed the summit's mandate. As Mark Halle of the International Institute for Sustainable Development puts it:

> *swirling the Plan of Implementation around in a shallow pan with the hope that some nuggets of gold will appear is an idle exercise. The few flakes of gold are largely offset by the mass of colourless mud* (Halle, 2002).

Stories from the Summit Preparations

So how did we arrive at the fragmented, largely unsatisfactory pinnacle of the summit? We can learn a good deal by going back through the preparatory process and identifying the development of critical themes which can help us to understand the Johannesburg outcomes better. Two stories in particular throw some light on the ideological and power-based conflicts evident in the WSSD process:

- the Global Deal;
- 'Type 2' partnerships for sustainable development.

The Global Deal

At the outset it was agreed that the summit should establish a 'global partnership to achieve the objectives of sustainable development' and 'reinvigorate, at the highest political level, the global commitment to a North–South partnership and a higher level of international solidarity' (UNGA, 2000). There was never any strong support for negotiation of major new international agreements along the lines of the Rio conventions on biodiversity and climate change. Rather, Johannesburg should achieve advances in two broad areas:

- recognizing sustainable development as an overarching set of policy goals and principles which could unite countries and define the terms for their collaboration;
- promoting action to implement existing commitments, through actions involving civil society, the business sector, government at different levels and so on – taking what was seen as a pragmatic approach to problem-solving and delivering change.

Box 1.1 WSSD terminology: a short guide

Type 1 outcomes: commitments and agreements negotiated by governments through the PrepCom process, resulting in the Johannesburg Plan of Implementation finalized at the summit.

Type 2 outcomes:

> *a series of implementation partnerships and commitments involving many stakeholders... These would help to translate the multilaterally negotiated and agreed outcomes into concrete actions by interested governments, international organizations and major groups* (opening statement by the chairman of the Third WSSD PrepCom).

Over 220 partnerships (with US$235 million in resources) were identified in advance of WSSD and about 60 partnerships were announced during the summit by a variety of countries.

Global Deal: a set of commitments and responsibilities to implement sustainable development. Led by governments and endorsed by heads of state, but incorporating activities involving business and civil society at all levels.

A number of key individuals and countries, most notably former Danish environment minister Svend Auken, went further and began to sketch out elements of a 'Global Deal' between North and South, which would tackle the unfinished business from UNCED by spelling out common goals and commitments and recognizing mutual responsibility for action between countries. At the UN Economic Commission for Europe (UNECE) regional preparatory meeting for WSSD in September 2001 the EU stated that:

> *in a spirit of partnership and solidarity and through a participatory process, we will seek to achieve a 'Global Deal' at the summit containing commitments by governments, as well as other stakeholders, that will result in concrete action to improve the implementation of sustainable development policies* (EU, 2001).

However, others at that UNECE meeting were less enthusiastic – the US and Russia would not accept the term 'Global Deal', stating that they were not clear what it implied and reserving their judgement until its proponents could present a more detailed proposal. This scepticism (on the part of the US at least) had hardened further by the time the second global preparatory meeting for WSSD (PrepCom II) took place in New York in late January–early February 2002. Although the EU was joined by others supporting the 'Global Deal' approach, adding their views on what might usefully be included in the balanced package of issues and interests, the head of the US delegation to PrepCom II, Jonathan Margolis, stated 'there isn't going to be a single Global Deal' in Johannesburg. 'We're not looking for these grand solutions that sound good from a rhetorical perspective, but rather we're looking for solutions that actually lead to concrete developments on the ground' (Wakefield, 2001).

Box 1.2 EU discussion paper on the Global Deal (December 2001)

Outcome:

- The Global Deal is a balanced package taking into account the three pillars of sustainable development.
- It should build on what already exists.
- The actions foreseen have to be built on what already exists; these include a focused, concrete and pragmatic package of actions contributing to the accelerated implementation of Agenda 21 and the Millennium Development Goals/international development targets (MDGs/IDTs)

Follow-up:

- It should serve as a mechanism to ensure real follow-up by all involved partners to the results of the WSSD.
- It needs to involve all major groups.

Value added:

- It should not reopen Agenda 21
- Only actions where progress can be made should be included.
- An excessively broad agenda could mean a lack of focus and progress.

Further discussion is needed, within and between the different regions to ensure that the Global Deal takes into account the priorities defined in the preparatory process, on the following elements:

- Should the Global Deal be a single package, or might it encompass different types of subsidiary/regional/sectoral agreements (ie be an umbrella)?
- How would the Global Deal include commitments by the business sector and civil society?
- How could a platform be created that constructively engages civil society and business to both contribute to and benefit from a Global Deal (eg given that there is already a 'Global Compact')?
- What should be the role of the governments in the Global Deal in establishing a framework for action?

Source: EU (2001)

The scope of these 'grand solutions' is evident in a speech given by Mohammed Valli Moosa, South African minister of environmental affairs and tourism, in March 2002. He asserted that:

> *the power of the [Global Deal] concept lies in its integration of economic, social and environmental issues. Economic issues – trade, finance, investment, technology transfer – are therefore a crucial part of the Johannesburg agenda* (Valli Moosa, 2002).

In the event, the US (with tacit support from a handful of countries including Australia and Japan) effectively exerted a veto on the wishes of those trying to initiate an ambitious attempt to bring together relevant international policy activities under the umbrella of sustainable development.

NGOs and other stakeholders were a little slow to join this debate, perhaps preferring to wait and react to detailed Global Deal proposals, which never materialized, rather than endorse the concept and then have to back away from the specifics. The EU can also be criticized for failing to counter cynicism from many, including G77 countries, who pointed to failures to deliver promises (explicit and implicit) made during the UNCED process and asked what was different this time.

The US therefore succeeded in removing the overarching notion of a deal which could challenge existing power structures and 'business as usual' and focused attention on isolated delivery mechanisms – 'solutions on the ground' which could be delivered by a combination of government, private sector and civil society action.

The effect the US line had on the WSSD process was to strip away any chance that the summit might recognize sustainable development as central to the set of policy goals for international collaboration on economic, social and environmental issues. And in turn there was now little chance that the UN could adopt this agenda as its mandate for a radical reappraisal of the purposes and functions of international institutions and processes. It took a long time for these impacts to be fully apparent, but the central elements of the Global Deal are wholly absent from the final WSSD Plan of Implementation. In its place is the piecemeal approach envisaged by the US, which implies that the fundamentals are sound and only relatively minor adjustments are necessary.

Type 2 partnerships

In the absence of a strong inter-governmental framework for action, the 'concrete developments on the ground' advocated by Jonathan Margolis assumed a rather different significance. At PrepCom II and subsequently, the grounds for contention shifted – in place of a debate on whether or not major revisions to the institutional architecture for economics, society and environment should be agreed was argument over whether inter-governmental negotiations and commitments were important at all. The US government made it clear that the summit should focus predominantly on identification of Type 2 partnerships and that agreement of a consensual text was not essential. An internal US position paper argued that 'in focusing on negotiated text, the CSD [ie the PrepCom] loses the opportunity to focus its efforts on operational sustainable development success stories'.

As a result of this tacit downgrading in expectations and the emerging US strategy, serious misgivings were expressed at the possibility that partnerships could come to replace government commitments and obligations (SDIN, 2002). Most governments (notably the EU and South Africa) were careful to state that 'Type 2' should not supplant 'Type 1'. Any proposed collaboration should enhance the implementation of priorities established in the text negotiated by governments – even if this text ended up being largely a repackaging of existing commitments because it would not be possible to drive through a new consensus. In order to clarify the concept, WSSD Bureau vice chairs Jan Kára and Diane Quarless issued an explanatory note which provided some general guidelines for Type 2 partnerships, proposing that they should (WSSD Bureau, 2002):

- achieve further implementation of Agenda 21 and Millennium Development Goals;
- complement globally agreed Type 1 outcomes and not substitute government commitment;
- be voluntary in nature and not be subject to negotiation within the PrepCom;
- be participatory, with ownership shared between partners;
- be new initiatives, or, in the case of ongoing initiatives, demonstrate added value in the context of the summit;
- integrate economic, social and environmental dimensions of sustainable development;
- be international (global, regional or sub-regional) in scope and reach;
- have clear objectives, and set specific targets and time frames for their achievement; and
- have a system of accountability, including arrangements for monitoring progress.[1]

These guidelines helped by providing a pragmatic yardstick for assessing the value of particular initiatives and their validity as WSSD Type 2 partnerships. They did not really help to clarify the underlying ramifications of Type 2 for WSSD and, beyond that, for the UN system as a whole.

The problem for many with the Type 2 model did not derive from an innate antipathy towards partnerships involving civil society, the business sector and governments, although numerous cautionary examples were cited and reservations expressed about the broader implications of this approach. The central dilemma was whether official recognition of such partnerships strengthened inter-governmental commitments or marginalized them. Could a summit where the main evidence of progress was a collection of initiatives which aimed to deliver elements of sustainable development be called a success? And if so, didn't this let governments off the hook by shifting the focus from their responsibility to provide leadership and legitimacy to global commitments?

A number of developing country government delegates were also extremely suspicious about the implications of the Type 2 approach. One South American official likened the development to 'a whole new form of conditionality', through which donor governments would be able to oblige recipient countries to accept involvement of multinational companies in provision of basic utilities by linking funding to a Type 2 package. A coalition of Southern governments lobbied until the end of the summit process against the adoption of partnerships as one of the official WSSD outcomes. Their misgivings were based on the fear that this development would reduce the pressure on donor countries to provide additional direct financial support for sustainable development in the South.

The UN Monterrey Conference on Financing for Development had already provided some substance to these concerns. The US government and the EU pledged significant increases in Official Development Assistance. However, the EU did not move away from its current practice of tying aid, placing questionable obligations on recipient countries, while the US took the opportunity to put forward a unilateral 'compact for development', which President Bush claimed would lead to 'greater accountability'. 'We must tie our aid to political, legal and economic reform, and by insisting on reform we do the work of compassion', he said. 'Pouring money into a failed status quo does little to help the poor. Liberty and law and opportunity are the conditions for development' (Bush, 2002). Although he uses the term accountability, this seems to go only one way – the US is not interested in accountability to internationally negotiated standards and commitments on sustainable development, as has been clear in the WSSD process.

In considering the outcomes of Johannesburg, one commentator suggested that 'the US missed a real opportunity':

> *Despite widespread international criticism for its rejection of an apparent international consensus on many environmental issues, the US brought to Johannesburg promising and much-needed new approaches – such as partnerships among government, industry and environmentalists – that could help address festering world problems. Unfortunately, by refusing to commit itself to targets and timetables, the US failed to force other countries to take its ideas seriously, and to begin a transformation of the debate about sustainability* (Lempert, 2002).

Others would conclude that these two aspects of the position taken by the US in WSSD negotiations were entirely consistent, and that they reflect hostility towards multilateralism and continued belief in market-based solutions to social and environmental problems. This understanding made it very difficult for other advocates of the partnership approach to make a coherent case for a more balanced mix between commitments endorsed by governments (Type 1) and actions carried out by a mix of governments and other actors to achieve those goals (Type 2). If the US did not see this as a necessary objective then what likelihood was there that it would become the basis for agreement?

Discussion of Type 2 partnerships continues to be contentious for a number of reasons. First, there is the fear that this focus will marginalize inter-governmental decision-making on sustainable development and put in its place 'coalitions of the willing' which involve major companies and other organizations but are less accountable to the needs and wishes of the world's poorest people. Second, there is the fear that global partnerships could favour major multinational companies in the provision of services such as water and energy and serve as a vehicle for market expansion at the expense of existing providers but with no clear long-term benefits for the countries concerned. Third, there is the fear that the term 'partnership' masks a whole range of power imbalances between the actors involved which will not be tackled without strong political leadership and commitment to the principles of transparency, accountability, equality and sustainability (see for example SDIN, 2002).

For others this shift has been seen in a more positive light. The World Resources Institute (WRI) wrote that:

> *This summit will be remembered not for the treaties, the commitments, or the declarations it produced, but for the first stirrings of a new way of governing the global commons – the beginnings of a shift from the stiff formal waltz of traditional diplomacy to the jazzier dance of improvisational solution-oriented partnerships that may include non-governmental organizations, willing governments and other stakeholders* (WRI, 2002).

Many of those involved in Type 2 partnerships are similarly positive, contrasting the difficulty of making progress through UN negotiations with the opportunities partnerships offer to make real progress towards existing commitments such as the Millennium Development Goals.

To a large extent this case remains unproven. It will be a critical litmus test for the UN Commission on Sustainable Development to increase the credibility of Type 2 partnerships – and by extension of the WSSD process as a whole – by demonstrating that:

- they are really making a difference, increasing the amount of available resources rather than merely diverting funds from other sources;
- they are enhancing accountability, increasing the means by which civil society can influence actions which have impacts on their livelihoods; and
- they can be assessed independently and credibly – and criticized as ineffective, or as window dressing, or even as counterproductive, when necessary.

Parallel Events and Activities

Much has changed in ten years. At the Rio Summit, the majority of international non-governmental participants were from Europe or North America. In Johannesburg, representation was much more diverse, with significant numbers from other African countries, Southeast Asia and China, and the Arab countries, to name just a few. NGO participation at UNCED was predominantly from the environmental movement, while at WSSD there were events and organizations addressing issues of equity and human rights, land ownership, development, corporate accountability, social justice and so on – and consequently less to suggest that the summit was principally about environmental issues.

Partly as a result of this diversity it proved difficult to present consensual NGO positions along the lines of the Alternative Treaties negotiated by NGOs in Rio. It also highlighted the fact that, for many summit participants, the critical policy areas addressed at national and international levels were not really up for negotiation in Johannesburg. Many of the events and the position statements agreed during the summit focus on economic issues and the work of the World Trade Organization, the World Bank, the International Monetary Fund, the EU's Common Agricultural Policy and so on – highlighting the challenges which were not addressed at WSSD in mainstreaming sustainable development.

There was also significant progress in civil society engagement with the negotiations: the Sustainable Development Issues Network (see www.sdissues.net) provided a much more democratic and effective focus for interaction with the summit process than had existed at UNCED, which built on lessons learnt from global conferences in the years since 1992 and from annual sessions of the CSD. The large international environment and development NGOs collaborated well in the newly created 'Eco-Equity Coalition', which produced daily newsletters and held joint press briefings from PrepCom III onwards. Issue coalitions such as the Indigenous Peoples Caucus succeeded in having their priorities reflected in the final WSSD texts (in this instance through having the term 'indigenous peoples' included in the Political Declaration, where previously governments would not accept the autonomy implied by 'peoples'). IUCN ran a summit-long programme of meetings, presentations, workshops and panels at their Environment Centre which often put the inter-governmental process to shame and provided a welcome respite for jaded officials.

From the local government, scientific and business communities there was a notable emphasis on using the summit to stimulate real debate on the tricky aspects of sustainable development. The business programme did address the issues and problems to be confronted by those attempting to become better corporate citizens while blatant instances of corporate 'greenwash' were largely absent. The Science Forum broke new ground by bringing together researchers, policy-makers and civil society to explore the role of scientific research in sustainable development – and the difficulties presented by current decision-making structures and knowledge gaps.

Whether these activities significantly compensate for the lack of progress in the official process is doubtful. But they do signal a welcome willingness to carry forward debate, commitments and action in the absence of inter-governmental leadership, which has implications for the future.

UN Follow-up to WSSD

Our challenge is that a political process which has been good at defining policy frameworks and goals must now show itself as being effective, also, in maintaining the pressures for implementation. It is a new type of challenge, but it is very necessary that we respond to this. We cannot treat the processes of implementation as if they can be handled in an entirely non-political manner. And it is very important that the CSD use its strength, which is its capacity to bring so many diverse actors together and the openness that it has to civil society, the way in which it has embraced the notion of partnerships, to really focus, not just on policy development, but on implementation (Desai, 2003).

At its 11th session in April–May 2003, the CSD faced some complex tasks. Agreement had to be reached on a programme of work for the next decade which would allow governments and others to follow up the commitments made at WSSD. The ways in which the CSD works had to be reviewed in order to ensure that its structure effectively promotes action and engages key players. And the link between global policy debates and implementation of existing commitments at ground level had to be strengthened. In short, many of the unresolved issues from WSSD identified above were on the agenda.

The formal negotiations at the 2003 session dealt mainly with agreement of a work programme for the next 15 years, and with the ways in which sessions of the CSD would be conducted in future. The turn-out was a little disappointing – the ministers present were overwhelmingly from environment departments, and officials from development or planning ministries (particularly from European countries) seemed less engaged than during the summit process or at previous CSD sessions. Civil society groups were also quite sparsely represented, and those present were largely from organizations with an environmental focus rather than from those prioritizing economic, social or developmental issues.

Perhaps because the right people were not present, there was little discussion on some of the broad policy contexts which are shaping multilateral collaboration. Conflict and militarization were not addressed, despite the situation in the Middle East. There was little attention paid to the implications of the Millennium Development Goals, the objectives of which are increasingly being used to shape international cooperation, despite the absence of any strong environmental focus there; the growing significance of World Bank-led Poverty Reduction Strategies in shaping donor relations with least developed countries was not really considered, although these are seen by many development agencies as much more important than country strategies for sustainable development.

These gaps can largely be explained because this was essentially an organizational session, and so there was little opportunity for substantive discussion on broader issues. A number of ministerial interventions did take a wider perspective, though the CSD offered little opportunity for serious debate. It remains to be seen whether in its future work the CSD can prove to be a serious forum for political debate and pragmatic information sharing which could enable it to contribute to these higher-profile policy processes.

In many ways, a global forum for politicians, civil servants and representatives from civil society organizations is one of the worst contexts in which to get to grips with the challenges of putting the Johannesburg agenda into action at national or local level.

The strength of the CSD to date has been its function as a political forum, bringing together government ministers to discuss and (sometimes) reach agreement on issues of global significance. Left to market mechanisms, or the accountability of unelected organizations, there is no means by which the interests of individuals and communities – let alone of future generations – can be represented in these global deliberations. It is not sufficient for the UN to conduct technocratic or bureaucratic assessments of the challenges to be confronted; it has to find means by which to strengthen the accountability of those with power to those who are affected by their decisions.

BOX 1.3 KEY OUTCOMES FROM CSD11

1   A two-year work cycle, to include an 'implementation' session and a 'policy' session – governments will only negotiate text in the second year.
2   Thematic clusters of issues for future years:
   •   water, sanitation and human settlements (2004–2005);
   •   energy, industrial development, air pollution and climate change (2006–2007);
   •   agriculture, rural development, land, drought, desertification and Africa (2008–2009);
   •   transport, chemicals, waste management, mining, ten-year programme on sustainable consumption and production patterns (2010–2011);
   •   forests, biodiversity, biotechnology, tourism, mountains (2012–2013);
   •   oceans and seas, marine resources, small island developing states, disaster management and vulnerability (2014–2015);
   •   overall appraisal of implementation of Agenda 21 and the Johannesburg Plan of Implementation – JPOI (2016–2017).
3   Cross-cutting issues to be considered in each work cycle – using the section headings from the JPOI (poverty eradication, changing unsustainable patterns of consumption and production, protecting and managing the natural resource base, etc).
4   A voluntary system of reporting for Type 2 partnerships.
5   A greater emphasis on regional activities – particularly through new 'regional implementation fora'.
6   New organizational approaches, including the learning centre and partnerships fair, as ways to share experience and good practice.
7   Election of a new chair for 2003–2004: Norwegian environment minister Borge Brende.

However, there were also areas CSD11 did not really tackle:

•   UN system coherence on sustainable development issues (could be taken up by the UN Economic and Social Council – ECOSOC);
•   trade and sustainable development – particularly relations with the WTO and its ongoing work;
•   corporate accountability – not incorporated in the CSD's future agenda, despite its prominence in WSSD;
•   strengthening the national reporting process to allow voluntary 'peer review' to develop between interested countries (opposed by the US and G77).

Sustainable development is also about equity – finding ways in which limited resources as well as costs and burdens can be more fairly distributed, as the title of this book, *Survival for a Small Planet*, suggests. This also presents problems which require political solutions at all levels of governance, and a significant role for the CSD as the only international political forum focusing on sustainable development.

A further aspect of the CSD's work also depends upon significant political engagement. The bringing together of social, environmental and economic discourses which sustainable development entails requires engagement of a diverse range of actors and creation of innovative ways of working which go beyond the confines of inter-governmental agreement. This shift is evident in the new activities agreed for the CSD. But the legitimacy of these activities still derives most clearly from the endorsement and support of governments, and from the extent to which politicians, as well as other influential actors, are prepared to demonstrate leadership in using the space created at the international level in effective ways, in order to create the contexts in which real improvement is possible at national and sub-national levels.

And, finally, political engagement is essential if sustainable development is to be seen as a central focus for multilateral cooperation in the decades to come. The problems to be confronted in realizing this goal are enormous; the impacts of that other global 'coalition of the willing' based on what Jan Pronk terms the 'security paradigm' in Chapter 2 of this book have yet to be fully realized; the messages emerging from Johannesburg are often muddled and incoherent – and yet sustainable development remains the only rational basis for consensus between different countries, peoples and interest groups that is fair and far-sighted. Let's hope this potential doesn't wither on the vine in the years after WSSD.

Routes Forward

At Johannesburg we entered into a solemn pact with future unborn generations not to destroy our beloved planet Earth. We also entered into a deal with the poor and hungry to ensure social and economic development. Now, the poor watch and wait to see whether hunger, disease and global warming will be tackled with the same vigour displayed by some on the military front (Valli Moosa, 2003).

The rest of this volume presents a diverse range of perspectives on priorities for action and ways in which the international community could make progress towards sustainable development. Many of the authors were personally involved in the WSSD process, and their chapters reflect this experience. But the focus of the book as a whole is very much on future challenges – on ways in which the international community could build on the successes of Johannesburg, and also salvage renewed direction and purpose from the summit's shortcomings. Hopefully it can provide some useful food for thought for all those involved in attempts to translate the rhetoric of sustainable development into reality.

Notes

1   See also the 'Guiding Principles for Partnerships for Sustainable Development ("Type 2 Outcomes")' tabled by the vice chairs but not formally endorsed by governments at the Bali WSSD PrepCom, available at www.johannesburgsummit.org/html/documents/prepcom4docs/bali_documents/annex_partnership.pdf, accessed 31 March 2003.

References

Bush, G (2002) 'A New Compact for Development in the Battle Against World Poverty', remarks made on 22 March 2002,at the United Nations Financing and Development Conference, Monterrey, Mexico, available at http://usinfo.state.gov/journals/itgic/0402/ijge/gj01.htm, accessed 31 March 2003

Desai, N (2003) 'Statement to the Commission on Sustainable Development 11th Session by the UN Under-Secretary-General for Economic and Social Affairs', New York, 28 April 2003

EU (2001) 'Towards a "Global Deal": A First Overview of Views and Opinions and some Initial Thoughts', draft discussion paper, 17 December 2001, available at www.anped.org/docs/EU%20WSSD%20Global%20Deal.doc, accessed 31 March 2003

FOEI (Friends of the Earth International) (2002) 'Clashes with Corporate Giants: 22 Campaigns for Biodiversity and Community', Amsterdam 2002, available at www.foei.org/publications/corporates/clashestext.html, accessed 31 March 2003

Greenpeace/WBCSD (2002) 'Call to Action', Johannesburg, 28 August 2002, available at http://archive.greenpeace.org/earthsummit/wbcsd/, accessed 31 March 2003

Halle, M (2002) 'Johannesburg Plus 0.166 – a Perspective on WSSD as the Dust Begins to Settle', speech to the World Council of Churches, Geneva, 5 November 2002

Lempert, R (2002) 'Missed Opportunities in Johannesburg', UPI Press, 22 October 2002, available at www.upi.com/view.cfm?StoryID=20021021-095122-6514r, accessed 31 March 2003

SDIN (Sustainable Development Issues Network) (2002) 'Taking Issue: Questioning Partnerships', Paper No 1 March 2002, available at www.sdissues.net/SDIN/docs/TakingIssue-No1.pdf, accessed 31 March 2003

Sharma, A, Mahapatra, R and Polycarp, C (2002) 'Dialogue of the Deaf', *Down to Earth*, Centre for Science and Environment, Delhi, 30 September 2002, pp25–33

South African Government (2002) 'A Proposed Approach to Action-Oriented, Time-Bound Outcomes for the WSSD', non-paper, 3 April 2002

UNGA (2000) Resolution 55/199 'Ten-year Review of the Progress Achieved in the Implementation of the Outcome of the United Nations Conference on Environment and Development', para17b, 20 December 2000

UN Secretary-General (2003) 'Follow-up to Johannesburg and the Future Role of the CSD – The Implementation Track', report of the secretary-general for consideration by CSD11, 18 February 2003, available at www.un.org/esa/sustdev/csd11/sgreport.pdf, accessed 31 March 2003

Valli Moosa, M (2002) 'Linking Doha, Monterrey and Johannesburg: A Global Deal to Eradicate Poverty and Inequality and Promote Sustainable Development', address by South African minister Valli Moosa to the UNDP Seminar on Financing of Global Public Goods, Crowne Plaza Hotel, Monterrey, Mexico, 19 March 2002

Valli Moosa, M (2003) 'Opening Address by the Chairman to the 11th Session of the UN Commission on Sustainable Development', New York, 28 April 2003

Wakefield, J (2001) 'Energy Initiative Urged for Johannesburg Summit', Scidev.net, 10 December 2001, available at www.scidev.net/news/index.cfm?fuseaction=66&language=1

WRI (World Resources Institute) (2002) 'WRI Expresses Disappointment over Many WSSD Outcomes', Washington, DC, news release, 4 September 2002, available at http://newsroom.wr.org/newsrelease_text.cfm?NewsReleaseID=135, accessed 31 March 2003

WSSD Bureau (2002) 'Further Guidance for Partnerships/Initiatives ('Type 2 outcomes') to be Elaborated by Interested Parties in Preparation for the World Summit on Sustainable Development', explanatory note by the vice chairs Jan Kára and Diane Quarless, April 2002, available at www.johannesburgsummit.org/html/documents/prepcom3docs/summary_partnerships_annex_050402, accessed on 31 March 2003

Chapter 2

Security and Sustainability[1]

Jan Pronk, IIED chair and former UN secretary-general's special envoy for WSSD

Why was the World Summit on Sustainable Development in Johannesburg, 2002, different from the Earth Summit (UNCED 1992) in Rio de Janeiro, and less appealing? Why did we not place the future at the heart of our deliberations? Why didn't we really address questions concerning the destiny of the Earth, the needs of poor people and the risks confronting future generations? Was it a lack of imagination? Was it due to old-fashioned, impotent machinery and procedures within the UN system? Was it scepticism, a lack of political will, a lack of insight into changed world conditions or a lack of capacity to translate new insights into a new approach? Or have we become obsessed by the risks of today: security questions and the war against terrorism?

Maybe it was all of that. But the most important reason is that fundamental disagreements exist concerning the concept of sustainability itself, despite a superficial consent reached during talks and negotiations. There is a general public disbelief, an overall doubt, about whether the direction advocated or chosen is the right one and a complete uncertainty over whether there are better alternatives. The result is political alienation and a climate of distrust in many countries: people do not trust their leaders, leaders disregard people's needs, people are suspicious about values, models and doctrines propagated by governments. Uncertainty, disbelief, distrust, alienation and fear – this is far beyond mere disagreement.

A Paradigm Dispute

Throughout history, dominant paradigms have been contested. The paradigms of those in power are always different from the paradigms of the non-elite. However genuine paradigm disputes can help in fighting for common ground between interest groups at a higher political level. They can help to disarm powerful elites, and undermine their bias in favour of the status quo, by focusing on the longer-term interests of society. This is true for paradigm disputes both within nations and worldwide. In the field of international development cooperation a major dispute of this nature took place after decolonization in the 1960s and after the UN Conference on the Human Environment in Stockholm, in 1972. There was a risk that the newly won independence of the young nation states would not be followed by a reasonable degree of political and economic autonomy. The answer was a threefold new paradigm: self-reliance plus the fulfilment of basic human needs plus a new international economic order. None of the three became reality. Instead the world experienced a period of neo-colonialism, widening gaps between rich and poor. In the 1980s this led to complete stagnation. Gamani Corea spoke about 'the lost decade for development' (UNCTAD, 1987). The South was told to adjust to new realities set by the North. There was no international cooperation to address world problems such as mounting debt burdens, a deteriorating environment and increasing world poverty. All efforts were paralysed by the last convulsions of the Cold War between East and West until 1989, when the end of the Cold War created new perspectives for the peoples of all nations, A new paradigm for development cooperation emerged, again defined with the help of three concepts: democracy, eradication of poverty and sustainable development.

So, when we came together in Rio de Janeiro for the UN Conference on Environment and Development in 1992 the mood was positive. There was room for change: change for the good – freedom, democracy, human rights, disarmament, peace, development and the protection of the environment. No wonder that the new paradigm of sustainability was widely endorsed: progress for the present generation in all respects and everywhere, without discrimination, but on the understanding that successive generations would be entitled to the same opportunities. We would be obliged to use the resources at our disposal in such a way that they could be fully sustained or renewed for the benefit of our children and grandchildren. After Rio we were optimistic, but the optimism did not last long. The world lacked the capacity or the will to translate the new dream into reality. Between the fall of the wall in Berlin in 1989 and the summit in Rio in 1992 there was a fair amount of political will. But domestic conflicts in many societies and the erosion of the international public system were weakening the capacity to bring about democracy, poverty eradication and sustainable development. Good governance became a mantra that drowned out the call for sustainable development.

Conflict and Globalization

The new conflicts rose mostly within nations, not between them. Some were not new at all, but re-emerged – often after decades of silence. The power struggle between East and West led to a tacitly agreed demarcation of influence, to preserve the status quo, which in turn paralysed conditions in the South and prevented change. Economic conflicts can be managed within a reasonable period of time, by a good combination of economic growth and (re)distribution of assets and income, creating a perspective of progress for the present generation. However, cultural, social, ethnic, religious or sub-national domestic conflicts are rooted deeply in society.

Cultural conflicts, accompanied or sharpened by economic inequalities, outlive generations. They are less manageable than economic conflicts, because there is no way out by means of sharing or redistribution. In an economic conflict there is always a feasible win–win solution: the right path of investment, growth and distribution can make all parties gain. An economic increase of one party does not necessary have to result in a welfare loss for others. Cultural identity conflicts are different. Identities are defined in terms of absolute positions, not in terms of shares of total potential welfare. A stronger position of one group in a society – whether a tribe, an ethnic group, a religious denomination, a social class, a sex, a tongue, a colour, a caste, a nationalistic clan, or any group defining its identity in other than purely economic terms – always means that another group will lose. Welfare is a relative concept; it can be increased through intelligent distribution. Power is an absolute concept; total power cannot be increased by means of redistribution. Only when cultural conflicts are not seen as power conflicts but as identity conflicts can a solution be possible, provided that each group considers its identity not threatened but enriched through interaction with the other. Cultural confrontation has to be transformed into cultural exchange. But as long as this is not the case, such conflicts are longer lasting, less manageable and more violent than either economic conflicts or international disputes.

Over the past decade, violence has not been limited to the original location of the conflict. It has been brought to other countries by the same forces that brought about globalization. That was the second major new phenomenon in the 1990s. Globalization was not discussed in Rio; it had not been discovered. Of course internationalization was not new: there had been intercontinental transport, foreign investment and trade, international finance, imperialism and colonization, world wars, efforts to build international alliances, a League of Nations, and the UN itself.

Globalization was not a new process – we had seen it for centuries and had witnessed a stronger pace in the four decades since the Second World War. But in the final decade of the last century it got a new shape. Internationalization had been an economic and a political process, steered and fostered by means of concrete decisions of policy-makers and entrepreneurs. It was man-made. But somewhere in the 1990s internationalization turned into globalization. It got a momentum of its own, became less a consequence of demonstrable human decisions, more self-contained and self-supporting. The driving force was twofold. First, there was technological advance, enabling full and fast information and communication everywhere, physically and virtually. Second, there were economic global markets linking production, investment, transportation and trade, advertisement and consumption anywhere in the world to any other place. The result was a disregard for national frontiers, a strengthening of global corporations and an erosion of nation states.

Globalization became a cultural affair as well. A reality in the mind of the people: time differences and long distances are no longer barriers for communication. Technology has solved this. What used to be far away has come close – 'the death of distance'. Actual distance and time difference are no longer relevant, only the distance between human minds counts. In the WSSD conference centre in Sandton, Johannesburg, most of us felt that our air tickets, cellphones, emails, credit cards and CNN connected us with people in comparable conditions in cities abroad, rather than with AIDS victims on the African continent; landless and jobless people in southern Africa.

Global Apartheid

Many people are excluded. Globalization is neither coherent nor complete. In the 1990s globalization was boosted by new technologies, rising expectations and a mounting demand from the global market. This unprecedented growth could have helped to enlarge the capacity of the international community to address poverty and sustainability questions. It did not. Instead, globalization led to even more unbalanced development and less sustainable development. Globalization made international cooperation lopsided by directing political attention mainly towards facilitating the workings of the world market and neglecting welfare, social justice and environmental issues.

What has this meant for the poor? During long periods of capitalist expansion poor people were exploited. But they had an opportunity to fight back, because the system needed them: their labour and their purchasing power, the power to buy the goods produced by the system and thereby sustain the very system that exploited them. This common strength of the poor helped to modify exploitation. Development became potentially beneficial to the poor. There was hope in the prospect of incremental improvement. Everybody within the system was entitled to such a perspective. Everybody had the right to hope. We have to conclude that hope is no longer justified. Globalization has changed the character of capitalism. There are more people excluded from the system than exploited in the system. Those who are excluded are seen as dispensable. Neither their labour nor their potential buying power is needed. That is the reason why they cannot fight back any more. They have lost a perspective. If you believe that your life is worse than your parents' and that there is no hope that your children will do better, then there is no cause for optimism whatsoever.

For many people this is today's reality. They have no land to work on, no job, no credit, no education, no basic services, no security of income, no food security, but ever more squalor, an ever greater chance of being affected by HIV/AIDS, a house without electricity, water and sanitation. Despite unprecedented world economic progress during the last decade, for about 2 billion people there is only the experience of sinking further and further into the quicksand of complete poverty. In Johannesburg President Mbeki called this 'global apartheid'.

The gap between rich and poor in the world can no longer be explained in terms of a strikingly unequal distribution of income and wealth which could be modified through world economic growth and a better distribution of the fruits of growth. The gap appears to have become permanent. Rich and poor stand apart, separated from each other. Under the apartheid regime in South Africa people were either white or black. So, they were part of the system, or they were not. Today people belong to modernity, or they do not. The world of modernity is Western in origin, but stretches out towards islands and pockets of modernity in the East and in the South. The worlds of modernity are linked with each other by means of modern communication. Through the culture of modern communication people feel that they belong to modernity, that they are part of it, part of the globalized, uniform, Western, neo-liberal culture of mass-consumption, materialism, images and virtual reality. That modern world is separated from the world next door, physically sometimes just around the corner, but far away in terms of communication, mentality, experience and consciousness: poverty, hunger, unemployment, lack of basic amenities in the shanty towns, in the countryside and at the periphery, where pollution is permanent, where the soil is no longer productive, water scarce and life unhealthy.

Poor People Have to Live in the Worst Places of the Earth

'A global human society based upon poverty for many and prosperity for a few, characterized by islands of wealth surrounded by a sea of poverty is unsustainable', President Mbeki has said (Mbeki, 2002). Indeed, this is apartheid. On the one side security and luxury, on the other deprivation, hardship and suffering. At the beginning of the new millennium, for many people life has never been so good. At the same time, for many millions more in our global neighbourhood life is not liveable.

Security and luxury on the one side of the fence are being sustained and protected by continuing the squalor, suffering and poverty elsewhere. Not by exploiting the poor (though there still is exploitation – low commodity prices and inadequate wages for migrant labour) but because the poor are excluded. The Western world is afraid that they will cost more than they can contribute. They do not fit into cost–benefit calculations. People living in the slums of Calcutta, Nairobi and Rio de Janeiro, AIDS victims in Africa, landless people in Bangladesh, subsistence farmers in the Sahel, illegal migrants crossing the Mediterranean; all of them lack the capacities needed to contribute to the modern global economy and the buying power for its products. That is why these people are considered dispensable. Well-to-do people are not interested in the ideas of the poor, let alone their feelings or their fate. The poor are a burden and should not try to come close. They are excluded by the connected from the islands of wealth created by globalization. They are deprived of space and soil, in particular good soil. They are deprived of water, forests and natural resources. They are burdened by sky-high debts. Their enterprises do not have fair access to global or national markets, which favour foreign companies, providing them with more licences to operate, higher credits and tax holidays. Globalization takes away living space. The poor are told to stay in, or return to, their homelands, perhaps in occupied territories, separated from each other by arbitrary or economic boundaries drawn by those who have access to resources, capital and technology.

The pace of globalization has made winners and losers. Real losers and those who see themselves as losers. Globalization is shaking established structures and cultures. Some have the skills to gain access to the modern world markets. For others, it is either sink or swim. Many of them, economic asylum seekers for instance, are struggling with the waves of modernity and sink into the undercurrent of the new dynamics. For other people, single females with children in Africa for instance, modernization means uprooting. In the past their existence was fragile, now it is shattered. They are dragged down by the current of globalization.

Resistance

Others resist. Such resistance can take different forms: protest, economic action, migration, forming alliances or a political counter-offensive at a high level. It can also imply the strengthening of a vulnerable culture or an effort to tie religion with politics. It can result in violence, first against those within that culture who choose in favour of modernity and assimilate themselves into the foreign, Western culture. Later on violence may be directed at the foreign culture itself. That is a final stage. The more the centre of globalization disregards the periphery, not only the economic and social needs of the periphery, but also its traditions, culture, religion and aspirations, the harsher the resistance. Western promotion of individualism – 'each man for himself' – is seen by many as arrogant, as an insult. The excluded feel not only poor and dispossessed, but also defeated, humiliated and resentful.

In the 18th century a similarly haughty attitude from the elite brought about a revolution. Today revolt is in the air. 'If you don't visit a bad neighbourhood, it will visit you', Thomas Friedman wrote (Friedman, 2003). That visit can take different forms. One is migration to the towns. Another one is crime and violence in any metropolis with a dazzling city centre next to barrios and shanty towns of breathtaking poverty. A third reaction can be terrorism. Migration does not lead to crime, and crime does not result in terrorism, but all three are consequences of uprooting. Even when there is no direct link between poverty and violence, systematic neglect of aspirations and feelings of injustice create conditions within which violence can flourish. People may acquiesce to violence when they feel humiliated, personally and as a group, once they feel that they are not taken seriously, not respected or recognized as a culture or as a society, once they feel excluded by the new world system. Then they may give a willing ear to calls for violence. Some approve silently, others give support or shelter. Others show themselves receptive to a message of violent action. 'Why not', they may think, 'if the world does not leave us an alternative?'

Those who feel that the system does not care about them may try to seek access to the system, try to clear themselves a way into the system. That has been the aspiration of migrants and of emancipation movements. Often they have been successful. But if your experience is that the system not only ignores you, but brushes you aside, doesn't want you, cuts you off, excludes you, then you may become inclined to consider it your turn to turn away from the system. 'If the system doesn't want me, then I do not want the system' is a form of logic. People who come as far as this do not even seek access to the system any more. They turn their back upon the system, denounce that system. One step further is to resist and oppose it, to want it to be undermined, then to attack and undermine it themselves.

Poverty does not lead necessarily to violence. But poverty, exclusion and neglect, the perception of being seen as a lesser people with an inferior culture, being treated as dispensable by those who have access to the market, to wealth and power, together will lead to aversion, resistance, hate, violence and terrorism; resistance against globalization, which is perceived as perverse, as a curtailment of living space, as occupation; aversion to Western dominant values, which steered that process of globalization in the direction of global apartheid; hate against leaders of that process and against those who hold power within the system; violence against its symbols; deadly violence against innocent people within that system; unscrupulous, unsparing violence, fanatically believing: 'this is the only way'.

Is it wholly incomprehensible that people who consider themselves desperate become receptive to the idea that they have been turned into extremists by a system beyond reach? One step further and they become receptive to the arguments of fanatics; they have nothing to lose in a battle against a system that is blocking their future. One more step and they believe that they will gain by sacrificing themselves in that battle. It is hideous, beyond justification, but the notion exists. It should and can be fought, but the most effective way to do so is not by resorting to counter-violence alone, but by taking away the motives and reasons that people may have when surrendering to the temptations of fanatics.

Most people, however poor and desperate, dislike violence. They are disillusioned, but in doubt. Many people in the world have developed a love–hate relationship with the West and its culture. They do not want to make a choice for or against the West unless they are forced to do so – for instance by the West itself. Then resentment overtakes doubt.

After 11 September 2001, world leadership has the task of disarming the fanatics without alienating those who doubt. As was pleaded by UN Secretary-General Kofi Annan when he received the Nobel Peace Prize, that requires building a sustainable, democratic and peaceful world society, within which humanity is seen as indivisible. That concept of sustainability, Kofi Annan added, ought to be based upon the dignity and inviolability of all human life, irrespective of origin, race or creed.

Lifelines

That is what was really at stake in Johannesburg – universal access to basic categories of sustainability: health, water, biodiversity, agriculture and energy.

Health means survival; water is life... Biodiversity gives us a lifeline to the past as well as the future. It is the ultimate guarantee of the continuity of life. Agriculture provides people with food, work, an income and a home. Energy is the lifeline with progress: a more efficient use of resources, more food, more work, a better home. Water, energy, health, agriculture and biodiversity – WEHAB – they form a string of lifelines. Together they give human survival a meaning and life a sense of direction, by freeing people from the fight for mere survival, to overcome the constraints set by space and time, to enable them to reflect on the sense and meaning of human existence, to divide labour and exchange the fruits of labour, to philosophize, write poetry, make love, create images, tell stories, collect knowledge, play games. A sustainable world society means that people are free to do all this together with other people, within the family and with partners in society, coming from different backgrounds, with different cultures, different experiences, different insights, different languages, and to share all that with each other.

Water, energy, health, agriculture and biodiversity. Together they are the lifeline between people and the planet. They shape the essential conditions for a sustainable development of human life, provided of course that they themselves are being preserved, sustained and developed in equilibrium with each other. That is crucial if we are to halve the number of people living in poverty or eradicate it altogether. But those conditions for sustainability can only be met if there is a common determination towards the goal, common values and a shared belief concerning the system within which the endeavour should take place, full agreement about rights and duties, a willingness to comply with the norms and to live up to the principles, being confident that all this will be adhered to by everybody else, whether rich and powerful or not. Not only is the task itself complex, but so is the setting within which the task has to be accomplished. That cannot be imposed by a government or a bureaucracy. It can only be achieved together with all other partners in society, bottom up, in a participatory approach, so that each and every individual and all social groups can trust that all will benefit more or less equally from a common endeavour to make life worth living, now and in the future.

If we look back to the last decade of the 20th century, we have to acknowledge it failed to fulfil the promises of 1989 and 1992, when we were optimistically heading towards the end of the millennium. It was not a decade of new international sustainable development cooperation. During that period we saw globalization resulting in ever-greater ecological distortions, a sharpening of inequalities, a greater conflict potential and a weakening of the capacity of the polity to deal with these concerns, rather than a strengthening of that capacity. One might call that stumbling into disaster. Economic conflicts have been complicated by religious and cultural conflicts, violence could not be contained but has spread around the globe and all this became further complicated by the violence of terrorism.

Since 11 September 2001 the world stands at a crossroads. The choice is between two paradigms: security or sustainability. Security is exclusive: 'our' security, which we presume to be threatened by others – outsiders, foreigners, potential enemies – and which we try to protect through exclusion. The other paradigm, sustainability, is inclusive: a safe and secure place for all human beings, a safe habitat, a safe job, secure access to food, water and health care, secure entitlements to resources which are essential for a decent and meaningful life, worthy of human beings. Sustainability as an inclusive concept implies the mutual trust that justice will be maintained and secured for all people, without any discrimination. Sustainable development is the ultimate guarantee of mutual security.

In international policy, security is the dominant idea: more exclusion, pre-emptive strikes, retaliation, more violence, more terrorism, war. Going for absolute security kills. Embracing sustainability sows the seeds of life.

Notes

1   Adapted from the Pastrana Borrero Lecture, United Nations Environment Programme, New York, 19 November 2002.

References

Friedman, Thomas (2003) Quoted in online newsletter available at: www.[bs.org/newshour/bb/middle_east/july-dec03/iraq_8-19.htmlm 19 August 2003
Mbeki, President Thabo (2002) Statement at the opening of the World Summit on Sustainable Development, Johannesburg, 26 August 2002
UNCTAD (1987) 'Corea Calls for New Development Consensus', press release

Chapter 3

The Trade and Environment Agenda Post-Johannesburg

Mark Halle, IISD and Nicola Borregaard, RIDES

The World Summit on Sustainable Development (WSSD) in Johannesburg provided an opportunity for the global community to assess progress towards sustainable development in the decade since the Rio Summit in 1992, and to agree on actions aimed at spurring momentum towards that ultimate goal. This chapter addresses two issues. First, it explores why trade liberalization has become controversial in the years since the conclusion of the Uruguay Round in 1995, focusing particularly on the emerging challenges of environment and sustainable development for the trade regime. Second, it concentrates on how to build on the results of WSSD to influence the multilateral trading system so that it is more supportive of sustainable development goals.

Trade Liberalization, Growth and Equity: The Key Issues

Devotees of sustainable development know that lasting environmental progress cannot be achieved unless the pressing development problems facing the poorer countries – and the poor within countries – are addressed. Further economic growth is required to generate the resources needed to combat poverty, improve human well-being and bring resource use within sustainable limits. While a case can be made in the richer countries for moving to a model of development that is much less capital, resource and energy intensive, it is difficult to imagine how most of the world can possibly move to such a model without first enjoying some solid economic growth.

The liberalization of trade has, in recent decades, provided the engine for impressive growth, with expansion of trade far outstripping overall economic growth. Trade is responsible for a significant proportion of recent global economic growth and there is potential for considerable further growth if the process of trade liberalization is allowed to proceed.

The United Nations Conference on Environment and Development – the Rio Conference – recognized this reality. Unable to meet or even come close to committing the financial resources needed to place the world community on a sustainable footing, the richer countries suggested that 'trade, not aid' might be the answer. A full chapter in Agenda 21 was devoted to how trade might be made to contribute to sustainable development, so that countries might 'grow their way out of poverty' through greater access to markets in the rich countries.

If the formula 'trade liberalization leads to economic growth, which leads to sustainable development' were invariably true, there would be massive support for further liberalization, and the trading system would not be facing the crisis of legitimacy it suffers today. Unfortunately, trade contributes to sustainable development only where trade policies and the policies governing social and environmental matters are in harmony and are mutually supportive.

Trade supporters are guilty of selling their case on the basis of aggregate statistics. Recent evidence suggests, however, that there are disturbingly negative links between global decisions and local effects. The real-life impact at the local level of decisions taken at the global level – even for the best of reasons – is emerging as a central issue in attempting to make trade liberalization support sustainable development goals.

Are Trade and Sustainable Development Compatible?

One of the more common clichés in the trade world is that there is no inherent contradiction between pursuing the goals of trade liberalization and those of development or the environment. Indeed, trade policy professionals will point to a range of ways in which more open trade contributes to social development or to environmental progress. Trade, development and environmental policies, we are told, need not be incompatible.

Indeed, trade can be good in a number of obvious ways. First, in generating economic growth, it makes available resources that can be used to address burning national or international issues. To the extent that it does generate such disposable income, it justifies the Rio bargain of greater trade to replace dwindling aid resources. Second, free trade augments competition, and breaks down protected markets that, generally speaking, are to the disadvantage of consumers. The competition is an incentive to innovate and to modernize, often replacing dirty and inefficient technology with more environmentally and worker-friendly technology. Third, participation in the wider world has also helped to spread notions of more transparent and democratic governance, respect for human rights, priority for social issues and a cleaner environment. Indeed, it is well established that public demand for environmental quality rises with economic status. Last, it obliges countries to review their policies, laws and regulations, often opening the way for outdated policies to be replaced.

However, this optimistic listing masks the fact that trade policy is rarely in harmony with development and environment policies, with the result that trade liberalization often has the effect of undermining policies in these other fields, or of impeding progress towards their realization.

The problem lies in the fact that trade policy generally reflects commercial interests. Few countries undergo an open and participatory process where commercial and other public policy interests are woven together to form a trade policy representing the wide range of national interests in a balanced way. Instead, trade policy tends to be strongly biased in favour of a narrow view of immediate commercial interests.

What counts is not what is possible in a hypothetical world, but what happens in reality. Encouragement can be derived not from imagining that some hypothetical state might one day be reached, but from measuring real progress towards that state. The in-built contradiction between the two is the source of growing frustration, and has led to a serious undermining of the credibility of the multilateral trading system and of the World Trade Organization (WTO), entrusted with its administration.

This is a recent phenomenon. For most of its history, the General Agreement on Tariffs and Trade (GATT – the predecessor of the WTO) attracted little attention. This is because it dealt almost exclusively with manufactured goods, and what happened at the border when these goods were traded. The mandate of GATT was almost exclusively within the undisputed field of trade policy, leaving development and environment policy in the realm of domestic decision-making, or to purpose-built regimes dealing with their international aspects.

The Uruguay Round – and the subsequent creation of the WTO to replace GATT – changed that for good, because it represented a massive expansion of the scope of trade policy, bringing it centrally into domains once reserved for domestic policy-setting. In a wide range of fields – food safety, product standards, standardization, intellectual property rights, services, environment – the Uruguay Round gave the WTO authority in areas that were, before that, the exclusive preserve of national governments, or of specific inter-governmental regimes. Add to that the power of the WTO's dispute settlement system, with its ability to impose sanctions on sovereign governments and to ensure that trade policy took precedence over other policies, and the formula for conflict was complete. Incompatibility between trade and other policies was not only a matter for academic interest, but for genuine alarm.

In the few years leading up to the WTO ministerial conference in Seattle and since, the debate has polarized. Free trade proponents continue to insist on the beneficial impacts of trade on both development and environment, and attribute problems to policy failures in other areas. Those sceptical of – or downright opposed to – further liberalization claim that it rests on a failed model linked to the now discredited Washington consensus, and insist that trade liberalization is nothing more than a tool, a vehicle, that should be subordinated to broader public policy goals.

The truth, as always, lies between the two. Trade and the trade rules are often blamed for problems the cause of which lies elsewhere. Trade liberalization has become a symbol of globalization, and of the insecurities associated with it, and ends up taking the blame for any aspect of the prevailing macroeconomic paradigm. It is often convenient to blame the trade rules for problems in fact caused by discriminatory domestic policies, by protectionist forces, or by competition among corporations.

Impact of Trade Liberalization

With trade policy in the ascendant, and with the Uruguay Round bringing trade policy into the realm of domestic decision-making, it has become increasingly evident that trade liberalization has had a negative impact on development and environment.

First, trade liberalization has served an economic model, described as the Washington consensus, which promised rapid growth in exchange for rapid liberalization. While this promise has often been fulfilled in the aggregate, it has led to a model of development that has deepened the inequities among and within countries. This in turn has led to the marginalization of countries, communities and populations, to the worsening of some development indicators, and to the degradation of the environment that too often accompanies poverty. It is a model that relies on massive consumption of energy and natural resources, contributing to the progressive recession of sustainable development goals.

Second, trade liberalization challenges the sovereignty of governments to establish their own domestic approaches to development and to set their own standards for environmental quality. Trade liberalization has a powerful standardizing effect, and the standards adopted tend to be those suited to the developed countries. Recent experience with the North American Free Trade Agreement (NAFTA) suggests that trade rules are having a 'chill effect' on new regulation; governments are afraid that new environmental or social regulations will land them in trade disputes with their partners.

Third, there are in-built contradictions between the trade rules and other international conventions, for example between the provisions of the WTO agreement on Trade-Related Intellectual Property Rights (TRIPs) on the one hand, and the Convention on Biological Diversity at the multilateral level, or Brazilian and South African legislation on essential medicines, on the other. In the case of a dispute, it is almost always the politically more powerful trade rules that prevail.

Fourth, recent studies suggest that trade liberalization increases pressure on developing countries to export their natural resources. This increase in direct exploitation of natural resources is taking place in an environment largely unguided by clear rules or codes of conduct at the international level, leading to serious negative impacts on developing country environmental policies.

Fifth, trade liberalization favours the commercial sector, and the exporters in particular. It similarly offers advantages to export-based products over others, and to exporting countries over others. This further consolidates the commercial sector and increases its political influence, undermining the ability of governments to seek appropriate balances in the public good.

The Rio Bargain Betrayed

If the general public began to focus on the impacts of trade liberalization only after the Uruguay Round brought trade policy into the living room, the experience of developing countries dates back to Rio. The promises inherent in the 'Rio bargain' were taken seriously; growing out of dependency will always be preferable to living on international alms. Developing countries started to join GATT on a large scale during the Uruguay Round. In the seven years since WTO was established to take over from GATT, membership has expanded to 140; the vast majority of new members come from developing countries or economies in transition. Since WTO is a consensus-based organization, it might have been expected that the transformation would be accompanied by a sharp rise in the priority accorded to development issues in the trade context. Sadly that is not the case.

The results of the Uruguay Round were aggressively sold to the developing countries on the grounds that everyone would come out ahead. Although there would be some who benefited more, no country would be left behind. Very rapidly after the round was concluded, however, it became clear that the benefits from liberalization would not be automatic and depended on putting conditions in place domestically to take advantage of the new market openings. This in turn depended on ... *development*. It was predicated on access to investment, access to technology, existence of an adequate policy, regulatory and institutional infrastructure, and the human capacity to understand where the openings lay and how they could be exploited. In the absence of these, many developing countries found they had thrown open their own markets without being in a position to take advantage of the modest openings that the rich country markets now afforded them.

To this must be added the fact that liberalization in the fields that would provide most benefit to developing countries was either very modest (eg agriculture), deferred (eg textiles), or plagued by bad-faith implementation (eg textiles, anti-dumping). The trade liberalization generated in the Uruguay Round was potentially beneficial to all countries. In reality, it benefited those already privileged countries that were in a position to take advantage of the new market openings.

In response, the developing countries developed an implementation agenda, seeking assistance both to develop their capacity to take advantage of the new trade opportunities, and to deal with the development problems that the lack of capacity was generating. Little progress was made, and attempts to link agreement on a new round to progress on implementation failed with the general collapse of Seattle.

Seattle tripped up the momentum of trade liberalization, but not for long. The same issues were back on the agenda less than two years later, at the WTO Ministerial Meeting in Doha (Qatar), in November 2001, at which a new round of multilateral trade negotiations was launched. While the work programme adopted there is entitled the Doha Development Agenda, there is a genuine fear that this might be window dressing rather than a real commitment to addressing the current imbalances in the trading system.

BOX 3.1 BENEFITS OF FURTHER LIBERALIZATION?

Why should developing countries even consider agreeing to further liberalization? Aside from strong and persistent pressure from the more powerful countries, there are three reasons:

1   Still ahead are prospects for liberalization in the areas that could be of strong benefit to the developing countries – especially the prospect of greater market access for their agricultural and textile products. Without further negotiations, these prospects will not be realized.
2   Although liberalization has yielded more benefits to the richer countries, it has nevertheless provided developing countries with solid development benefits as well. Developing countries fear that an anti-liberalization stance will strengthen the hand of protectionists and 'freeze in place' the current situation of inequity.
3   Lack of progress at the multilateral level will not halt liberalization, but shift it to regional and bilateral trade processes in which developing countries have even less relative power, and which tend to be dominated by one or two 'giants' (eg the US in the Americas).

Trade and Environment after Doha

The fourth ministerial meeting of the WTO took place in Doha, Qatar, in November 2001. Unlike the third ministerial meeting in Seattle, which ended in failure, the Doha meeting reached agreement on a programme of work – the Doha Development Agenda – that will occupy the trade policy community over the coming years. It includes a range of items that will be negotiated, another set of issues that will be prepared for negotiation, and a further range of issues that will be the subject of particular attention.

This corresponds to the way the trading system has always worked. Issues that are admitted to be relevant are first studied; once they are mature, they move to a second phase – that of framing the negotiation agenda; once the agenda is clear, the issues are placed on the table for negotiation.

Doha represented an advance for the environment in the trade context. A number of environmental issues were admitted into the first-class cabin – they have been accepted for negotiation; others moved up to business class – the framing stage; and many more were kept on board for further examination. It must also be said that there are some threats to the environment in the Doha agenda – some issues were left on stand-by, on a badly overbooked flight.

This progress was largely unexpected. Since the WTO and its Committee on Trade and Environment (CTE) were first set up in 1995, the formal trade and environment agenda remained unchanged through three ministerial meetings, and little visible progress had been made. A range of environmentally related disputes in the WTO, and in particular the famous 'shrimp–turtle' case, deepened developing country suspicion and their determination to resist the extension of the environmental agenda in the WTO.

A combination of deft manoeuvring by the European Union and the normal trade-offs needed to secure concessions in other areas, led to a breakthrough on the environment in the Doha agreement. Henceforth, the environment is considered not only a topic permanently relevant to trade, it is now also a topic for negotiation. In other words, environment is a topic on which countries that wish to see stronger environmental safeguards will have to be prepared to make trade-offs with countries not so convinced of the wisdom of placing environment at the centre of trade policy.

This breakthrough is undoubtedly more significant for its symbolic value than for the substance of the environmental concessions so far secured. Indeed, the negotiation agenda is extremely limited in scope, with built-in restrictions on how far the negotiators can expand the purview of the negotiations.

Even if the agenda is successfully completed, it is far from sufficient to ensure full coherence between trade and environment policies at the national and global levels. And it is very far from enough to ensure that trade liberalization contributes optimally to sustainable development. That would require action over a much broader front, and would no doubt require a re-examination of a number of the premises and assumptions on which the entire trading system is based.

Still, some progress was made in realigning the WTO in support of sustainable development. Reference to sustainable development in the preamble of the Doha declaration is stronger and more definitive than similar text in the Marrakech agreements that ended the Uruguay Round. And for those who doubt the value of non-binding preambular language, past practice has shown that it is referred to in trade disputes and, in some cases (eg shrimp–turtle), appears to influence the outcome considerably. More important, the CTE and the WTO Committee on Trade and Development (CTD) have been given a watching brief over the entire Doha Development Agenda, from an environment and development perspective, respectively. Issues important to the environment are, of course, spread right across the negotiation agenda, so that this brief is potentially of great significance if it is well used. The CTE can take care that environmental interests are advanced in the negotiations on agriculture, services, intellectual property rights, subsidies and the many other issues that have either an environmental dimension, or an impact on the environment. How, or indeed whether, this review process can lead to recommendations to the negotiators is still far from clear.

So Doha turned a corner on trade and environment. The argument is no longer whether environment belongs in the WTO, but rather how it will be dealt with. The countries that resisted introducing environmental concerns must now turn their attention to how their own environmental interests might be advanced in the trade context, and what advantages they might secure in exchange for concessions to those who believe ardently in environmental progress. Nobody knows how the environment agenda will play out in the WTO, because the game is new and unfamiliar.

What WSSD Could Not Do

UN mega-conferences have been following a law of diminishing returns over the past two decades. The Summit on Financing for Development in Monterrey was long on rhetoric but very short on commitment. And, in terms of concrete outcomes that can be measured, counted or ratified by parliaments, WSSD was no better. If anything, it was worse.

Predictably, those who hoped to secure at WSSD what they failed to achieve in Doha or Monterrey were disappointed. Doha was the forum for securing concessions on the trade agenda and what was achieved there represents a difficult and delicate balance. Monterrey could not do anything to upset or even tilt that balance. Nor could WSSD. It was not able to trump Doha, despite the larger number of countries represented. It failed to secure any concessions on trade that could not be secured at Doha, with a few minor exceptions, outlined below. And it was not able to reverse any of the decisions taken at Doha. Those who hoped that it might were dreaming.

What WSSD Did Do

Doha created space – political and negotiating space – to study, frame an agenda for, and negotiate issues that arise at, the trade and environment interface. Further, it advanced the notion that sustainable development may be considered a goal to which the process of trade liberalization should contribute and against which trade proposals might increasingly be judged.

For the moment, this space is only loosely occupied. It was to be hoped that Johannesburg would focus on how to occupy that space in a way likely to advance sustainable development goals and reinforce the synergy between the worlds of trade and environment policy. What, in fact, was achieved?

Most significantly, WSSD beat back a concerted attempt to make multilateral environmental agreements subsidiary to the trade rules, a move that would have been a disaster for international environmental cooperation. While the exact interaction between the two sets of rules remains unclear, each is deemed to be equally valid in relation to the issues they address. Beyond this, WSSD adopted some language that may allow environmental concerns to be reinforced in the trade context. This included:

- a strengthening of the call to phase out harmful subsidies, including the elimination of 'subsidies that contribute to illegal, unreported and unregulated fishing and to over-capacity';
- a renewed call to promote the 'mutual supportiveness' of multilateral environmental agreements (MEAs) and trade rules, along with recognition of the 'importance of maintaining the integrity of both sets of instruments';
- an emphasis on liberalizing markets for 'organic products' in the context of the negotiation on environmental goods and services;

- a strong plea to strengthen and extend capacity building on the relationship between trade and sustainable development, including a focus on sustainable resource management and reversing the instability of commodity prices;
- a decision to negotiate, in the context of the Convention on Biological Diversity, 'an international regime to promote and safeguard the fair and equitable sharing of benefits arising out of the utilization of genetic resources'.

WSSD tried, with the limited success noted above, to shove the Doha agenda into a broader framework of sustainable development. It might have done better to focus on structuring the sustainable development community's response to Doha, enhancing its ability to take advantage of the openings created by the Doha agenda, and working out how to expand that space in the course of the trade negotiations now under way. Now that WSSD is over, is any of this still attainable?

A Positive Trade Agenda Post-WSSD

The Doha agenda offers considerable scope for positive interaction between the sustainable development community and the trade policy community, just as it represents a number of dangers. The following are a number of suggestions on ways in which the sustainable development community might reinforce the former, while avoiding the latter.

Sustainable development as the goal of trade liberalization

The Doha preamble states that:

> *we are convinced that the aims of upholding and safeguarding an open and non-discriminatory multilateral trading system, and acting for the protection of the environment and the promotion of sustainable development can and must be mutually supportive.*

By implication, the WTO is saying not only that it recognizes protection of the environment and the promotion of sustainable development as compatible and equally valid with the goals of trade policy, but also that this compatibility must be ensured. The sustainable development community should focus on how that obligation might be met in practice. Further, for the first time, the Doha preamble speaks of the need for cooperation with other bodies, including the UN Environment Programme (UNEP).

This will require the sustainable development community to accept that an open and non-discriminatory multilateral trading system is a desirable goal for sustainable development. At the same time, the sustainable development community must insist that trade policy be supportive of sustainable development goals in fact and not just in theory. It should urge the WTO to adopt sustainable development as the clear and unequivocal goal for the trading system (IISD Viewpoint, 2001).

If such a goal is clearly established, it will be possible to insist on reviewing all present and proposed trade measures in light of their impact on sustainable development. Indeed, until there is an agreement on what end trade is designed to serve, controversy over trade liberalization is bound to continue.

Building capacity to occupy the spaces created by Doha

As noted above, Doha created new space for the environmental debate in the WTO. It has created a range of new opportunities for the sustainable development community to influence the trading system so that it is more favourable to sustainable development goals. That said, the sustainable development community is poorly prepared to take full advantage of the opportunities that exist. Capacity within the environmental community to advance sustainable development proposals in the trade policy arena is still extremely thin, especially in the developing countries. Yet, with over ten references to the need for capacity building in the Doha declaration and the WSSD Plan for Implementation, the millions being provided to the WTO technical assistance trust fund and the strong attention being paid to the need to build capacity to negotiate, very little attention is being devoted to building the capacity needed to pursue environmental or sustainable development objectives through the trading system. One of the few exceptions is the International Institute for Sustainable Development – International Centre for Trade and Sustainable Development (IISD-ICTSD) Trade Knowledge Network, now being expanded in collaboration with the IIED-led Regional and International Networking Group (Ring). The sustainable development community should push for a commitment to greatly expand capacity building programmes aimed at equipping the community to advance its interests in the multilateral trading system.

Securing parity between the WTO and MEAs

Ever since the Uruguay Round was concluded there has been a fear that the WTO might challenge trade measures taken pursuant to multilateral environmental agreements. At the same time, trade sanctions are essential in ensuring compliance with obligations under these conventions. As the experience of the WTO has shown, it is the threat of sanctions that gives the agreements teeth.

The issue of the link between the WTO and MEAs is now on the negotiating table and is probably the most urgent of the issues around which capacity must be built. There was a concerted – and nearly successful – attempt at WSSD to adopt language that would have placed the onus on the MEAs to demonstrate their compatibility with the trade rules. Now that this threat has been pushed aside – at least for the moment – the sustainable development community should promote a set of principles that might govern these negotiations. They include the following:

- MEAs are international undertakings signed by WTO member states and other governments, and are in no way subordinate to the international trade rules.

- Issues arising from the MEAs should be addressed by their own dispute settlement or governance mechanisms, and not by the WTO. The WTO should unequivocally state that its panels will not hear disputes arising from MEAs, until and unless the recourse mechanisms available through the MEAs themselves have been exhausted.
- The negotiations in the WTO should consider a blanket exemption for legitimate trade measures taken under an MEA, perhaps subject to respect for certain criteria (eg that they are the least trade-distorting of the measures available). These criteria should be developed in an independent forum involving the WTO and MEA secretariats, with appropriate representatives from government and civil society.
- The key inter-governmental organizations in the environment field and the key MEAs must have the right to attend negotiation sessions as observers.

At the same time, the sustainable development community should accept that, in implementing trade measures, MEAs should respect the WTO principles of transparency and non-discrimination. There is no necessary incompatibility between the WTO's wish for a level playing field and the objectives of environmental policy. In this respect, the Doha agenda carries risks in that it excludes consideration of cases between parties and non-parties to a convention when both are WTO member states. Also undesirable would be any attempt by the WTO to define what is a legitimate trade measure under an MEA.

Agriculture

After six years of pursuing a limited agenda on agriculture, Doha has launched the WTO into agricultural negotiations in earnest. This presents both opportunities and dangers for the environment. The declaration recognizes the concept of 'multifunctionality', that is, the notion that agriculture serves a variety of purposes beyond the production of agricultural commodities. And it appears to give scope for a series of environmental exceptions to the general rule of agricultural liberalization.

The sustainable development community should rally around a strategy to maximize the use of the environmental instruments available in agriculture, while helping to dismantle the barriers to developing country products and assisting them to adjust to the new environmental paradigms in agricultural production.

Subsidies: scope for a genuine win–win formula

Since its establishment in 1995, the WTO has had an agreement (the Agreement on Subsidies and Countervailing Measures) that determines how to evaluate subsidies for their trade-distorting effect. Only those that meet these strict criteria can be challenged. The environmental community has always been frustrated at the limited scope of this agreement, believing that the elimination of perverse subsidies represents a genuine meeting ground for the trade and sustainable development communities. Many subsidies are, indeed, bad for trade, bad for development and bad for the environment.

The Doha agenda opens a modest space for identification and elimination of perverse subsidies, starting with fisheries. The sustainable development community should not only organize the environmental community to come forward with ideas and recommendations in this area, but should also argue for the WTO to use the full scope of its agenda to create momentum behind a genuine move to progressively eliminate perverse subsidies.

Boosting cooperation on environmental standards

The Doha agenda calls for the CTE to frame an agenda on 'labelling for environmental purposes'. While vaguely worded, this refers to the need to agree on the range of standards, norms and rules that underlie the market or the consumer's ability to favour products that meet given environmental criteria. This has been controversial in the past, largely because of the fear that environmental standards would be used in a discriminatory manner. Now that environment is on the agenda, there is an urgent need not only to secure greater international cooperation on environmental standards, but also to ensure that developing countries are not put at a disadvantage as the application of these standards becomes ever more important for trade. The sustainable development community should agree on a strong upgrading of efforts to develop and apply a mutually compatible set of environmental standards, to favour standards that are non-discriminatory and support sustainable development, and to build capacity for developing countries to participate in the standard-setting process.

Intellectual property rights and traditional knowledge

The TRIPs Agreement has proved to be one of the most unpopular of the WTO disciplines, and has contributed in considerable measure to the poor public image enjoyed by the WTO in the sustainable development community. In a move that has enormous value as a precedent, Doha put the first crack in the TRIPs edifice, by forcing a relaxation of intellectual property protection for public health purposes. Indeed, the members agreed that a non-commercial objective was important enough to force this relaxation. The Doha agenda now calls for framing future action on other relevant provisions of TRIPs.

It is time for the sustainable development community to come together to agree on a clear, bold and specific agenda in respect of the WTO and intellectual property rights, beginning with recognition of measures to protect indigenous, traditional and communally held knowledge.

Investment

While Doha did not agree to launch negotiations on investment immediately, there is a strong likelihood that they will be initiated following the next ministerial meeting in the second half of 2003. Following the collapse of the Organisation for Economic Co-operation and Development (OECD) negotiations on a multilateral investment agreement, the sustainable development community has somewhat gone to sleep on the issue of investment liberalization. That is a dangerous slumber. Not only in NAFTA, but also in a rapidly expanding number of bilateral investment agreements, investors are securing rights with very few corresponding responsibilities, and in a way that is providing a strong disincentive for both social and environmental legislation in developed and developing countries alike. The sustainable development community must now mobilize a coalition to monitor closely all proposals for investment liberalization, to develop policy options and to begin briefing developing country negotiators on the dangers of what is currently being proposed.

Conclusion

The value of the Rio and Johannesburg processes was that they looked beyond competitive national and regional interests to the requirements of a world characterized by a healthy environment and a satisfactory standard of living for all. This idealism undoubtedly led both summits to fall short of their goals, but nothing that has happened in the past ten years suggests that the goal was wrong or that it was foolish to try.

Indeed, in the period between Rio and Johannesburg, we have lived through an era of unprecedented growth and prosperity, accompanied by an increase in poverty, marginalization and inequality. We have lived through the Asia crisis and the collapse of the Washington consensus. We have witnessed the crises of the World Bank, the International Monetary Fund (IMF) and the WTO. We have seen the massive backlash against globalization and the questioning of our economic models. We have lost faith in the generosity of the richer countries, which matched unprecedented prosperity with dwindling support for development cooperation.

There was, in theory, scope for considerable creativity in WSSD in respect of the trade and sustainable development interface, and the eight proposals outlined above should in no way limit the innovative spirit of the follow-up. Indeed, in part because the achievements of WSSD are so modest, creativity and innovation are needed more than ever in the trade policy world, which has not shown much openness to change even when the world has fundamentally changed around it.

This chapter makes a few simple points:

- The WSSD could not reopen, modify or reverse decisions taken at Doha. Attempts to do so were doomed to failure.
- Instead, the starting point for sensible follow-up action lies in the recognition that Doha has created considerable new space for a constructive debate between the trade and sustainable development communities.
- The sustainable development community should focus on how that space might best be occupied, how it might use the new openings to influence the Doha agenda in favour of sustainable development, and how capacity to do that might best be built.
- More than anything, the sustainable development community should aim to identify specific, implementable ideas cast in terms that the trade policy community can accommodate.

The WTO is not the hermetically sealed fortress that it used to be. There is scope for considerable evolution of the trading system towards sustainable development, but it requires an organized, capable and strategic sustainable community to spearhead that movement. It did not all come together at WSSD, but it could now.

Reference

IISD Viewpoint (2001) 'What is it All For? Setting Clear Goals for the World Trading System', August 2001, available at www.iisd.org/trade

Chapter 4

Moving Beyond Kyoto: Developing Countries, Climate Change and Sustainable Development

Adil Najam, Tufts University and SDPI, Saleemul Huq, IIED and BCAS and Youba Sokona, ENDA

Five years down the road from Kyoto, the protocol that bears that city's name is finally inching towards ratification. It has been a tortuous journey: the political process stands much bruised, and the substance of the protocol has been much diluted. While its eventual ratification will be a moment to celebrate, there is no cause to be complacent. Although the Kyoto Protocol is a step in the right direction, it is a very small step at best. Moreover, what was always a desirable but imperfect agreement has been made all the more imperfect by the fact that the world's largest polluter has decided to stay out of the agreement, while those who have agreed to join have demanded and received changes that have weakened the protocol considerably. It is time to begin thinking about the shape of the global climate regime in its post-Kyoto phase. This chapter begins doing so from the perspective of the developing countries of the South. The principal argument is that we need to return to the basic principles outlined in the Framework Convention on Climate Change in searching for a new North–South bargain on climate change. Such a bargain may be achievable if we can construct a new policy architecture that places sustainable development at its core.

The recent Conferences of the Parties (particularly COP-6 and COP-7) to the United Nations Framework Convention on Climate Change (FCCC) have managed to resuscitate what had seemed to be a sinking Kyoto Protocol, despite the US decision to abandon the agreement (Müller, 2002b). However, the decisions taken at these meetings leave the protocol riddled with all the many problems that had dogged the original agreement while further diluting its content significantly.

While the survival of the protocol may be something to celebrate, from the perspective of the developing countries of the South, the protocol, which had been imperfect to begin with, is now all the more flawed (Agarwal et al, 1999; Najam, 2001a). The buy-in to the protocol, including by developing countries, has largely come on the basis of the argument that 'getting something is better than getting nothing' and that, no matter how diluted, the protocol could become a first step towards 'bigger and better things'. While the eventual coming into force of the protocol would be a welcome step, no one doubts that it would be rather meagre progress (Malakoff, 1997; Najam and Page, 1998). Although the coming into force of the protocol is still not a certainty, it is becoming increasingly likely that it will be ratified by enough countries to come into effect sometime fairly soon (Müller, 2002a). This is largely because of the efforts of the Europeans who have pushed long and hard for the protocol to come into force even without the US. However, this has meant compromising on some of the key clauses of the protocol as it was originally negotiated, including on issues related to sinks and to carbon trading. In this bartering process, the so-called 'flexibility mechanisms' within the protocol have been flexed to the maximum (Agarwal et al, 2001).

So, where do we stand five years down the road from Kyoto? Is the world's climate any better off than it was five years ago? Are the developing countries any better off? Unfortunately the answer to the last two questions has to be negative. However, while much precious time has been lost, something valuable may still be salvaged. The purpose of this chapter is to take stock of the Kyoto Protocol from a developing country perspective.

The Kyoto process has been focused on – even obsessed with – the short-term need to launch the policy process and get the industrialized countries to agree to targets, no matter how meagre. It is time now to refocus on the longer-term objectives of the FCCC, particularly on its stated goals regarding sustainable development. In this regard, developing countries are now confronted by both challenges and opportunities.

The challenges emerge from the fact that developing country concerns, which had always been marginal to the thrust of the FCCC, have become even more marginalized in recent COPs as energy has had to be diverted to get reluctant Northern countries (those listed in Annex 1) to accede to the Kyoto Protocol. As the industrialized countries dragged their feet, the concerns of the developing nations have largely been lost in the dust. With the Kyoto dust now beginning to settle, it is time to bring these Southern concerns to the forefront once again. The focus on mitigation targets has been entirely logical since industrialized countries have been the principal contributors to the carbon build-up and remain the predominant carbon emitters (Müller, 2002a). However, the post-Kyoto period has been so consumed by getting Annex 1 countries to agree to what they had already agreed to at Kyoto that there has been little time or energy left for other issues, particularly those that are of greater interest to the South. This has only deepened the existing North–South split in global climate politics (Müller, 2002b). Moreover, in the desire to get the North to accede, the protocol has been structured in ways that could be detrimental to Southern interests once they also have to take on mandated commitments (Agarwal et al, 1999). For example, in deciding to reduce emissions as a percentage of 1990 emissions rather than setting targets for allowable emissions per capita, the structure of the protocol has created a system which benefits those with high current emissions rather than those whose current emissions are low. The system, if maintained, is likely to be detrimental to Southern interests since most developing countries have fairly low per capita emissions and are likely to be required to cap their emissions at lower levels than the current emissions of countries of the European Union or US (Agarwal and Narain, 1991; Najam and Sagar, 1998). For the most part, developing countries would have preferred a system based on maximum allowable emissions according to some negotiated formula and a clear focus on linking climate change and sustainable development (Banuri and Sagar, 1999; Najam, 2001a; Sokona, 2001).

The opportunity emanates from the fact that the case for making the link between climate change and sustainable development is already enshrined in the text of the FCCC (Rayner and Malone, 1998; Banuri et al, 2001). This focus was effectively sidelined in the operational provisions and marginalized in the Kyoto Protocol, which became very narrowly focused only on mitigative goals and emission reductions (Sagar and Kandlikar, 1997; Najam and Sagar, 1998). However, persistent protestations by the South have triggered a resurgent interest in trying to address the links between climate change and sustainable development (Müller, 2002b). It is still not too late to reorient the protocol towards the goals of sustainable development. The increasing interest in issues related to climate adaptability and the related focus on the social, economic and climatic resilience of vulnerable communities and ecological systems allow a good opportunity for this linkage to be strengthened (Munasinghe, 2000; Banuri et al, 2001; Huq and Sokona, 2001; Beg et al, 2002).

Southern Concerns

The original FCCC was not viewed as a great 'victory' by the developing countries, which wanted the convention to focus more directly on issues of historical responsibility, sought more immediate mitigative action and demanded adaptive assistance for the most vulnerable communities and countries (Dasgupta, 1994; Hyder, 1994; Rajan, 1997; Sagar and Kandlikar, 1997). Since then, the climate regime has become even less sympathetic to the concerns of the South (Agarwal et al, 2001; Huq and Sokona, 2001; Najam, 2001a). As already pointed out, this has largely been a case of neglect and inattention, rather than outright assault. For the most part, this has been a direct result of the overwhelming preoccupation of policy-makers, scholars and activists with getting Annex 1 countries to agree, and then accede, to the Kyoto Protocol. In focusing on this short-term objective, the longer-term goals of the FCCC – especially those related to sustainable development – have tended to slip. The result has been a systematic marginalization of the core interests of the developing countries.

While developing country governments and scholars have raised a number of specific concerns regarding the direction in which the global climate regime is evolving, these relate generally to three large categories of concerns:

1 The principle of inter- and intra-generational equity and responsibility which was so central to the discussions of global climate change up until the adoption of the FCCC has been sidelined in the discourse since then, especially since the Kyoto agreement.
2 The focus of the regime has become skewed towards minimizing the burden of implementation on polluter industries and countries, instead of giving priority to the vulnerabilities of the communities and countries at greatest risk and disadvantage.
3 The regime has now distinctly become a regime for managing the global carbon trade and has lost sight of its original mandate of stabilizing atmospheric greenhouse gas concentrations.

Let us explore each of these concerns separately.

Equity and responsibility between and within generations

First, issues of equity and responsibility between and within generations have been among the central themes in the policy as well as in scholarly discussions on global climate change (see Weiss, 1989; Agarwal and Narain, 1991; Jamieson, 1992; Gadgil and Guha, 1995; Shue, 1995; Najam and Page, 1998; Banuri and Sagar, 1999; Meyer, 1999; Baer et al, 2000; Carraro, 2000; Munasinghe, 2000; Müller, 2002a). The discussion on this issue was particularly heated during the years leading up to the FCCC. Although it still figures as a recurrent theme in the scholarly literature, it seems to have lost its salience in the policy discourse. Indeed, equity seemed to be among the first casualties of the Kyoto process, in which even the pretence of some form of equity between emission reduction targets was quickly abandoned amid the arbitrariness and global horse-trading on which the agreement was ultimately based (Reiner and Jacoby, 1997; Najam and Sagar, 1998). Even though the European Union has chosen a framework of burden sharing among its own members on the argument of equity and fairness, the Kyoto regime *as a whole* is devoid of a basis in equity and emanates, instead, from the basis of stated willingness and political expediency. For example, there is no clear reason a priori why the Kyoto Protocol set a target of 7 per cent below the base year emissions for the UK, 6 per cent for Japan and 0 per cent for New Zealand. The lack of a clear and predictable formula or basis for emissions reductions not only sets a bad precedent for the future but also leaves the developing countries without any clue about the basis on which they will be required to enter the regime at some future, unspecified date (Najam and Page, 1998).

The abandonment of the equity principle – particularly with regard to the least developed countries and in the context of the related principle of 'common but differentiated responsibility' – is of grave concern to the South. The regime's loss of interest in the principle of equity and responsibility only encourages the abuse of the principle by its members. Indeed, the essence of the term equity has been distorted by the US Congress which demanded 'equity' between the percentage emission cuts for Annex 1 countries and their developing country counterparts. It remains both comical and sad that, in the very same breath, the

US is both willing and able to deny any call for equity in the level of emissions per person. Even though the average American emits just under 20 tons of carbon dioxide per year while the average Indian emits less than 1 ton and the average Chinese around 1.34 tons, the US Congress wants each to reduce their emissions by an equal percentage but is loathe to even discuss the possibility of a regime that sets the same emission limits for each (Najam and Sagar, 1998). As the desire for efficiency overwhelms both equity and responsibility, the distinction between 'luxury' and 'survival' emissions is lost and any discussion of global or generational fairness becomes all but mute (Agarwal and Narain, 1991).

Priority of most vulnerable countries

On the second issue, the *Third Assessment Report of the Intergovernmental Panel on Climate Change* (IPCC, 2001; see especially Working Group II report) has made it abundantly clear that even if the Kyoto Protocol is implemented in full, the impacts of global climate change will start being felt within the next few decades and that the most vulnerable communities and countries are those which are already the poorest and least able to adapt to these changes. This is because the impact of climatic events is not only a function of the intensity of the event but of the resilience of communities – and the poorest communities tend also to be the least able to adapt (Downing et al, 1996). The threat is especially pressing for the least developed countries (LDCs) and the small island developing states (SIDS), where any economic development they may be able to achieve in the next few decades is in real danger of literally being swept away because of human-induced climate change. In the past, climatic hazards such as floods, cyclones and droughts may have been attributable to nature alone; in the future they will definitely have a component that is human induced. More importantly, it is also clear that the past contribution of these countries to the climate change problem is minuscule. In this regard, much is made of the fact that emissions from developing countries are growing with their development and that sometime in the next two decades the total emissions from all currently developing countries would equal the total emissions from all currently industrialized countries. Although stylized, this is factually correct. However, it needs also to be noted that, even in such a scenario, the vast bulk of the global population would still be living in developing countries, and each individual in the North would still be emitting far more proportionately than their individual counterparts in the South. The result is that those who have been least responsible for creating the crisis are most at risk from its ravages (Rayner and Malone, 1998; Banuri and Sagar, 1999).

The reconvened sixth COP at Bonn in 2001 did agree to set up a number of funds including the Climate Change Fund for capacity building and transfer technology, and the LDC Fund to assist least developed countries in climate change adaptation (Huq, 2003). While the intent of these funds is noble, it is difficult to place too much confidence in their potential, because: (a) they are voluntary, (b) they are to be managed via the still-controversial Global Environment Facility (GEF), and (c) they remain poorly funded (Huq and Sokona, 2001). Similarly, the solution proposed in the Kyoto Protocol –

participation in carbon trade via the Clean Development Mechanism (CDM) – is unlikely to benefit the poorest countries, because they are not positioned or likely to attract private sector funding in any case (Agarwal et al, 1999). It is quite conceivable that the CDM will follow the path of foreign direct investment: the much-trumpeted benefits will accrue to a handful of the larger developing countries, leaving the bulk of the South on the sidelines of the global carbon market (Banuri and Gupta, 2000).

Divergence from FCCC mandate

Third, and flowing directly from the above, is the concern that the so-called 'flexibility mechanisms' of the Kyoto Protocol have turned it into a global carbon trade regime that has lost sight of the original mandate of the FCCC, that is, the stabilization of atmospheric greenhouse concentrations. Significant problems with the Kyoto regime – including the issue of 'low-hanging fruit', trades in 'hot air', the exclusion of poorer countries and marginal groups, and the sheer inadequacy of the Kyoto targets (Najam and Page, 1998; Sokona et al, 1998; Agarwal et al, 1999; Banuri and Sagar, 1999; Meyer, 1999; Banuri and Gupta, 2000; Müller, 2002a) – have long been known and highlighted. These lingering concerns were tempered by the belief that despite all the holes in it, the protocol was a step in the right direction. However, it was and remains quite clear that the problems inherent in the protocol will need to be somehow addressed, and soon. Moreover, the concessions made in the last two COPs (especially on the issue of sinks) and the absence of the world's largest carbon emitter from the regime have made an already inadequate agreement all the more inadequate (Najam, 2001b). A Kyoto Protocol that, even counting the targets originally set for the US, would not have made much of a dent in global carbon stabilization (Malakoff, 1997) is likely to make an even smaller dent now that the US has exited the regime. In addition, the protocol has been made more flexible than ever through liberal latitudes in the provisions regarding the use of sinks and carbon trading to meet stipulated targets.

Most importantly, there is a danger that Kyoto has now become so much a mechanism for managing global carbon trade that the issue of real emission cuts for atmospheric carbon stabilization has been marginalized. This concern is most pronounced for the most vulnerable coastal countries for whom the delay in actual emissions cuts could have dire consequences; especially if the much touted flexibility mechanisms of the Kyoto Protocol fail to deliver the expected benefits of carbon trading. For the emitter countries of Annex 1, it makes full sense to pin their hopes on a successful global market in carbon trade; for low-lying LDCs most vulnerable to climate change, the possibility of failure, even if remote, is both unacceptable and unimaginable.

Southern Interests

While the South's concerns about the climate regime have evolved as the Kyoto Protocol has taken shape, the longer-term interests of the developing countries have remained relatively unchanged over the last decade or longer. While specific (and generally shorter-term) interests of particular countries and regions vary, the key interests of the South as a whole can be characterized within three categories:

1   The creation of a predictable, implementable and equitable architecture for combating global climate change that can stabilize atmospheric concentrations of greenhouse gases within a reasonable period of time, while giving all nations a clear indication of their current and future obligations based on their current and future emissions.
2   Enhancing the capacities of communities and countries to combat and respond to global climate change, with particular attention to adaptive capacity that enhances the resilience of the poorest and most vulnerable communities.
3   The efforts to combat global climate change and the pursuit of sustainable development are two sides of the same coin. For either process to work, each must reinforce the other. To be at all meaningful, any global climate regime must have sustainable development as a central goal – at the declaratory as well as operational levels. With climate change, sustainable development becomes an untenable proposition; with sustainable development, communities and people become more resilient and better able to adapt to climatic and other changes in their environment.

Let us explore each of these interests separately.

Long-term policy architecture

Most environmental issues are long-term issues. Climate change is particularly so. The test of any climate regime is not simply what it will or will not do in the next few years, but also what it is likely to achieve over the next many decades, even centuries. Any policy architecture put into place today is likely to remain with us for a very long time (Jacoby et al, 1998). It is, therefore, very important that the policy architecture we construct is robust enough to stand the political as well as the climatic tests of time. The Kyoto Protocol, even though it is a step in the right direction, leaves much to be desired in terms of its implications for long-term policy (Cooper, 1998). Moreover, as discussed earlier, the arbitrariness of the Kyoto targets and the lack of any objective basis for their selection leaves the countries of the world – developing as well as industrialized – largely directionless on what might be expected of them in the future (Najam and Sagar, 1998).

An alternative, more robust, architecture would be one which defines its targets not in terms of symbolic short-term measures, but long-term atmospheric stabilization; which gives all countries a clear signal on what is likely to be expected of them in the future; which is based on clear and objective principles derived directly from the FCCC; and which is seen to be fair and equitable by all countries, North and South. With the struggle for Kyoto's ratification now nearing completion and with its limitations having become all too clear in the course of this debate, there is an opportunity to re-initiate the discussion on the larger architecture of the future climate regime. This is not to suggest an abandonment of the Kyoto Protocol; rather, this is to build on the Kyoto promise by returning to FCCC basics. One potentially useful approach – although by no means without its own complications – is to move towards per capita emission targets and a 'contraction and convergence' policy scenario aimed at atmospheric stabilization in the post-Kyoto phase (Agarwal et al, 1999; Meyer, 1999). Even if such targets are 'adjusted' on some mutually accepted bases (for example, economic output per unit of carbon, climatic zones, population density, etc) they could lead to a more transparent and predictable regime that sends clear signals to all countries about the type of behaviour that would reduce the regulatory burden on them over time. Moreover, such targets could be applied to all countries, North and South, thereby responding to the US demand that all countries be treated equally by doing away with the 'class' structure of the current regime. Instead of a convoluted system of arbitrary percentage cuts for different countries, having a standard global emissions budget linked directly to atmospheric stabilization would not only be more elegant and equitable but also more manageable in the long term. Indeed, such a system could be a first step towards a more meaningful clustering of related agreements around a broader regime for all issues related to the atmospheric commons (Najam, 2000; Najam et al, 2002).

Social, economic and technical resilience

Moving to the second issue, 'capacity building', much like technology transfer, has been a much-abused term in the rhetoric of climate policy. Both North and South reiterate by rote the importance of building capacity, yet neither has shown much willingness to invest meaningfully in doing so (Banuri and Sagar, 1999). In introducing the twin concepts of 'adaptive' and 'mitigative' capacity (by working groups II and III, respectively) the third assessment of the IPCC (2001) has made a significant contribution to the policy discourse by outlining what types of capacities are required, by whom, and when. The most pressing challenge in this regard is to strengthen the social, economic and technical resilience of the poorest and most vulnerable against extreme climatic events. The priority must be on those countries that are climatically most vulnerable as well as economically impoverished and therefore unable to cope with or adapt to sudden and significant climatically induced disasters. This highlights the need to focus on issues of adaptation, especially in LDCs and SIDS where the threat of climate change is more immediate and intense while the ability to adapt is least developed (Huq and Sokona, 2001). As already mentioned, COP-6 has made a rather symbolic gesture in this direction by setting up a set of voluntary funds. However, there continues to be significant uncertainty about how much money will be available to these funds and how it will be used (Huq, 2003). The next step must be to fund these initiatives and to set up clear priorities for their use; depending on how large these funds are and how they use their endowments, they could be an important step towards aligning the climate change regime towards sustainable development.

While the developing country interest in capacity enhancement is self-evident, the new element is our growing understanding of *where* capacity needs to be enhanced and *what* capacities need to be supported and strengthened. In short, the capacity to adapt to climatic impacts (ie social, economic and technical resilience) is needed most desperately where the vulnerabilities are the most pronounced; that is, at the local and community levels (Bohle et al, 1994; Ribot et al, 1996; Burton, 1997; Rayner and Malone, 1998; Downing and Baker, 1999). Effective capacity building at this level will require a rethinking of both *how* we do capacity building and with *whom* we do it. The shift towards strengthening the social, economic and technical resilience of vulnerable local communities will come from working directly with civil society and community organizations. This will be more difficult as well as more expensive. However, this is an investment that can have pay-offs both for climate change and for sustainable development; each reinforcing the other.

Integrating climate policy and sustainable development

This brings us to the final, overarching and enduring interest of the South in the pursuit of sustainable development. Sustainable development must not be seen *only* as a Southern interest. It is not an opposition to the interests of the North or to the goals of the global climate regime. As the most recent IPCC assessment (IPCC, 2001) has made clear, the supposed dichotomy between the global objective of climate policy and sustainable development policy is false (also see Munasinghe, 2000). Combating climate change is vital to the pursuit of sustainable development; equally, the pursuit of sustainable development is integral to lasting climate change mitigation. The pursuit of sustainable development is a clearly stated goal of both the FCCC and the Kyoto Protocol (see, for example, the preamble and Articles 2 and 3 of FCCC and Articles 2 and 10 of the Kyoto Protocol). Yet, there has been a hesitancy from those operating in the 'climate arena' to deal earnestly with sustainable development. While the Third Assessment Report of the IPCC has included a chapter linking the two, the linkage is far from integrated into the bulk of the report (IPCC, 2001). The issue remained one of considerable contention during the drafting of the Third Assessment Report and subsequent attempts to initiate a special IPCC report on climate change and sustainable development failed after heated debate within the IPCC. In short, although climate change and sustainable development were nominally included in the Third Assessment Report because of developing country pressure, sustainable development is still far from being integrated into the climate change debate. While it is fair to celebrate the fact that sustainable development is now on the IPCC agenda, it would be unreasonable to claim that it has yet been incorporated in any meaningful manner.

The 1992 Rio Earth Summit clearly placed sustainable development as a common interest of all countries, developing as well as industrialized; a common interest around which related North–South bargains could then be built on other issues, including climate change. Unfortunately, this has not yet happened. The 2002 World Summit on Sustainable Development (WSSD) tried to reinstate the concept to its intended place at the centre of all environmental policy. A recent survey of more than 250 experts and practitioners from 71 countries rated climate change as the second most important issue (after poverty eradication) in terms of achieving sustainable development (Najam et al, 2002). It is time that those involved in climate policy recognize that sustainable development is similarly important to their goals. The post-Kyoto regime will be stronger if it forcefully re-establishes its links with sustainable development; it will certainly get more support from developing countries if it does. Ignoring sustainable development's importance to climate policy may or may not impact the future of sustainable development but will almost certainly adversely impact the future of the global climate regime. Stated most simply, sustainable development is needed because it can provide the conditions in which climate policies can best be implemented (Munasinghe, 2000; Beg et al, 2002).

Towards a Post-Kyoto Climate Regime

Five years down the road from Kyoto, and with the prospects of the protocol coming into force finally inching towards reality, is there an opportunity to move into a post-Kyoto phase of negotiation, one which could revitalize the global climate regime by expanding its intents and contents beyond the narrow confines of the Kyoto Protocol? Could a new climate bargain be struck which explicitly links the goals of combating climate change with those of sustainable development, designs a new and more inclusive architecture for the climate regime, and invests in meaningful capacity development for adaptation and societal resilience in the poorest and most vulnerable communities and countries?

Yes, it can. But only if governments, academics and activists from the South take the lead in actively seeking such change.

The lead for such a realignment of the climate debate will have to come from the governments of the South, since they are the principal demanders of such change (Sagar and Kandlikar, 1997; Najam and Page, 1998; Banuri and Gupta, 2000; Sokona and Denton, 2001; Müller, 2002a). Once the task of bringing the Kyoto Protocol into force is completed, we will have to start thinking about what is going to follow Kyoto. Developing countries which have essentially sat on the sidelines of the climate discussions for the last ten years have both the opportunity and the responsibility to become more active in this discussion, or even its leaders.

The world's attention is already directed towards them and seeks what the US has called 'meaningful developing country participation' in the climate regime. If the South remains as quiet and uninterested in this new phase as it was in the previous one, participation is likely to be 'thrust' upon it in terms of mandatory targets of some sort. On the other hand, developing country governments could seize this as an opportunity to change the terms of the discussion and of the regime by reopening the questions of regime architecture, of investments in adaptation, of historical responsibility, of equity in climate policy, and of meaningfully linking sustainable development policy to climate policy. The task of devising and putting forth proposals that match these interests lies squarely with negotiators from the South. Developing country negotiators will do well to start thinking about these issues. In the past, the South has been routinely reactive in its environmental negotiations with the North – far better at spelling out how existing regimes fail to meet their interests than at redefining those regimes (Najam, 1995). It is well past time that developing countries change their strategy. The post-Kyoto period provides them with at least an opportunity to try.

References

Agarwal, A and Narain, S (1991) *Global Warming in an Unequal World*, Centre for Science and Environment, New Delhi

Agarwal, A, Narain, S and Sharma, A (eds) (1999) *Green Politics: Global Environmental Negotiation-1: Green Politics*, Centre for Science and Environment, New Delhi

Agarwal, A, Narain, S, Sharma, A and Imchen, A (eds) (2001) *Green Politics: Global Environmental Negotiation-2: Poles Apart*, Centre for Science and Environment, New Delhi

Baer, P, Harte, J, Haya, B, Herzog, AV, Holdren, J, Hultman, NE, Kammen, DM, Norgaard, RB and Raymond, L (2000) 'Equity and Greenhouse Gas Responsibility', *Science*, vol 289, p2287

Banuri, T and Gupta, S (2000) *The Clean Development Mechanism and Sustainable Development: An Economic Analysis*, Asian Development Bank, Manila

Banuri, T and Sagar, A (1999) 'In Fairness to Current Generations: Lost Voices in the Climate Debate', *Energy Policy*, vol 27, no 9, pp509–514

Banuri, T, Weyant, J, Akumu, G, Najam, A, Roas, LP, Rayner, S, Sachs, W, Sharma, R and Yohe, G (2001) 'Setting the Stage: Climate Change and Sustainable Development', in *Mitigation: Climate Change 2001* (Third Assessment Report of the Intergovernmental Panel on Climate Change, IPCC), Cambridge University Press, London, pp73–114

Beg, N, Marlot, JC, Davidson, O, Afrane-Okesse, Y, Tyani, L, Denton, F, Sokona, Y, Thomas, JP, la Rovere, EL, Parikh, JK and Rahman, AA (2002) 'Linkages between Climate Change and Sustainable Development', *Climate Policy*, vol 2, nos 2–3, pp129–144

Bohle, HG, Downing, TE and Watts, MJ (1994) 'Climate Change and Social Vulnerability: Toward a Sociology and Geography of Food Insecurity', *Global Environmental Change*, vol 4, no 1, pp37–48

Burton, I (1997) 'Vulnerability and Adaptive Response in the Context of Climate and Climate Change', *Climatic Change*, vol 36, nos 1–2, pp185–196

Carraro, C (ed) (2000) *Efficiency and Equity of Climate Change Policy*, Kluwer Academic Publishers, Dordrecht

Cooper, RN (1998) 'Toward a Real Global Warming Treaty', *Foreign Affairs*, vol 77, no 2, pp66–79

Dasgupta, C (1994) 'The Climate Change Negotiations', in I Mintzer and JA Leonard (eds) *Negotiating Climate Change: The Inside Story of the Rio Convention*, Cambridge University Press, Cambridge, pp129–148

Downing, TE and Baker, T (1999) 'Drought Vulnerability: Concepts and Theory', in D A Wilhite (ed) *Drought*, Routledge, New York

Downing, TE, Watts, MJ and Bohle, HG (1996) 'Climate Change and Food Insecurity: Toward a Sociology and Geography of Vulnerability', in TE Downing (ed) *Climate Change and World Food Security*, Springer, Heidelberg

Gadgil, M and Guha, R (1995) *Ecology and Equity: The Use and Abuse of Nature in Contemporary India*, Penguin Books, New Delhi

Huq, S (2003) 'Climate Change and Adaptation Funds: How Should they be Spent?', *Climate Policy*, vol 2, no 2–3, pp243–246

Huq, S and Sokona, Y (2001) *Climate Change Negotiations: A View from the South. Opinion: World Summit on Sustainable Development*, International Institute for Environment and Development, London

Hyder, TO (1994) 'Looking Back to See Forward', in I Minstzer and JA Leonard (eds) *Negotiating Climate Change: The Inside Story of the Rio Convention*, Cambridge University Press, Cambridge, pp201–226

IPCC (2001) *Climate Change 2001 – Third Assessment Report of the Intergovernmental Panel on Climate Change* (three volumes), Cambridge University Press, London

Jacoby, HD, Prinn, R and Schmalensee, R (1998) 'Kyoto's Unfinished Business', *Foreign Affairs*, vol 77, July/August, pp54–66

Jamieson, D (1992) 'Ethics, Public Policy, and Global Warming', *Science, Technology, and Human Values*, vol 17, no 2, pp139–153

Malakoff, D (1997) 'Thirty Kyotos Needed to Control Warming', *Science*, vol 278, p2048

Meyer, A (1999) 'The Kyoto Protocol and the Emergence of "Contraction and Convergence" as a Framework for an International Political Solution to Greenhouse Gas Emissions Abatement', in O Hohmeyer and K Rennings (eds) *Man-Made Climate Change: Economic Aspects and Policy Options*, Physica-Verlag, Heidelberg

Müller, B (2002a) 'The Global Climate Change Regime: Taking Stock and Looking Ahead' in *Yearbook of International Co-operation on Environment and Development 2002/03*, Earthscan, London

Müller, B (2002b) 'A New Delhi Mandate?', *Climate Policy*, vol 2, nos 2–3, pp241–242

Munasinghe, M (2000) 'Development, Equity and Sustainability in the Context of Climate Change', in M Munasingha and R Swart (eds) *Proceedings of the IPCC Expert Meeting on Development, Equity and Sustainability, Colombo, Sri Lanka 27–29 April*, IPCC and World Meteorological Organization, Geneva

Najam, A (1995) 'International Environmental Negotiations: A Strategy for the South', *International Environmental Affairs*, vol 7, no 2, pp249–287

Najam, A (2000) 'The Case for a Law of the Atmosphere', *Atmospheric Environment*, vol 34, no 23, pp4047–4049

Najam, A (2001a) 'Deal or No Deal', *Down to Earth*, vol 10, no 11, pp50–51

Najam, A (2001b) 'The Case Against GEO, WEO or Any Other EO', in D Brack and J Hyvarinen (eds) *Global Environmental Institutions: Arguments for Reform*, Royal Institute for International Affairs and Earthscan, London

Najam, A and Page, T (1998) 'The Climate Convention: Deciphering the Kyoto Protocol', *Environmental Conservation*, vol 25, no 3, pp187–194

Najam, A and Sagar, A (1998) 'Avoiding a COP-out: Moving Towards Systematic Decision-Making Under the Climate Convention: An Editorial Essay', *Climatic Change*, vol 39, no 4, ppiii–ix

Najam, A, Poling, JM, Yamagishi, N, Straub, DG, Sarno, J, DeRitter, SM and Kim, EM (2002) 'From Rio to Johannesburg: Progress and Prospects', *Environment*, vol 44, no 7, pp26–38

Rajan, MK (1997) *Global Environmental Politics*, Oxford University Press, Delhi

Rayner, S and Malone, E (eds) (1998) *Human Choices and Climate Change*, Batelle Press, Colombus, Ohio

Reiner, DM and Jacoby, HD (1997) 'Annex I Differentiation Proposals: Implications for Welfare, Equity and Policy', MIT Joint Program on the Science and Policy of Global

Change, Report No 27, Massachusetts Institute of Technology, Cambridge, Massachusetts

Ribot, JC, Najam, A and Watson, G (1996) 'Climate Variation, Vulnerability and Sustainable Development in the Semi-Arid Tropics', in JC Ribot, AR Magalhaes and SS Pangides (eds) *Climate Variability, Climate Change and Social Vulnerability in the Semi-Arid Tropics*, Cambridge University Press, Cambridge, pp13–51

Sagar, A and Kandlikar, M (1997) 'Knowledge, Rhetoric and Power: International Politics of Climate Change', *Economic and Political Weekly*, 6 December, p3140

Shue, H (1995) 'Equity in an International Agreement on Climate Change', in RS Odingo, AL Alusa, F Mugo, JK Njihia, A Heidenreich and A Katama (eds) *Equity and Social Considerations Related to Climate Change*, ICIPE Science Press, Nairobi, Kenya

Sokona, Y (2001) 'Marrakech and Beyond', *Down to Earth*, vol 10, no 11, p53

Sokona, Y and Denton, F (2001) 'Climate Change Impacts: Can Africa Cope with the Challenges?', *Climate Policy*, vol 1, no 1, pp117–123

Sokona, Y, Humphreys, S and Thomas, JP (1998) 'What Prospects for Africa?' in J Goldemberg (ed) *Issues and Options: The Clean Development Mechanism*, UNDP, New York

Weiss, EB (1989) *In Fairness to Future Generations: International Law, Common Patrimony, and Intergenerational Equity*, Transnational Publishers, Dobbs Ferry, New York

Chapter 5

Financing Sustainable Development: Is There Life after Johannesburg?[1]

Adil Najam, Tufts University and SDPI

The year 2002 provided the international development community with two important chances to influence significantly the direction of development financing – especially financing for sustainable development. We are likely to remember both as missed opportunities.

The first was the United Nations International Conference on Financing for Development (FfD) and the second was the World Summit on Sustainable Development (WSSD). In their run-up, there was a sense in developing countries in particular, and among all those concerned with issues of international development, that the substance of these summits and the fact that they came back-to-back were of considerable significance. However, despite the many obvious and deep links between the agendas of these two 'super meetings' – especially in terms of issues related to financing sustainable development – it was both surprising and rather disturbing that there was only half-hearted interaction between the two.

A clear environment vs development divide seemed to be at work. Despite the 'SD' in its title, WSSD was seen as a predominantly 'environmental' event and FfD was quite clearly a meeting about economic growth and international aid. This very visible chasm between the two was a sad, but probably true, commentary on the state of sustainable development as a policy construct (Najam, 2001).

This chapter looks at the one issue that was central to both FfD and WSSD, financing for development, and outlines the challenges and opportunities that lie before us. In using the two conferences as the context, the chapter highlights key questions that have come to the fore during the build-up to and at these major events. The chapter is written in the belief, mistaken as it might turn out to be, that despite the very meagre achievements of the two conferences, it is still possible to seek a convergence of the overlapping themes in the follow-up phase.

Focusing on 'Demand-side' Legitimacy

The world of development finance is twice cursed. The persistent and deepening crisis about the *amount* of finance available for development assistance is compounded by growing doubts about the *efficacy*, or even appropriateness, of the use to which these limited resources are put. (The debate on the effectiveness of aid has raged long and hard: a sampling of various arguments may be seen in Hancock, 1992; Bandow and Vasquez, 1994; Cassen, 1994; Rich, 1994; Smillie, 1995; World Bank, 1998; South Centre, 1999; Randel et al, 2000; Morrissey, 2001.) It is not only that the pie is small and shrinking, but there is also a lurking suspicion that it is being utilized less than effectively. The result is a vicious cycle: the lack of legitimacy that results from ineffective use of available resources serves to reinforce the existing tendencies towards shrinking financing.

The premise of this chapter is that the dynamic can be reversed into a virtuous cycle. Strengthening the legitimacy and effectiveness of the development process on the ground could attract increased resources into public development activities. This builds directly on a framework proposed by Tariq Banuri and Erika Spanger-Siegfried (2001) which calls for the replacement of the current preoccupation with 'supply-side' issues (trying to increase the inflow of financial resources into development activities) with 'demand-side' issues (enhancing the capacity of individuals, communities, governments and development institutions to access and effectively utilize financial resources).

Policy-makers and academics who look at issues of financing for development, including sustainable development, tend to be principally concerned with expanding the resource flows into development, particularly through state-centric channels. For example, the discussions during the FfD process were largely preoccupied with issues of resource mobilization, both internationally and domestically. Similarly, a key concern of WSSD was the abject failure of the international system to mobilize the resources that would have been needed even to begin implementing Agenda 21. While these are, of course, very legitimate and pressing concerns, much less attention was paid during either discussion to the effective use – or lack thereof – of the resources that were available. Indeed, the sizeable endowments available to the World Bank and the International Monetary Fund (IMF) seem to have triggered correspondingly little change in the global developmental profile; the world continues to become an ever-more unequal and ever-more unsustainable planet (see UNDP, 1999; South Centre, 1999). For its part, the Global Environment Facility (GEF) that had caused such anguish to Rio negotiators seems to be suffering simultaneously from having insufficient resources to meet its mandate and being unable to spend the scant funds that it does have (Agarwal et al, 1999). Something is terribly wrong, and it is not just the amount of funds available for sustainable development.

This is not to suggest that resource mobilization is not important. It does, however, suggest that questions of legitimacy and effectiveness of resource use are also important and have a direct bearing on questions of mobilization. The first port of call in this regard is the variety of mechanisms created to channel resources into sustainable development. This challenge should have been equally central to the agendas of FfD and WSSD but has been marginalized, if not ignored, in both discussions.

Can these issues of legitimacy be brought back to the centre of subsequent discussions on financing for sustainable development? Doing so will require a re-articulation of the discourse on at least three interrelated levels: the legitimacy of the goals of financing, the legitimacy of the actors involved, and the legitimacy of the measures by which we gauge success or failure.

Goals: What Counts?

Financing seems to have become a goal in itself. The tenor of development discussions in general, and multilateral environmental negotiations related to sustainable development in particular, has become so routinized and the arguments so predictable that the issue of financing has become all but delinked from the goal that it is supposed to achieve. Rather than being tied directly to a global public good (see Kaul et al, 1999; World Bank, 2001) – such as climatic stabilization, maintenance of biodiversity, creation of sustainable livelihoods – financing has been reduced to nothing more than an act of charity. The North is implored by the South to throw a few crumbs of pity and benevolence because the South is poor, not in lieu of the South supplying a global public service (Banuri, 1992; Najam, 1995; Agarwal et al, 1999). While the North is understandably averse to any mention of 'compensation' for its environmentally irresponsible behaviour in the past, the result of distancing financing from the goal that it is directed towards is rather perverse. From the North's perspective, there is no compulsion to actually deliver on promises made nor any grounds for insisting on proper utilization; after all, this is merely charity and charity cannot be accounted for or be accountable. For the South, there is the humiliation of having to hold out the beggar's bowl but also the sense that how they use the alms given to them should ultimately be their own business (Agarwal, 1992; Najam, 1995).

A more useful way to conceptualize the issue would be through an explicit contractual arrangement between those who are to supply a global public good and those who are willing to pay a certain price for that service. For example, Anil Agarwal and his colleagues at the Centre for Science and Environment in India (Agarwal et al, 1999; see also Agarwal and Narain, 1991) have proposed such a schema for considering the maintenance of the global climate system – a service that the poor of the world provide by keeping their emissions low. They then propose a transfer of resources from the 'over-emitters' to the 'under-emitters' as a fee for the provision of this service. Conceptually, the beauty of such a framework is that the transfer of resources would be made directly to those who are actually providing the service rather than to the treasury of the country in which they live. Properly implemented, with such a mechanism the transfer would benefit not the elites in the South whose own emissions may be no different from those in the North, but the poor in these countries who are actually providing the global public service.

While implementing any particular initiative, such as that above, would require significant design innovations in the implementation regime, the point to be made here concerns the need to link directly the provision of financing to the goal that it is supposed to serve. This entails more than simply earmarking funds for particular purposes or creating financing mechanisms for selected priorities. It would require explicit identification of certain environmental services as global public goods and a mechanism where those who benefit from these public goods transfer resources to those who provide or maintain the services. Financing, therefore, would not be the 'end' but the 'means' to larger socially desirable goals.

The key goal of concern to us is sustainable development. Financing for sustainable development is particularly sensitive to questions of scale and scope; the availability of large amounts of money for a small number of large projects may be less useful than the availability of relatively small amounts of money for a large number of relatively small initiatives (Sachs, 1999). A meaningful emphasis on the goal of financing for sustainable development necessarily broadens the focus from just the amount of financing that is available to the goal of that financing – that is, sustainable development. Importantly, it allows other important questions to be asked: for what purpose are the resources going to be used, who will they be channelled and disbursed through, and how will the effectiveness and legitimacy of this use be gauged? In the current discourse, such questions, even when asked, are marginalized as the spotlight remains fixed on the quantity of financial flows – whether private or public, non-concessionary or concessionary.

Institutions: Who Counts?

The principal systemic question related to financing for sustainable development concerns the institutions through which such financing is channelled. The legitimacy and efficacy of such institutions (including the World Bank, the IMF, the United Nations system and NGOs) was central to the agenda of the FfD process and has also been discussed within the WSSD context. The questions, however, have tended to be rather limited in scope concentrating mostly on the familiar issues of governance, including management, representation and transparency. While these are important questions, a set of more fundamental questions regarding the legitimacy and effectiveness of these institutions needs to be added to the debate.

Irrespective of other differences one may or may not have with international financial institutions (IFIs), it has become increasingly clear that they operate at a very different scale from that at which the problem happens. Efficient as they might be in disbursing amounts in the US$1 million-plus range, they tend to be not only uninterested in, but actually incapable of, operating effectively in the range of thousands, let alone hundreds of dollars. Given their costly procedures and personnel, such institutions do not have the ability to operate effectively at the medium and small scale, the scale at which so many sustainable development initiatives reside (Rich, 1994; Banuri and Spanger-Siegfried, 2001). Similar problems of scale apply to many national financial institutions and, indeed, to large international NGOs (Clark, 1991; Edwards and Hulme, 1996; Najam, 1999). The hurdle is not one of ideological persuasion or intent, it is simply a question of capacity. The institutions that are *best* suited for raising large amounts of international finance are *least* suited to disbursing money at a level where sustainable development is most likely to happen.

The problem could, of course, be solved by simply passing on this financing to a set of intermediate institutions (local NGOs) were it not for the significant problems of accessibility. Most discussions of institutional transparency focus on the operational secretiveness of international institutions, particularly IFIs (the main concern revolves around the danger of inappropriate decisions being taken, sometimes consciously, under the veil of secrecy). However, the issue of accessibility is intrinsically tied to transparency. In addition to being non-transparent, IFIs tend to be inaccessible; not only for would-be watchdogs, but also for potential beneficiaries. This relates directly to the question of scale raised above. While IFIs are incapable of operating at the 'ground level' of sustainable development because of their in-built pathologies of scale, those who are operating at the ground level are denied entry to elevated levels by barriers of accessibility and often lack the capacity to operate in that environment (Clark, 1991; Hulme and Edwards, 1996; Najam, 1996).

The challenge here is that IFIs and their national counterparts have tended to be as resistant to learning to talk to intermediate NGOs as the latter have been hesitant to converse with IFIs. In essence, the institutional chain that could have been the conduit for financial resources flowing to the appropriate level has a huge gap within it which only entrenches the existing tendency, and even incentive, to siphon off the financing at levels higher than those where it might make the most sustainable development impact. The challenge is one of mismatched institutional capacities. Institutions that can access global financial resources are constrained by their inability to operate at the level where sustainable development initiatives can most meaningfully be undertaken; and those who are able to operate at that level are either unable to raise the resources they need or are denied access to those who have such resources, often both.

Information: How we Count?

Institutions involved in financing for development, including financing for sustainable development, tend to see themselves very much as part of the *financial system*, rather than a development system. The distinction is more than semantic. Financial institutions are assessed, and should be assessed, according to financial criteria. However, such criteria are not entirely appropriate for gauging the performance of development institutions. Unfortunately, it is not only institutions such as the World Bank and IMF but also those such as the GEF and many NGOs that increasingly insist on measuring their efficacy and legitimacy in terms of their financial strength rather than their developmental impacts (Edwards and Hulme, 1996; Najam, 1996).

World Bank staff members, for example, are very fond of reminding their audiences that they are, after all, a 'bank' and that their rates of recovery would be the envy of any financial institution. It is quite clear that they would. What is less clear is how much of a virtue this is for a development institution (Rich, 1994). GEF reports are similarly detailed in terms of how much money has been put into the fund and how much has been disbursed. The impact this investment has had on fostering sustainable development is less clearly articulated (Agarwal et al, 1999). There seems to be a clear sense that those entrusted with development financing are far more comfortable being managers of money than facilitators of development. They certainly seek the validation of their 'performance' in terms of the former. To be fair, this tendency is not restricted to IFIs but is equally prevalent in agencies of national government and in many NGOs which are just as determined to highlight 'dollars spent' rather than meaningful discussions of how this relates to the actual achievement of – or even attempted achievement of – sustainable development (Clark, 1991; Najam, 1996). In all cases the 'means' (financing) are decoupled from the 'end' (sustainable development) not only in how claims are made for financing but also in how the institutional efficacy is accounted for. This tendency has contributed greatly to the deepening crisis of legitimacy of development finance.

Unfortunately, institutions at all levels (international, national, local) care most deeply about that which they can count. It is not surprising, then, that we find a fairly developed culture of accounting for finances but only half-hearted attempts at measuring development impacts. This is not something that can be shooed away by recounting the well-rehearsed lamentation about all the known difficulties in trying to 'define' sustainable development. It is a question of making explicit the sustainability goals that we seek to achieve, determining some measures (quantitative or qualitative) to gauge the achievement of those goals, and holding those responsible (IFIs, national governments, NGOs) accountable against these goals.

To use an analogy from the private sector, just as financial markets have well-developed systems of financial disclosures and credit rating, the development system needs corresponding systems of both disclosing the implementation variables and rating development impacts. While it is useful and necessary to have sound and accessible *financial* information and monitoring for development finance regimes, it is even more useful and necessary to have sound and accessible *development* information and monitoring of these regimes. Sustainable development reporting initiatives, therefore, are of prime importance in rationalizing the discussions on financing for sustainable development and moving the discussion away from a preoccupation with financial performance to more fundamental concerns about sustainability performance.

A Final Word

The key point this chapter seeks to make is that the global community needs to take a fresh look at the entire system of financing for development and reorient it towards a decidedly (sustainable) development orientation. Here we have identified only a few key elements of such a reorientation.

Such an enterprise cannot be easy since it would challenge the now entrenched 'financing' orientation of the regime. One must begin with a re-articulation – or at least a reaffirmation – of the principal goal: sustainable development. Doing so with any degree of honesty will necessarily require a re-examination of the institutions that are entrusted with the financing for the sustainable development agenda and lead to the conclusion that, while these institutions are certainly a part of the institutional chain that might deliver sustainable development, they are incapable of doing so in and of themselves. An expanded institutional framework that incorporates intermediary and local NGOs (by providing them access and investing in their capacities) will be absolutely critical if the goal of sustainable development is to be taken seriously. Finally, such institutions (at all levels) will need to be invested in with a different set of performance measurements: measures which gauge the ability of institutions to deliver on their developmental goals rather than focus on financial accounting alone.

Notes

1   A version of this chapter was published in the journal *Progress in Development Studies*, vol 2, no 2, pp153–160, 2002.

References

Agarwal, A (1992) 'The North–South Environmental Debate: Off to the Next Round', *Down to Earth*, vol 15 (July), pp33–36

Agarwal, A and Narain, S (1991) *Global Warming in an Unequal World*, Centre for Science and Environment, New Delhi

Agarwal, A, Narain, S and Sharma, A (eds) (1999) *Green Politics: Global Environmental Negotiation-1*, Centre for Science and Environment, New Delhi

Bandow, D and Vasquez, I (eds) (1994) *Perpetuating Poverty: The World Bank, IMF, and the Developing World*, Cato Institute, Washington, DC

Banuri, T (1992) 'Noah's Ark or Jesus's Cross?' working paper WP/UNCED/1992/1, Sustainable Development Policy Institute, Islamabad

Banuri, T and Spanger-Siegfried, E (2001) *Strengthening Demand: A Framework for Financing Sustainable Development*, International Institute for Environment and Development (IIED) and Regional and International Networking Group (Ring), London

Cassen, R (1994) *Does Aid Work?* Oxford University Press, London

Clark, J (1991) *Democratizing Development: The Role of Volunteer Organizations*, Earthscan, London

Edwards, M and Hulme, D (eds) (1996) *Beyond the Magic Bullet: NGO Performance and Accountability in the Post-Cold War World*, Kumarian Press, Hartford, Connecticut

Hancock, G (1992) *Lords of Poverty: The Power, Prestige, and Corruption of the International Aid Business*, Atlantic Monthly Press, New York

Hulme, D and Edwards, M (eds) (1996) *NGOs, States and Donors: Too Close for Comfort?* Saint Martin Press, New York

Kaul, I, Grunberg, I and Stern, M (eds) (1999) *Global Public Goods: International Cooperation in the 21st Century*, Oxford University Press, New York

Morrissey, O (2001) 'Does Aid Increase Growth?' *Progress in Development Studies*, vol 1, no 1, pp37–50

Najam, A (1995) 'International Environmental Negotiation: A Strategy for the South', *International Environmental Affairs*, vol 7, no 2, pp249–287

Najam, A (1996) 'NGO Accountability: A Conceptual Framework', *Development Policy Review*, vol 14, no 1, pp339–353

Najam, A (1999) 'Citizen Organizations as Policy Entrepreneurs', in D Lewis (ed.) *International Perspectives on Voluntary Action: Reshaping the Third World*, Earthscan, London, pp142–181

Najam, A (2001) 'The Case Against GEO, WEO or Any Other EO', in D Brack and J Hyvarinen (eds) *Global Environmental Institutions: Arguments for Reform*, Royal Institute for International Affairs and Earthscan, London

Randel, J, Germany, T and Ewing, D (eds) (2000) *The Reality of Aid, 2000: An Independent Review of Poverty Reduction and Development Assistance*, Earthscan, London

Rich, B (1994) *Mortgaging the Earth: The World Bank, Environmental Impoverishment, and the Crisis of Development*, Beacon Press, Boston, Massachusetts

Sachs, W (1999) *Planet Dialectics: Explorations in Environment and Development*, Zed Books, London

Smillie, I (1995) *The Alms Bazaar: Altruism Under Fire*, International Development Research Centre, Ottawa

South Centre (1999) *Financing Development: Issues for a South Agenda*, South Centre, Geneva

UNDP (1999) *Human Development Report 1999*, Oxford University Press, New York

World Bank (1998) *Assessing Aid: What Works, What Doesn't, and Why*, Oxford University Press, New York

World Bank (2001) *Financing for Development*, background paper prepared by the staff of the World Bank and the International Monetary Fund, World Bank and IMF, Washington, DC

Chapter 6

Global Public Goods: Some Key Questions

Keith Bezanson, Institute of Development Studies, University of Sussex

The notion of 'global public goods' (GPGs) has recently assumed centre stage in the international agendas of policy-makers. At the same time, GPGs have become a subject of extensive new academic study and scholarship. An urgent need is to link the two by examining academic discussions on GPGs in the context of actual and ongoing policy processes.

Such a bridging effort seems especially important at this time for two reasons. First, political and social pressures are mounting for the financing of a wide range of new initiatives in the name of GPGs. Second, there is currently considerable disagreement on the value and potential of an international public goods approach to addressing global concerns. The considerable enthusiasm expressed by some scholars and policy-makers contrasts sharply with the serious reservations of others. Indeed, there are many who go so far as to express alarm about claims being made in the name of global goods and about what they view as the 'fuzziness' of the concept of a global public good (GPG), especially when it is inscribed into policy processes.

The main question is of a practical nature and centres on whether the concept of global public goods can advance thought and action on common concerns that affect a large portion of humanity. This raises a number of challenges for clarity on three interrelated sets of factors associated with the growing attention paid to GPGs.

The first of these factors involves the very idea of a public good. The idea of a public good originates in the academic discipline of economics where it is accorded an exacting technical definition. There are major difficulties in extending it beyond its narrow economic scope and applying it at a global level. The second factor is globalization. The usual assertion is that the requirement for the provision of GPGs is increasing as a function of globalization. Yet, globalization is a paradoxical phenomenon of numerous definitions and few tight conceptual boundaries. The third factor is the system of international development cooperation that has been placed at the centre of demands to ensure the provision of GPGs. This system finds itself under greater stress today than at any time since its launch over 50 years ago.

Each of these factors has its own share of conceptual imprecision and ambiguity, contradictory interpretations and competing viewpoints, and each is in a stage of rapid evolution. Their convergence makes attempts at developing integrative conceptual frameworks problematic and risky. This is further compounded by the rapid pace of intellectual production and of policy shifts in relation to issues such as HIV/AIDS, peace and security, and climate change, among others, which bear directly on the conception of global public goods and their financing.

These difficulties and risks may be formidable, but for policy-makers they make all the more urgent the need for a conceptual framework that integrates the key factors affecting the definition, delivery and consumption of GPGs. Viewed positively, the potential pay-offs from such a framework, particularly in terms of better and more effective policies to address common concerns, may be substantial. Viewed negatively, the lack of conceptual clarity could lead to misguided policies and involve high opportunity costs. In addition, the very nature of public goods requires a conceptual framework that makes clear that it is not possible to escape values, preferences, interests, asymmetrical knowledge and power relations in defining global public goods and in arranging for their provision. Without policy processes that take all these factors into consideration, declarations that something is a GPG are essentially empty rhetoric.

The key questions that need to be asked and for which a conceptual framework is required are outlined below.

To What Extent is the International Public Goods Approach Useful in Addressing Global Common Concerns?

To quite a significant extent. Indeed, by focusing attention on the limitations of current political, legal, institutional and financial arrangements for addressing global problems, the GPGs approach has already made an important contribution. However, there is a need for pulling together a growing number of disparate conceptual contributions, to reach consensus and broad agreement on definitions, and to move from the intellectual to the policy arena. In a sense, this would be similar to what happened with the concept of 'sustainable development' during the last decade. Initially it generated a lot of controversy and debate, but gradually it became more precise, policy-oriented and widely accepted.

How Should the Process of Defining Global Public Goods be Approached?

With restraint, circumspection, rigour and patience. Current practice has led to grouping all manner of global concerns, aspirations or desirable situations under the title of 'global public goods'. Absent definitional precision, this could soon render the term meaningless. Also, the more focused the definition, the greater the possibility of deriving useful policy implications and of mobilizing financial resources. This requires the adoption of rather stringent conditions regarding the reach of cross-border spillovers or externalities, and the degrees of non-excludability and non-rivalry. The distinction between 'core' and 'complementary' GPGs, together with the components of an 'idealized international public goods delivery system', can be of help in this task.

How Should Choices be Made on which International and Global Public Goods to Provide?

By emphasizing the political nature of these choices. The determination of what are international public goods and which ones have priority for provision involves a multiplicity of actors with different interests and agendas. The international community of nations, corporations and civil society associations face difficult choices in setting priorities, allocating all types of scarce resources (political capital, attention of key decision-makers, institutional and organizational capabilities, finance), and in mobilizing support for such choices. The lack of public spaces specifically devoted to discussion, negotiation and agreement on such matters can be seen as a major shortcoming of the current international system.

A possible response to this might be the establishment of an 'international and global public goods' entity, preferably of a temporary nature and within the UN system, whose function would be to debate these issues systematically and to give recommendations on priorities and on the structure of international public goods delivery systems.[1]

It would, of course, be no easy task to reach consensus on whether halting the spread of HIV/AIDS is more or less important than conserving biodiversity, or on whether maintaining peace and security should take precedence over abating climate change or maintaining global financial stability. Such choices, however, are currently being made – albeit implicitly – without much discussion and without attention to the asymmetries that are inherent in international power relations. The establishment of such an international entity may be seen as a first step to redress this situation.

How Can the Widest Possible Participation be Ensured in the Design and Implementation of International Public Goods Delivery Systems?

It cannot unless better institutional arrangements are put in place. The varying extents to which countries – as well as firms, associations and individuals – benefit from and contribute to the production of an international public good lead them to assign different priorities to externalities, spillovers, degrees of excludability and other characteristics of international public goods. Identifying and responding to such diversity of demands requires highly inclusive institutional arrangements, capable of processing a multiplicity of viewpoints and of ensuring the participation of all relevant stakeholders, while at the same time avoiding glaring inconsistencies and maintaining overall coherence. In this regard, the perception that arrangements for the provision of some public goods are an imposition of rich donor countries and Northern NGOs reduces their legitimacy, creates ownership problems and conspires against the active involvement of those who actually produce the international public good. Therefore, discussions and negotiations regarding the definition, provision and financing of international public goods should involve the participation and cooperation of as many of the affected stakeholders and constituencies as possible.

This is not happening and will not happen in the absence of mechanisms to build and support the capacity of developing country stakeholders – which are usually at a disadvantage – for active and meaningful participation in the design and operation of GPGs regimes. Such mechanisms could take the form of a general 'participation fund' along the lines proposed by the United Nations Development Programme (UNDP), or of specific participation financing tied to an individual GPG. They would allow reaching out to researchers, academics, intellectuals and informed representatives of civil society in developing countries, whose participation in decisions affecting the provision of GPGs could also be considered, in itself, as an international public good.

How Can Global, Regional, National and Local Interests be Aligned so as to Ensure that Effective Actions are Taken to Ensure the Supply of an International or Global Public Good?

By creating appropriate incentive systems and financing mechanisms. A great variety of state, private and civil society actors must be involved in the provision of a GPG, all the way from raising awareness about its importance at the global level down to the specific activities that actually produce or consume it. The regimes associated with it should establish rules, regulations, incentives, financing mechanisms and procedures to influence their behaviour and motivate their active involvement in the provision of the public good. Yet, it may not be enough to focus on the explicit policies directly associated with an international public good delivery system; other international, national or local policies can thwart its purpose and contain, in effect, an array of 'implicit' public goods policies that neutralize efforts to provide it. For example, energy pricing policies may stimulate the consumption of fossil fuels and undermine emissions reduction programmes, agricultural and forestry policies may override biodiversity conservation efforts, and intellectual property regulations may constrain the ability to halt the spread of HIV/AIDS. In addition, well-designed and properly aligned incentive systems could help in avoiding free-riding and the under-provision of international public goods.

Aligning the activities of the variety of public, private and civil society agents that intervene in an international public goods delivery system is a complex task that requires substantive policy analysis and administrative capabilities. These are not always found in international organizations and may be available only to a limited extent in the national and local governments, private sector and civil society institutions of developing countries. Therefore, it is essential to strengthen their capacity to contribute to the design and operation of an effective international public goods delivery system. At the international level, it is important to reinforce UN bodies and other regional organizations, and to avoid an excessive reliance on the multilateral development banks (MDBs). As indicated in the preceding sections, the MDBs should have an important but not primary role in the provision of global public goods, for they must balance this role with their central functions of financial intermediation and national capacity building aimed at reducing poverty and improving living standards. At the same time, MDBs should include international and global public goods concepts and practices in their operations, and particularly, in their policy dialogues with borrowers and grantees.

What is the Best Way to Approach Financing Issues in an International Public Goods Delivery System?

There is no single 'optimal' approach to the financing of global public goods. While some general principles and questions are useful in the examination of financial issues and alternatives (eg to what extent can the externalities be internalized? Could a market be created? Could international fees or taxes be levied? How far down along the continuum from global to local should a GPG stretch?), a singular set of appropriate financial arrangements will apply for each specific international public good. This implies the adoption of a systematic 'case-by-case' approach to the identification and choice of financing mechanisms. Nevertheless, a few guidelines can be inferred.

First, even in cases where externalities can be internalized and market-based instruments established to provide incentives for private agents to engage in the production of a GPG, public intervention, including public financing, will be required. This is because the proper operation of an international public goods delivery system requires transparency, openness, accountability and an effective regulatory framework. These good governance features require public financing. Thus, a certain amount of public financing will be required for market mechanisms to deliver GPGs.

Second, public funding is and will remain by far the main source of financing for GPGs. The scope for private sources, including both profit and not-for-profit corporations and individuals, is important and growing, but the amounts generated are likely to remain quite modest in comparison to public funding. Moreover, there is a much higher degree of uncertainty with regard to predictability and sustainability of funding from private sources. There is, in the end, no substitute for public funding of GPGs.

Third, to the extent that the numerous proposals and calls for the provision of GPGs become operational (ie regimes are established for their delivery), more stable and predictable sources of public funding for such goods will be essential. Existing arrangements of voluntary contributions (United Nations) or regular replenishments (Global Environment Facility – GEF) are weak and unreliable and will not provide the security of regime essential for an expanded provision of GPGs. Thus, if the international system evolves to the provision of GPGs on a widespread basis, international taxation, fees and levies become essential, indeed inevitable.

Fourth, there is a need to separate clearly those resources allocated to development assistance in general, which would benefit primarily the recipient countries, from those used in the provision of GPGs, which benefit developed countries at least as much as developing countries. The financing of international and global public goods should not come at the expense of development assistance flows, and particularly those directed to the poorest developing countries.

How Can Uncertainty, Time Lags and the Dynamic Character of International Public Goods be Dealt With?

By being flexible, adaptive and adopting a learning stance. In the relatively short time that international and global public goods issues have acquired prominence, and despite the confusion and controversy that have accompanied their eruption on to the international scene, an informal collective learning process appears to be under way. Even as the concept of public goods has become a moving target, intellectual contributions are now building on one another and academic and policy-oriented debates are focusing on the most relevant of these. However, if the concept of international and public goods is to realize its potential, it will be necessary to put in practice a broader and more operational collective learning process.

This would involve treating initiatives to provide international and global public goods as experiments from which to learn. Temporary and highly focused institutional arrangements involving multiple stakeholders may be a way to proceed without undue rigidities and without committing excessive amounts of resources. Such arrangements would have to be monitored and evaluated continuously, with the aim of spreading best practice (this could be a task for a possible 'international and global public goods' entity at the UN). Without too much exaggeration, enhancing the learning capacity of the international community to improve the provision of international and global public goods may be itself considered as a public good.

In the last analysis, transforming a most promising approach – international and global public goods – into an effective instrument for dealing with common global concerns will require, beyond instituting a collective learning process, very strong leadership along with forward-looking countries, institutions and persons committed to the goal of global equity and sharing the responsibility of realizing such potential.

Notes

1   For example, it may be possible to create a temporary Working Group as part of the follow up to the UN Conference on Financing for Development to address these questions.

Chapter 7

Towards Better Multilateral Environmental Agreements: Filling the Knowledge Gaps[1]

Adil Najam, Tufts University and SDPI

The last couple of decades have seen hectic negotiations pertaining to multilateral environmental agreements (MEAs). While many people have celebrated the resulting sense of activity, others have lamented the lukewarm commitments enshrined in many MEAs and the lack of implementation – this has led to a sense of 'MEA proliferation' leading to 'negotiation fatigue'.

Indeed, many have voiced strong frustration with the lack of tangible outputs and meaningful connections between MEA activity and the rest of the world. MEAs have been characterized as distant from local realities, too self-referential, having few direct links to actual events and current initiatives. There is a growing feeling that the world of MEAs is so detached that it cannot be an engine or initiator of real change for sustainable development. On the other hand, MEAs have been among the most visible manifestations of the inter-governmental community's interest in sustainable development; so much so that nearly all MEAs now advertise the achievement of sustainable development as their ultimate objective. Indeed, even the World Trade Organization (WTO) has recently begun claiming sustainable development as one of its defining goals. There remains, however, a disconnect between the proclaimed interest of MEAs in achieving sustainable development and their ability to do so on the ground.

How can this disconnect be addressed? This chapter seeks to begin answering this question by reviewing ways in which better research partnerships could strengthen existing and emerging MEA regimes in the service of sustainable development.

The recent interest in improving the coherence between MEAs, as a way of devising more efficient and streamlined structures for global environmental governance, is a welcome development. However, the discussion is sometimes defined too narrowly. There is a need for 'coherent MEAs' as much as there is for 'MEA coherence'. Moreover, coherence has to be substantive as well as procedural. While pooled secretariats and joint negotiations for related MEAs are certainly good initial steps, the ultimate goal must be firmly rooted in the content of MEAs, rather than just their procedures.

Towards a Framework: Who does What, When?

Let us begin by laying out a framework for understanding the role of research in the MEA life cycle. If all policy is really about putting theory into practice, then research has to be the lifeblood of good public policy. Research is particularly important to international policy on issues of high indeterminacy such as environment and sustainable development. The term 'research' could conceivably include so much as to become meaningless. It is important, therefore, to organize our understanding of research into meaningful categories. There are multiple ways to think about research in terms of MEAs, each useful in different contexts and each highlighting different aspects of the research needs.

Three ways of understanding and categorizing the role of research in MEAs are of particular importance. The first looks at the suppliers of research to the MEA process and responds to the question, '*who* is doing the research?' The second looks at the substance of research on MEAs and responds to the question, '*what* type of research is it?' The third focuses on the stage in the MEA cycle in which the research is being done and responds to the question, '*when* is the research being done?'

Who? Categorizing by research supplier

There are multiple actors that provide research related to MEAs: formal and informal, solicited and unsolicited, public and private. Each research supplier has particular core strengths and tends to produce research with particular qualities. Although research suppliers often cross neat categories, and their core strengths can sometimes be debatable, the public perception of these core qualities is nonetheless important. The key research suppliers in the MEA life cycle can be divided into four broad categories:

Research by academia

The actor most closely associated with 'research', of course, is academia. Even though academia may no longer be the biggest provider of research on MEAs, it is very often the first port of call for those seeking such research. This is not only because research is a 'primary function' for academics but also because academics stake a claim to being a source of *independent* and peer-reviewed analysis, a claim that may not always be entirely true, but which cannot readily be denied because it is more true for academia than for other research suppliers.

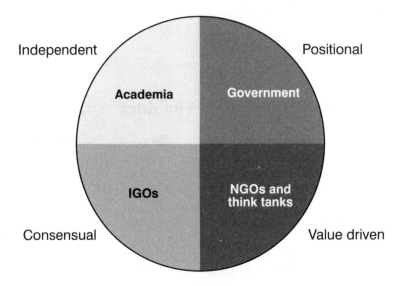

Figure 7.1 *Who: different research suppliers have different core strengths*

Research by governments

Governments are a less noticeable but significant source of research on MEAs. The core strength of research by governments is that it is explicitly or implicitly *positional*. Not only does it provide information about particular countries, but in doing so it provides insights about the positions that those countries are likely to take on particular issues.

Research by inter-governmental agencies

Inter-governmental agencies – including MEA secretariats – have become major suppliers of research. They produce mountains of in-house and contracted research that ranges from papers prepared internally, to outsourced research, to dedicated research enterprises such as the assessments and special reports of the Intergovernmental Panel on Climate Change (IPCC). A core quality of such research is that it tends to reflect *consensual* positions since these agencies are owned by all governments.

Research by NGOs, think tanks, business groups, etc

Non-governmental, non-academic sources are now among the largest suppliers of research related to MEAs. Some of it is, in fact, very 'academic' and is done by academics themselves. Such research is often sponsored by or done directly for governments or inter-governmental agencies. However, the defining feature of such research is that it is explicitly *value driven*. This is not to say that other research suppliers do not have values, nor that such research is any less robust. However, unlike research from other suppliers, it tends to be based on the explicit sets of values that drive their sponsoring institutions.

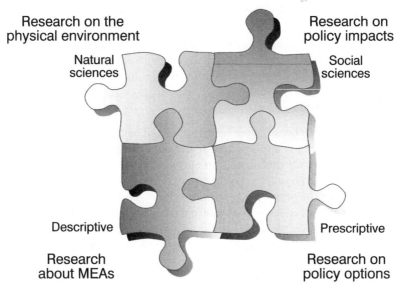

Figure 7.2 *What: different types of research are required*

What? Categorizing by research content

A categorization by substantive research content would differentiate between the types of research question being asked concerning an MEA. There are at least four distinct types of research, each with particular characteristics and requiring particular capacities. While there are overlaps between these various types of research, they are generally distinct and distinctively recognizable. More importantly, however, they build on each other: formally, by processes of cross-referencing during analysis; and informally by each setting agendas for the other:

Research on the physical environment

Research on the physical environment provides the scientific and factual basis for MEAs and includes research on changes in physical conditions and determinants of physical conditions. All MEAs need scientific research because that is the only way we know what is going on in the environment. Indeed, it is very often such research that places an issue on the international agenda, as happened quite dramatically in the case of stratospheric ozone depletion and climate change. For the most part, such research builds on disciplines of the natural sciences. Scholars usually play the leading role in conducting such research and, even when it is done by scholars residing in other sectors, it is often presented and tested academically.

Research on policy impacts

Research on policy impacts seeks to understand the physical and human impacts of policy. It is particularly important to MEAs and has recently drawn much attention under the heading of 'effectiveness' assessment. It includes research on the impacts of MEAs on social, economic, human and environmental conditions and builds heavily, but not entirely, on the social sciences. All four of the research suppliers identified above produce such research but from rather different motivations, and often with different results.

Research on policy options

Research on policy options has been characterized as 'part research, part policy' and seeks to identify and advocate particular policy options in terms of specific national or stakeholder interests. Innovation and evolution in MEA agendas often flow from such research. Good research in this category invariably builds on good research in other categories: the best tends to be transparent and explicit about its prescriptive or even partisan focus, and the worst tries to masquerade as belonging to one of the other categories. While such research also comes from all four of the identified research suppliers, governments and NGOs are usually the most heavily engaged in such research.

Research on MEAs

Research *on* MEAs includes research to understand why and how particular MEAs function, how they have developed or are likely to evolve, and how they might be improved. Such research tends to be descriptive in nature. It is often a lead-in to analyses of MEA impacts when it comes from academics and is a precursor to policy options when it comes from NGOs. It is also sometimes produced for purely pedagogical reasons to train participants in the MEA process, including NGO and government representatives. Such research is of particular value in terms of capacity building and can, therefore, have a direct bearing on MEA quality.

When? Categorizing by phase of MEA life cycle

There is significant research on exactly what constitutes the 'MEA life cycle' and various models have been posited of its various phases. Without going into the intricacies of this literature, we can identify three broad phases that are common in various models. While what is sometimes called the 'MEA life cycle' is generally represented as an ordered and staged cyclical process, the fact is that usually all three phases operate simultaneously and movement on any phase will spur and change the dynamics in the others:

Research during the agenda-setting phase

Research during the agenda-setting phase is characterized by *contestation*. It is generally a process where multiple ideas are floated and compete for attention. A few become the basis of further action, often with a call for more research or the initiation of policy negotiations. The process does not necessarily reach consensus, but it does narrow the field of issues and options to be seriously considered. Contestation often happens at two distinct levels. The first, led by

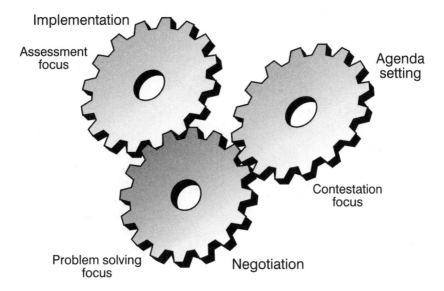

Figure 7.3 *When: different phases are motivated by different types of research focus*

academics, is based mostly on research about the physical environments and potential policy impacts. The second, usually led by NGOs, derives most nourishment from research about policy impacts and policy options. When governments and inter-governmental research join the chorus this usually implies that the issue is to be moved to the next stage. The contestation continues and usually adds new issues to the agenda as the process develops. A good example of this process was the early climate conferences which led to the near-permanent IPCC research structure. Over the years the IPCC deliberations have very clearly advanced the climate agenda as well as responded to its evolution due to other influences (see Figure 7.4, based on the IPCC *Third Assessment Report: Climate Change 2001* – IPCC, 2001).

Research during the negotiation phase

MEA research in the negotiation phase is quite frantic. While some elements of contestation remain, the purpose of contestation changes and is generally overwhelmed by a *problem-solving* focus. As is demonstrated in the climate change case, agenda setting – or, to be more exact, agenda refinement – continues with negotiation. Research conducted by or for governments becomes particularly important as understanding of different positions and policy options takes centre stage. While research findings from academic institutions and inter-governmental organizations also play critical roles in this process, NGOs are fairly active suppliers of research in this phase. Just as governments push policy options based on their national interests, NGOs and others push options based on their defining values.

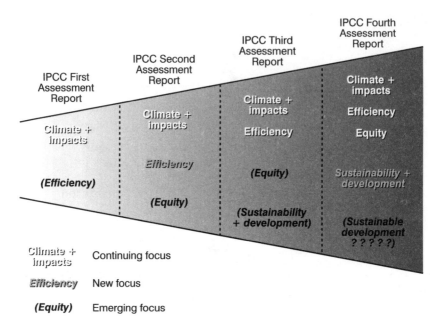

Figure 7.4 *The IPCC experiment: driving research; driving agenda*

Research during the implementation phase

Research on implementation lies at the conjunction of descriptive research on MEAs and research on physical and policy impacts. Most MEAs have only just begun to flirt with implementation. While some, like the Convention on International Trade in Endangered Species (CITES) or the Convention on Ozone-Depleting Substances, are in implementation phase, most (including, for example, the climate regime) are not, while some, like the Desertification Convention, are in the very early phases of implementation. The focus of the research related principally to implementation tends to be on *assessment* of progress, impact and effectiveness. This, of course, leads back to new research for agenda setting and negotiation based on these assessments. Inter-governmental organizations are (generally) major movers of such research, especially through the various assessments they require or contract. The other three players are also likely to be involved in such research, sometimes at the behest of inter-governmental agencies and often on their own.

A useful framework for identifying research needs can be constructed by using these three sets of categories and asking the question: *who* is best placed to do *what* type of research, *when* in the MEA life cycle? The important point to be made is not that one particular supplier or type of research is more important than the other; it is that better MEAs are likely to emerge if all research suppliers provide good research in their areas of comparative core strengths, if robust research is provided in all substantive categories, and if appropriate research inputs are made at each of the broad stages of the MEA life cycle. If research partnerships for sustainable development are to influence MEA coherence, then the partnerships must themselves be the product of a coherent strategy that builds on the strengths and synergies discussed above.

Towards Coherence

Applying this framework to the issue of enhancing MEA coherence in all its three dimensions, defined earlier, we begin to get a sense of where research partnerships are most needed and can add most value to the larger goal of sustainable development. An important distinction here is between better research for MEAs (which is usually demanded by the MEAs themselves) and research for better MEAs (which usually is not). While it is common to place more emphasis on the first, both are useful and the latter may ultimately be more important.

Improve the coherence of individual MEAs with their own sustainable development goals

Every MEA – and even the World Trade Organisation (WTO) – is now nominally committed to the goal of sustainable development. International institutions including the United Nations Development Programme (UNDP), the World Bank and most regional development banks have also internalized the language of sustainable development. While some MEAs (eg the Desertification Convention) and some institutions (eg UNDP) seem to have taken the concept more seriously than others, the original potency of the concept has largely been relegated to the realm of the rhetorical. Indeed, it has been argued that this wide-scale declaratory acceptance of 'sustainable development' has 'defanged' the concept of its operational intent in terms of actual policy action. Yet, the impressive declaratory inroads made for 'sustainable development' over the last decade provide the research community with both a responsibility and an opportunity. The responsibility flows from the fact that one of the reasons why MEAs have been able to avoid operationalizing their sustainable development mandates is that there is a severe paucity of research on exactly how particular MEAs impact or can impact sustainable development goals.

One example of the opportunities for research partnerships in this area relates to the Climate Convention. The links between sustainable development and climate change have been boldly proclaimed in the convention and have been hotly debated in the IPCC. However, they remain peripheral to the regime's actual design. A key research challenge is to begin to calculate the human, economic and environmental costs of adaptation as well as mitigation to the poorest communities and, equally importantly, to individual livelihoods. Such research is particularly important because the communities that are most vulnerable to climate change (eg coastal communities in developing countries and small island states) also have comparatively tattered safety nets and low resilience to severe climate change. In this case, as in just about all others, the major gaps in our understanding lie not so much at the international level, as at national and local levels. The particular research gap in this case relates to research on policy impacts and policy options. In both cases, NGOs – and particularly those located within the South and with links to the vulnerable communities – are best placed to fill this research gap, possibly with support from governments and inter-governmental agencies.

Improve the substantive coherence between different MEAs

In this case we are interested in research that can enhance the substantive coherence between various MEAs so that they can better serve the interests of sustainable development. This is important because MEAs have been compartmentalized by issues, whereas a defining feature of sustainable development is that 'everything is linked to everything' and many of the most important challenges as well as opportunities lie at the conjunction of different issues.

There are two particular research challenges in this area. The first is to identify the areas of substantive overlap that already exist and to initiate efforts of MEA clustering, pooled secretariats and joint negotiations in these areas. Early research in this area has already identified a number of 'natural clusters'. For example, issues related to the atmosphere are clearly a cluster that could be built by first pooling the Ozone and Climate Conventions and then linking these to other related issues where the science, as well as policy, will be advanced through natural synergies. Such clustering would also serve the extremely important purpose of easing the negotiation preparation pressure on developing countries which are being increasingly burdened by more frequent and more technically intense negotiations, for which they have neither sufficient resources nor sufficient capacities. Immediate research in this area will partly come from better understanding of the MEAs themselves, is likely to build on descriptive research and should be spearheaded by inter-governmental agencies, particularly the United Nations Environment Programme (UNEP).

The second area is to identify new contexts for potential linkage and eventual coherence. The immediate concern here is to link the evolving environmental provisions in the WTO to the existing provisions in MEAs. Some possible areas for positive coherence have been identified in the literature:

- coherence between intellectual property rights regimes established by the agreement on Trade-Related Intellectual Property Rights (TRIPs) and in key MEAs such as the Convention on Biological Diversity;
- coherence between the 'polluter pays' principle within MEAs and anti-dumping provisions within the WTO; and
- coherence between the 'special and differential' treatment clauses in the WTO and the 'common but differentiated responsibility' clauses within MEAs.

Research on such areas has begun to be pursued by inter-governmental organizations, especially the WTO. However, governments – particularly developing country governments – have a strong interest in pursuing opportunities for such coherence for sustainable development. In this regard, partnerships with academic scholars and NGO practitioners are likely to be useful since scholars who have an interest and expertise in both MEAs and the WTO are more likely to be found in academia and NGOs than in governmental or inter-governmental organizations.

Improve the procedural coherence between the structures of MEA management

Procedural coherence is important because it can lead to improved governance. Moreover, it is likely to reduce the pressures of an inefficient negotiating environment. As the number of institutions with a direct mandate for, or indirect influence on, global environmental issues has increased, it has become increasingly difficult for governments as well as civil society to keep track of the various, and sometimes contradictory, messages coming from these institutions. With MEA proliferation, a number of new environmental treaty secretariats have added to this cacophony. The result is not only a severe case of negotiation fatigue but also an overdose of research and reporting responsibilities being thrust on countries – particularly developing countries – in the name of better global environmental governance.

While some have been suggesting a 'superinstitution' for the environment, the problems inherent in the idea seem to outweigh its benefits. However, there are a variety of other, less drastic, mechanisms for improving the procedural coherence in global environmental governance. Some that have been discussed in the literature include:

- multi-issue panels for scientific assessment;
- a single location for all environmental secretariats;
- improved coordination between international environmental institutions;
- back-to-back negotiating sessions for related MEAs;
- pooled reporting requirements across various MEAs.

Improving procedural coherence will require research inputs, both in terms of better descriptive research on MEAs themselves, and in devising realistic and realizable policy options for operationalizing such coherence. Research partnerships between inter-governmental organizations and NGOs which specialize across a range of different MEAs could yield particularly useful dividends. A key element in this process is the role of capacity building. It is quite clear that many developing country governments lack critical capacities for the type of research that they need to negotiate better MEAs effectively; the first step in building such research capacity must be a comprehensive capacity audit to determine exactly which research capacities are needed and where.

Notes

1   The ideas presented in this chapter have benefited greatly from written contributions from Saleemul Huq, Fannie Mutepfa, Enoch Okpara, Krystyna Swiderska, Camilla Toulmin and Konrad von Moltke; discussion with Taghi Farvar, Atiq Rahman and George Varughese; and comments from the participants of a Workshop on Research Partnerships for Sustainable Development held at Cambridge (UK) on 18–19 July 2002. Their contribution is gratefully acknowledged; all responsibility for the content and its shortcomings remains with the author.

References

IPCC (2001) *Third Assessment Report: Climate Change 2001*, Intergovernmental Panel on Climate Change, Geneva

Chapter 8

The International Framework for Action: Is the CSD the Best We Can Do?

Simon Upton, chairman of the OECD Round Table on Sustainable Development

There *is* an international framework for action in support of sustainable development. It is vast, complex and sustains a huge amount of diplomatic activity and engagement by civil society. It has grown over the years and is, inevitably, in a constant state of redefinition as our understanding of the issues evolves. It would be very easy, in writing about the international framework, to become lost in a description of its elements, their synergies and their dysfunctions. It would be necessary to review, comprehensively, the mandates and interrelationships of agencies such as the United Nations Environment Programme (UNEP), the Global Environment Facility (GEF), the Food and Agriculture Organization (FAO) and the secretariats of the various multilateral environmental treaties, not to mention the raft of inter-governmental agencies dealing with the financing of development. It is likely that any attempt to propose improvements would stand a high chance of gravely prescribing the need for better coordination and integration of its constituent agencies and instrumentalities. The polysyllabic fog of international institutionalese quickly starts to gather.

This chapter eschews any such analytical trail. That is not to say that such an exercise is not important. Given the realities of international diplomacy and the deeply vested interests in the status quo, an architecture resembling the present one is where we start from and it is unlikely to undergo radical change unless the world feels the immediate pressure of threats or challenges that demand swift responses. Neither institutions nor negotiating cultures are given to revolutionary change. So integrate and coordinate better we must.

This analysis attempts, rather, to ask how we might like to think about 'action' at the international level, and leave the nuts and bolts of the institutional and negotiating game to those who know them best.[1]

I write as a former New Zealand minister and as a former chairman of the Commission on Sustainable Development (CSD). My interest is in how the attention and interest of policy-makers (ie elected governments) can be maintained at the global level.

Such people have built the framework that we have. They are also prisoners of it. The average span in office of a cabinet minister is a mere fraction of the career span of many of those who operate the levers of that framework. Politicians come and go through a revolving door. Gaining traction over their domestic institutions is for many a sufficient challenge; coming to grips with institutions of international governance is another thing again.

If by 'action' we mean presiding over the operation of the status quo, then the transitory nature of elected governments is no problem. If by 'action' we mean trying to galvanize an agenda and retain the ability to respond to new challenges and/or discard activities on the basis of newly acquired knowledge, the barriers to effective governance by accountable politicians are huge. Quite aside from the complexity of negotiations between a very large number of parties, the quantity of information available to, on the one hand, the managers of the web of institutions we have spun and, on the other, the ephemeral elected 'governors' of the institutions, is stacked hopelessly in favour of the former. The problem is not that those who preside over the current institutions are reluctant to act. The problem is that they often lack a clear mandate and, even where there is one, it covers only a part of the field of action.

The question then is: how can we secure a vantage point above the web of institutions and negotiations to survey priorities gauge the quality of international initiatives and, where appropriate, identify points of policy leverage? The search for such a vantage point is strongly influenced by the nature of the international agenda that has been unleashed.

The idea of international action for sustainable development received its biggest boost at the time of the Rio Conference on Environment and Development. Until then, inter-governmental action had focused on specific environmental issues (such as tackling the release of ozone-depleting compounds or the use of drift nets by fishermen) or the development of legal jurisdiction in novel areas (the Law of the Sea). With the Rio Conference, an extremely broad agenda brought to the negotiating table not just new prospective environmental conventions but a much wider array of issues such as the management of inter-generational risks and the sustainability of consumption patterns.

In addition, these concerns were juxtaposed with the development ambitions of a large number of countries and the relationship between North and South that should dominate the response to pressures on the global environment. In short, the socio-economic dimension of trying to promote an ecologically sustainable human footprint was given equal status with the environmental dimension. One result of this ambitious coupling of biophysical and economic issues (captured in the 27 Principles of the Rio Declaration and Agenda 21)[2] was to highlight the inadequacy of any single existing agency in which such diverse, cross-cutting issues could be pursued. The upshot was the UN Commission on Sustainable Development (CSD).[3]

Given the sheer breadth of Agenda 21, it is scarcely surprising that countries felt the need to institute a follow-up mechanism. It was not so much a case of needing to attend to unfinished business (such as the fate of the Forest Principles) as a case of needing to make sense of business barely begun. If conferences can launch paradigm shifts (and the jury on that must remain out for the present), much more sustained and concentrated effort is required to bed them down.

In broad terms, the United Nations describes the CSD's role as threefold:

- reviewing progress on the implementation of the outcomes of the Rio Conference (most notably Agenda 21);
- elaborating policy guidance and options for future initiatives aimed at achieving sustainable development; and
- promoting dialogue and building partnerships for sustainable development not just between governments and inter-governmental organizations, but with non-governmental organizations (NGOs) embedded in civil society at large.

Operating in accordance with the resolution of the General Assembly which established it (47/191),[4] the CSD has, over the decade since Rio, settled into a cycle of annual meetings, each of which has addressed a cluster of related issues from within Agenda 21. A ministerial segment to the meetings has attempted to respond to the General Assembly's call to 'consider emerging issues and to provide necessary political impetus to the implementation of the decisions of the [Rio] conference and the commitments contained therein'. The annual meetings have also provided a focus for a very wide, and varying, group of non-governmental interests to come together, share ideas and try, from the margins, to influence the political players who pass fleetingly through the CSD's meetings.[5]

There is not room here to attempt a comprehensive list of the outcomes of the nine sessions of the CSD that have been held since Rio. There have undoubtedly been some useful conclusions. And the adoption of a multi-stakeholder process in contrast to the traditional inter-governmental encounters remains a uniquely progressive feature of the CSD's modus operandi. But few would pretend that the Commission has generated the sense of urgency and engagement raised at the time of the Rio Conference.[6]

This should not necessarily be interpreted as a shortcoming of the process. In the first place, many of the biggest issues that broke upon the scene at Rio have been carried forward in dedicated processes such as the negotiation of protocols to the Climate Change and Biodiversity Conventions. In the second place, there has probably been a healthy realization that many of the most significant challenges rely on cooperation and collaboration at regional and sub-regional levels rather than the global level.

That said, there has been an ongoing current of debate about 'global governance' over the last decade which suggests that the present arrangements remain problematic in the minds of many people. Proposals have ranged from re-examining and strengthening the mandates of existing agencies such as

UNEP to the creation of completely new entities like a World Environment Organization.[7]

Ten years on from Rio it is not unreasonable to ask whether the CSD as it is currently configured can sustain itself as a forum in which the many strands of the sustainable development debate can be usefully advanced. Any review of the CSD's effectiveness should include a consideration of three questions:

1   Is it a forum where emerging issues related to sustainable development can be swiftly placed on the international agenda and explored in a sufficiently substantive way to give decision-makers a crisp and authoritative basis for action should they wish to proceed?
2   Does the CSD process really engage non-governmental groups, institutions and expertise in an open, frank way?
3   Does the CSD have real political-level buy-in?

My short answer to each question would be no, or insufficiently. In the first place, the CSD has become ensnared in the wider machinations of the UN system. Despite the fact that its only function is to report to the Economic and Social Council (which in turn can only report on to the General Assembly), the deliberations of the CSD are treated as though they are a major inter-governmental negotiation in which significant national interests are at stake.[8] Of course, to the extent that they are part of the New York-based calendar, CSD sessions are caught up in wider intra-UN debates. As such, collateral damage flowing from sensitivities in other areas is visited upon them.

For those who insist that progress at the global level is only made in very small incremental steps, this is by no means a demoralizing conclusion. What may seem to activists to be a consensus-driven process leading to lowest common denominator outcomes, is to professional negotiators a guaranteed way of ensuring that sectoral enthusiasm is not permitted to sweep away a wider pursuit of national interests.

But it is doubtful whether this long, slow diplomatic game lends itself to the catalytic role that at least some of the CSD's sponsors envisaged for it. Slow and tortured negotiations make sense if legally binding rules and processes are to issue from the process. But where the ambition is an agenda-setting role in which national interests are expressly reserved, it has to be asked whether the negotiating mind-set can sustain the interest of members, let alone the engagement of those NGOs which are not always initiated into the arcane rituals of international diplomacy.

The engagement of the non-governmental community (including business) has proved particularly difficult. On the one hand, the annual meetings of the CSD provide a rationale for a very broad range of different interest groups to gather at the same time to exchange views and information – and, hopefully, engage the interest of politicians. On the other hand, the formal process of 'multi-stakeholder dialogues' has frequently been a stilted affair with little to show for all the preparations that many have, in good faith, undertaken.[9]

Finally, there is the lack of political buy-in to the CSD process. This goes right back to the preparation of meetings which is left largely in the hands of diplomats. The memberships of the bureaux that organize the meetings are normally chaired by a minister supplemented by a handful of New York-based representatives from permanent missions. And there is very little expectation that the preparation for meetings involves the substantial engagement of relevant ministers. This is perhaps not unreasonable given the fact that, in comparison with the negotiation of real binding legal instruments, little appears to be directly at stake at CSD meetings. But the result is very low expectations on the part of policy-makers who are urged to attend CSD to keep the sustainable development agenda alive.

The best case that can be made for ministerial attendance at meetings of the CSD is the opportunity to engage a wide cross-section of opposite numbers and stakeholders, frequently in the margins. It is not a particularly strong reason. The world is awash with international conferences and seminars, many of them much smaller, more focused and untainted by the negotiating mind-set that pervades the UN system.

Can we do better? It is a fair question to ask, ten years after the Rio Conference. To do so, countries would have to make up their minds whether they wanted the CSD to be a catalyst for giving exposure to genuinely new and challenging issues, or a forum that seeks through negotiation to bring pressure at the margin to all the pre-existing agendas that have their homes in other agencies. One thing is clear to me: trying to *catalyse* issues by negotiation is doomed to failure through terminal boredom. A majority of countries have made it clear that they have no enthusiasm for new institutions and agencies. Those who do, have tended to shroud them in proposals to transform existing agencies. Few if any seem prepared to advocate getting rid of any. So there is a real risk that – without some decisive engagement by key players – the safe mediocrity of the status quo will be the default position.

As a former chairman of the CSD, I would resist such a conclusion. Without a significant change in format, the CSD stands little chance of galvanizing action. But then, neither do any of the other agencies – given their roles and mandates – have the capacity to engage debate across traditional policy borders. My solution would be to use the CSD as a mechanism to set about purpose-built, time-bound commissions to bring into the open some of the emerging international environment and development issues for which there is, for whatever reason, no obvious suitable forum.

The idea would be to set up investigatory commissions whose role it would be to report in depth on the substance of issues of rising concern and to outline dispassionately the range of conceivable solutions that the international community could consider coalescing around. To make an impact, the membership of such bodies would need to encompass:

- *active* ministerial participation (not necessarily drawn from the CSD's 53 members but reflecting the need for regional balance);
- officers of the relevant inter-governmental organizations at the highest level;
- a small number of technical experts of the highest quality to give each commission its own independent investigative firepower.

The brief of such commissions should be to canvas the opinion of all interested sectors of civil society in addition to member governments. While the expectation should be that such commissions should seek to clarify the problem definition and narrow the range of disagreement on remedies, they should avoid any analytical dilution caused by an attempt to reach a negotiated consensus. The robust description of remaining differences will be a better basis for describing the terrain that any future formal negotiations will encounter.

To avoid the potentially life-sapping negotiation of terms of reference for commissions, the CSD should only spell these out in general terms. The members of the commissions should be left considerable latitude to define the boundaries of their enquiries in response to the submissions they receive. Their reports to the CSD should provide the bulk of the substance to be discussed at meetings of the CSD. In other words, the current dreary negotiated preparatory processes would be replaced by the focused deliberations of ministerially led enquiries. Requiring them to generate a finished report would provide meetings of the CSD with something of substance to debate – in the presence of its authors and many of those they have consulted along the way. And by insisting that commissions report within a maximum of three years, the policy relevance of their findings would be ensured.

Ministerial membership of commissions must be insisted upon. Only they can confer the legitimacy needed to make reports back to the CSD that cannot simply be ignored. If ministers are going to invest time in their conclusions, they are going to want them to be addressed substantively by their peers. The corollary of this is that ministers are only going to engage on this sort of basis if it is explicitly understood from the outset that the status of what they are doing is without prejudice to national interests and devoid of any negotiating significance. If reports led to subsequent attempts to negotiate treaties then they would have to take the hard road of traditional diplomacy.

CSD-spawned commissions would simply be a way of placing new issues on the international agenda – or re-energizing old ones – without prejudice to any parties. They would leave final decision-making authority firmly in national hands while being a visible recognition of the fact that, in a rapidly globalizing world community, many problems cannot be tackled exclusively behind closed borders. There is no immediately obvious precedent for the approach being advocated here. But two recent international initiatives – the World Commission on Dams (WCD) and the Commission on Macroeconomics and Health (CMH) – provide support for the view that purpose-built commissions can make a difference.

In the case of the World Commission on Dams, some 53 organizations spanning governments, international agencies, private corporations, NGOs and foundations provided financial assistance (without strings attached) to a particularly high-powered team chaired by a South African minister, Kader Asmal.[10]

The WCD's brief was twofold: first, to review the development effectiveness of large dams and assess alternatives for water resources and energy development; and second, to develop internationally acceptable guidelines for the development and management of dams. The WCD tackled a thorny and contentious issue that, if not eliminating disagreement, provided a body of analysis that no future debate or development could afford to ignore, as well as practical guidance to a wide range of parties. In short, it moved the issue forward. While it was not formally a report to any single agency, its immediate audience was, self-evidently, those agencies in the development business.

By contrast, the Commission on Macroeconomics and Health was formally commissioned by the Director-General of the World Health Organization (WHO) and reported to her. But like the WCD, it enjoyed the sponsorship of a range of governmental and private philanthropic institutions, all of whom shared an interest in its conclusions, in addition to WHO.[11] Chaired by Professor Jeffrey Sachs, its membership encompassed a range of experts drawn from political, inter-governmental and academic backgrounds. In 150 accessible pages, it generated an up-to-date, policy-relevant framework for focusing on the relationship between health and economic development. Like the report of the WCD, Professor Sachs's report has become an essential reference point for politicians and non-governmental players who wish to engage on these issues.

In both cases, time-bound commissions provided both depth of analysis and a 'way through' timely issues that have begged champions. Whether the conclusions are in either case 'definitive' is beside the point. The two reports turn a spotlight onto an important issue and provide the sort of basis for informed debate that should make inter-governmental fora (like the CSD for instance) much better focused than they currently are.

Both commissions provide a basis for re-thinking the role of the CSD as a mechanism for keeping the difficult, cross-cutting issues at the heart of sustainable development on the agenda. If sustainable development is to be genuinely about development *and* containing the negative side-effects or externalities that can be ultimately self-defeating, then such commissions would need (as the two examples above illustrate) to go beyond problem definition to elaborating the range of practical, cost-effective solutions needed to make progress. This will in many cases broach issues relating to developmental and technical assistance since many environmental pressures of global concern (such as the destruction of forests) have their roots in specific regional development imperatives.

It is obvious from the outline of this proposal that the number of issues under consideration at any one time would be very much smaller than the potential array of issues outlined in Agenda 21. This is deliberate. Ten years on from Rio two things have become much clearer. The first, already mentioned, is that a relatively small number of issues require, for their solution, truly international action. The adage 'think global, act local' is profoundly wise. Even if people wish to advocate global solutions to many problems, there are simply no adequate governance mechanisms to attempt them – and no likelihood that they are going to be created in the foreseeable future. *Thinking* about global problems may be all that we can do. Our actions – for both ecological and human reasons – may only make sense at a local or at most regional level.

Second, there is a much greater level of realism about the limits to how much can be meaningfully absorbed at any one time by either bureaucracies or decision-makers. The ability of even reasonably well-resourced countries to devote the needed human resources to the array of issues canvassed at Rio has been stretched. And even where there are few material constraints, the ability to engage political attention across a wide range of fronts has often been overestimated. It is one thing to go through the motions of grafting 'sustainability' concerns into every corner of national and international life (and there have been some heroic examples). It is entirely another to engender the sort of focused political commitment that any sense of prioritization requires.

With national councils for sustainable development well established in many countries, CSD as a catalyst for action could do worse than focus – as only it can – on those pressing issues that affect the global commons and in respect of which international law has at best only partial coverage and in many cases none. There are challenges enough posed to the oceans and atmosphere – and their interaction with biophysical systems at the planetary level – without spending scarce financial and diplomatic resources on issues that can only ever be solved at the local level.

Neither is there any shortage of unfinished negotiations or completed treaties that have yet to come into force which could benefit from some sustained analysis – not to mention agreements in force that are simply inadequate and need to be either rewritten or significantly upgraded.[12]

Notwithstanding the commitment of vast diplomatic resources, the Framework Convention on Climate Change and its (thus far unratified) protocol failed to dent the rising track of greenhouse gas emissions. Similarly, notwithstanding the Biodiversity Convention, forest destruction continues apace in many parts of the world. These are much quoted instances. But there are many others. Take, for instance, the Agreement to Promote Compliance with International Conservation and Management Measures by Fishing Vessels on the High Seas, which would give teeth to the FAO's ambitious code of conduct. Completed in 1995, the agreement still lacks the 25 acceptances needed to enter into force. Unsustainable practices persist on the high seas. And it has to be said that even the entry into force of the agreement would not of itself solve anything to the extent that the flags of a large pool of non-signatories provide a means of escape for those who would seek to raid the ocean commons.[13]

Instances such as this highlight the stark reality that bodies of negotiated international law guarantee nothing of themselves. Implicit in that observation is the fact that unsustainable practices – both within territorial jurisdictions and in the global commons – will not be tackled by treaties and regulation. Those formal mechanisms will only gain traction when there is effective national and regional governance, and that in many cases is inextricably linked to hard issues of economic and social development. Thus it is important that any global level initiatives in support of sustainable development are firmly rooted in an understanding of the drivers of *unsustainable* development. This is the multidisciplinary perspective that would need to inform any commissions mandated by the CSD as proposed. It is the genesis of the CSD in the Rio process that should make it the obvious forum in which to initiate action of this type.

Conceiving of the CSD as a catalyst for action would make it a vantage point from which priorities could be identified and the quality and integration of international initiatives could be assessed. Above all, it would at least enable the analysis of genuinely global issues in an integrated way. We live in a world of nation states with competing – and sometimes irreconcilable – national interests. As such, there is no escaping the essentially inter-governmental nature of any attempts to respond to the global challenges. But the need to negotiate our way patiently through them should not blind us to the fact that economic and social development paths impose footprints that do not stay behind closed borders. Nor are they, frequently, the intended or even the predicted consequences of human activity.

If we can at least free our approach to problem analysis from the prism of nationally conceived interests – as this transformation of the CSD proposes – we may achieve a more transparent and fairer basis for amending and furthering the norms on which international relations are based.

Postscript

In the course of the Johannesburg Summit, the role and function of the Commission on Sustainable Development came to be considered. The conclusions of the summit (as reflected in the Plan of Implementation) were extremely cautious. Negotiators agreed that the role of the commission should be 'strengthened' but the general reader would be challenged by the text of the implementation plan to identify just what this 'strengthening' might entail.

Readers familiar with the past work of the commission would no doubt be surprised to learn that 'reviewing and monitoring progress in the implementation of Agenda 21 and fostering coherence of implementation, initiatives and partnership' could be described as 'an enhanced role'. Similarly a call for 'focus on the cross-sectoral aspects of specific sectoral issues' and the provision of 'a forum for better integration of policies, including through interaction among Ministers dealing with the various dimensions and sectors of sustainable development through the high-level segments' simply begs the question: what on earth has the commission been doing these last ten years if it hasn't been doing this? The only 'concrete' procedural proposal made was to limit 'negotiating' sessions of the commission to every two years.

Fortunately, as is so often the way with negotiated texts, the genius of such inscrutable recommendations is their coded ability to leave open options for the future. So it is a relief to discover that the Report of the Secretary-General on the 'Follow-up to Johannesburg and the Future Role of the CSD' (UN Secretary-General, 2003) takes an imaginative and lateral inspiration from these anodyne words. The recommendation that 'negotiations' should become a biennial affair is used to construct a much more interesting approach to engaging relevant parties in the process of reviewing implementation and identifying priorities for future deliberation and action.

Most encouraging is the observation in paragraph 45 that:

> *... a number of proposals were made regarding the creation of issue-oriented time-bound Sub-Commissions or Task Forces involving a limited number of representatives of countries, international institutions and major groups to provide inputs to the CSD. Such Sub-Commissions or Task Forces, if initiated and funded by interested parties, could make valuable inputs to the work of the Commission and raise the profile of sustainable development issues in the public eye.*

And again, in paragraph 75 under the heading of maintaining high-level political engagement, it is suggested that:

> *Another possibility could be for interested governments to organize inter-sessional meetings or processes involving relevant Ministers from other interested countries together with leaders of international organizations and major groups, to generate innovative ideas or policy approaches to address specific issues on the CSD agenda.*

The motivation to establish such commissions or task forces would not, of course, necessarily depend on determinations of the CSD. The willingness to assemble 'coalitions of the willing' is as likely to arise from the interests and expertise of the various players as it is from some negotiated list of priorities. Indeed, there are good grounds for suspecting that 'willing' coalitions – in other words, countries and stakeholder groups with a real desire to get on with the job – are more likely to arise organically than as a result of some formal process. But to the extent that they do – and their joint analytical skills and practical expertise as change agents throw new light on the issues – they can only enliven the CSD's workings.

Rather than seek to manage the future work programme too closely, the CSD would do well to accept for debate and scrutiny the widest range of findings that engaged members of the international community are prepared to refer to it. The Secretary-General's liberal and intelligent response to the cautious recommendations of the Johannesburg Summit is to be welcomed.

Notes

1   The difficulties of managing sustainable development at the national government level, though not within the scope of this chapter, should not be underestimated either. The need to develop a whole-of-government approach to the matter is pressing. A recent OECD report highlights the substantive and serious problems in ensuring policy coherence and integration at the national level (OECD, 2002).
2   Agenda 21 and the Rio Declaration can be downloaded from www.un.org/esa/sustdev/agenda21.htm and www.un.org/documents/ga/conf151/aconf15126-1annex1.htm.
3   Factual information about the CSD is located at www.un.org/esa/sustdev/csd.htm. The full reports of the CSD and the Rio outcomes can be accessed via www.un.org/esa/sustdev/csdpast.htm. Rather surprisingly, the extent of academic interest in the work of the commission has been relatively limited. A useful overview is provided by Tornberg (2000), Wagner (1999) and Young (2000).

4   The full resolution may be downloaded at www.un.org/documents/ga/res/47/ares47-191.htm.

5   The reports of the work of the CSD since its creation can be accessed at www.un.org/esa/sustdev/csdpast.htm.

6   Verdicts on the CSD's success are mixed. For a positive account of its achievements, see Dodds (2001). For a more caustic critique see Agarwal et al (2001).

7   The literature on the environmental and sustainable development governance issues, including the creation of a World Environment Organization is expanding. For a good overview of the main ideas behind the concept see Biermann (2000), Esty (1994), Whalley and Zissimos (2001) and Farr (2000). Critical surveys of the issue include Auer (2000), Bolton (2000), Hassan (2001) and Velasquez (2000) .

8   Discussions in early 2003 on the future mandate of the CSD have included the notion that the CSD's future plan of work might alternate negotiating sessions with years in which discussions on 'implementation of existing commitments' would take place. While this is welcome, it does not obviate the relevance of the points made in this chapter.

9   The WSSD process was threatened with, among other things, an NGO walk-out over the perception that certain countries were seeking to derail progress and downgrade consultative processes within the wider CSD framework. For more details see in particular, UN Wire (2002), ENS (2002) and Bridges Weekly Trade News Digest (2002).

10 The World Commission on Dams was formed following a meeting initiated by the World Bank and the World Conservation Union (IUCN) in 1997. Although originally focusing on a study of the World Bank's dam-building record, the process expanded into an independent review led by 12 commissioners drawn from government ministries, the private sector and civil society. A full-time professional secretariat was established to support the WCD's work, along with a 68-member advisory forum and thousands of contributors who analysed and commented on the final report. Funding for the project was drawn from more than 30 companies, NGOs, governments and individuals. More detail on the WCD, its structure and the full report of its findings can be found at www.dams.org/. There are a number of assessments available of the work of the WCD, including in particular: Bird (2000), Dubash et al (2001), Navalawala (2001), Parasuraman and Sengupta (2001), Bradlow (2001) and McCully (2001). See also www.dams.org/report/reaction.htm for an overview of a range of responses by international financial institutions and others to the WCD report.

11 In May 1999, the World Health Organization and the UK's Department for International Development (DFID) organized a meeting called 'World Health Opportunity: Developing Health, Reducing Poverty'. The meeting underlined the point that health is an issue of importance to macroeconomic specialists and as a consequence, WHO established the Commission on Macroeconomics and Health (CMH) in January 2000. The CMH's two primary and interrelated objectives were to analyse the impact of health on development and to examine the modalities through which health-related investment could have a positive impact on economic growth and equity in developing countries. It recommended a set of measures designed to maximize poverty reduction and economic development benefits of health sector investment. More particularly, its key recommendation was that the world's low- and middle-income countries, in partnership with high-income countries, should scale up the access of the world's poor to essential health services, including a focus on specific interventions. The CMH comprised six working groups, and a professional secretariat. The CMH was funded by more than ten

governmental agencies and foundations (WHO, 2002). More information about the CMH and WHO's role in its creation may be accessed by following the links from www.who.int/home-page/. The full report can be downloaded at www.cid.harvard.edu/cidcmh/CMHReport.pdf. Assessments of the report and its utility can be found at www.guardian.co.uk/Archive/Article/0,4273, 4324170,00.html and www.cid.harvard.edu/cidinthenews/articles/FT_010902.html. More academic sources analysing the report have yet to emerge.

12 There are, currently, in excess of 50 worldwide multilateral environment and sustainable development-related agreements, not including the protocols and amendments related to these. If the protocols and amendments are included (and many of these are important in their own right, eg the Montreal Protocol), the figure approaches 100. To these may be added more than 100 regional agreements (or more than 160 if supplementary protocols and amendments are included). The diplomatic resources required to manage the discussions related to these agreements are obviously enormous. Yet, a cold hard look at the actual implementation rates of these agreements is sobering. Fully a third of the more than 220 worldwide and regional multilateral environment and sustainable development-related agreements and their various protocols/amendments have not actually been implemented. Furthermore, the number of international organizations tasked with managing these agreements is growing. Currently, the FAO, UNEP, WHO and more than ten individually established secretariats for specific agreements manage the worldwide multilateral arrangements with a plethora of regional secretariats managing the sub-international level agreements (OECD, 1999, 2001).

13 For more information on this agreement see www.fao.org/fi/agreem/codecond/codecon.asp#AGREEM.

References

Agarwal, A, Narain, S, Sharma, A and Imchen, A (eds) (2001) *Global Environmental Negotiations 2: Poles Apart*, Centre for Science & Environment, Delhi, pp169–222

Auer, MR (2000) 'Who Participates in Global Environmental Governance? Partial Answers from International Relations Theory', *Policy Sciences*, vol 33, pp155–180

Biermann, F (2000) 'The Case for a World Environment Organization', *Environment*, November

Bird, J (2000) 'A Global Water Policy Arena – The World Commission on Dams', *Water Law*, vol 11, part 6, pp208–216

Bolton, R (2000) 'Should We Take Global Governance Seriously?', *Chicago Journal of International Law*, vol 1, part 2, pp205–221

Bradlow, DD (2001) 'The World Commission on Dams' Contribution to the Broader Debate on Development', *American University International Law Review*, vol 16, part 6, pp1531–1572

Bridges Weekly Trade News Digest (2002) 'PrepCom II Falters in Lead-up to WSSD', *Bridges Weekly Trade News Digest*, vol 6, no 13, 9 April

Dodds, F (2001) 'Reforming the International Institutions', in F Dodds and T Middleton (eds) *Earth Summit 2002 – A New Deal*, 2nd edn, Earthscan, London, pp320–324

Dubash, N, Dupar, M, Kothgari, S and Lissu, T (2001) *A Watershed in Global Governance? An Independent Assessment of the World Commission on Dams*, WRI, Washington, DC

Environmental News Service (2002) *Johannesburg Summit Preparations Bog Down*, 8 April, available at www.ens-newswire.com/ens/apr2002/2002-04-08-03.asp, accessed 2 September 2003

Esty, D (1994) 'The Case for a Global Environmental Organization', in P B Kenen (ed.) *Managing the World Economy: Fifty Years After Bretton Woods*, Institute for International Economics, Washington, DC, pp287–309

Farr, K T (2000) 'A New Global Environmental Organization', *Georgia Journal of International and Comparative Law*, vol 28, part 3, pp493–525

Hassan, P (2001) 'Elements of Good Environmental Governance', *Asia-Pacific Journal of Environmental Law*, vol 6, issue 1, pp1–11

McCully, P (2001) 'The Use of a Trilateral Network: An Activist's Perspective on the Formation of the World Commission on Dams', *American University International Law Review*, vol 16, part 6, pp1453–1475

Navalawala, BN (2001) 'World Commission on Dams: Biased?' *Economic and Political Weekly*, 24 March, pp1008–1010

OECD (1999) *OECD Environmental Data*, OECD, Paris

OECD (2001) *Environmental Performance Reviews*, OECD, Paris

OECD (2002) *Governance for Sustainable Development: Five OECD Case Studies*, OECD, Paris

Parasuraman, S and Sengupta, S (2001) 'World Commission on Dams: Democratic Means for Sustainable Ends', *Economic and Political Weekly*, 26 May

Tornberg, J (2000) 'The United Nations Commission on Sustainable Development', *New York Law School Journal of Human Rights*, vol 17, part 33, pp957–968

UN Secretary-General (2003) 'Follow-up to Johannesburg and the Future Role of the CSD – The Implementation Track', report of the Secretary-General for consideration by CSD11, 18 February 2003, available at www.un.org/esa/sustdev/csd11/sgreport.pdf, accessed 31 March 2003.

UN Wire (2002) *Consensus Eludes Preparatory Meeting*, 8 April, available at www.unwire.org/unwire/20020408/25368_story.asp, accessed 2 September 2003.

Velasquez, J (2000) 'Prospects for Rio + 10 and the Need for an Inter-Linkages Approach to Global Environmental Governance', *Global Environmental Change*, vol 10, pp307–312

Wagner, LM (1999) 'Negotiations in the UN Commission on Sustainable Development: Coalitions, Processes and Outcomes', *International Negotiation*, vol 4, no 2, pp107–131

Whalley, J and Zissimos, B (2001) 'What Could a World Environmental Organization Do?' *Global Environmental Politics*, vol 1, no 1, February, pp29–34

WHO (2002) *Macroeconomics and Health: Investing in Health for Economic Development*, WHO, Geneva

Young, J (2000) 'Education at the Commission on Sustainable Development: The Perception of the International Community', *The Environmentalist*, vol 20, pp169–178

Part 2

National and Local Governance

Chapter 9

National Sustainable Development Strategies

Stephen Bass and Barry Dalal-Clayton, IIED

New Thinking and Time for Action

New thinking on strategies for sustainable development emphasizes multi-stakeholder processes, continuous learning and improvement, and effective mechanisms for coordinating strategic planning. International endorsement of the principles underpinning this new thinking would help all countries to make progress, especially following the key concern for such strategies shown during the World Summit on Sustainable Development (WSSD) in Johannesburg in August–September 2002.

Recent international reviews (OECD DAC, 2001; UN DESA, 2002a,b; OECD/UNDP, 2002) and debate have revealed how national strategies for sustainable development can offer *systems* to integrate many initiatives – and keep sustainable development on everyone's agenda. Old notions of strategies as perfectionist 'master plans', which are invariably imposed from outside, are being dispensed with. The new approach to strategies is very timely.

The challenge of sustainable development

Since the Rio Earth Summit in 1992, the international community, national and local governments, private sector organizations, NGOs and others have struggled to find ways to operationalize sustainable development. Achieving this has remained elusive.

Sustainable development means treating the issues of poverty, environmental management and social issues together, in the face of many difficult challenges. But how can environmental protection, poverty alleviation and moneymaking objectives be integrated in practice – or trade-offs made if integration is impossible? How can long-term needs *really* be balanced with short-term imperatives, especially when change is so unpredictable? How can local demands be treated alongside broader national and global requirements? And how do you get a decision-making process 'with the maximum possible participation' (as called for by Agenda 21) that does not impose substantial costs in time or money?

In effect, social, environmental and economic issues of almost unprecedented complexity need to be tackled at several levels in ways, that are not merely conceptually neat, but also encourage significant behavioural and institutional change.

Moving towards sustainable development presents tremendous challenges. Important structural changes are needed to the ways societies manage their economic, social and environmental affairs. Different countries may settle for different solutions, but all will have to make hard choices. Strategies for sustainable development are about making and implementing such choices, in a realistic, effective and lasting way.

Early strategic planning approaches

Earlier strategic planning efforts that professed to address the issue of sustainable development did not really get to grips with the above challenges. From the World Conservation Strategy in 1980, to Agenda 21 in 1992, the sustainable development texts that emerged from international processes tended to be overwhelming in their all-encompassing nature, with an emphasis on comprehensive sets of objectives. Many approaches were largely environmental and did little to integrate social and economic dimensions, and often the focus was on producing documents with little effective implementation. A similar approach was followed by sectoral initiatives towards sustainability (for example, the UN Inter-governmental Panel/Forum on Forests produced over 250 'proposals for action').

Such massive agendas have tended to be ignored: no one person or group is interested in all items in the list of 'what should be done'. They were also too vague or too remote from day-to-day realities of 'how to do things': investment, trade and production, and consumption. No wonder that many of the earlier national approaches – national conservation strategies (NCSs), national environmental action plans (NEAPs) and so on – have been treated at best as checklists, or as encyclopedias of ideas, to turn to whenever the occasional policy space or financial opportunity emerges to do something 'green'.

Until recently, there has been little guidance on strategies. The assumption that they are plans has been unchallenged. At the 1992 Earth Summit, governments made a commitment to adopt national strategies for sustainable development. The understanding at the time was that some kind of integrated master plan was the way forward: 'the strategy should build upon and harmonize the various sectoral, economic, social and environmental policies and plans that are operating in the country' (Agenda 21, Chapter 8, para 8.7). However, it was also understood that international precepts should not be imposed, and that successful strategies would be 'country-driven'.

In the past, many strategic planning initiatives had limited practical impact because they focused on the production of a comprehensive document as an end product, and such documents have often been left without implementation.

Targets

Five years after the Earth Summit, the 1997 Special Session of the UN General Assembly set a target date of 2002, when 'the formulation and elaboration of national strategies for sustainable development that reflect the contributions and responsibilities of all interested parties should be completed in all countries' (United Nations, 1997, para 23). Significantly, the special session also introduced an emerging idea of strategies as processes – 'important mechanisms for enhancing and linking national capacity so as to bring together priorities in social, economic and environmental policies'. Again no real guidance was offered, but countries were nonetheless urged to go about the task.

The Millennium Development Goals include one to 'integrate the principles of sustainable development into country policies and programmes and reverse the loss of environmental resources' (UNGA, 2001, Goal 7, target 9).

Most recently, the Plan of Implementation agreed at WSSD recommits governments to taking action on national sustainable development strategies (NSDSs).

States should:

> *(a) Continue to promote coherent and coordinated approaches to institutional frameworks for sustainable development at all national levels, including through, as appropriate, the establishment or strengthening of existing authorities and mechanisms necessary for policy-making, coordination and implementation and enforcement of laws;*

> *(b) Take immediate steps to make progress in the formulation and elaboration of national strategies for sustainable development and begin their implementation by 2005. To this end, as appropriate, strategies should be supported through international cooperation, taking into account the special needs of developing countries, in particular the least developed countries. Such strategies, which, where applicable, could be formulated as poverty reduction strategies that integrate economic, social and environmental aspects of sustainable development, should be pursued in accordance with each country's national priorities* (United Nations, 2002, para 145).

Learning from past experience

Recent UN and Organisation for Economic Co-operation and Development (OECD) initiatives have been developing guidance on effective strategies for sustainable development. As in any field, it is clear that leadership and innovation in sustainable development are derived from many sources. It would certainly be a conceit to view centralized national strategies as the only means to bring it about. Earlier reviews by IUCN and IIED (notably Carew-Reid et al, 1994; Dalal-Clayton et al, 1994; Bass et al, 1995; Dalal-Clayton, 1996) and a more recent intensive consultation exercise in eight developing countries supported by the OECD (OECD DAC, 2001) showed that there have been some valuable results from the earlier approaches to sustainable development strategies. Most significant have been their roles: in improving awareness of sustainable development issues among a wide range of stakeholders; in developing sustainable development pilot projects; in setting up environmental authorities where these were missing; and in coordinating/integrating authorities and fora concerned with sustainable development. But the OECD work (OECD DAC, 2001) and a recent international forum hosted by UN Department for Economic and Social Affairs (UN DESA, 2002a) and the Government of Ghana, supported by the UK Department for International Development (DFID), the United Nations Development Programme (UNDP) and the Danish Government, were also significant in looking more widely for sources of leadership and innovation, not assuming that existing one-off strategies were the only pointers to the future.

Given circumstances of continuing change, it is now clear that effective strategies require systematic and iterative processes of learning and doing. They do not have discrete beginnings or ends. Establishing a new or stand-alone strategic planning process would rarely be recommended.

It is now accepted that, instead, an NSDS should improve the integration of social and environmental objectives into key economic development processes. In other words, a set of locally driven, continuing processes, rather than an encyclopedia of possible actions (most of which will interest only a few people). The OECD Development Assistance Committee (DAC) policy guidance on NSDSs offers the first official definition of a strategy:

> *A coordinated set of participatory and continuously improving processes of analysis, debate, capacity strengthening, planning and investment, which seeks to integrate the short- and long-term economic, social and environmental objectives of society – through mutually supportive approaches wherever possible – and manages trade-offs where this is not possible* (OECD DAC, 2001).

The OECD, and latterly the UN International Forum, actively looked for those mechanisms that individual countries had found most effective in identifying and debating sustainable development issues, in planning experiments, in changing policy towards sustainable development and associated roles, and in monitoring sustainable development in ways that lead to improved action. Some NCSs, NEAPs and Green Plans offered some of these mechanisms. But there were other sources of innovation, too, especially in the regular planning system, in corporate investment, in public–private partnerships, and in community development and decentralization initiatives. These other initiatives responded to different everyday pressures – local as well as (increasingly) global – and were often uncoordinated with one another. But they pointed to desirable characteristics of a strategy for sustainable development, if they could somehow be brought together.

Common principles and characteristics

The OECD work established a set of principles for NSDSs. Building on these, the UN International Forum on NSDS, held in Ghana in November 2001, agreed a number of characteristics common to sustainable development strategies in both developed and developing countries (UN DESA, 2002a,b).[1] These principles and characteristics can be summarized as:

- integration of economic, social and environmental objectives;
- coordination and balance between sector and thematic strategies and decentralized levels, and across generations;
- broad participation, effective partnerships, transparency and accountability;
- country ownership, shared vision with a clear time frame on which stakeholders agree, commitment and continuous improvement;
- developing capacity and an enabling environment, building on existing knowledge and processes;
- focus on priorities, outcomes and coherent means of implementation;
- linkage with budget and investment processes; and
- continuous monitoring and evaluation.

The International Forum further confirmed that:

> *effective national sustainable development strategies have common characteristics, but that they take different forms depending on national and local conditions... For example, established frameworks such as a National Vision, National Agenda 21, a Poverty Reduction Strategy (PRS) or a Comprehensive Development Framework (CDF) can all provide a good basis to build on for taking strategic action towards sustainable development. The particular label applied to a national sustainable development strategy is not important as long as the common characteristics of the strategy are adhered to* (UN DESA, 2002a).

Strategies should be learning systems

The emphasis is now on demand-driven processes rather than top-down agendas. 'Strategy' is increasingly being used to imply a continuous (or at least iterative) learning system to develop and achieve a shared vision, rather than a one-off exercise. The associated challenges are now more clearly about institutional change – about generating awareness, reaching consensus on values, building commitment, creating an environment with the right incentives, working on shared tasks, and doing so at a pace with which stakeholders can cope. The means to do this are integrated systems: of participation, analysis, debate, experiment, prioritization, transparency, monitoring, accountability and review. All countries will have some elements of these systems within existing strategic planning mechanisms. The challenge is to find them, bring them together and strengthen them.

Putting an NSDS into operation would, in practice, most likely consist of using promising, existing processes as entry points, and strengthening them in terms of the key principles and characteristics listed above.

Establishing a coordinated system

An NSDS should be seen as a set of coordinated mechanisms and processes to implement the principles and help society work towards sustainable development – not as 'master plans' which will get out of date. This will help to improve convergence between existing strategies, avoid duplication, confusion and straining developing country capacity and resources. Indeed, a sustainable development strategy may best be viewed as a system comprising various components:

- regular multi-stakeholder fora and means for negotiation at national and decentralized levels, with links between them;
- a shared vision, developed through such fora, incorporating broad strategic objectives;
- a set of mechanisms to pursue these objectives in ways that can adapt to change (notably an information system with key sustainable development indicators; communication capabilities; analytical processes; international engagement; and coordinated means for policy coherence, budgeting, monitoring and accountability);
- strategic principles and locality- or sector-specific criteria, indicators and standards adopted by sectors and stakeholders, through legislation, voluntary action and market-based instruments, etc;
- pilot activities – from an early stage – to generate learning and commitment;
- a secretariat or other facility, with clear authority and powers, to coordinate these mechanisms; and
- a mandate for all these activities from a high-level, central authority such as the prime minister's office and, to the extent possible, from citizens' and business organizations.

Strategies: a shared challenge in the North and South

The problems faced by developing and developed countries in preparing strategies for sustainable development are usually quite different. Most developing countries are occupied with economic development, poverty alleviation and social investment. Developed countries face problems caused by high levels of industrial activity, movement and consumption (for example, pollution and congestion).

Countries have consequently approached strategies from different perspectives and pursued them through different means. In the North, the focus has been on institutional reorientation and integration, regulatory and voluntary standards and local targets, environmental controls, and cost-saving approaches. The South has been concerned with creating new institutions and 'bankable' projects. Clearly they have much to learn from each other's experiences. Both now face a stronger challenge, in a globalizing world, of encouraging responsible business and investment – and therefore of well-organized private sector participation in NSDSs. Governments urgently need to address several key uncertainties if they are truly serious in meeting the international target for sustainable development strategies.

First, are bureaucrats willing to do things differently; to think and behave in new, open, participatory ways that provide for dialogue and consensus building; to agree what is needed and how to get there? There is a need to identify those motivations that will encourage bureaucrats to work differently.

Second, are institutions willing to work in support of each other to achieve cross-sectoral integration and synchronization? There is a need to identify and support the constructive institutional relationships and experiments that exist.

Third, and perhaps most critically, political will must be generated to support such approaches. The NSDS principles and system are designed to continuously improve such political will, but an NSDS will require bold leadership to kick the whole process off.

Time to seize the opportunity

Sustainable development strategies emerged as a fundamental issue at WSSD, where countries and organizations gave considerable thought to how they might organize themselves to operationalize the agreements embedded in the WSSD Plan of Implementation. The guidance resulting from both the UN and the OECD processes provides a timely and effective way forward at national to local levels. They offer a 'fitness for sustainable development' diagnostic and a 'gap analysis' to identify processes and mechanisms that are missing. Because national strategies are now understood as being based on what works from civil society, private sector and government sources, they should be able to spur countries on to real institutional change by clarifying the issue as one of 'identify and scale up' rather than 'start again'. Because the new thinking on national strategies treats NEAPs, poverty reduction strategy papers (PRSPs), CDFs and so on as optional means to an end, rather than as ends in themselves, it encourages an inclusive approach that should be able to defuse tensions between these 'branded' initiatives. By emphasizing integration with budget/investment processes, and by seeking clarity of goals and evidence of priorities, effective strategy processes are also more likely to attract investment than in the past.

National strategies can provide many 'entry points' for concerned civil society and business groups. Many such groups are seeking effective means of engagement with one another and with government. There are limits to what even the best corporations and NGOs can do on their own, especially in the absence of a forum to debate integration and trade-offs with one another and with government. It is clear that the emerging, pragmatic approach to national strategies has dispensed with the notion of a government-led plan and replaced it with a government-facilitated process. This process integrates many functions (debate, information-gathering, analysis, decision-making, experimentation, role changes, policy changes, monitoring and review) and incorporates principles of inclusiveness and innovation; thus it is an efficient and equitable way to bring together concerned groups. In short, it offers a practical way to keep sustainable development on everybody's agenda. 'Ultimately, sustainable development is not something that governments do for people; it is something people achieve for themselves through individual and collective change' (Cielito Habito).

Bridging the Knowledge Gap in SD Strategies

'Strategy fever': an opportunity or a threat?

Despite the advances noted above, many difficulties are still evident in efforts to deliver change through existing strategic approaches. Even the largest countries today are facing a form of 'policy inflation' through the sequential performance of multiple strategy exercises. In brief, these include:

For poverty alleviation

PRSPs are the predominant approach, promoted by the World Bank (as part of requirements for securing debt relief). Many bilateral development agencies have accorded PRSPs a central place in their support to developing countries. The World Bank's particular requirements have meant that existing 'home-grown' poverty strategies may have been received, displaced and/or superseded by the PRSP (ODI, 2001).

For environmental conservation

The environmental conventions spawned by the UN Conference on Environment and Development (UNCED) each demand some form of national response. The predominant frameworks include national biodiversity strategies and action plans under the Convention on Biological Diversity (CBD), national communications under the Framework Convention on Climate Change (FCCC), national action plans under the Convention to Combat Desertification (CCD), and national forest programmes to implement the Inter-governmental Panel on Forests (IPF) Proposals for Action. In some countries, frameworks that were developed in the 1980s and early 1990s – NEAPs and NCSs – are still in operation. These do not relate to international obligations, but NEAPs are often strongly associated with the World Bank (OECD/UNDP, 2002).

For an integrated approach to sustainable development

Three recognized frameworks are predominant, and one 'organic' option has emerged in practice:

- At local level, Local Agenda 21s have been developed in over 6400 local districts or municipalities, as means to put Agenda 21 into action. Some of these have led to significant innovation and changed behaviour.
- The national-level equivalent is the NSDS, but far fewer of these have been developed. There has never been a strong international political push for NSDSs, in spite of their centrality to Agenda 21 recommendations and being made an international target in 1997 at a UN Special Session (Rio +5). Indeed there were no official UN guidelines until 2001.
- In 1999, the World Bank introduced the concept of the CDF as a means to ensure integrated development, and initiated CDF pilot projects in 12 countries. But this approach has now been largely subsumed under the

international focus on PRSPs (CDF principles are applied in heavily indebted poor countries (HIPC)) (OECD/UNDP, 2002).

- Other integrated approaches to sustainable development have developed more organically, most notably the evolution of those environmental strategies (for example, in Pakistan) which have progressively had to deal with social and economic issues during implementation, or through the evolution of national development plans, which have had to face up to pressing social and environmental concerns (as in Thailand).

A recent global study reveals key problems with most strategies

The two examples above came from an important study of many strategy types by eight developing countries[2] and the OECD Development Assistance Committee (OECD DAC, 2001). This study revealed remarkably similar problems, which may be summarized as follows:[3]

- A large number of strategies were not *country-led* but were induced or even imposed by external agencies. ('A long form to fill in if we are to get aid' was how one minister described one major strategy process.)
- In developing countries, different external agencies pushed their own strategy 'brands', leading to *competition*, 'policy inflation' and overburdening of local capacities.
- Consequently, many strategies were not *integrated* into a country's mainstream decision-making systems (notably government economic planning and private sector investment decisions). Potential incentives for effective local institutions and mechanisms to contribute to, or make use of, the strategy, were missed. The results, therefore, were frequently mere 'planners' dreams', with little political, civil society or business commitment and demand for further action.
- There were often few links between *policy and on-the-ground realities*, so that policy debate did not learn from the field, and people in the field did not participate in debate. As a result, opportunities to link progress in both areas were missed.
- Very many strategies were little more than wish lists, lacking clear *priorities* or achievable targets. The strategies' determination to be comprehensive was a source of both strength (awareness of linked issues) and weakness (lack of focus). This was partly due to inadequate research to inform priorities and solutions, or the progressive removal of the researcher from the priority-setting process. As a result, no one was interested in – or felt responsible for – the complete wish list, and those at the 'centre' felt paralysed by too many proposals.
- There was often a very narrow base of *participation*, usually because of lack of time and resources, no recognized means to identify the stakeholders that counted most, and weak rules on participation processes and outcomes. Any participation was often late in the process. As a result, *consensus* was forced, fragile or partial; few people felt a sense of 'ownership'.

- *Information* employed was often out of date, repeating old analyses and not challenging existing assumptions, with inadequate time and resources available. *Analytical methodologies* were not often up to the holistic tasks, or were inadequately tried, tested and trusted. Existing *sources of (local) knowledge* were often overlooked in favour of the analyses of (external) strategy consultants. As a result, credibility has often been low because the knowledge was not measured in terms of its relevance, utility and accountability to local stakeholders. In the earliest strategies – such as some NCSs and NEAPs – analysis was quite innovative as there were fewer imposed norms and frameworks. But in the worst cases, pieces of 'analysis' have even been cut-and-pasted from one country strategy to another; these served more to push the point of view of the external 'drivers' of the strategy than to assess local needs and solutions. Most strategies of all types have given less attention to these issues than others; as a result, strategy decisions were light on new information and innovation.

These common failings have discredited the concept of 'strategies', and the term has begun to be synonymous with external concepts rather than locally owned policy processes and commitments. Yet the transition to sustainable development *will* require some kind of coordinated, structured (ie strategic) response that deals with priorities, that can manage complexity and uncertainties, and that encourages innovation. Tackling the knowledge limitations will be key.

A case study on information analysis and research in PRSPs

A study by the Overseas Development Institute (ODI) concluded that, in the majority of PRSPs, 'data quality and research capacity utilization/development has been very weak', although this is beginning to change with, for example, the setting up of longer-term PRSP research studies on key themes (ODI, 2001).

Most of the PRSP development processes to date have been relatively rapid affairs, with little chance to do anything more than bringing together existing data. For example:

> *[In the Senegal PRSP] due to the compressed time frame, the thematic groups had only about two months to formulate terms of reference, analyse findings, and submit its final report... As a result, the quality of the analysis ... was not very high* (Phillips, 2002).

> *Even full PRSPs have significant deficiencies in their poverty profiles, including lack of specificity about key categories of poor people* (Thin et al, 2001).

In some countries, much data exists but is underutilized, for example in Rwanda and Ghana; in the latter the statistics bureau has not been involved in the PRSP. The Pakistan PRSP has not used research material from the parallel Participatory Poverty Assessment, feeding accusations that the process is intended to impose knowledge, rather than to generate it (Zehra, 2002). Where data has been used, it has often been old, for example, in Tanzania, where household survey data was ten years old (Whaites, 2002).

Where economic changes are rapid, communities can enter or leave conditions of poverty over a short time. Frequent monitoring and research, to correlate conditions of poverty with policies and other interventions, are needed to develop and improve strategies. But PRSPs have not adequately assessed the available capacity to do this, or provided resources to utilize and build capacity (ODI, 2001; Whaites, 2002).

Those engaged in most PRSP processes are now aware of the need for improving the quality of data gathering and poverty mapping, for capacity building, and for participation in monitoring and evaluation. Many new household surveys (to help with outcome assessments) have been commissioned. Some will complement these with 'lighter' survey instruments including participatory approaches (to pick up evidence on intermediate processes). These participatory approaches are part of the PRSP programme in several countries, such as Mali, Mozambique and Tanzania. In the medium term this will significantly improve the prospects for diagnostic work during PRSP implementation (ODI, 2001).

It is also vitally important to develop research programmes that can, over time, understand the dynamics of linked poverty and environment problems, and the processes that work in solving them. The need for continuing research is barely covered in documents addressing PRSPs to date. Poverty 'observatoires' are being established in some African countries, but the question is whether they are set up in such a way as to stimulate demand for data use and analysis. In Uganda, the location of a technical poverty research unit close to the Ministry of Finance (responsible for the PRSP – itself a useful strategic decision) has helped (ODI, 2001).

A case study of research in Pakistan's National Conservation Strategy

A highly comprehensive mid-term review of Pakistan's NCS was conducted eight years into its implementation (Hanson et al, 2000). In relation to research, it revealed some progress:

- Pakistan's NCS formulation marked perhaps the first major effort to research the environmental aspects of national development.
- Recognizing the need for a continuing research programme linked to the NCS, the Sustainable Development Policy Institute (SDPI) was established in 1992 to serve as a source of expertise and advisory services for government, private sector and non-governmental initiatives in support of their work on the NCS.
- SDPI has encouraged stakeholders to take an enquiring approach to sustainable development, and it has trained policy researchers in interdisciplinary methods.
- SDPI is also facilitating the flow of international institutional knowledge and research on sustainable development into Pakistan in addition to contributing research in the programme areas recommended by the NCS.

However, it also revealed failings – mainly in the absence of a baseline, consistent monitoring, recording and evaluation (MRE) of NCS performance. Consequently:

> *The NCS cannot learn and adjust, a considerable weakness in today's climate of rapid change… Good MRE likely would have changed the prevailing perception of the NCS being a static reference 'document' to appreciation of its potential as a dynamic process to improve future economic, ecological and social well-being* (Hanson et al, 2000).

The review stressed the need to invest more in research in the planned process of transforming the NCS into a full sustainable development strategy. It suggested:

- a network of research institutions, centred on SDPI;
- a regular 'state of environment' report coupled with a national conference;
- regular 'state of environmental stakeholders' surveys of awareness, commitment and judgements of priority issues;
- an independent 'watchdog' (or report), perhaps involving SDPI;
- a 'balance sheet' of environmental assets related to the costs of inaction; and
- regular macroeconomic scrutiny and strategic environmental assessment.

Research should now form a real driver of the strategy, the challenge being to strike a balance between 'pushing advice' on important upcoming issues that are not fully appreciated yet by stakeholders, and reacting to the 'demand pull' of routine policy processes when they call for advice (Hanson et al, 2000).

Sustainable development is knowledge-intensive, covering a vast terrain

The case studies have indicated how sustainable development requires a continually updated understanding of many issues. Much knowledge already exists, but needs to be identified, applied and kept under review. Underlying assumptions or 'myths' need to be tackled. Gaps in knowledge need to be identified. Processes of innovation need to be generated when new problems emerge. Particular research programmes need to be put in place to organize the exploration of this vast terrain. Box 9.1 outlines what such research needs to cover.

Key issues to be addressed

Breadth and complexity of issues

Some challenges arise from the broad extent and multiple dimensions of the many themes on which knowledge is required: their inherent complexity, their frequently wide geographical extent, their multiple interactions, and the speed, scope and uncertainty of change. There is potentially so much that could be

Box 9.1 Scope of research needed for sustainable development

Understanding poverty in its various dimensions: poor people's access to financial, physical, natural, social and human assets; their conditions of vulnerability, resilience and opportunity; their associated rights and powers; and well-being relative to others. Both aggregate and stratified information is needed. Of particular importance is understanding the nature of chronic poverty, that is, identifying those people or groups who seem 'immune' to development efforts from one generation to the next.

Understanding environmental conditions: the extent of particular ecosystems, and their productive capability (yields or waste assimilation capacity), diversity and current use; and both the potential hazards they face and the actual degradation being caused. It is especially important to identify the status of ecosystems of importance to human well-being and to the main economic sectors (eg farm systems, or air and water quality), and to identify those under most threat.

Understanding multiple links between poverty and environmental conditions: There are few simple, linear and one-way relationships. While at one time it was felt that poor people destroyed the environment, it is now generally realized that people are poor because they do not have effective access to environmental benefits and to means to sustain them. Simple development myths are bandied about in the absence of dynamic and locally specific information. Isolating the major causes is nearly always a matter of long-term research, independent from any vested interests, coupled with transparent debate processes and a high-level mandate to get to the (sometimes ugly) truth.

Understanding change and possible future scenarios: Uncertainties abound, but one thing is certain: sustainable development will *not* be described by the end-point illustrations offered by the average sustainable development strategy. Change is constant in economic, social and environmental systems, and disequilibrium is often on the increase, especially in small and vulnerable communities and countries. Sustainable development requires the ability to assess vulnerabilities and sources of resilience in relation to uncertain changes. Scenario planning provides rigour to test resilience (it is not a forecasting exercise). Yet sustainable development research too often bases its conclusions on existing conditions or (at best) an extrapolation of current trends.

Understanding stakeholder powers, capacities, needs and motivations: An assessment of the particular powers (or lack of them) of stakeholders is crucial both to an understanding of each sustainable development issue (who are the dominant and the marginalized) and to the structuring of strategy processes (who needs to be involved to remedy problems and realize opportunities).

Understanding policy- and decision-making processes: including the institutional, legislative and administrative drivers and dynamics of development. In sustainable development strategies, for example, stakeholders establish an intention to undergo a participatory process to renegotiate goals and their own roles in achieving them. Research is needed to identify which are the most promising existing mechanisms for this. Subsequently, the strategy process itself, and all of its components, need to be well understood for the strategy to keep on track.

Understanding practice – the impacts of 'solutions': There is a vast range of field-based innovation at the interface between economic, environmental and social systems. Much more effort is needed to assess such innovations, their impact and the conditions that make them a success. This helps to avoid the cult of the 'local success story', the 'miracle cure', or the 'demon to be exorcised'. It is too easy to say 'this local project is good, so we'll have a hundred more of them' without understanding the particular context and enabling policy and institutional conditions. Policy should be improved by knowing what works on the ground, why, where and when.

Understanding and testing theories of the development process: Development agencies tend to favour fashions and miracle solutions, which are replete with assumptions. 'Sustainable development' itself can be viewed as a hypothesis, requiring research to establish the right integration and trade-offs, to assess impacts, to review whether the process has worked, to make adjustments as necessary, and to revisit assumptions, fashions and theories.

investigated. This calls for interdisciplinary (and not just multidisciplinary) ways of working, for prioritization, for sampling, for multi-stakeholder partnerships (to surface different kinds of knowledge and apply comparative advantage) and for international collaboration (both to tackle global problems and to get to grips with common local problems).

Key strategy drivers exhibit an urge to simplify and to spend money quickly – and 'forget' research

There is frequently a call to 'get on with it, and not to waste time on further research', especially in the international 'development business'. Research is frequently supported only so far as it supports the prevailing paradigm or improves its efficiency; research on local conditions for success and failure is a rapid affair at best.

Baseline/change information is not collected

As touched on above, there are practical supply-side problems for research. These include information availability, reliability and currency. The right kind of information (especially time series) tends to be unavailable, because it has not been a policy priority or has been difficult to obtain.

Methodologies

There are problems of both methodology availability for complex issues and process monitoring, and adequate understanding, experience and skills in them. Many of the methodologies promoted for researching sustainable development issues (eg OECD/UNDP, 2002) are themselves at the forefront of research and are not yet routinely applied.

Participatory research: transaction costs

Participatory approaches, combining stakeholders' knowledge and reflection with organized research programmes, should be the core of strategy research. But they are expensive to put in place (even though systems are often available, they are unused by many strategies).

Researchers are uncoordinated

Research capacities and resources available for sustainable development research are often limited or fragmented in many countries. There are also challenges relating to its organization and its financial, professional and policy independence. The poverty research community and the environment research community tend to be very separate, with different political- and paymasters, and there are few incentives and methodologies to enable working together.

Low policy demand for 'research'

Any lack of poverty, environmental or sustainable development information, or biases in it, tends to reflect skewed policy priorities. Low demand tends to be for three reasons:

- The status quo is favoured and change is feared (common with local elites, who may prefer myths to be perpetrated than truths revealed).
- Change is favoured and local reality is ignored (common with external parties such as the development bank economists and others driving the strategy process, who prefer their prevailing paradigms to prevail over local knowledge and innovation).
- All stakeholders agree on 'higher' priorities. In the case of strategies, participation is agreed as a priority but is often undertaken in a way which squeezes out the room for genuine enquiry (as a token or a fashion).

A 'continuous improvement' approach can link sustainable development strategies with research and action

It is becoming clear that there are both mutual needs and potentials for improved research–policy–practice links. *Strategy processes* that effectively link all the centres of debate and decision-making – government, business and civil society – on a continuing basis, will lead to demand for relevant sustainable development research. *Research programmes* that bring together many sources of knowledge in effective interdisciplinary methodologies on a continuing basis will lead to better strategies.

A practical approach for doing this is the 'continuous improvement' framework. This integrates research and policy actors in a step-by-step, learning and adaptation process of change driven by multi-stakeholder groups; see Figure 9.1. There is emerging political agreement that this is the right approach to strategies, through both the NSDS policy guidelines developed by the OECD and eight developing countries (OECD DAC, 2001) and guidelines developed by the UN (UN DESA, 2002b). These apply to all forms of strategy aiming at sustainable development, including poverty and environmental strategies.

Key differences between the older 'master plan' strategies and the new 'continuous improvement system' thinking, derived from OECD and UN reviews, are summarized in Table 9.1.

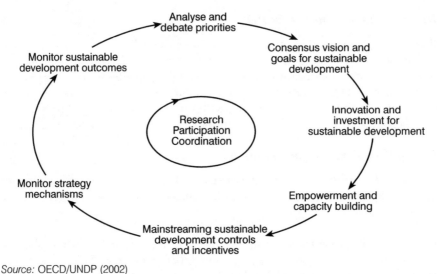

Source: OECD/UNDP (2002)

Figure 9.1 *A 'continuous improvement' approach to sustainable development strategies*

Some principles for strategy research, based on 'what works'

The continuous improvement approach to strategies offers greater scope for research and vice versa. But it has implications for how research is done. Drawing principally on OECD/UNDP (2002), a number of research principles for sustainable development strategies can be proposed:

1   **A coherent, continuing programme:** Sustainable development research should be a central component of the strategy, reflected in the strategy's formal mandate.
2   **Ownership:** Multi-stakeholder groups should design the information-gathering, analysis and research process themselves, to ensure ownership of the strategy and its results.
3   **High-level support:** The research programme should be commissioned, agreed and endorsed at the highest level, involving recognized policy and research authorities, thus increasing the chance that the research will be used.
4   **Good research coordination:** Many players should be involved, sharing the knowledge they gain. If one research institution coordinates the work, there should be considerable space for others to contribute from the poverty and environmental research communities and sources of local knowledge.
5   **Stakeholders doing their own analysis:** Groups affected by key issues should be enabled and encouraged to engage in research and analysis themselves. Special efforts should be made to identify 'who counts most' and involve them, with a focus on groups who are often marginalized from policy- and decision-making but who may hold critical (and often ignored) knowledge.

Table 9.1 *Changing approaches to strategies*

From	To
Develops and implements a single 'master plan' for sustainable development (that gets increasingly out of date)	Builds a system of coordinated mechanisms and processes dealing with sustainable development priorities step by step
Fixed ideas and solutions	An adaptive, learning system offering coherence between activities
One-off initiative	A continuous process
Management based on precedent or evidence only	Also experimentation and managing uncertainty
State alone is responsible	Society as a whole is responsible
Narrow participation	Multi-stakeholder approach
Focus on outputs (projects, laws, etc)	Focus on outcomes (impacts) and the quality of participation and management processes
Sector-based research and planning	Partnerships and integrated research and planning
Focus on costly 'projects' (and a consequent dependence on external assistance)	Focus on cost savings and domestically driven and financed investment and development

Sources: Adapted from OECD/UNDP (2002) and Dalal-Clayton and Bass (2002)

6   **Existing capacities:** Most of the research tasks should be implemented by bringing together and supporting existing local centres of information, technical expertise, learning and research.

7   **Criteria for prioritizing research:** Priorities should be addressed, to avoid the expansion of the number and types of issues addressed in the strategy beyond any ability to handle them. The issue may be a priority if it:
  * is an opportunity/threat to poor people's livelihoods and/or key economic sectors;
  * is an opportunity/threat to key ecosystem assets and processes;
  * reflects established public concerns and is visible to them;
  * has a major learning/extension/multiplier effect;
  * is an international obligation;
  * is timely in relation to a pending decision;
  * is 'researchable' – can be defined in terms of clear questions, with a good chance of coming to swift completion, successful conclusions and adoption of results.

8   **Accessible and participatory methods of research:** These should be selected to bring multiple dimensions together and, where relevant, to engage decision-makers in local 'learning by doing'. Those that are conducive to interdisciplinary ways of working include:
  * environmental and social impact assessment;
  * strategic environmental assessment;
  * multi-criteria analysis;
  * decision analysis;

- scenario development and foresighting;
- cost–benefit and cost-effectiveness analysis;
- risk assessment methodologies;
- participatory and action research approaches.
9 **Partnerships:** Partnerships between researchers should be established to enhance economies of scale; to pool research, participation and communications capacities; to undertake interdisciplinary approaches; to share intellectual resources; and to attain a higher policy profile. The utility of different models of research partnerships should be compared, especially those that were designed to link closely with policy.

The political move towards 'participation' can help

Moves towards strengthening research in strategies have been far less prevalent than the strengthening of participation. Today's strategy initiatives are invariably more multi-stakeholder, and more consultative, than even in the recent past. But the full utility of participation in each of the many tasks in a sustainable development strategy has not always been recognized. The OECD and UNDP studies have shown that *effective* participation is, in fact, closely bound up with knowledge utilization and generation; it brings together more people in uncovering knowledge and researching problems and solutions. This reality needs to be considered in future strategy initiatives. In other words, 'knowledge generation matters' as much as the current paradigm of 'participation matters', and they are connected.

Outside the confines of formal research commissioned by policy-makers, improvements in policy are frequently made through forms of participation that alter the language and perceptions of decision-makers, and that introduce issues and innovations that were not anticipated. This occurs not just through 'supply-driven' partnerships of researchers with common research interests but also through 'demand-driven' partnerships of researchers with other stakeholders. There is a considerable literature on the workings of policy communities, epistemic communities, advocacy coalitions, issue networks and so on, which describe these formal and informal partnerships (see Lindquist, 2001). Such understanding needs to be brought into the concept of sustainable development strategies, so that they can seek out such partnerships and give them the space and time to explore sustainable development and create innovations. This broader approach to sustainable development knowledge identification, utilization and learning could achieve greater efficacy and credibility than the short-term, externally driven strategy model of brief, commissioned analyses of pre-set issues:

> *Strategies have to be grounded in the politics, the policies, the programmes, the practices, the paradigms, the performance measures, and the pathologies that preoccupy both the populace and the policy-maker* (Banuri, 1999, quoted in Hanson et al, 2000).

Notes

1   The International Forum comprised 73 expert participants from 31 countries, developing and industrialized, and drawn from government, civil society, the private sector and international agencies.
2   Bolivia, Burkina Faso, Ghana, Namibia, Nepal, Pakistan, Tanzania and Thailand.
3   Similar findings were made by ODI (2001) and the country studies for UN DESA (2002b).

References

Bass, SMJ and Dalal-Clayton, DB (2001) *Strategies for Sustainable Development: Meeting the Challenge*, Opinion Paper for the World Summit on Sustainable Development, International Institute for Environment and Development, London

Bass, SMJ, Dalal-Clayton, DB and Pretty, J (1995) *Participation in Strategies for Sustainable Development*, Environmental Planning Issues No 7, International Institute for Environment and Development, London

Carew-Reid, J (ed) (1997) *Strategies for Sustainability: Asia*, IUCN in association with Earthscan Publications, London

Carew-Reid, J, Prescott-Allen, R, Bass, S and Dalal-Clayton, DB (1994) *Strategies for National Sustainable Development: A Handbook for their Planning and Implementation*, International Institute for Environment and Development (IIED), London, and World Conservation Union (IUCN), Gland, in association with Earthscan, London

Dalal-Clayton, DB (1996) *Getting to Grips with Green Plans: National Level Experience in Industrial Countries*, Earthscan, London

Dalal-Clayton, DB and Bass, S (2002) 'Recent Progress and New Thinking on Strategies for Sustainable Development', paper presented at the Annual Meeting of the International Association for Impact Assessment, 15–21 June 2002, The Hague, IIED, London

Dalal-Clayton, DB, Bass, S, Sadler, B, Thomson, K, Sandbrook, R, Robins, N and Hughes, R (1994) *National Sustainable Development Strategies: Experience and Dilemmas*, Environmental Planning Issues No 6, International Institute for Environment and Development, London

Hanson, A, Bass, S, Bouzaher, A and Samdani, GM (2000) *Pakistan's National Conservation Strategy: Renewing Commitment to Action. Report of the Mid-Term Review*, Ministry of Environment, Local Government and Rural Development, Islamabad, November 2000

IIED/UNDP/DFID (2002) 'National Strategies for Sustainable Development: New Thinking and Time for Action', Opinion Paper for the World Summit on Sustainable Development, International Institute for Environment and Development in cooperation with United Nations Development Programme and UK Department for International Development, IIED, London, available at www.iied.org/pdf/wssd-09-nssd.pdf

Lindquist, EA (2001) *Discerning Policy Influence: Framework for a Strategic Evaluation of IDRC-supported Research*, IDRC, Canada

Lopez Ornat, A (ed) (1997) *Strategies for Sustainability: Latin America*, IUCN in association with Earthscan, London

ODI (2001) *PRSP Institutionalization Study: Final Report*, submitted to the Strategic Partnership with Africa, 15 October 2001, Overseas Development Institute, London

OECD DAC (2001) *The DAC Guidelines: Strategies for Sustainable Development: Guidance for Development Cooperation*, Development Cooperation Committee, Organisation for Economic Co-operation and Development, Paris, available at www.SourceOECD.org

OECD/UNDP (2002) *Sustainable Development Strategies: A Resource Book*, Organisation for Economic Co-operation and Development, and United Nations Development Programme in association with Earthscan, London

Phillips, W (2002) 'All for Naught? An Analysis of Senegal's PRSP Process', in A Whaites (ed) *Masters of Their Own Development? PRSPs and the Prospects for the Poor*, World Vision International, Monrovia, California

Thin, N, Underwood, M and Gilling, J (2001) *Sub-Saharan Africa's Poverty Reduction Strategy Papers from a Social Policy and Livelihood Perspective: A report for DFID*, Oxford Policy Management Group, Oxford

United Nations (1997) *Programme of Action for the Further Implementation of Agenda 21*, 19th UN General Assembly Special Session, New York

United Nations (2002) 'Plan of Implementation of the World Summit on Sustainable Development', adopted on 4 September 2002, UN doc A/CONF.199/20, available at www.johannesburgsummit.org/html/documents/summit_docs/131302_wssd_report_reissued.pdf

UN DESA (2002a) *Report of an Expert Forum on National Strategies for Sustainable Development*, meeting held in Accra, Ghana, on 7–9 November 2001, Department of Economic and Social Affairs, United Nations, New York, available at www.johannesburgsummit.org

UN DESA (2002b) *Guidance in Preparing a National Sustainable Development Strategy: Managing Sustainable Development in the New Millennium*, background paper no 13 (DESA/DSD/PC2/BP13), submitted by the Division for Sustainable Development, Department of Economic and Social Affairs, United Nations, to the Commission on Sustainable Development acting as the preparatory committee for the World Summit on Sustainable Development Second preparatory session, 28 January – 8 February 2002, New York, available at www.johannesburgsummit.org

UNGA (2001) *Report of the Secretary-General: Road Map towards the Implementation of the United Nations Millennium Declaration*, A/56/326, 6 September 2001, United Nations General Assembly, New York

Whaites, A (ed) (2002) *Masters of Their Own Development? PRSPs and the Prospects for the Poor*, World Vision International, Monrovia, California

Wood, A (ed.) (1997) *Strategies for Sustainability: Africa*, IUCN in association with Earthscan, London

Zehra, M (2002) 'The PRSP Experience in Pakistan: Concerns for Sustainable Development', paper presented at workshop organized by BMZ, Germany, *Beyond the Review: Sustainable Poverty Alleviation and PRSP: Challenges for Developing Countries and Development Cooperation*, 13–16 May 2002, Berlin, available online at www.qtz.de/poverty-conference/dokumente/results/sustainability/maheen%20 zehra%20-%20pakistan.doc, accessed 2 September 2003

Chapter 10

Striving for Good Governance in Urban Areas: The Role of Local Agenda 21s in Africa, Asia and Latin America

*Gordon McGranahan, IIED, Liliana Miranda, Ecocuidad,
David Satterthwaite, IIED and Luz Stella Velasquez, IDEA-UN*

One of the most significant innovations in addressing urban environmental problems in recent years has been the emergence of a new kind of city-wide initiative to address environmental problems: Local Agenda 21. Although more common in Europe and North America, there are growing numbers of cities with Local Agenda 21s in Africa, Asia and Latin America. This chapter draws on case studies of Local Agenda 21s and Local Agenda 21-like activities in Manizales (Colombia), Ilo and Chimbote (Peru), Nakuru (Kenya), Durban (South Africa), Jinja (Uganda), Windhoek (Namibia), Rufisque (Senegal) and Durban (South Africa).[1]

Local Agenda 21s came out of the 1992 UN Conference on Environment and Development (also known as the Earth Summit) held in Rio de Janeiro. They were seen as the means by which local action plans could be developed within each city and town to implement the many recommendations that were within Agenda 21, the 'action plan' that government representatives endorsed at the conference. Their importance was reinforced at the World Summit on Sustainable Development in Johannesburg in 2002. In his opening address, the secretary-general of the summit, Nitin Desai, highlighted Local Agenda 21s when referring to the concrete successes of the intervening decade: 'We know that there have been some successes – that there is heightened awareness, and that there have been many concrete achievements, particularly in communities which have established Local Agenda 21s' (Desai, 2002).

The Local Agenda 21s implemented since 1992 have particular importance for three reasons:

- They represent concrete experiences that have sought to address the many environmental problems associated with urban development – and many have considerable achievements.
- Most are locally developed and driven, not developed or imposed from outside, and they generally rely more on locally generated resources than external resources. Some of the most successful Local Agenda 21s (for instance those in Ilo in Peru and Manizales in Colombia, with which two of the authors have been involved) relied almost entirely on locally generated resources.
- They support (and reinforce) 'good local governance' for environment and development. In Latin America in particular, the more successful Local Agenda 21s have been associated with politicians and civil servants with strong commitments to democratic practices, greater accountability to citizens and partnerships with community organizations and non-governmental organizations (NGOs).

Their Strengths: Combining Good Governance with Action

At their best, Local Agenda 21s provide a means by which environmental issues become more integrated within the planning and management of an urban area. They usually involve the development of a particular document – the Local Agenda 21 – but the significance of the document should be that it was developed through a broad, inclusive consultation process that draws in all key interests ('stakeholders') and that provides an efficient and equitable means of reconciling conflicting or competing interests. The consultation process, with its potential to secure more cooperation between the different government agencies (including local offices of national or provincial agencies), NGOs and community organizations is as important as any documents produced.

A critical outcome of the consultation process should be agreements on priorities and on actions and partnerships to implement them. For instance, in Manizales, it led to the development of a local environmental action plan (Bioplan-Manizales) which became integrated within the municipal development plan and municipal budget. It included measures to improve waste management (including recycling), to combine reducing the risk of landslides (the city is in a mountainous region) with the development of eco-parks throughout the city and to improve public transport. Each district (comuna) within the city developed its own local agenda and included measures to address particular local problems; for instance in the poorest district, Olivares, this included micro-credits for local environmental enterprises and measures to increase local employment while protecting the district's architectural heritage. The city has also been developing an innovative indicators programme – the environmental traffic lights – and a decentralized system of observatories to monitor progress. In Ilo, Peru, the quality of the environment has been transformed through some 300 projects financed and implemented through partnerships between the municipal government and community-level management committees. Despite the fact that the city's population expanded more than sixfold since 1961, there have been major improvements in the quality of the urban environment including housing, provision for water and sanitation, green areas, sewage treatment and land management (see Box 10.1 for more details).

Local Agenda 21s can also integrate what is often termed the 'brown' environmental health agenda with broader 'green' ecological concerns (McGranahan and Satterthwaite, 2000). This integration has generally proved difficult within conventional, local government-directed environmental plans. Local Agenda 21s have particular importance for combating global warming, since measures to reduce greenhouse gas emissions are only likely to be acceptable to local populations in low-income nations if developed through consultative processes and integrated with measures to address local environmental concerns. This includes concerns for the most basic environmental health necessities such as safe, sufficient water, adequate provision for sanitation and drainage, and regular services to collect and safely manage household wastes. At least 600 million urban dwellers in Africa, Asia and Latin America live in homes and neighbourhoods with such inadequate provision for these that their lives are continually at risk. This includes hundreds of millions who have no access to safe water and tens of millions who have no provision for sanitation at all – and so must resort to defecation in the open or into plastic bags (Hardoy et al, 2001).

Their Weaknesses

Perhaps the main worry for Local Agenda 21s is the relatively few instances of success. Virtually all national governments formally endorsed Agenda 21 and so committed themselves to supporting the development of Local Agenda 21s in each settlement. This means that by 1996, most local authorities in each country should have undertaken a consultative process with their populations and achieved consensus on a Local Agenda 21. Thus, there should be tens of thousands of Local Agenda 21s that were put in place six years ago and that are now being implemented. But there is little evidence of Local Agenda 21s being developed in most low-income nations.

Another worry is that most examples of good practice in Local Agenda 21s come from cities where there have been major improvements in the quality and accountability of local governments. Local Agenda 21s were the means by which improvements were achieved but it was the change in local government that was the critical reason for their success. Certainly in Ilo and Manizales, national decentralization programmes and support for elected local authorities (and mayors) underpinned their success. In addition, in both cities, the innovations pre-date 1992. Local Agenda 21s can assist local political reform but they cannot replace it. Local Agenda 21s can ensure better use of limited resources – as in Ilo – but they do not, of themselves, increase investment capacity. Most urban governments in low- and middle-income nations remain weak and ineffective; many have little accountability to their citizens. This means little scope for Local Agenda 21s to become the vehicle for real consultative processes (as outlined in

Agenda 21). Or even if they do, the Local Agenda 21s may founder on the very limited investment capacity of local governments.

A third worry is that by being 'local', they may not deal with the transfer of environmental burdens across each locality's boundaries. Cities can develop very high quality environments by transferring their environmental costs to other people and other ecosystems. For instance, many wealthy cities import from distant places all the goods whose fabrication involved high inputs of energy and water and high levels of pollution and hazardous wastes. The environmental costs of their consumption are concentrated elsewhere. The mobility and comfort of their citizens is underpinned by high levels of private automobile use and energy use, which may cause few local environmental problems but means high levels of greenhouse gases and thus contribution to global warming with its many environmental costs. This is a greater worry for Local Agenda 21s in high-income nations, since these generally have a much larger transfer of environmental burdens. Local Agenda 21s need regional and national frameworks to support the action needed to address regional and global environmental goals.

The Origin of Local Agenda 21s

As noted above, the term Local Agenda 21 comes from Agenda 21, the document formally endorsed by all government representatives attending the UN Conference on Environment and Development (the Earth Summit) in 1992. Agenda 21 was the most substantive document to come out of this conference and it was meant to form the action plan for governments to integrate environment and development. Local Agenda 21s were to be the means by which each locality (including each city and town) developed its own sustainable development plan. The text of Agenda 21 recognizes that such local action plans are central to its achievement:

> *Because so many of the problems and solutions being addressed by Agenda 21 have their roots in local activities, the participation and cooperation of local authorities will be a determining factor in fulfilling its objectives. Local authorities construct, operate and maintain economic, social and environmental infrastructure, oversee planning processes, establish local environmental policies and regulations and assist in implementing national and sub-national environmental policies. As the level of governance closest to the people, they play a vital role in educating, mobilizing and responding to the public to promote sustainable development* (para 28.1).

Although this might overstate the actual role of most local authorities, the recognition of the role they should have in both development and environmental management is important. Agenda 21 also lists two objectives for local authorities: that they should undertake 'a consultative process with their populations and achieve a consensus on a Local Agenda 21 for their community'; and that they should be encouraged to implement and monitor programmes which aim to ensure that women and youth are represented in decision-making, planning and implementation processes. It is worth noting that these objectives are not so much on what Local Agenda 21s should include but on how they should be organized, especially the local consultation processes to ensure that all groups are involved (Lafferty and Eckerberg, 1998).

The fact that virtually all governments committed themselves to implementing Local Agenda 21s in 1992 does not, in itself, mean much. In all the global UN conferences held since the 1972 UN Conference on the Human Environment, government representatives have formally endorsed a great range of recommendations, most of which have been ignored or hardly implemented. It is worth recalling that most of the world's governments committed themselves in the mid-1970s to ensuring that all their populations would have access to safe water and adequate provision for sanitation by 1990. The 1980s was even designated by the United Nations as the 'International Drinking Water Supply and Sanitation Decade'. Yet hundreds of millions of rural and urban dwellers still lack access to safe water and adequate provision for sanitation, 11 years after the target date. But in the case of Local Agenda 21s, there is evidence of considerable innovation in urban areas in different continents. There are also new initiatives to encourage city governments to share their experiences (including more conferences, journals and newsletters) and a new interest in urban development by many international agencies.

Experience to Date

Local Agenda 21s have varied enormously from place to place. This is not surprising, since the relevant chapter of Agenda 21 did not – and indeed could not be expected to – specify in detail how the consultation process should be developed and implemented. Even within an individual city, there can be a multiplicity of Local Agenda 21 initiatives, displaying different organizational forms, interpretations of sustainable development and modes of action. This diversity is increasingly seen as a potential source of strength, though it does make it difficult to generalize about what has been achieved.

Three additional examples, illustrating the variety of ways in which Local Agenda 21s can take shape, are given below:

Building on local partnerships in Rufisque, Senegal

Decentralization in Senegal has devolved to local authorities many of the responsibilities taken up in Local Agenda 21s. Local stakeholders, including local authorities, NGOs, community-based organizations and private enterprises, had already been engaged in a range of collaborative efforts to improve local conditions that conform to the recommendations of Agenda 21. With the assistance of an international NGO centred in Dakar, Environnement et Développement du Tiers Monde (ENDA-TM), these efforts helped to provide the basis for an attempt to develop a more formal Local Agenda 21.

Round tables for a sustainable Penang, Malaysia

As one of its first steps towards a Local Agenda 21, the Sustainable Penang Initiative organized a series of round tables, centred on different aspects of sustainable development. These round tables brought together a range of stakeholders, provided the basis for the 'Penang People's Report' (centred on a series of sustainable development indicators), led to a variety of local initiatives, and fed into the more formal Penang Strategic Development Plan 2000–2010. The initiative was led by the recently established Socio-Economic and Environmental Research Institute (SERI), a state think tank for sustainable development.

Sustainable development planning in Durban, South Africa

Durban's Local Agenda 21 programme was initiated in 1994, and local government structures have been the driving force for the programme since its inception. Durban's administrative structure and boundaries have changed radically since 1994, but the international origins of the Local Agenda 21 concept helped to provide a politically neutral platform for pursuing sustainable development at the local level. The Local Agenda 21 has set up a range of stakeholder groups. For their State of the Environment and Development Report, for example, there were three key stakeholder groups: an interim steering committee, a larger advisory committee and a local government-centred inter-service unit network. The Local Agenda 21 programme has also engaged in a series of consultation exercises linked to particular projects and initiatives. Two examples of the potential of Local Agenda 21s are given in Box 10.1.

As yet, it is too soon to judge the significance of the Local Agenda 21 movement. Thousands of urban centres may report that they have developed a Local Agenda 21 but many are neither participatory nor effective. Some are no more than a document setting out the goals or plans of some government agency which was developed with little consultation with citizens and for which there is little interest or capacity to implement. Some may simply be conventional development plans renamed. Others may be the result of one or two workshops, which also result in little action. Others may include admirable consultative processes and well-developed goals, yet founder on the very limited capacity of the city authorities to work in partnership with other groups and to plan, invest and coordinate the investments and activities of other agencies (including those of higher levels of government). And all city authorities, regardless of how effective they are, will have difficulties incorporating those aspects of sustainable development that respond to the needs of future generations or to limiting the environmental costs that are passed on to 'distant elsewheres' (to use William Rees' term, in his discussion of cities' 'ecological footprints') (Rees, 1992).

Drawing from the as yet limited documentation of experiences to date, the following points seem relevant:

- **The more successful Local Agenda 21s were possible because of some coincidence of key local and national changes** (see for example López Follegatti, 1998) especially decentralization, which gave more scope for local action, even if it often did not transfer public resources, and strengthened local democracy. This was important for both of the examples given in Box 10.1. It is no coincidence that most innovative Local Agenda 21s are in cities with strong local democracies. Much of the innovation in Local Agenda 21s has been the result of local rather than national or international initiatives.

- **Many Local Agenda 21s have been spurred by citizen action to address particular environmental hazards** as in Ilo, where all citizens wanted action on the very high levels of air pollution and the other environmental costs generated by the Southern Peru Copper Corporation. A Local Agenda 21 was developed in Chimbote, Peru, to counter a threat to a park/tree nursery and the industrial pollution from a steel mill and local fish-meal processing industries (Foronda, 1998). These environmental problems helped to mobilize citizen action, which then evolved into a coalition that now seeks to address a wider range of environmental problems. Indeed, effective Local Agenda 21s depend on an active and committed civil society that is prepared to engage in local issues and seek ways to work with local authorities (Miranda, 2001).

- **Local Agenda 21s can be much strengthened if local governments and businesses see them as part of a strategy to attract and hold new investment.** For instance, the richness and diversity of the ecology in and around Manizales and the area's great natural beauty are obvious assets on which the city can build its tourism base. Even for cities that are seeking to attract industry, a reputation for good environmental management need not be a disadvantage and can be turned into a strong advantage, as the good environment makes it attractive for employees and as an efficient government ensures that infrastructure and services are available for enterprises.

- Many innovative experiences benefited from long-term political support. So often, good long-term initiatives set in motion by one mayor are immediately reversed or changed by his or her successor. Ilo's success owes much to the fact that six successive mayors have supported and developed the innovations set in motion by its first elected mayor in the early 1980s.

- Local NGOs or universities often have important supporting roles. For instance, the local NGOs, Labor in Ilo and Natura in Chimbote, were instrumental to their successes. The National University in Manizales has had a central role in the formulation and development of Bioplan-Manizales and in supporting its implementation and monitoring.

In Peru, one reason for the innovation in Local Agenda 21s in many cities has been the support they received from Ecociudad (Miranda and Hordijk, 1998). This small, Peruvian NGO has taken on the role of encouraging and supporting local authorities to develop Local Agenda 21s. This is assumed to be a task for national governments, but in this instance there was little interest from national

---

BOX 10.1 EXAMPLES OF LOCAL AGENDA 21S

Manizales (Colombia): A local environmental action plan (Bioplan-Manizales) was developed with widespread consultation and this has become integrated into the municipal development plan and the municipal budget. It includes measures to protect and revitalize the city's rich architectural heritage, improve public transport (partly funded by a tax on petrol), reduce the risk of landslides (the city is in a mountainous region) and relocate the population living on steep slopes at high risk of landslides. The relocation programme was linked to the development of eco-parks throughout the city, some on land that had slopes that were too dangerous for permanent settlements and others with important ecological functions; for instance one integrated into the city's watershed and another focused on protecting biodiversity. Many of these eco-parks were managed by community associations. Community-based environmental initiatives helped to generate jobs; for instance managing eco-parks, running tree nurseries and increasing recycling. More localized environmental action plans have also been developed; for instance the action plan for Olivares commune (one of 11 communes in Manizales and also the one with the lowest average income) identified the commune's main environmental problems and also the area's environmental resources on which the agenda built. The city also developed an innovative indicators programme, the 'environmental traffic lights', through which progress in each of its 11 communes are tracked with regard to social conditions, community involvement, natural resource use, energy efficiency and waste management. Data on current conditions and trends in each commune are displayed in public places. They are called environmental traffic lights because, for each indicator, public boards show whether conditions are improving (green), getting worse (red) or stable (amber). The monitoring of progress is helped by environmental observatories in different parts of the city (Velasquez, 1998).

Ilo (Peru): In this port city in southern Peru, the environment has been transformed over an 18-year period with major improvements in the quality of housing, and liquid and solid waste management, and in provision for water, sanitation, garbage collection, electricity, paved streets and green areas. Some 300 projects have been financed and implemented through partnerships between municipal government and community-level management committees. The local authorities have a land development programme which ensures land for housing is available to low-income households, and so Ilo avoided the problem of rapidly expanding illegal settlements, even though the city's population has expanded more than sixfold since 1961. A large coastal area within the city has been reclaimed for public use (the municipal authorities helped to move the industries, settlements and institutions that were located there) and this now includes a pier, tree-lined walkways, play spaces and an amphitheatre. There has been a long fight with a copper factory that was set up in Ilo some 40 years ago which generates high levels of solid waste and air pollution. Citizen pressure forced the company to stop polluting the local bay and dumping wastes on local beaches although reducing the very high output of sulphur dioxide has been more difficult. Development plans for the city occur within a coherent environmental plan, which is developed through consultation with different groups and is supported by a commission with representatives drawn from many agencies and sectors (López Follegatti, 1998).

---

government in playing this role. This NGO has encouraged many local authorities to develop local agendas and has organized workshops and exchanges to allow such authorities to share their experiences. It has advised many local authorities on how to develop Local Agenda 21s and developed manuals and other documents to help guide them. It has also developed new courses with universities. In effect, it is supplying the services governments should provide but rarely do. It is perhaps symptomatic of new alliances and partnerships that it was a small local NGO that developed strong working relationships with the official, elected authorities in many of Peru's cities.

As more Local Agenda 21s become documented, it will become easier to understand the kinds of policy and institution that make them more effective. One significant tendency is that a large share of innovative Local Agenda 21s are outside large cities and national capitals. For Ilo, its physical distance from Lima, the national capital, and its relatively small size may have been an important protective factor. For large cities, it is more difficult to get an effective city-wide Local Agenda 21 if the city is made up of many municipalities (and usually with different political parties in power in the different municipalities) and vested interests that benefit from lax environmental management are more powerful. Capital cities are particularly problematic as national and local government agencies have different priorities and are, so often, in conflict.

The Shared Goals that Local Agenda 21s can Work Towards

In addition to the overarching goal of contributing to sustainable development, Local Agenda 21s have a number of shared goals that relate to their consultative process:

- **Institutionalizing consultation, participation and accountability.** Local Agenda 21s should be organized in such a way as to develop a broad consensus on the key problems and how these should be addressed. As such, they help to broker agreement between diverse groups in which all citizens have a real say in how resources are used. Environmental planning moves into the public arena as it shifts from being something determined or driven by professionals to something discussed and influenced by public consultation (Haughton, 2000).
- **Integrating concerns for environment and for development.** Local Agenda 21s should allow citizens' concerns for environmental quality to become more influential in government, both in the use of public resources and in government regulation and control of private sector development. Where significant sections of a city's population suffer serious environmental health problems – for instance from industrial pollution or lack of provision for water, sanitation, drainage and garbage collection – by being inclusive, the Local Agenda 21 should help to ensure that these problems receive a higher priority. They should also guard against too elitist or middle-class concerns for the environment.
- **Ensuring that plans are driven by local concerns based on knowledge of local resources and ecosystems** – although they should take into

account regional concerns (for instance a locality's production of waste may damage resources in a neighbouring locality) and national and global issues, particularly regarding resource use and waste generation.

- **Ensuring coordination and cooperation between different government agencies** – as they involve the different public bodies or agencies active within any locality (including those responsible for infrastructure and service provision, land use planning and management and environmental regulation).

- Tapping what one former US president referred to as that **'vision thing'** – for instance pride in a locality's natural resources and cultural heritage, and in the quality of its governance (including its Local Agenda 21) and a commitment to protecting resources for the future. This has been particularly significant in Ilo since the Local Agenda 21 of this small, relatively poor, isolated small city has attracted international recognition which in turn has helped to encourage and support it. It has also helped the city authorities and its citizens in their attempt to get the local copper foundry to reduce its very high sulphur dioxide emissions.

The Diverse Environmental Challenges that Local Agenda 21s Need to Address

Despite their unifying goal of pursuing sustainable development, Local Agenda 21s inevitably face very different environmental challenges in different localities. To some degree, this reflects each locality's specific geography and history. There are some systematic environmental differences related to affluence. These differences are summarized in a very simplified form in Figure 10.1.

Country-wide studies indicate that household sanitary conditions tend to improve with wealth, that concentrations of various outdoor air pollutants increase and then fall, and that contributions to carbon emissions increase. More generally, the most critical environmental burdens associated with urban affluence tend to be more dispersed and delayed with indirect effects on human welfare, while the most critical environmental burdens associated with urban poverty tend to be more localized and immediate with direct consequences for human health. These tendencies are by no means strong enough to justify prejudging the priorities for a city on the basis of its economic status, but they do illustrate the importance of not letting the priorities of affluent cities dominate local agendas in less affluent settings.

In pursuing sustainable development, Local Agenda 21s should ideally combine a concern for the local as well as global burdens, for present as well as future needs, and for impacts on humans as well as those on natural systems. While this presents a challenge in every locality, it tends to take a different form in very low-income urban centres (where the present needs tend to be more pressing) and affluent urban centres (where the burdens on future generations tend to be heavier). Local Agenda 21s in low-income urban areas do tend to place less emphasis on ecological burdens and what are often described as

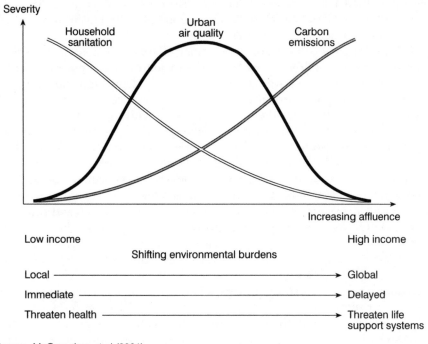

Source: McGranahan et al (2001)

Figure 10.1 *Affluence and the urban environment*

'green' issues, particularly when they are locally driven. This is sometimes taken to reflect an unwillingness on the part of local authorities in low-income countries to move beyond the 'brown' environmental health agenda. The more serious danger, however, is that international support for Local Agenda 21s may mistakenly over-emphasize the importance of the 'green' agenda in low-income settings.

The International Challenge of Supporting Local Agenda 21s

International support for Local Agenda 21s should help to meet other key goals espoused by international agencies such as strengthening and supporting local democracy and addressing the environmental problems that cause or contribute to poverty. Indeed, perhaps the best international support for Local Agenda 21s is long-term support for the development of more competent, effective, accountable city and municipal authorities.

The very name Local Agenda 21 implies international engagement. If the best way forward were simply to let local authorities get on with solving their own problems, there would be little point in even coining the term. Organizations such as the International Council for Local Environmental

Initiatives (ICLEI) have made a concerted effort both to draw attention to the importance of local authorities in the international arena and to create a network that can support new local initiatives.

There is also a growing recognition among international donors of the need for more support for urban areas (especially to address urban poverty) and for more support for 'good governance' at local level. Many international donors gave very little support to urban areas over the last two decades. In part, this was because of the difficulties they face in working with local governments (or because recipient governments at national level were reluctant to let them do so). In part, it is also because of inappropriate definitions of poverty which greatly understated the extent and depth of poverty in urban areas and drew attention away from those aspects of poverty that require 'good local governance' to address them. However, the last few years has seen increasing numbers of international donors developing urban programmes and strategies.

Most donors recognize the importance of supporting better urban governance. Most also recognize the need to support civil society, both in supporting the work that community-based organizations and local NGOs can do and in supporting a more productive engagement between civil society and local authorities. But there are large gaps between good intentions and success. Most donor support goes to national governments, not local governments. It is also politically difficult for any international donor to support long-term processes of strengthening more accountable, effective local government – which after all is taking power and resources away from the national government with whom this support has to be agreed. Finally, the pressure on donors to define their own strategies and demonstrate their own successes has led to a situation where local environmental strategies supported by donors often reflect the donor's own approach as much as they do the local authority's. This can undermine a Local Agenda 21 and shift its focus from the pursuit of locally articulated goals to the pursuit of internationally available funds.

If international support for Local Agenda 21s is to be successful, the following are important:

- Having a functional Local Agenda 21 is viewed favourably when making decisions about national and international financial assistance.
- The consultation processes of existing Local Agenda 21s should be employed to increase stakeholder participation in international funding decisions that are likely to affect the capacity of local authorities to pursue their agendas.
- The encouragement by international donors of participatory consultative processes within cities must be backed by support for addressing the priorities they identify. There is some tendency for international agencies to support local consultative processes without either having the funds and means to support the implementation of what these local processes identify, or making it clear from the outset that such funds will not be available.
- Suitable means should be found to finance initiatives emerging from Local Agenda 21s, and to evaluate them. Among the challenges here is the need for donors to encourage Local Agenda 21s to be accountable 'downwards'

to citizens and their community organizations, as well as 'upwards' to the donors.

One of the main attractions of Local Agenda 21s for international donors – that they are likely to result in reduced regional and global environmental burdens – also brings a risk. Attempts to convince local groups that it is in their self-interest to reduce their 'ecological footprint' can seem to be (and indeed can be) manipulative. Promoting a national or global agenda and overstating the local benefits can undermine the participatory character of Local Agenda 21s. There are potential synergies between improving local conditions and reducing larger-scale environmental burdens, and it is appropriate that national and international agencies should try to tap such opportunities. However, if Local Agenda 21s are to achieve an open and transparent character, it is important that regional, national and international (as well as local) interests are explicitly identified. It is also important to recognize that urban centres that have managed to address their own local environmental problems in an equitable and efficient manner are likely to be the best partners in international efforts to address global environmental challenges.

Notes

1   Certain sections of this chapter also draw on Satterthwaite and McGranahan (2000).

References

Desai, N (2002) *Opening Address to the World Summit on Sustainable Development, Johannesburg, 26 August 2002*, available at www.johannesburgsummit.org.

Foronda, FEM (1998) 'Chimbote's Local Agenda 21: Initiatives to Support its Development and Implementation', *Environment and Urbanization*, vol 10, no 2, October, pp129–147

Hardoy, JE, Mitlin, D and Satterthwaite, D (2001) *Environmental Problems in an Urbanizing World*, Earthscan, London

Haughton, G (2000) 'Information and Participation within Environmental Management', *Environment and Urbanization*, vol 11, no 2, October, pp51–62

Lafferty, WM and Eckerberg, K (eds) (1998) *From the Earth Summit to Local Agenda 21: Working Towards Sustainable Development*, Earthscan, London

López Follegatti, JL (1998) 'Ilo: A City in Transformation', *Environment and Urbanization*, vol 11, no 2, October

McGranahan, G and Satterthwaite, D (2000) 'Environmental Health or Ecological Sustainability? Reconciling the Brown and Green Agendas in Urban Development', in C Pugh (ed) *Sustainable Cities in Developing Countries*, Earthscan, London

McGranahan, G, Jacobi, P, Songsore, J, Surjadi, C and Kjellén, M (2001) *The Citizens at Risk: From Urban Sanitation to Sustainable Cities*, Earthscan, London

Miranda, L (2001) 'Civil Society and Urban Environmental Improvement; A Peruvian NGO's Perspective', paper presented to the Danida Workshop on Improving the Urban Environment and Reducing Poverty, 5 December 2000, Copenhagen, unpublished

Miranda, L and Hordijk, M (1998) 'Let us Build Cities for Life: The National Campaign of Local Agenda 21s in Peru', *Environment and Urbanization*, vol 10, no 2, October, pp69–102

Rees, WE (1992) 'Ecological Footprints and Appropriated Carrying Capacity', *Environment and Urbanization*, vol 4, no 2, October, pp121–130

Satterthwaite, D and McGranahan, G (2000) 'The Importance of Local Agenda 21s', *City Development Strategies*, no 3, pp6–10

Velasquez, LS (1998) 'Agenda 21; A Form of Joint Environmental Management in Manizales, Colombia', *Environment and Urbanization*, vol 10, no 2, pp9–36

Velasquez, LS (1999) 'The Local Environmental Action Plan for Olivares Bio-commune in Manizales', *Environment and Urbanization*, vol 11, no 2, pp41–50

Part 3

Equity and Sustainable Development – Towards New Ways of Working

Chapter 11

Environment and Human Rights: A New Approach to Sustainable Development

*Maria Adebowale, Capacity Global, Chris Church, ANPED,
Beatrice Nduta Kairie, ELCI, Boris Vasylkivsky and
Yelena Panina, Eco-Pravo Kyiv*

This chapter examines the background to current discussions on environmental and human rights. It suggests that the lack of success of many of the Rio initiatives makes it appropriate to consider new approaches, and that such approaches should be rooted in recognition of an inalienable right to a safe and healthy environment. It first considers the need for environmental human rights and looks at what such rights might be. It includes perspectives from different nations and regions, and highlights the UN Draft Principles from 1994. It also considers the issue of globalization and suggests that environmental human rights could play an important part in this debate. The chapter concludes by assessing prospects after the 2002 World Summit on Sustainable Development (WSSD).

The central conclusion is that this is a very appropriate time to be considering these issues and that there is a need for debate leading to a convention that will for the first time put these rights in a clear legal framework. It welcomes the moves by the UN Commission on Human Rights (UNCHR) and the UN Environment Programme (UNEP) to work together on these issues and stresses the need to build upon decisions reached at the 2002 Summit.

Introduction

The issue of 'environmental human rights' or the human right to a safe and healthy environment is not a new one. It has been suggested that the development of concern for human rights and for the environment have been two of the key processes which characterized the 20th century. Much more must be done before the rights set out in the UN Universal Declaration of Human Rights can be fully realized for all people, yet the principle that 'human rights should be protected by the rule of law' is still universally recognized. This protection of human rights by the rule of law remains one of the keystones for democratic expression, within a framework that guarantees legal action while fostering dialogue.

We would suggest that the principles of human rights, the right to life and the right to development, cannot be realized in the absence of the right to a healthy environment. Many international agreements since the 1972 Stockholm Conference have talked about such a right. Some 60 nations have constitutions or pieces of legislation intended to ensure this right, although there is little evidence of work to make this happen.

Over the last few years there has been increasing interest in these issues, including work by the Northern Alliance for Sustainability (ANPED) to build links with NGOs and other agencies in all parts of the world. Further work by organizations involved in projects such as the Access Initiative and ongoing activities of groups such as the Argentinian Centro de Derechos Humanos y Medio Ambiente (CEDHA) have also raised awareness.

This chapter seeks to provide an introduction to the issue. It firstly outlines the need for such rights and then provides some background.

A Brief Overview: Human Rights and the Environment

Work towards sustainable development is increasingly recognizing the importance of a human rights approach. This should not be surprising: the protection of human life in relation to health, culture and living standards is central to any social, environmental or economic programmes. The right to life cannot be realized without the basic right to clean water, air and land. A human rights approach allows the quality of life of people, in particular the most vulnerable, to be integrated into environmental decision-making.

There are two main approaches to human rights and the environment:

- the use of existing human rights; and
- the need for new human rights for a safe and clean environment.

The rights we have already are:

- civil and political; and
- economic, social and cultural.

Civil and political rights provide for moral and political order. Such rights include the right to life, equality, political participation and association. They are couched most clearly in the Universal Declaration of Human Rights (1948) and

International Covenant on Civil and Political Rights (1966). When realized, civil and political rights are fundamental to guaranteeing a political order supportive of sustainable development. They can protect civil mobilization around environmental protection and equity.

Economic, social and cultural rights are often referred to as 'second generation' rights. These provide substantive standards for an individual's well-being. The International Convenant on Economic, Social and Cultural Rights (1966) provides an example. The covenant provides, among other things, the right to health, which recognizes the need for environmental improvement. It also provides for self-determination including the right of all peoples to manage their own natural resources. These second generation rights often have a direct bearing on the human and environmental condition.

Although existing first and second generation rights can provide for a degree of global and environmental protection if effectively mobilized, they are indirect environmental rights. They therefore suffer from a lack of clarity and precision on environmental protection and equity. What is required to strengthen the use of universal human rights is direct policy, legislation and institutional changes which recognize a specific right to a healthy environment and which take into account both substantive and procedural issues.

The Need for Environmental Rights

It is over 30 years since the UN Conference on the Human Environment, in Stockholm in 1972, put environmental issues on the international agenda. Since then there has been much hard work to protect and improve the environment globally, nationally and locally. There has been much progress, but it is clear that in all parts of the world our environment is under threat and that many problems are becoming more serious. The UN Conference on Environment and Development (UNCED) in 1992 recognized these problems and sought to resolve them through Agenda 21 and the various UNCED conventions.

Work on implementing these conventions, which are based on the principle of 'common but differentiated responsibility', has gradually revealed that these 'less than perfect bargains' have:

- failed to place constraints on national strategies that may lead to unsustainable growth;
- failed to ensure the implementation of national framework laws and enforcement strategies such as national environmental action plans (NEAPs);
- failed to control perverse state resource use and damaged inter-generational equity; and
- increasingly revealed the inadequacies of funding by those agencies which fund strictly environmental work that does not consider socio-economic factors.

It is failures such as these that have led to calls for a new approach to sustainable development. A further driver for change has been the increased pressure resulting from globalization. It is clear that non-mandatory ('soft law') agreements are an inadequate basis for ensuring effective control of these processes.

The need for change has been acknowledged, but some will question whether the introduction of inalienable human rights to a safe environment is the way forward. It has been suggested that adequate rights already exist. This is simply not the case. There are a few key international rights, but substantive rights to a safe environment are still largely implied rather than explicit. In theory, existing human rights legislation should protect our environment, but this does not happen in practice.

Many groups have tried to use human rights legislation to protect the environment, such as the 'right to life' defined by Article 2 of the European Convention on Human Rights (ECHR), which states that 'everyone has a right to life protected by law'. Most attempts to do this have been unsuccessful, although some successful cases exist. We believe that this is an inadequate way to provide for our rights.

Defining Environmental Rights

We suggest that any discussion of environmental human rights must encompass three areas of work:

- the right to a clean and safe environment;
- the right to act to protect the environment;
- the right to information and to participate in decision-making.

Different organizations across the world are approaching these issues in their own ways, but there are some commonalities:

The right to a clean and safe environment

These are 'substantive' rights. They are the most basic rights, and the hardest to define. Many organizations would support the idea that 'clean water and food security' are 'basic human rights' (quotes from UNEP, 1999). The UN Draft Principles from 1994 (see Appendix 1) spell out what these might be in more detail.

The right to act to protect the environment

This right is inherent in the UN declaration and associated conventions, through the right to organize and to free assembly. This right is under threat in many nations. The 'Just Earth' campaign run by the Sierra Club and Amnesty International USA have highlighted many such examples.

The right to information, to access to justice and to participate in environmental decision-making

These rights enable citizens to play an active part in creating a healthy environment, and they are directly linked to the key points in several UN conventions and declarations. In Europe these rights are enshrined in the UN Economic Commission for Europe (UNECE) 'Aarhus Convention' (the European Convention on Access to Information, Public Participation and Access to Justice in Environmental Decision-Making; see below); other regions will need to consider how best to deliver these rights within local circumstances.

These rights do not exist in isolation: they cannot be seen as separate from other human rights or from other issues linked to poverty, economic and social exclusion. A human rights perspective to sustainable development moves from the 'traditional green' issues to a wider approach to protecting the most vulnerable in society. Most recently WSSD agreed that:

> *Peace, security, stability and respect for human rights and fundamental freedoms, including the right to development, as well as respect for cultural diversity, are essential for achieving sustainable development and ensuring that sustainable development benefits all* (United Nations, 2002, para 5).

This is a vague formulation, and it is not substantiated by more detailed assertions of rights elsewhere in the agreed text. Nevertheless, supplemented by more detailed interpretations these rights can provide a platform for environmental and sustainable improvements which are likely to benefit the most marginalized people, the poor, women and minorities. The human rights perspective facilitates policies that have a strong impact on poverty and exclusion for reasons of gender or race. The right to information, justice and participation within the sustainable development context includes rather than excludes people who have felt excluded from the traditional green movement agendas. Environmental human rights support a bottom-up approach. Active involvement and shared control, by the people and states most affected by a degraded environment, is fundamental at local, national and global levels.

The UN Draft Principles

In 1994 the 46th session of the Commission On Human Rights (Sub-Commission on Prevention of Discrimination and Protection of Minorities) received a report entitled 'Review of Further Developments in Fields with which the Sub-Commission has been Concerned on Human Rights and the Environment'. This was the final report prepared by Fatma Zohra Ksentini, the Special Rapporteur on this issue appointed in 1989.

Ksentini's work focused initially on the issue of toxic wastes and dumping of these wastes in poorer nations (an issue which was high on the international agenda in the late 1980s). Her work broadened during the research on this and became a major overview of environmental rights. The final report included a full analysis of environmental rights and legislation at a national level.

The report also suggested that: 'For many years environmental problems were almost exclusively considered from the standpoint of the pollution in one part of the world, ie the industrialized countries'.[1] The report identified the need for new approaches to these problems.

Most significantly the report concludes with a set of 'Draft Principles for a Declaration on Human Rights and Environment'. These provide the best overview of how substantive rights might be defined and are attached as Appendix 1. These principles were discussed in 1994 on the release of the report but were not taken forward. Since then developments in this field make it an appropriate time to revisit these issues and principles.

National and Regional Instruments

A European perspective: the Aarhus Convention

The 'Aarhus Convention' is the UNECE European Convention on Access to Information, Public Participation and Access to Justice in Environment Decision-Making. This convention was agreed at the Environment for Europe Ministerial Conference in 1998 and came into effect on 30 October 2001. It states that 'every person has the right to live in an environment adequate to his or her health and well-being'. But the right to know how bad the environment is, to take part in decision-making and to be able to go to court do not on their own guarantee this right to an 'adequate environment'.

There have been some proposals to turn the Aarhus Convention into a global agreement. This is an inappropriate way to develop work in this field and is unlikely to be acceptable to many nations. However, the underlying principles regarding access and participation are exactly those referred to in Principle 10 of the Rio Declaration. These remain crucial to the long-term development of environmental rights, and in the aftermath of WSSD, taking forward Principle 10 is emerging as a significant focus for a joint programme of work between UNEP and the office of the UN High Commissioner for Human Rights, recently endorsed at UNEP's 2003 Governing Council meeting.

A Southern perspective

Agenda 21 rightly points out that unsustainable consumption and production patterns in richer nations are the 'major cause of continued environmental degradation'. While this is primarily a Northern issue, there are issues for poorer nations. There is a need for an acknowledgement by some Southern governments that they are also responsible for the continued loss and depletion of natural capital, mainly by failing to implement convention obligations.

The prevailing situation in many of the poorest states involves:

• poor management of resources with inequality of access and ownership;

- promulgation of weak environmental laws which are subject to manipulation by the executive and a failure to implement the laws;
- inability to implement convention obligations and to integrate and manage them into public policies and programmes;
- lack of state accountability in use of natural capital and use of political power to frustrate environmental policies and programmes;
- lack of local control over resources; the removal of decision-making authority or ownership is still a problem;
- continued marginalization of pastoral and rural communities and urban migrants; and
- a failure to acknowledge the role of women as environmental managers and a lack of involvement of women in development and execution of programmes (although major steps have been taken in some countries, such as Uganda).

The domestic pressures of poverty and inequality still prevail. These factors indicate a general failure to respond to the Rio conventions (and particularly the Convention to Combat Desertification), whose underlying goal is to improve conditions in particular at the community level. There is an urgent need for a new approach. If such an approach is based on a human right to a healthy environment, then it will link into and support initiatives that address other inequity issues.

A UK perspective: the Human Rights Act 1998

Traditionally the UK rights to a healthy environment have been protected indirectly through rules and regulations regarding private property, environmental protection and human health. These rules and regulations are provided for through either common law or acts of parliament. There is no substantive right to a healthy environment and until recently there was no law which illustrated an understanding of environmental justice. For example, the Environmental Protection Act 1995, the cornerstone of UK environmental law, does not provide for or recognize a direct right to a healthy environment.

Two recent developments which could play an instrumental role in developing some of the principles of environmental rights are the Human Rights Act 1998 and the Aarhus Convention (see above).

The Human Rights Act 1998 brings into UK domestic law the 'rights and freedoms guaranteed under the European Convention on Human Rights'. So far as it is possible to do so, primary legislation and subordinate legislation must be read and given effect in a way which is compatible with the convention rights. This shows how a new convention could be brought into effect. Although the act does not provide for expressed environmental rights it can be used to protect environment and equity in a human rights context. It is possible to use all the provisions to challenge cases of environmental injustice, but the ECHR provisions which are considered the most advantageous, in the context of environmental justice, are: the right to life (Article 2), the right to a fair trial (Article 6), the right to respect for private and family life (Article 8), and the right to freedom of expression (Article 10).

Arguably, such existing human rights provide a multi-faceted definition of environmental rights and justice, but using human rights, civil or social, to protect environmental rights is difficult for two main reasons. First, the rights do not relate directly to the environment and are not precise enough. The Human Rights Act 1998, for example, does not provide for an express environmental right, and a right to 'a healthy and adequate environment' is currently highly subjective. Second, using human rights to provide assistance in environmental equity depends upon a judiciary familiar with environmental and human rights law as well as experience of the issues raised when dealing with environmental rights.

The use of the Human Rights Act for environmental justice cases is in its early stages. However, its potential to attack environmental inequity and act as a catalyst for an environmental justice movement is recognized among UK NGOs and government.

A US perspective: the Environmental Justice Movement and the Executive Order

In the US the human rights approach to sustainable development is best reflected by the strong Environmental Justice movement. The movement began as part of the civil rights movement by ethnic minority groups – black, indigenous and Hispanic community groups – across the USA, culminating in a direct environmental equity movement in the 1980s and 1990s. The main premise of this movement is to achieve equitable distribution of environmental risks across 'racial' and social lines. The movement has strong support and involvement from the most vulnerable in American society, in particular among 'people of colour'. This developed out of concerns, backed up by much research, that hazardous installations such as toxic waste dumps and polluting factories were mostly sited in areas where most of the population were poor and from ethnic minority groups. As a result, minority neighbourhoods were suffering disproportionately from the impact of industrial and hazardous waste facilities.

The movement calls for a fair treatment: this implies that no person or group of people should shoulder a disproportionate share of the negative environmental impacts resulting from the execution of domestic and foreign policy programmes.

In 1992, as a direct response to calls for laws on environmental equity, the US Environmental Protection Agency created an Office of Environmental Justice. In February 1994 President Clinton signed Executive Order 12898, 'Federal Actions to Address Environmental Justice in Minority Populations and Low-Income Populations'. The order recognizes the right for any one group, in particular minority and low-income populations, not to suffer 'the disproportionately high and adverse human health or environmental effects of their programmes, policies and activities'. As a result of the order, the Environmental Protection Agency has an environmental justice strategy in operation.

Globalization and Rights

Many environmental problems have international causes, and in recent years many organizations have become concerned about the consequences of economic globalization and the inequitable sharing of the Earth's resources. The complex pressures of globalization have resulted in increased influence of international markets and have changed macroeconomic structures and national policies, with new pressures on natural resources and ecosystems, and the development of unsustainable levels of consumption. There has been little attempt at an international level to address the long-term environmental costs of these destructive policies on sustainable human development.

While the desire to open new markets for those currently excluded may be an acceptable aim, there have been a number of cases where trade liberalization has cut across national attempts to improve environmental quality. The use of international law to undermine environmental action has been a factor in generating much of the opposition to globalization and has led to a loss of confidence in international institutions.

It is suggested that one way to ensure that such globalization is properly controlled is to strengthen international organizations. We believe there is a need for stronger international environmental organizations and agreements, and we recognize the work being done by many bodies to consider whether it is best to strengthen existing bodies or to develop some new structures.

Whatever happens we believe that, if such organizations are to have real powers, they will need to be rooted in international law and in human and environmental rights. We therefore suggest that adoption of international environmental rights should be part of the process of ensuring that globalization is controlled so that it leads to sustainability.

The 2002 World Summit on Sustainable Development

By the time of the UN Rio +5 Special Session in 1997 there was a recognition that many of the key issues were not being adequately addressed, that funding that was central to turning Agenda 21 into a real programme of action was not being made available, and that governments were failing to implement what they had signed up to. Work towards the 2002 Summit therefore developed with a much more limited perspective than pre-Rio.

Central to this work has been a recognition that, over a decade later, many of the key indicators continue to worsen, and that action on poverty will need to be central to the policy framework emerging from WSSD. The issue of human and environmental rights is entirely supportive of that work, with a recognition that the poorest overwhelmingly live in the worst environments and that issues such as safe water and food security are central to work on both poverty and environment.

These priorities were reflected in the activities of ANPED and a range of other non-governmental and inter-governmental organizations in preparation for the summit. Thus in 2001 the UNCHR reaffirmed that human beings are at the centre of concerns for sustainable development and that they are entitled to a healthy and productive life in harmony with nature. The UNCHR also affirmed that the illicit movement and dumping of toxic and dangerous products and wastes constitute a serious threat to the human rights to life and health of individuals, particularly in developing countries that do not have the technologies to process them.

It has to be said that the final outcome from WSSD was disappointing. References to environmental rights were bracketed (that is, unresolved) at the final preparatory negotiations for WSSD, in Bali in June. In the agreed Johannesburg Plan of Implementation and the Johannesburg Declaration on Sustainable Development, the references to the links between human rights and the environment in relation to sustainable development were further watered down. The most relevant paragraph graphically illustrates the way in which negotiating governments weakened the proposed association between environment and human rights:

> *Acknowledge the consideration being given to the possible relationship between environment and human rights, including the right to development, with full and transparent participation of Member States of the United Nations and observer States* (United Nations, 2002, para 169).

The deletion of a draft paragraph, which contained a reference to 'Rio Principle 10', and the severe weakening of paragraph 169 was a great disappointment. Furthermore, reference to the continued work programme for UNEP and the Office of the UN High Commissioner for Human Rights (UNHCHR) was deleted, and as a result the mandate for the UNHCHR has been called into question.

This places organizations which have been active in this area in a difficult position. One cause for optimism is the coalescing of a truly global coalition of civil society organizations concerned with these issues. The Human Rights and Environment Caucus grew tremendously during the WSSD PrepComs. By the end of the summit over 50 organizations were active members.

Conclusions

Current environmental issues require new approaches. The linking of human rights to environmental priorities is an acknowledgement that conservation will not be successful without human development. A range of diverse actions is required at both national and international level, with inalienable human rights providing the basis for such action.

Such an approach requires a new focus on governance and accountability, and provides the underlying principles to support that focus. New rights under Principle 10 of the Rio Declaration will strengthen the role of civil society, enabling national and local organizations to play their part in that governance and to influence resource use and allocation more effectively.

The links between human welfare and resource exploitation are strong. These links need to be openly addressed to provide a common base under international law for all future action on sustainable development. While rights issues have been divisive in the past, the multiplicity of national actions in this field suggest that this may be a common basis for action. Even if there is not agreement on these key issues, it is important that a public debate takes place at the highest level so that all those interested can see where the agreements and disagreements exist.

Notes

1   'Immediately after the Stockholm Conference, perception of environmental problems was limited to a specific geographical area, the industrialized countries, and reduced to the simplest of terms, pollution' (Sahnoun, 1987).

References

Sahnoun, M (1987) 'Environnement et développement', *Revue Algérienne des Relations Internationales*, no 8, OPU, Algiers

UNEP (1999) *Global Environment Outlook 2000*, Earthscan, London

United Nations (2002) 'Plan of Implementation of the World Summit on Sustainable Development', para 5, adopted on 4 September 2002, UN doc A/CONF.199/20, available at www.johannesburgsummit.org/html/documents/summit_docs/131302_wssd_report_reissued.pdf

Appendix 1: Draft Principles for a Declaration on Human Rights and the Environment

(as included in the 1994 Special Rapporteur's Report to the UNCHR)

Preamble

Guided by the Charter of the United Nations, the Universal Declaration of Human Rights, the International Covenant on Economic, Social and Cultural Rights, the International Covenant on Civil and Political Rights, the Vienna Declaration and Programme of Action of the World Conference of Human Rights, and other relevant international human rights instruments,

Guided also by the Stockholm Declaration of the United Nations Conference on the Human Environment, the World Charter for Nature, the Rio Declaration on Environment and Development, Agenda 21: Programme of Action for Sustainable Development, and other relevant instruments of international environmental law,

Guided further by the Declaration on the Right to Development, which recognizes that the right to development is an essential human right and that the human person is the central subject of development,

Guided by fundamental principles of international humanitarian law,

Reaffirming the universality, indivisibility and interdependence of all human rights,

Recognizing that sustainable development links the right to development and the right to a secure, healthy and ecologically sound environment,

Recalling the right of peoples to self-determination by virtue of which they have the right freely to determine their political status and to pursue their economic, social and cultural development,

Deeply concerned by the severe human rights consequences of environmental harm caused by poverty, structural adjustment and debt programmes and by international trade and intellectual property regimes,

Convinced that the potential irreversibility of environmental harm gives special responsibility to prevent such harm,

Concerned that human rights violations lead to environmental degradation and that environmental degradation leads to human rights violations,

Declare the following principles:

Part I

1   Human rights, an ecologically sound environment, sustainable development and peace are interdependent and indivisible.
2   All persons have the right to a secure, healthy and ecologically sound environment. This right and other human rights, including civil, cultural, economic, political and social rights, are universal, interdependent and indivisible.
3   All persons shall be free from any form of discrimination in regard to actions and decisions that affect the environment.
4   All persons have the right to an environment adequate to meet equitably the needs of present generations and that does not impair the rights of future generations to meet equitably their needs.

Part II

5   All persons have the right to freedom from pollution, environmental degradation and activities that adversely affect the environment, threaten life, health, livelihood, well-being or sustainable development within, across or outside national boundaries.
6   All persons have the right to protection and preservation of the air, soil, water, sea-ice, flora and fauna, and the essential processes and areas necessary to maintain biological diversity and ecosystems.

7   All persons have the right to the highest attainable standard of health free from environmental harm.

8   All persons have the right to safe and healthy food and water adequate to their well-being.

9   All persons have the right to a safe and healthy working environment.

10 All persons have the right to adequate housing, land tenure and living conditions in a secure, healthy and ecologically sound environment.

11 (a) All persons have the right not to be evicted from their homes or land for the purpose of, or as a consequence of, decisions or actions affecting the environment, except in emergencies or due to a compelling purpose benefiting society as a whole and not attainable by other means.
    (b) All persons have the right to participate effectively in decisions and to negotiate concerning their eviction and the right, if evicted, to timely and adequate restitution, compensation and/or appropriate and sufficient accommodation or land.

12 All persons have the right to timely assistance in the event of natural or technological or other human-caused catastrophes.

13 Everyone has the right to benefit equitably from the conservation and sustainable use of nature and natural resources for cultural, ecological, educational, health, livelihood, recreational, spiritual and other purposes. This includes ecologically sound access to nature.
    Everyone has the right to preservation of unique sites consistent with the fundamental rights of persons or groups living in the area.

14 Indigenous peoples have the right to control their lands, territories and natural resources and to maintain their traditional way of life. This includes the right to security in the enjoyment of their means of subsistence.
    Indigenous peoples have the right to protection against any action or course of conduct that may result in the destruction or degradation of their territories, including land, air, water, sea-ice, wildlife or other resources.

Part III

15 All persons have the right to information concerning the environment. This includes information, howsoever compiled, on actions or courses of conduct that may affect the environment and information necessary to enable effective public participation in environmental decision-making. The information shall be timely, clear, understandable and available without undue financial burden to the applicant.

16 All persons have the right to hold and express opinions and to disseminate ideas and information regarding the environment.

17 All persons have the right to environmental and human rights education.

18 All persons have the right to active, free and meaningful participation in planning and decision-making activities and processes that may have an impact on the environment and development. This includes the right to a prior assessment of the environmental, developmental and human rights consequences of proposed actions.

19 All persons have the right to associate freely and peacefully with others for purposes of protecting the environment or the rights of persons affected by environmental harm.

20 All persons have the right to effective remedies and redress in administrative or judicial proceedings for environmental harm or the threat of such harm.

Part IV

21 All persons, individually and in association with others, have the duty to protect and preserve the environment.

22 All States shall respect and ensure the right to a secure, healthy and ecologically sound environment. Accordingly, they shall adopt administrative, legislative and other measures necessary to effectively implement the rights in this Declaration.

These measures shall aim at the prevention of environmental harm, at the provision of adequate remedies, and at the sustainable use of natural resources and shall include, inter alia,

- collection and dissemination of information concerning the environment;
- prior assessment and control, licensing, regulation or prohibition of activities and substances potentially harmful to the environment;
- public participation in environmental decision-making;
- effective administrative and judicial remedies and redress for environmental harm or the threat of such harm;
- monitoring, management and equitable sharing of natural resources;
- measures to reduce wasteful processes of production and patterns of consumption;
- measures aimed at ensuring that transnational corporations, wherever they operate, carry out their duties of environmental protection, sustainable development and respect for human rights; and
- measures aimed at ensuring that the international organizations and agencies to which they belong observe the rights and duties in this Declaration.

23 States and all other parties shall avoid using the environment as a means of war or inflicting significant, long-term or widespread harm on the environment, and shall respect international law providing protection for the environment in times of armed conflict and cooperate in its further development.

24 All international organizations and agencies shall observe the rights and duties in this Declaration.

Part V

25 In implementing the rights and duties in this Declaration, special attention shall be given to vulnerable persons and groups.

26 The rights in this Declaration may be subject only to restrictions provided by law and which are necessary to protect public order, health and the fundamental rights and freedoms of others.

27 All persons are entitled to a social and international order in which the rights in this Declaration can be fully realized.

Chapter 12

The Politics of Radical Partnerships: Sustainable Development, Rights and Responsibilities

Charles Secrett, former executive director, Friends of the Earth UK

Development is about welfare and power. The global political economy is failing to deliver the conditions under which basic needs and the prospect of fulfilling lives can be met by most of the world's population – or by future generations – as unique global commons and primary ecosystems are rapidly degraded, and essential democratic requirements for progress are denied by government and politics.

Despite talking about a community of global interests and partnership between governments and society, the G7 and the EU dominate multilateral bodies and back laissez-faire policy prescriptions which make worse these failures of development. They benefit disproportionately from unfair terms of trade and unequal global commons resource allocations, at the expense of poor countries and the regenerative capacity of environmental systems worldwide. They use their political and economic hegemony to gradually impel developing nations to open up vulnerable markets, and agree to unprecedented access by unaccountable corporations and the use of key natural resources to satisfy Northern consumers. In return, they offer minimal debt relief and inadequate development aid. The result is growing instability and insecurity: economic colonization of Southern assets, perpetually disenfranchised subsistence communities and the loss of sovereignty for countries which, lacking capacity and authority, cannot compete. Power is not the same as leadership.

What sort of common interest partnerships are these? No wonder the South is battling back, determined to secure what they need. And so, inter-governmental agreements increasingly end in disarray. The protracted problems over issues such as the principle of 'common but differentiated responsibilities' in the negotiation of the Johannesburg Plan of Implementation is merely the latest example.

Ultimately, the embedded inequalities of decision-making, resource use and wealth between nations drive global development problems: the build-up of climate change, disintegrating habitats and species extinctions, swelling economic migration and sinking public confidence. Global problems need global solutions, and mutually supportive relationships between states and civil societies. Instead, we have deep division and bitter disagreement between governments, North and South, and between transnational companies and communities. Neither side can afford the continuous environmental, social and political upheavals that result.

It is time to draw up and implement a new social contract between citizens and the state, and a new international concordat between governments, in order to secure the fundamental entitlements for well-being, which every person and every nation requires to prosper. Statutory rights and enabling institutions are primary tools of political economy which can address environmental and civil inequities through democratic and fair methods. Rights are enforceable, but also depend on the exercise of responsibilities by society. At the global and national levels, new sustainability rights, rules and adjudication bodies can forge the radically different partnerships between government, companies and communities that are needed to underpin the rewritten social contract and revised political concordat. This should be the business of the UN in follow-up to the Johannesburg Summit, and its focus on the double-barrelled crisis of entrenched poverty and environmental degradation. This builds stability and security. Sustainable development is about justice and well-being for all.

The Crisis of Development

As is obvious to concerned public officials and citizens worldwide, if not captains of industry and trade negotiators, development is failing to deliver … big time. The *Global Environment Outlook 2003* (*GEO 3*) (UNEP, 2002) is the latest survey to confirm that business-as-usual policies are not working for the common good, for the poor, for the environment or for future generations. The thoroughly documented plunder, pollution and dismantling of climate, land and ocean ecosystems, the deep disparities in access and use of natural resources between regions, the huge numbers of people living in poverty, and the growing gulf in standards of living, technological capacity and political authority between have and have-not nations create intolerable and unsustainable ecological, economic and social stresses. This is the crisis of development. It can be cured by good governance: a mix of representative government and participative politics acting in the public interest.

Well-being

Development that fosters progress is about increasing and improving well-being for people. Progress depends on both quantitive gains, such as in standards of living, and qualitative benefits, such as improved quality of life. Well-being is a complex, fuzzy state, whose definition and character vary to a significant extent between different societies, cultures and individuals in their pursuit of satisfaction and happiness. That is part of human diversity – a good thing, worth respecting and celebrating. However, there are fundamental requirements for a fulfilling life which are common to humanity. Basic needs must be satisfied for everybody, whatever their status. Reasonable standards of living and quality of life must be practically attainable for anyone. Democratic rights and freedoms for all must be upheld. As Amartya Sen, the Nobel prize-winning development economist, has shown, achieving the conditions for sustainable development (ie sustainability) is about securing essential political and civil liberties through democratic governance, as much as it is about environmental protection, economic management and resource distribution.

These development imperatives are difficult to achieve, and harder to maintain. How such universal human requirements are more precisely defined and realized raises significant and vexatious questions of political economy in every society and across the family of nations: questions about authority, accountability and entitlement. What are the relative responsibilities of government, business and individuals in allocating valuable resources and managing common property assets, like the global commons estate? Who has rights to what, and how should they be secured? When and why should government intervene in the marketplace? Can citizens effectively hold governments and corporations to account? How should sovereignty be divided between international, national and local arenas of policy influence and decision-making? Securing well-being is about exercising power responsibly; using economic and political authority to determine democratically and fairly who gains or loses out, and why.

The post-Cold War consensus among the industrial powers – predominately Northern governments and transnational companies – is to go for full-blooded economic globalization, liberalized trade and capital flows, and the privatization of state assets.

Light touch government will free invisible hands in the marketplace, development opportunities and investment will spread, prosperity will flow, and standards of living will rise as more and more people enjoy the fruits of a growing global economy.

Or so the trickle-down argument goes. But many authorities, including the victims who lose out on the critical resources they need to prosper and who are effectively kept out of decisions which set the rules of engagement, profoundly disagree. In and around meetings of the World Economic Forum, World Bank, International Monetary Fund (IMF) and the World Trade Organization (WTO) (and in 2002 during the World Summit on Sustainable Development process), deprived countries and communities are resisting, refusing to accept exclusion.

The Denial of Rights

The fact is that laissez-faire policy agendas, and the political apparatus that results, are not very good at fostering development that maximizes opportunities for well-being. It is true that, since the Reagan–Thatcher era when market priorities first gripped tight on finance, trade and aid agencies, one-fifth of the global population have gained significant material benefits and political advantages. Absolute levels of financial wealth have also soared to reward a distinctly privileged minority. It is also true that, on average, the world is growing richer and people are living longer. But these gains have come at too high a price, and mask the inequities of resource use and decision-making between nations, corporations and communities that underpin the global development crisis. As a recent UN Human Development Report summed up:

> *The greatest benefits of globalization have been garnered by a fortunate few. A rising tide of wealth is supposed to lift all boats, but some are more seaworthy than others. The yachts and ocean liners are rising in response to new opportunities, but many rafts and lifeboats are taking on water – and some are sinking* (UNDP, 2002).

The richest 20 per cent of the population have secured 90 per cent of economic consumption on their 'yachts and liners', under these discredited development models and policies. They are also responsible for 70 per cent of climate pollution, 80 per cent of natural resource waste and 95 per cent of toxic waste production. Meanwhile, over 4 billion people survive on the proverbial US$2 a day, consistently unable to meet basic needs. This vulnerable majority are least equipped to cope with the adverse economic and social impacts of destabilized ecosystems, and disrupted environmental services and product flows. They are also least able to compete for scarce natural resources in the marketplace.

There are other substantive reasons of political economy why four-fifths of humanity remains in either relative or absolute deprivation, mostly to do with the character of nation states themselves. They include undemocratic regimes, entrenched elites, corrupt and inefficient public sector administrations, unfair land ownership, and inadequate manufacturing, service and technical capacity. But the prevailing international order makes it nearly impossible for have-not societies to succeed. Fair shares for all are not yet on the menu.

Institutional Inequities

The entwined workings of the WTO, World Bank and IMF illustrate this point neatly. Organisation for Economic Co-operation and Development (OECD) governments, personified by the US, the EU and Japan, insist that the WTO manages international trade according to a binding legal framework that guarantees nation state rights to trade freely, and company rights of access to markets with minimal interference. Member states give up a certain amount of national economic and political sovereignty so that the WTO itself can set global trade rules, adjudicate over disputes and enforce market rights. But there are no such enforceable statutes which enable countries and communities to protect critical natural resources … or exercise economic sovereignty over local market conditions … or hold corporations accountable and liable through mandatory rights of redress and compensation, when their operations and products cause demonstrable harm to the environment or human health.

Instead, WTO procedures are deemed to take precedence over other inter-governmental decisions that affect trade, such as the many multilateral environmental agreements (MEAs) which curb business activities. Under the Doha Declaration, WTO members have decided to negotiate among themselves over the relative mandates of existing trade rules and the MEAs, drawn up by other bodies, with which they clash. There is no independent global authority to decide the conflicting merits of pursuing liberalized trade over environmental protection or natural justice, either generally or on a case-by-case basis. Instead, the free trade body will decide. Given the in-built market and political bias of WTO rules, custom and practice, the eventual settlement is likely to resemble the predictable findings of a kangaroo court.

Developing countries are expected to prosper economically by trading on their comparative advantages of substantial timber, water, land, fish, ores and other natural capital stocks. But such export-oriented development has led to the over-production of primary commodities at generally low and volatile prices, and increasingly exhausted ecosystems. Poor countries compete with each other to supply industrial economies, while trying to prise open protected Northern markets and pay off development loans from Northern governments, private banks and agencies like the World Bank and IMF. Free trade politics and the economics of comparative advantage overwhelmingly benefit the already rich and powerful, whose raw material and natural resource imports grow cheaper as their loans are redeemed, at the expense of the poor and weak, and the environment.

In these market conditions, some 500 companies, the great majority incorporated in the North, have grown to master almost two-thirds of world trade. Having manipulated trade agreements to secure unprecedented access and de facto control for their companies over natural resources and commodities produced by other nations, the industrialized countries are leading the charge through the WTO to force developing countries through statutory mandate to open up their relatively protected and nationally owned agricultural, financial and service sectors. De jure command by the North over critical global resources for development is absolutely unacceptable to the deprived South.

The vicious cycle of downward development prospects is made worse as Northern governments use majority voting rights in the World Bank and IMF to stipulate further that developing countries should liberalize markets, cut public spending and privatize utility, health and education services as conditions for additional lending and aid. As with commodities, Northern companies are best placed to dominate market share and profit. Overall, the free trade agenda amounts to a triple whammy against the developing world.

No such levers impel the G7 or other industrial nations to play fair according to existing rules – let alone fulfil their environmental, economic and social responsibilities to their own citizens, disadvantaged nations and future generations. As necessary and relatively effective as they are in helping to rein in these abuses of power, campaign groups and an investigative media are no substitute for secure entitlements to well-being for those in need. Northern governments continue to default on aid and technical transfer obligations made to developing nations. They maintain massive domestic subsidies for unsustainable energy, transport and agricultural industries. And they close their own markets to Southern and other competitors when that suits domestic priorities. The gospel according to Smith and Ricardo is a relative, not absolute, testament of market faith for the free trade proselytizers.

As befits a religiously charged economic superpower, the US is the most ardent believer in globalized free trade, and one of the worst offenders. Isolationist foreign and economic policy decisions – such as failing to adhere to global agreements freely entered into or acknowledge global authorities democratically decided upon – are invariably justified as morally right for Americans, if not the world. In adolescent political cultures, muscle often chokes off reason and responsibility.

In February 2002, the pro-WTO US introduced a series of WTO-illegal tariff and trade barriers against cheap steel imports to protect uncompetitive domestic producers. Yet the US continues to fight sustained trade wars against other countries' attempts to protect key sectors and consumers from American food products, such as hormone-treated beef and GM crops deemed threatening to human or environmental health. A couple of months later, Congress passed a Farm Appropriations Bill, whose subsidy increase alone to American farmers amounted to some US$70 billion. The net effect will be to intensify further monotype food production, swell surpluses that are liable to be dumped cheaply on world markets, and so make it harder still for developing nations to compete globally, sell produce and meet needs.

The screaming paradox is that the US is the only country whose political economy was originally founded upon, and remains centred on, the defence and implementation of universal human rights for all citizens. But 2004 is an election year, and votes at home take precedence over international obligations for legislators seeking another term in office.

OECD countries are conservatively estimated to spend up to US$75 billion annually subsidizing fossil fuel use, the principal cause of global warming. At least five nation states will cease to exist in some 50 years, as a result of the consequent rise in sea levels. Tuvalu is already negotiating with New Zealand to accommodate its soon-to-be-displaced people. The Intergovernmental Panel on Climate Change anticipates that some 200 million climate refugees will similarly flee low-lying coastal zones in countries like Bangladesh, Egypt and the Philippines. Where will they go – to the EU, China, the US? At the Bonn Climate Summit, industrial countries pledged just US$500 million in aid to help developing countries reduce their own emissions and adapt to climate change. Is this fair compensation? Is it right?

For poor people, the slow and intermittent trickle of market-sanctioned opportunities to progress materially is no substitute for statutory environmental and economic rights of resource protection, access, use and sovereignty, upheld by the rule of law and democratically weighted institutions. Future generations can lay claim to similar rights of entitlement. Their well-being too will depend on inheriting a stable, fully functioning biosphere, with ecosystems and species populations at least as diverse, healthy and productive as those bequeathed to the present generation. These are reasonable expectations, which a sustainable development agenda should fulfil, but business-as-usual policies do not.

There is no question that fairly managed trade, which accounts for and accommodates social and environmental needs and entitlements, is indispensable for spreading prosperity in poor countries. The private sector has the capital, know-how and technology to deliver the economic means for sustainable development. But the rules governing the global marketplace, which force poor countries and small- and medium-sized enterprises to compete with rich countries and dominant transnational corporations on a legally equal footing, have to be changed in order to overcome the institutionalized inequities which drive unsustainable development.

The UN process on sustainable development is designed to address failures of political economy like these. The starting point is the Brundtland Commission assessment that sustainable development is about 'meeting the needs of the present generation without compromising the ability of future generations to meet their needs' – an innocuous definition stuffed with meaning. The Earth Summit blueprints for sound biosphere management and good governance (Agenda 21 and the Rio Declaration), and embryonic global statutes for implementation (the Climate and Biodiversity Conventions), lay the foundation for progressive international relations, and sustainable development entitlements, rights and responsibilities to be more precisely articulated and allocated between countries, companies and communities. This is globalization that can work.

Sustainability and Justice

Meeting the needs of the present generation while ensuring that future generations inherit the capacity to meet their needs is a comprehensive development objective. No one is excluded. It means being able to meet every basic need for all people – not just some needs, some of the time, or simply those of the relatively rich. This aim requires that any of the irreplaceable means by which needs are met must be secured and sustained, now and for the foreseeable future. And that includes maintaining the unique environmental services and goods (or critical natural capital), such as a stable climate or diverse ecosystems and their product flows, which all people require and will continue to require. To sustain critical capital, overall pollution loads and resource take must be kept within the tolerance limits of the biosphere and its primary ecosystems. Otherwise they will collapse.

Needs are the basic requirements for a decent life. For humanity, they include *physical needs* like decent homes, and uncontaminated and sufficient food, air, water, land and other natural materials; *economic needs* like energy, transport, waste minimization and other public service infrastructures, work and shops; *social needs* like vibrant, stable and secure communities, and good health; and, *aesthetic, mental and spiritual needs*, such as unspoilt and diverse environments, education, tranquillity and beauty. Critical natural capital and many other productive environmental resources are required, and used directly and indirectly, to meet these needs. Standards of living and quality of life are dependent on environmental resources. People also satisfy them through human creativity and invention. But art, culture, science and technology can only complement – they are no substitute for – nature's unique and irreplaceable contribution.

Humans also have civil and political needs which must be satisfied. They include the freedoms of information, of expression, of assembly and of movement; sovereign decision-making over community resources; authority to hold liable and seek redress from those causing harm to themselves or the assets they depend upon; and, meaningful participation in public policy decisions. These needs are not absolute, and cannot democratically be satisfied at the expense of the well-being of others. Representative and fair institutions are required to mediate and adjudicate between conflicting claims, and to safeguard the interests of the vulnerable. A sustainable political economy, whether at global, national or local levels, has to marry social justice and equity with economic development and environmental protection, in order to enable people to meet needs fairly.

Unfair Shares

There are other angles to the justice–sustainability matrix. Northern industrial nations clearly owe a substantial ecological debt to their developing country colleagues. Like the laziest sort of welfare state beneficiary, the North lives off the wealth of the South. The debt can be calculated by our historic and continuing unfair take of scarce and limited global commons capacity and natural resource stocks, frequently gained on the cheap, and the damage we do to other peoples' natural environments. The fact is that Northern consumption, and the lifestyles of the rich, are subsidized by squandering the environmental capital of the poor. For deprived communities, the ecological footprint left by industrial predation feels like the stamp of a jackboot.

The US uses 30 per cent of global oil production and emits nearly 25 per cent of global carbon emissions to satisfy the needs of just 4 per cent of humanity, its citizens. Republican and Democrat administrations alike keep taxes artificially low on subsidized petrol, diesel and coal, and refuse to sign the Kyoto Protocol to a convention negotiated in good faith. The average carbon emission of each American citizen is 6 tonnes per year; the average for Mozambique is 0.01 tonne, and for China 0.85 tonne. The distribution is neither environmentally sustainable, economically sensible nor justifiable politically. While the US is the worst offender in this case, all other industrial nations similarly take much more than their fair share of the limited capacity of the climate system to safely absorb a certain amount of pollution without disruption. As we do for critical natural resources like water, land, food, timber, minerals, metals, ores and fish.

The economic costs of the total misappropriation of global commons resources between North and South are substantial: the size of the 'carbon debt' alone owed by industrial nations has been conservatively estimated by Friends of the Earth at US$1,500 billion, and the damage caused by current climate-related disasters (hurricanes, droughts, floods) is reckoned at US$200 billion a year. Southern nations suffer the highest death tolls, economic disruption and numbers of displaced people from these disasters. Reallocating and redistributing critical natural resources on an equitable basis will help repay the debt, and free up essential resources, including pollution sink capacity, for currently disadvantaged nations to meet their economic development needs.

As access to environmental resources is unequally divided between rich and poor, so the impacts of environmental degradation are unevenly clumped. Pollution and resource waste hit poor people hardest. Already, impoverished communities in both Northern and Southern nations suffer the worst effects of polluted water and air, unwholesome or insufficient food, contaminated land, noise, and health-threatening factory and exhaust emissions. In the UK, at least 4.5 million households suffer from 'fuel poverty', unable to stay warm and dry in winter, which causes on average 30,000–60,000 premature winter deaths annually. Twenty per cent of the population cannot afford to buy healthy food. And, in 1999, 82 per cent of carcinogenic factory emissions occurred in the most deprived 20 per cent of neighbourhoods. Climate refugees are merely future confirmation of current realities.

Injustices cut across generations in a number of ways, apart from reducing the capacity of the environment to provide unique resources. Inter-generational inequities that erode the ability of our progeny to meet their needs are also imposed by activities like radioactive and toxic waste production, which impose costs on the future with no discernible benefits ... by worsening adverse environmental trends, whose costs mount over time, such as species extinctions, primary deforestation and climate change ... by the loss of irreplaceable genetic materials and capital as species are extirpated and numbers shrink to remnant populations ... and by novel technologies with unknown long-term effects, such as the badly controlled use of poorly understood genetically modified organisms and persistent synthetic chemicals, which threaten the health of environmental systems, wild species and human metabolisms alike.

Environmental Entitlements

Overall, four types of natural capital entitlement for well-being can be identified, which are denied to many under prevailing development agendas and market conditions. Development priorities, trade rules and market boundaries must be redrawn to ensure the fair distribution and allocation of these entitlements. Otherwise, sustainable development is not possible.

First, there is **the human entitlement to a productive, diverse and fully functioning biosphere:** the continuing destabilization and degradation of the global commons estate and common property resources, such as healthy oceans and resilient climate systems, threatens the well-being of every citizen, and is exacerbated by significant and unjustifiable disparities in pollution loads and resource take across nations.

Second, **the nation state entitlement to a fair share of critical natural resources:** rich industrialized countries wield disproportionate power in economic, trade and other inter-governmental institutions, and too often use that muscle at the negotiating table and in the marketplace to deny vulnerable nations equal access to and use of the raw materials and natural resources, including wild gene capital, required for development.

Third, **the citizen entitlement to natural assets required to meet basic needs:** poor communities with few if any political rights and productive assets are most at risk from significant global change largely created by others, and are most denied the opportunity to meet basic needs and other fundamentals for well-being by the prevailing international order and their own governments.

Fourth, **the inter-generational entitlement to each of the above three:** future generations are deprived of irreplaceable capital in the form of stable, productive, healthy and diverse ecosystems and natural resource stocks, as the present generation consumes and erodes primary forests, coral reefs, non-renewable minerals and metals, freshwater resources, fish stocks and the like, causing unprecedented rates of species extinction, primary habitat destruction and pollution. They too will demand democratic forms of global governance, and civil liberties and freedoms.

Entitlements are secured by rights, and maintained by responsibilities freely exercised under the rule of law. The denial of fundamental rights for well-being runs like a fault line through the social contract between citizens and states. The four universal entitlements to critical natural capital should be translated into statutory sustainability rights, as part of the rules-based framework for democratic decision-making throughout the global economy and nation states. But government cannot do everything. Equally important, civil society actors must exercise corresponding responsibilities to ensure that these sustainability rights can be fully realized. This is the basis for meaningful partnerships between government and society, where each supports the other. The contract needs rewriting.

Sustainability Rights and Responsibilities

Rights are the legal guarantee of the means and opportunities for citizens to meet their needs for a fulfilling life. In the same way that the global commons and other common property resources must be fairly allocated and distributed, so corresponding rights must be defined and responsibilities assigned to government and within society. There is a moral and political imperative to do so, and a strong business case.

Citizens need sustainability rights to secure development opportunities based on engagement, critical resource use and shared sovereignty, mediated by democratic institutions and processes. Guaranteed sustainability rights will empower citizens and enable them to interact as genuine partners with government and business. The development policy alliance between large companies, development agencies and government ministries, which ranges from the politically incestuous and corrupt to the useful and democratic, has led to the rapid accumulation of de facto and de jure rights for companies. This corporate rights grab poses a substantial threat to citizen, nation state and future generation well-being.

Rogue companies that legally profit from unjustifiable rules and market conditions to deny nation state or citizen rights and entitlements should be legally restrained. In 1998, the US-based Ethyl Corporation sued the Canadian government for banning a proven carcinogenic petrol additive produced by the company, won US$13 million compensation, and overturned the ban. In the US, Monsanto is allowed to sue farmers who inadvertently grow plants fertilized by wind-blown or insect-carried pollen from patented GM crops licensed to their neighbours. Investor rights, included in the 1994 North American Free Trade Agreement (NAFTA) and dozens of other bilateral trade treaties, were intended to protect foreign investors from arbitrary interference or expropriation of property. They are now used by clever lawyers from companies such as Mobil, Vivendi and Enron subsidiaries to sue developing country governments for millions of dollars over previously inviolable sovereignties, like setting tax rates, regulating privatized services and enforcing environmental and health standards.

Under NAFTA, such claims go to arbitration panels consisting of trade lawyers, who invariably sit in closed session whatever the wider public interest. Is this justice in action? In recent years, there has been widespread public opposition in India and Brazil against the forced introduction of patented GM crops; in Argentina, Bolivia and Ghana against the takeover of public water services by US and European companies; and in southern Africa against the pricing policies of foreign pharmaceutical companies for essential drugs.

The inflexible one-size-fits-all approach of economic liberalization policy eradicates market diversity, and makes it hard for developing nations to build up infant industries, promote local employment, protect cultural diversity and restrict resource imports. Economic subsidiarity, where communities can shape their own local markets within internationally agreed parameters (eg over fair shares in global assets, human rights and environmental limits), should be accounted for by global trading arrangements. WTO rules should be amended to ensure that environmental and human health priorities, nation state authority over global companies operating within their borders, and the right of communities to determine local market conditions take precedence over simplistic transnational demands to exploit commercial opportunities to buy and sell as they see fit.

The Business Case

Business leaders invariably shy away from government intervention. But a political economy which regulates and provides for fundamental development requirements also creates market stability and policy certainty. This is so because, in order to tackle the deep-rooted development crisis and satisfy future generation needs, long-term development strategies must be responsibly coordinated through negotiated agreements. As the policy boundaries of the market are redrawn, new environmental standards set and entitlement rights enforced, a level playing field is created that favours best practice companies and discriminates against the cowboys who undercut by slashing costs and corners. Supportive tax and spending regimes should reward companies that operate sustainably and penalize companies that do not. This is the future for markets. Fighting to perpetuate trade and other economic inequities is the corporate losers option.

Companies already suffer severe reputational damage when they trample over innate environmental and civic rights. Witness the impact in recent years of concerted citizen-driven consumer and shareholder campaigns against brand leaders like Monsanto, Shell, Nike and McDonald's, and a host of lesser-logo companies. Executives often forget that market forces work both ways. The grievances of inequity will ensure that civil resistance to overweening corporate power consolidates and grows in Northern and Southern markets, if governments and companies fail to correct perpetrated wrongs with enacted rights and responsible behaviour.

In the 21st century, good business will increasingly mean making money by working to high environmental and social corporate standards. Employees prefer this sort of company, and loyalty and productivity rise alongside customer satisfaction. Management time and money is saved, as campaigners focus elsewhere and expensive defensive PR budgets become unnecessary. Bad publicity melts away. Shareholders appreciate benefits like these. Just development is profitable development.

By liberating dormant assets, rights-based development can also enable the 4 billion people now virtually excluded from the global economy to participate meaningfully, opening up new market and business opportunities. People without credit, resources and capital have little means, apart from labour and the land they use, to prosper themselves. As Peruvian development economist Hernando de Soto argues, giving poor people formal ownership rights to the land they live on, or do business on, transforms dead capital into wealth. Statutory 'access and use' natural asset rights, combined with complementary national policy initiatives such as a principled system of property law and development services, both catalyse the growth of, and jump-start entry into, these emerging markets.

The Limits to Voluntary Action

In the run-up to the Johannesburg Summit, industry lobby groups like the International Chamber of Commerce, the World Business Council for Sustainable Development and Business Action for Sustainable Development urged the adoption of public–private partnerships between UN agencies, governments, companies and NGOs. The purpose of these so-called 'Type 2' voluntary agreements is to foster dialogue between stakeholders in development, and encourage project-based solutions financed by business. The aim is to compensate for the spectacular failure of government to implement Agenda 21 since the Rio Earth Summit. Laudable goals, and therein lies the danger. While carefully designed projects can address specific local development problems, they cannot substitute for concerted government action across markets and business at large. Companies like the voluntary approach because it keeps legal entitlements for communities and polluter-pays taxation at bay. It also helps build images of good corporate citizens in action, without requiring fundamental change to unsustainable activities or reform of unequal trading arrangements.

But the voluntary approach only works if all players are equal and there is a genuine communal agenda. Corporations have the advantage of size. In 1999, the five largest transnationals, including Exxon and General Motors, achieved sales greater than the combined incomes of the world's 46 poorest countries. Today, 51 of the 100 largest economies are corporations and only 49 are nation states. Ford Motor Co sales are bigger than Poland's gross national product (GNP). With instant free movement of capital, and decision-making structures and operations that span continents, transnationals can and do escape effective oversight jurisdiction by national government and weak international statutes. Without statutory sustainability rights, citizens and communities have insufficient safeguards against the overweening power and influence of behemoths like these, seeking profits.

Too much power is easily abused, even as many companies genuinely try to improve reputations and performance. Some transnationals, like BP, Ford and Shell, have begun significant stakeholder initiatives and environmental improvement programmes company-wide. But when the fundamental business remains environmentally unsustainable and effectively unaccountable to citizens and government, then reform must be mandatory.

The necessary distinctions for good governance between state authority and industry power have become muddled and opaque through cosy cohabitation. Government must fulfil its duties to society in part by independently managing markets and the private sector to help achieve the common good, as well as encourage reasonable competitive advantage and entrepreneurial flourish. But state responsibilities have become corrupted by the marketplace: ministers and officials hand over the results and products of publicly funded research and development programmes for private companies to patent and exploit, without fair recompense to the public purse ... inadequately resource and empower independent state regulatory agencies ... maintain perverse tax and subsidy codes which favour entrenched and unsustainable business operations ... allow industry representatives to dominate government advisory committees, oversight agencies and standard-setting bodies ... assume liability for environmental, human health or economic harm caused by company operations ... and do not safeguard citizen entitlements against unjust corporate power.

In the same way that previous generations sought to separate church and state in order to improve government and secure good governance, so it is time to separate corporation and state. Sustainability rights help to do so by levelling the playing field and securing essential entitlements.

Types of Rights

Rights can be defined in two classes: inalienable rights and enabling rights. **Inalienable rights** for sustainable development should be constitutionally guaranteed, to be interpreted by an independent judiciary and only very rarely adjusted by legislators. This is because these rights are about delivering universal human requirements for well-being. They include the right to live in and enjoy a productive, diverse and fully functioning biosphere ... the right of equal access to and use of environmentally sustainable global commons capacities and assets ... the general right to a clean and healthy environment, and specific rights to unpolluted air, pure water, wholesome food, uncontaminated land and tranquillity. Inalienable rights should secure and sustain the entitlements of nation states and future generations to fair shares in available global commons resources, while observing the tolerance limits of ecosystems and conserving the capacity of critical biological capital to maintain itself.

Inalienable rights are extremely powerful tools of political economy. They allow judges to overrule elected governments and order changes to laws, standards and other acts of public bodies deemed to infringe upon or otherwise offend fundamental human needs. But government will always be imperfect in the real world. There will always be a quivering tension between the checks and balances that link the judiciary, legislature and executive: an unavoidable fact of political economy. Exercising judgement over what is right and wrong is not the sole prerogative of the courts. It is equally the responsibility of politicians and citizens. Someone after all has to choose, monitor and hold the adjudicators to account. The price of democracy really is eternal vigilance. Ensuring that the dynamic equilibrium between judicial, political and citizen authority serves sustainable development goals is also a function of the progressive partnerships required in a modern state.

Enabling rights empower people to actively and meaningfully engage in their political economy, and to use democratic bodies to defend or secure the means to fulfil needs. They include rights to know about the state of environmental systems, as well as proposed development schemes or plans which threaten entitlements ... the right to determine local market conditions that allow small-scale enterprises to compete with large-scale companies ... the right to public sector infrastructure and services that enable citizens to minimize their own ecological footprints ... the right to protect and conserve environmental systems from adverse development and commercial activity ... the right to hold corporations accountable and liable for business operations which harm human health or disrupt critical ecosystem functions, and rights of redress and compensation ... and the right to participate in public policy decision-making and standard setting. In some cases, representative government will enforce such rights on behalf of citizens. After all, it is practically impossible for everyone to decide everything. In others, citizens will use the opportunities of democracy to act for themselves.

More than one type of policy package can deliver enabling rights effectively, depending on political, economic and social circumstances that vary over time.

From left to right to green, competing political parties and their supporters prefer different mixes of state intervention and social or market provision. Enabling rights are best enacted through legislation, standards, tax codes and/or general policy as appropriate, because they require more flexible implementation than constitutional fiat. Voters choose which they prefer at regular intervals. These policy instruments can be adjusted as governments change and elections shuffle up a different mix of ruling and opposition parties in the legislature and executive.

Civic Responsibilities and Good Governance

Individuals, like governments and corporations, have other responsibilities to exercise for sustainability. Statutory guarantees of essential development entitlements and rights to well-being are only one part of the revised bargain between citizens and the state, albeit the most important to rectify in present circumstances. Equally necessary is a civil commitment to actively use the opportunities of democracy to pursue the common good. No man or woman is an island unto themselves, unless they decide to become a hermit. One household's warm home and fast car is another household's battering storm and lapping waves on the doorstep. We are social animals, and depend on each other whether we like it or not.

It is no use relying solely on government to create a sustainable world. It takes more than that – governments have limitations. They cannot do everything. Nor should they be allowed to: the all-providing state is a dictatorship. Passive, complacent and apathetic citizens breed bad governments and irresponsible companies. Tackling climate change, deforestation and the waste of natural resources, for example, or creating political economies where poor communities and countries can prosper, depend on personal choices of lifestyle, economy and politics as much as they do on institutions, laws, spending and taxes.

Ultimately, it is citizens, not governments or companies, who have power. Government may exercise authority on our behalf, and companies may do what they can to influence and determine government priorities. But no government can survive without the endorsement of the electorate. And no company will stay in business, unless its stakeholders endorse what it does, makes and sells. On the high street, the consumer is king and queen. In the boardroom and at the AGM, the CEO and directors are subservient to investors and shareholders. Through the ballot box, voters rule.

Throughout its 40 chapters, Agenda 21 emphasizes that participatory democracy goes hand in hand with representative government in creating and securing the means and opportunities for sustainable development and progress. Good governance depends on active and aware citizens, in political arenas and public markets, as much as accountable, responsible and democratic government. Both are necessary; neither is sufficient. In the final analysis, this is the basis for the radical and progressive partnerships between government and civil society, and between community and community, that the social contract for sustainability requires to take effect.

Private lives depend on community efforts. But people as well as nation states need the supportive architecture of a sustainable political economy to address the crisis of development and the denial of opportunity and means for well-being. Statutory rights are the bedrock upon which the framework stands and the political enticement to social responsibility. Both classes of development rights and the entitlements they protect should be guaranteed through a new UN Convention on Sustainability Rights and other inter-governmental statutes, such as a new Treaty on Corporate Accountability and Liability. These should be enacted through accountable multilateral agencies, governed by member states. Similarly, nation states need to cement these rights in and through their own constitutions, legislatures and judiciaries. In many nations, and at the international level of government, the successful application of sustainability rights will require new institutions and/or reform of existing bodies to monitor, adjudicate and enforce them fairly.

Sustainability and State Reform

UNCED was the largest gathering of heads of state and world leaders ever. In Agenda 21, they agreed a compelling global action plan for sustainable development. Similarly, through the Rio Declaration on Environment and Development, governments endorsed the principles of environmental, economic and social rights and responsibilities for citizens and states, which are needed to translate sustainability goals into practical laws, management regimes and trading arrangements.

No government has repudiated these agreements – although most have done precious little to reform their political economies accordingly. Nevertheless, the official global mandate for sustainability is still alive. But, as Chamberlain infamously discovered, pieces of paper are only as good as the institutions and actions that make them real. Mandates mean nothing without consistent intent and application. What is generally missing is the apparatus of government, model environment–development agencies and mutually supportive international relations capable of delivery. But there is a precedent, which enabling institutions should build upon.

The Climate Change Convention Model

The Climate Convention is the best example of governments turning the Rio Declaration prerequisites for sustainability, and fundamental human entitlements for well-being, into international statute and implementation.

The convention decrees that overall pollution loads must be reduced to within climate system tolerance limits to avoid adverse impacts on society and ecosystem regeneration and productivity. The needs of future generations for diverse and productive ecosystems and a stable climate must be accounted for in emission reduction targets. Targets must be timetabled, so that progress can be measured. The nations most responsible for climate change pollution (Annex 1 countries) must act first and reduce emissions the most. Developing countries are allowed, for a time, to continue polluting while they favour economic development to meet citizen needs. Rich countries are expected to help poor nations to modernize their economies and reduce emissions, through appropriate technology transfers, capacity building and aid flows. The convention also recognizes that the resource use efficiencies required to cut greenhouse gas pollution will catalyse technical innovation and create new business markets. Collective emission reductions are seen as an economic and social opportunity, not a drag on development prospects.

The convention is based on the principle of 'common but differentiated responsibilities' – agreed at the Rio Summit but one of the main stumbling blocks between Northern and Southern governments negotiating the Johannesburg Plan of Implementation – and is slowly making it work in practice. Most importantly, the convention recognizes that global commons capacity (here, available climate sink space) should be shared between nations and generations, and that common property assets (the maintenance of healthy and diverse ecosystems, dependent on a stable climate, and their continual flow of unique environmental products and services) are needed by both rich and poor countries, and present and future generations. The convention understands that these are universal entitlements for well-being, to which all have a fundamental right.

Of course, this is no guarantee that governments will behave responsibly. It took a decade of painfully slow negotiations between competing blocks of nations, united only by their vested interests, before the Kyoto Protocol was signed; and only then to commit to very low, first-step emission targets. Special pleading, the abrogation of responsibility and leadership by industrial nations, and brinkmanship to the bitter end characterized the approach of most delegations for most of the 1990s. But the breakthrough in Bonn was helped by the convention's decision-making structure. Ratification depends on sufficient nations agreeing to implement: 55 nations have to do so, representing at least 55 per cent of total current emissions. The formula is sufficiently flexible so that no small group from the industrial nations, oil and coal producers or the G77 can hold up agreement indefinitely. Implementation is not dependent on either market action or regulation; both have a part to play, as binding emission reduction targets and tradable pollution quotas are set within a diminishing overall emissions cap, designed to eventually lower greenhouse gas loads within tolerable climate system limits.

The convention is not perfect, but it represents a paradigm shift in environmental management, development policy and political economy. Uniquely in international law, its clauses embrace the essential common interest (political, economic and environmental) imperatives and mutually supportive multilateral arrangements, which are necessary to equitably satisfy ecosystem requirements for regeneration and productivity, and present and future generation development needs. The convention rejects both the free market approach and decision-making dominated by a powerful few. But it has established an institutional and policy framework that sets out to encourage sustainable and fair global trade, where dynamic markets, economic productivity and commercial opportunity are bound by democratic authority, accountability and entitlements for the common good.

Its impact can be judged by the accelerated efforts of US motor manufacturers like Ford and General Motors to develop low-carbon fuels, and oil giants like Exxon-Mobil diversifying into renewable energy supplies, despite the isolationist reluctance of a Republican administration to endorse the Kyoto Protocol. Throughout the 1990s, these companies spent millions of propaganda dollars through the Global Climate Coalition industry lobby group rubbishing climate science and warning of economic catastrophe if the convention was enacted. They failed. Now they know where market opportunity and consumer demand lie and do not want to be left behind by their European and Japanese competitors. How long now before the US, Canadian and Australian administrations play ball?

In the final analysis, the convention was ratified and the Kyoto Protocol passed because of three factors, which significantly grew in influence during the 1990s. First, sufficient compelling scientific evidence of the likely threats of climate change and sea-level rise, and rising public concern, persuaded governments to invoke the precautionary principle and start enacting 'no-regrets' domestic policy responses, like renewables and energy efficiency programmes. Second, emerging markets for low- or no-carbon power supply, technologies, products and fuels opened up in response to consumer demand and nation state regulations and fiscal policy in the energy, housing and transport sectors. Third, after the breakdown in negotiations at the Hague Climate Meeting in 2000, campaign groups, media commentators and voters, particularly in Europe, demanded action and emission cuts from their elected representatives. Each factor was driven by citizen expectations. People really do have power, if they choose to use it.

Institutional Reforms

The Climate Convention should become the working model to reform the decision-making, policies and programmes of the WTO, World Bank, IMF and other finance and development agencies, and become the basis of future multilateral environment, trade and development agreements.

Financing for sustainable development programmes is a perpetual problem. Nation states are reluctant to use tax-payers' money to fulfil their global development responsibilities. Donors invariably tie disbursements through the World Bank and its regional counterparts, or in the IMF, to political and economic conditions that recipient nations must accept. The size of loans also helps to determine voting rights. A new source of independent money is needed. Introducing the 'Tobin Tax' on global financial flows and currency speculation is the obvious candidate. These are mostly generated by industrial power banks and investment houses, and cause many of the shocks and disruptions to financial markets and exchange rates which destabilize Northern and Southern economies. These substantial funds are sufficient to finance costed sustainable development priorities, and would allow the reorganization of development bank decision-making on equitable lines between North and South. At a stroke, many of the current political and economic disparities which hamstring the World Bank and the IMF, and bring both agencies into disrepute, would disappear. The World Bank needs a new role, and global development needs a new bank. It should administer and disperse Tobin Tax funds, according to sustainable development priorities set by its newly constituted and globally accountable board of directors. The first UN Conference on the Environment, in Stockholm in 1972, approved the principle of international 'automaticity' for environmental purposes: that is, the principle of raising money for global environmental programmes through an international taxation system. Post-Johannesburg, the UN should get to grips with how to implement and benefit from this system.

At least two other new international bodies will be required for sustainability entitlements and rights to work in practice. The United Nations Environment Programme (UNEP) tries hard to do its job, but has no authority and little funds. It issues warning cries about environmental instability, but can do little to redress the problems. Some 70 per cent of all multilateral environmental agreements are only partially implemented or have not been implemented at all. The UN needs a Global Environmental Protection Agency (GEPA) to enforce these statutes and negotiate new ones as appropriate. It should have equal authority to the WTO and should take over responsibility from the World Bank for dispersing Global Environment Facility funds.

Finally, the UN should establish a global Court of Justice to monitor the application of the proposed Convention on Sustainability Rights, enforce global sustainability entitlements and adjudicate between conflicting claims of other bodies, like the proposed GEPA and WTO.

Nation states have already set a persuasive precedent in releasing equivalent sovereign authority to the WTO to facilitate global trade. Reforms like these are necessary to develop a democratic international order capable of addressing the crisis of development and the denial of fundamental entitlements and rights. These arrangements should be the basis for developing the new international concordat between nations that transforms sustainable development theory and agreements in principle into real world practice.

Policy Targets and Fair Shares

In order to reallocate and redistribute global commons and other critical common property development assets for present and future generations, policy-makers have to figure out how much is available and what a fair share is. The concept of 'environmental space', originated in 1991 by Friends of the Earth Netherlands and the Wuppertal Institute (WuI) in Germany, and now applied widely by Friends of the Earth International (FOEI), is a policy calculus which enables them to do so robustly.

The environmental space method (ESM) initially estimates the overall resource take and pollution load which an environmental system can sustain and still maintain its productive natural resource flows and regenerative capacity.

The ESM assesses whether these assets are fairly shared out between and within generations. It combines estimates of critical natural capital stocks (eg timber, water, land, ores) and the tolerance limits (eg regeneration rate, sink capacity) of ecosystems in order to set equitable (per capita) shares for development in the present. Similarly, fair shares of future stocks and tolerance limits are worked out, based on future population estimates, and assigned for future generation use.

If all nations met their development needs with an equivalent pollution load to the UK, we would need the climate sink space of $8^1/_2$ planets to maintain climate stability. Rounding out the figures to make the illustration easier, 5 billion people emitted 20 billion tonnes of CO_2 in 2001, at an average of 4 tonnes per citizen. To achieve a 50 per cent cut in total CO_2 emissions of 10 billion tonnes by 2050, with an estimated global population of 10 billion people, means a fair per capita share of 1 tonne CO_2 emitted per person by then. In 2001, the UK population of 50 million people emitted 0.5 billion tonnes CO_2, or 10 tonnes each. Thus, assuming a stable UK population by 2050, the UK has to reduce its overall CO_2 emissions to 0.05 billion tonnes – or a 90 per cent cut on 2001 levels – in order for its citizens to take no more than their fair share of available climate sink space of 1 tonne per person by 2050.

ESM thus enables policy-makers to set environmentally sustainable and equitable resource use and pollution load targets, for individual nations to achieve as they see fit, on a sector-by-sector basis over determined periods: for example, to reduce carbon emissions by an estimated 60–80 per cent on 1990 levels by 2050, with each nation progressively moving towards its fair share emission rate, and using legal standards and fiscal policy to do so. ESM is an essential prerequisite to make the so-called 'contraction and convergence' approach, now attracting the attention of Climate Convention delegations, viable.

The ESM has been applied by FOEI/WuI to calculate global, national and future allocations for a wide range of critical natural resources. Nations that currently take more than their fair share of resource take and sink capacity must reduce, and develop more efficiently to cut resource consumption and pollution loads accordingly. Factor 10 increases in energy and material use efficiency are eminently achievable over a generation or less, and will help industrial economies to improve economic efficiency, and spur innovation and technological development. Deprived nations gain their fair share of the liberated natural resources and sink space in global commons systems, build economies on these critical development assets and improve their development prospects accordingly.

Conclusion

Given the state of the world and past history, many people and politicians believe that delivering sustainable development and universal public well-being is an impossible vision, more suited to angels in heaven than humans on Earth. I don't think so.

Humanity has the cultural and scientific resources, capital infrastructure, technology, business capability, policy tools, wealth and a still-functioning and bountiful biosphere to realize the public conditions for all citizens to enjoy fulfilling and satisfying livelihoods (private and personal happiness is another thing entirely). The failures of development are political and relative, not immutable or absolute. It may take a generation or two, and plenty of mistakes and learning, but sustainability can be achieved. The alternative is too depressing to contemplate, as the comparative 'Markets First', 'Policy First', 'Security First' and 'Sustainability First' scenarios analysed in *GEO 3* (UNEP, 2002) spell out. So, awesome challenge, yes; impossible prospect, no.

The common-good partnerships between government, business and civil society, which are addressing the climate threat, should be deepened and broadened to turn sustainability rights and entitlements into real-world political, economic and social advantage. The evidence of mounting environmental disaster on land and in the oceans, and unsustainable poverty, is even more compelling than the threat of climate change. We see millions go hungry every day, and watch them die. No one can deny that ecosystems like primary forests and coral reefs are disappearing, because they are being destroyed all around us. The sound alternative models of political economy and the embryonic framework of institutions and statute are there to build on, and correct the fundamental failures of development.

The imperative is to muster the leadership to implement Agenda 21, the Rio Declaration on Environment and Development and the Johannesburg Plan of Implementation. Post-WSSD, governments should shift perspective, agree a robust process to deliver these global commitments, and negotiate proposed enabling mechanisms such as the institutional, financial and statutory reforms outlined above. Doing so can make manifest the social contract for sustainability and the democratic international concordat, both of which treat nation states and civil society as equal partners reliant on a healthy biosphere. Development is then best placed to realize community well-being fairly, and fulfil the public interests that bind present and future generations. Isn't this a world order worth striving for?

References

UNDP (2002) *Human Development Report 2002*, OUP, New York
UNEP (2002) *Global Environment Outlook 2003*, Earthscan, London

Chapter 13

The Age of Globalization

Tariq Banuri, SEI Boston

Financing was a central theme in the UN Conference on Environment and Development (UNCED) in 1992, and 11 years later it remains an outstanding issue, the resolution of which will determine whether the world begins to move towards sustainable development. But 2003 is not 1992; even in the long sweep of history, a decade can make all the difference.

This is the age of globalization, with all the hope, danger and cynicism that have come to be associated with this word. In contrast, 1992 can only be described as the age of optimism and innocence: it came at the end of the deepest depression in industrialized countries since the 1930s; it was also the end of the lost decade for development. It marked the end of the Cold War and according to some the end of history. Optimism was in the air; there were visions of a new global compact between the North and the South producing a future of tranquillity, justice, cooperation and development. In retrospect at least, UNCED negotiations (as well as, albeit to diminishing degrees, the UN summits that followed soon after) appear remarkable for the optimism of the participants, their willingness to place trust in agreements, their faith in the ultimate commitment of the global community to the ideals of justice and equity, and consequently their dedication to cooperative action.

These hopes and commitments have evaporated – not because the promised economic growth did not take place, but precisely because it did. 2002 marked the end of a decade of dramatic economic expansion led by extraordinary developments in information technology. But this has led to more problems than solutions: a wider gap between the rich and the poor, recurrent global economic instability, increasing economic concentration, and, in addition to all this, the shadow of war, a shadow that makes ideals superfluous, replaces trust with instrumentalism, and engenders anxiety and fear.

The political mood is also different. Jean Baudrillard (2001) dubs the politically quiescent 1990s as the period of 'la grève des evenements' (literally 'an events strike', translated from a phrase of the Argentinian writer, Macedonio

Fernandez) to suggest that in the new millennium the strike is off. Baudrillard's preoccupation is with the terrorist attack of 11 September 2001, which he interprets as anti-globalization, as well as its immediate fallout, the Afghanistan war, which could well go down in history as the first war of globalization, nearly a century after the imperial war of 1914–1918. Regardless of how one interprets 11 September, however, the fact is that challenges to globalization have been growing. Increasingly militant protests at Seattle, Nice, Genoa and elsewhere have already forced the elite of the world to shift their meetings to less public venues and more authoritarian countries.

The conventional treatment of financing for sustainable development was premised on a pre-globalization world-view. Its preoccupations were the relationships between nation states, the flows of funds between countries and particularly between governments, national economic growth, and intra-national income inequality. In a globalized world, the pertinent questions are different: they relate to the legitimacy of mobilizing resources for development, for depressed areas, for the protection of vulnerable regions and communities, and for reducing global (not national) inequalities in income and wealth.

Taking Globalization Seriously

In order to be able to talk about global development or global finance, let us imagine the world as a single country.

What would this country look like? To begin with, it is a 'multinational' and unevenly governed country. It is also an unequal country – indeed, more unequal than any country in existence today. It is, in many ways, an apartheid country, where the elite invoke liberty and fraternity but secure their privileges through unabashed instrumentalism and naked power; where people are not free to travel from one region to the other, and if they do, are subject to arbitrary search and harassment; and where the affluent areas are protected from the poor hinterland by sophisticated disciplinary mechanisms. It is also a country with a dual economy, the shiny factories and offices of the elite world contrasting sharply with the slums and sweatshops of the non-elite regions; the former affluent, generally large in scale, well organized and economically aggressive and the latter a host of informal and semi-formal enterprises, organized under traditional arrangements, based principally around biomass, and integrated minimally if at all into the larger market.

Yet, it is not a country without hope. Like other developing countries, which saw an optimistic ideology, 'development', sweep across their societies at their 'tryst with destiny' – independence from colonial rule – the world too has acquired a language to nurture optimism. It is called globalization.

In short, the world would look very much like many developing countries; not a country like Switzerland or Norway, rather, an amalgam of apartheid-era South Africa, pre-liberalization China and contemporary Afghanistan.

Caveats and Questions

Many people have difficulties with the notion of the world as a single country. The world is far too chaotic and diverse, they would argue; it has neither a legitimate government nor a 'political community', that is, a shared sense of solidarity and responsibility. But when it comes right down to it, this messiness, diversity, weak government and low level of solidarity are not dissimilar to many developing countries. The extreme examples are war-torn countries (Angola, Afghanistan, Liberia), which are criss-crossed by ethnic, religious, linguistic and other divisions, some areas run by warlords, others self-governed by local communities, leaving a fairly small area under the direct control of a 'legitimate' state. Even countries that are otherwise peaceful come close to this image. On paper they have formal governments but in practice the writ of these governments does not run much beyond the brightly lit streets of the capital city; elsewhere, they cede authority to an informal system of governance run by landlords, politicians, policemen and businessmen, often with the tacit support of external interests.

Furthermore, notwithstanding the impression of messiness, the world *does* have order, a system of governance – even if not a single formal government. Oran Young (1994) argues, for example, that:

> *the achievement of governance does not invariably require the creation of material entities or formal organizations of the sort we normally associate with the concept of government. Once we set aside our preoccupation with structures of government, it is apparent that governance is by no means lacking in international society, despite the conspicuous absence of a material entity possessing the power and authority to handle the functions of government for this society as a whole* (Young, 1994 cited in Bigg, 2001, p23).

The problem of political community is trickier. The prevailing wisdom denies the existence of any solidarity and responsibility at the global level; it describes relationships between states as lying exclusively in the domain of instrumentalism and naked self-interest. According to Tom Bigg:

> *The notion that some form of order exists at the global level constitutes a direct challenge to the various realist schools of international relations, which share the supposition that relations between states are characterized by anarchy which is only mitigated by some form of equilibrium in the power at their disposal* (Bigg, 2001, p21).

Bigg goes on to argue that although neo-realist theorists would recognize the possibility of cooperation between states, this is more likely in areas of 'low politics' (environment, welfare, human rights) than 'high politics' (Bigg mentions only security, but presumably finance would be included here); and that the extent of such cooperation is limited by the benefit participating governments expect to accrue to them, or the damage they might expect to avert by participating.

Having said that, however, it is now increasingly recognized that global decisions are determined by more complex processes, and that they involve a larger group of actors besides governments: NGOs, business and labour groups, academic scholars and the media. The rise of global public policy networks (Reinicke et al, 2000) suggests that global decision-making has moved out of the exclusive domain of governments. At the global level, the conventional test of government – the demonstration that decisions taken or conclusions arrived at are more than a reflection of the wishes of the participants with traditional power capabilities – is fulfilled both positively and negatively. On the one hand, the speed and complexity of global problems are such that few governments have the capacity to make decisions without seeking professional input, political participation and legitimacy from the involvement of external actors. On the other hand, while governments (like other powerful groups) certainly continue to have enormous power to block decisions – and while government personnel can still siphon public resources for private uses – their ability to pursue and realize the public interest has become increasingly dependent on popular acceptance and legitimacy. The difference between democratic and authoritarian governance is no longer restricted to the form of the government but extends also to its substance, effectiveness and reach.

In other words, not only do governments voluntarily seek external advice, they find it difficult to accomplish anything without such involvement. James Rosenau has argued that the key difference between governance and government is that the former functions only if it is accepted by the majority, whereas the latter can function even in the face of widespread opposition (Rosenau, 1992). True, but there is a large distance between being able merely to *function* and being able to *accomplish* anything of consequence. Rosenau's test is largely inconsequential. A more relevant test would be to ask whether there is a difference between government and governance in terms of the capacity for accomplishment. The answer by and large is no.

The upshot of this discussion is that, in the age of globalization, it makes sense to project the world as a single country, and to ask questions regarding the agenda of sustainable development as well as its financial needs, not from the perspective of a value-free and irresponsible inter-state system. Rather, the approach suggested here, and which has been implicit in many arguments for foreign aid as well as responsible investment, is that of a single country.

The question then is how should the global community express its commitment to social equity and environmental conservation? This casts the entire debate in a different light and indeed challenges conventional wisdom, which appears to have strong roots in the instrumentalism of the colonial period. A brief comment on the historical continuity from the 19th to the 21st centuries may be in order here.

Globalization Redux[1]

A recent authoritative study demonstrates that the forcible incorporation of smallholder production into commodity and financial circuits controlled from overseas undermines food security, confiscates local fiscal autonomy, and integrates millions of tropical cultivators into the world market at the cost of 'a dramatic deterioration in their terms of trade'. This is not a description of contemporary conditions. It is the account of the historian Mike Davis of the world under the British Empire in the 19th century (Davis, 2001). The historical continuity of what made, and keeps, a huge part of the world poor is astonishing.

Since the 1960s every attempt by developing countries to engage with the global economy on terms that would help them develop, such as managing investment, regulating foreign multinationals and stabilizing commodity prices, has been resisted and opposed. According to Joseph Stiglitz, Nobel prize-winner and former chief economist at the World Bank:

> *Countries find themselves in situations where they are having policies imposed on them. It is not unlike the 19th century opium wars when countries were told to open up their markets and this threat was backed up by military force. Now it is an all-or-nothing deal. Either you do it the Washington consensus way or we will exclude you* (Elliott, 2001).

This is another echo from the 19th century when, according to Davis:

> *From about 1780 or 1800 onward, every serious attempt by a non-Western society to move over into a fast lane of development or to regulate its terms of trade was met by a military as well as an economic response from London or a competing imperial capital.*

Globalization in the 19th century was on the terms of the then dominant power, Britain, which claimed it as the discharge of the white man's burden. Britain argued for example that it had rescued India from 'timeless hunger'. It is the sort of rescue that India could have done without. The structural adjustment of India by the British Raj and its knock-on effect in China wrecked indigenous coping strategies. Thirty-one serious famines occurred in the 120 years of British rule in India, almost twice the total number of 17 recorded in the previous 2000 years.

What Have we Learnt from Conventional Development?

The age of globalization is in the last instance the age of *global* development, and as such it has much to learn from the experience of national development. The idea of economic (or social) development as a key component of the goal and purpose of governments is a recent one. Even more recent (and apparently still controversial) is inclusion of sustainable development in the goals and purposes of the global community of policy-makers. Yet until now, this goal has been viewed in a rather arm's-length manner.

However, there is much that is negative in the experience of development. Development was always and everywhere preoccupied with industrialization, and rarely with poverty eradication or social equity. The African thinker, Abdul Rahman Babu, argues that Africa would do well to imitate not the prescription but the experience of the West. The Western experience of modernization, he argues, was built on three pillars – agriculture, textiles and construction – namely the activities needed to feed, clothe and house people. In the West the three key sectors still underpin all other economic activity and are still heavily protected. In developing countries, International Monetary Fund (IMF) policies undermine these very sectors. They encourage African states to export raw materials, undermine subsistence agriculture and local businesses, and turn societies into markets for imported food and irrelevant consumer goods.

Babu argues that Africa should protect these three essential sectors, and not embark on further development until it has increased the capacity to save. Others, who have provided innovative leadership in the creation of sustainable livelihoods, do not go as far as Babu, but they too argue that for a community to grow, it needs to create a sustainable basis for its growth. This requires an investment in the social capital of the community, as well as the development of a robust base of savings.

There are those who argue that poor communities in general and the African poor in particular have no savings capacity, but there is considerable empirical evidence to the contrary. Community development programmes, micro-credit programmes and rural support programmes in south Asia invariably result in creating a savings tradition as well as supportive financial institutions. In Africa, as Jacques B Gelinas shows in *Freedom from Debt* (Gelinas, 1998), the failure is that of the big state and international banks, which have placed Africans in bondage to foreign creditors. The result is a vacuum in the domestic financial savings sector. 'Finance, like nature, abhors a vacuum', says Gelinas, and so micro-finance institutions have stepped in. Grameen Bank in Bangladesh, the Tontines in Cameroon or the Naam groups in Burkina Faso have done more than mobilize finance; they have mobilized women, the outcasts of the banking world.

It is important to recognize also that the savings tradition requires time and effort. On the eve of the industrial revolution (1760–1780), British investment constituted little more than 5 per cent, but certainly less than 10 per cent, of gross domestic product (GDP). In other words, after roughly 5000 years of city civilization, it was still necessary for the (then) most advanced economy to devote *90 per cent* of its economy to immediate consumption. Only after an initial breakthrough was achieved were higher shares of income devoted to investment. Developing countries will have to do the same.

There is also the argument that developing countries have to 'catch up'. But with whom and with what? Japan 'caught up' 150 years after the UK; Sweden 50 years after the rest of Europe. Needs are always relative. The first priority is to escape from debt bondage, feed, clothe and house people. Only then can development be considered as a genuine priority.

Concluding Comments

This chapter has argued that we should approach the world as if it were a single country. This approach places at the centre the responsibilities of various institutions and individuals. It provides a new window to interpret income transfers, implementation and development. The existing inter-state system is not only not oriented towards such problems, but its very instrumentalism creates problems for implementation as well as envisioning.

The change in approach also provides a new way of apprehending both the importance and the potential of development finance. Rather than view it as a form of charity from one nation to another, the perception of the world as a single country invokes the idea of mutual commitment and responsibility. Thus, instead of focusing on how to mobilize cheap resources, it asks how to create a broad-based societal legitimacy for development finance. From this, it is a short step towards the notion of mutual responsibility and institutional transparency. This can provide the basis for a consensus over both finance and development.

Notes

1   This section was contributed by Ann Pettifor and Andrew Simms.

References

Baudrillard, J (2001) 'The Spirit of Terrorism', *Le Monde*, 2 November 2001

Bigg, T (2001) 'The Impact of Civil Society Networks on the Global Politics of Sustainable Development', draft PhD thesis, City University, London

Davis, M (2001) *Late Victorian Holocausts – El Niño Famines and the Making of the Third World*, Verso, London

Elliott, L (2001) 'An Eye-Opener for the Blindfolded', *The Guardian*, 1 October 2001

Gelinas, JB (1998) *Freedom from Debt*, Zed Books, London

Reinicke, W, Deng, F, Beener, T, Gershman, J and Whitaker, B (eds) (2000) *Critical Choices: The United Nations, Networks, and the Future of Global Governance*, International Development Research Center, Ottawa

Rosenau, JN (1992) 'Governance, Order and Change in World Politics', in JN Rosenau and EO Czempiel (eds) *Governance Without Government: Order and Change in World Politics*, Cambridge University Press, Cambridge, pp1–24

Young, O (1994) *International Governance: Protecting the Environment in a Stateless Society*, Cornell University Press, Ithaca, New York

Chapter 14

What does the Feminization of Labour mean for Sustainable Livelihoods?

Nazneen Kanji, IIED and Kalyani Menon-Sen, UNDP India

The Feminization of Labour

It is only now, a decade and a half after the global acceptance by most countries of economic liberalization and market-oriented growth as strategies of choice for development, that reports of their negative impacts are being recognized as reliable. There is now sufficient evidence that these processes, particularly in the South, have resulted in greater inequalities in income and assets between and within countries. It is difficult to arrive at general statements about the specific effects of liberalization and market orientation on women, since these are mediated by the level of development, forms of integration into the world economy and pre-existing socio-economic inequalities in a particular country. Nevertheless, and despite country-specific variations, the phenomenon of 'feminization of the labour force' is emerging as a common theme in discussions of the ways in which global economic changes and market-led growth have impacted on women.

The term 'feminization of labour' is used in two ways. Firstly, it is used to refer to the rapid and substantial increase in the proportions of women in paid work over the last two decades. At the global level, about 70 per cent in the 20–54 age group are members of the paid workforce. In developing countries as a group, the figure is lower at 60 per cent (United Nations, 1999). These figures do not capture women's participation in rural and urban informal sectors in developing countries, which is usually less visible and therefore undercounted. However, this low wage informal sector continues to be an important employer of poor women in developing and transition countries (Mehra and Gammaye, 1999). The trend in the feminization of labour has been accompanied by a shift in employment from manufacturing to services in developed countries, and from agriculture to manufacturing and services in developing countries.

With the exception of Africa, women's employment has grown substantially faster than men's since 1980. With a stagnating (or slightly decreasing) male labour force participation rate, the difference between male and female participation rates has shrunk considerably in many regions (United Nations, 1999).

The term 'feminization of labour' is also used to describe the flexibilization of labour for women and men, a fallout of the changing nature of employment where irregular conditions once thought to be the hallmark of women's 'secondary' employment have become widespread for both sexes. Informal activities, subcontracting, part-time work and home-based work have proliferated while rates of unionization have declined (Standing, 1999). In the South in particular, standard labour legislation has applied to fewer workers, because governments have either not enforced it or abolished it outright, or because existing legislation is weak and enterprises have been able to circumvent and bypass it.

The deregulation of labour markets, fragmentation of production processes, de-industrialization and emergence of new areas of export specialization have all generated an increased demand for low-paid, flexible female labour. This chapter focuses on women's participation in manufacturing and agricultural exports in the South, drawing out the specific policy implications of the feminization of labour. We will then look at the broader, common issues and their implications for sustainable livelihoods.

The Feminization of Labour: Industry

Where poor countries have achieved an expansion of non-commodity exports, there has been relative growth in female-intensive sectors of industry. The lower the income level of the economy, and/or the greater the concentration of

---

BOX 14.1 WHY ARE WOMEN DISADVANTAGED IN THE LABOUR MARKET?

- Women workers continue to be primarily responsible for reproductive and domestic work, which is perceived to be their primary function. This perception reinforces structural barriers that prevent women from accessing education, training, land and productive assets. Women's double workload also restricts their time and mobility for productive work, and limits their choices of income-earning activities.
- Women are perceived to be 'secondary' earners so that men often have priority over women in the allocation of opportunities for paid employment.
- Women do not have equal access to productive resources and services. Because they are largely dependent on self-employment for which land, capital, technology and labour are critical, lack of access constrains their productivity and reinforces the stereotype that they are inherently less productive than men.

clothing production and electronics assembly in export production, the greater the employment-creating effects of trade have been for women (Fontana et al, 1998, p47). Subcontracting and supply links between formal sector enterprises and small workshops are widespread, indicating an even higher increase in informal jobs.

In parts of the Caribbean, Central America, south and Southeast Asia, light industry export-processing zones have employed labour which is overwhelmingly young and female. There is considerable debate on the effects of pay and conditions on women's livelihoods and well-being, particularly in the longer term. Some researchers have argued that the overall effect for women is positive given the choices they face in their given contexts. They contend that earning a wage increases women's bargaining power and 'status' within their households as well as providing resources to meet household needs (eg Lim, 1990). Kabeer (2000), in her investigation of women garment workers in Bangladesh, argues that women have moved from the margins of the labour market to a more central, better paid and more visible place in the economy.

Other researchers have emphasized the poor wages and working conditions, the precariousness of the work and the fact that mainly younger women without children are given these opportunities (Elson and Pearson, 1981; Pearson, 1998).

The longer-term benefits for women are even less clear. Women may stay locked in at relatively low levels of pay and skills in the export sector, becoming increasingly discriminated against as export production is diversified and/or mechanized. To take some examples, the share of women in export-processing zones has fallen off markedly in Singapore, Mexico (Fontana et al, 1998) and the Dominican Republic (Pineda, 2000).

Advocacy efforts to reduce discrimination against women in labour markets and to improve wages and working conditions in export activities have to tread a fine line. There are definite risks in taking local action to demand compliance with labour standards and codes of conduct, since countries which are shown up as non-compliers risk penalties. If the most negative aspects are stressed, then there may be unanticipated losses for the poorest countries and advantages for countries better able to meet higher standards. In many cases, workers' organizations themselves may oppose efforts to implement strict codes.

BOX 14.2 THE PHILIPPINE GARMENT INDUSTRY

The establishment of industries in the countryside has opened employment opportunities to many educated young women and men. Employers, however, prefer young women, often because of gendered notions of docility, nimbleness and flexibility. The new jobs come at a cost. Foreign investment has been attracted by the state on several premises: tax breaks, cheap labour and protection from labour organization. While it is true that more factories in industrial estates or export-processing zones pay the legislated minimum wage than those outside, wages are kept low. Moreover, job security is non-existent and women lose their jobs when they get pregnant. On the job, women have been vulnerable to sexual advances of foreign employers who think that local women are 'easy' or need the job too much to refuse them.

Source: Jeanne Illo (2001, pp3/4).

BOX 14.3 THE SELF-EMPLOYED WOMEN'S ASSOCIATION (SEWA), AHMEDABAD, INDIA

SEWA was founded in 1971 and registered in 1972 as a trade union movement for women in the informal sector. A few thousand women subsequently established the SEWA bank as a cooperative to provide poor self-employed women with access to credit and financial services and to reduce their dependence on exploitative moneylenders.

SEWA has strategically used the collective bargaining tools which have characterized many trade union movements. However, in areas where there are few prospects for employment, traditional unionizing techniques do not work. In such situations, SEWA has worked at the grass-roots level to form village organizations. SEWA helps women to run their own organizations, form cooperatives and bargain collectively in the marketplace.

Perhaps more important than access to credit, SEWA has concentrated on empowering women to use their resources more effectively. In the villages of Gujarat and in the city markets of Ahmedabad (where SEWA has its headquarters), women are speaking out more, taking leadership roles and realizing how far they can go when they have collective bargaining power for wages, better working conditions, combating domestic violence, or improving education and family health.

Source: Adapted from SEWA homepage: www.gdrc.org/icm/sewa.html

---

The international adoption of labour standards, enforced through official machinery, will not have any impact on the informal sector, where women are predominant. Without complementary measures, the divisions between protected and unprotected workers could increase. Support needs to be given to working women's organizations which cover formal and informal sector workers, to improve their access to information on labour rights and to strengthen their ability to take collective action. SEWA, the Self-Employed Women's Association of Ahmedabad, India, is a notable example of an organization that uses such a strategy.

The Feminization of Labour: Agriculture

Trade liberalization in the South has fuelled recent agricultural policies that are geared to diversification and 'non-traditional' or high-value export goods. Some African examples include horticultural products and cut flowers in Kenya and Zimbabwe, tobacco in Mozambique and vanilla cultivation in Uganda.

In 'non-traditional' horticultural exports, low-paid seasonal female employment has had a crucial role in production in many countries in the South. When compared with industry, agriculture, particularly horticulture, requires higher levels of risk and greater flexibility if a consistent global supply network for fresh produce is to be maintained. The chain is organized in such a way that risk is offset by the more powerful players at the distribution end on to the more fragmented and heterogeneous producers operating in diverse locations to supply this fresh produce. As Barrientos (1999) argues, it is flexible seasonal

> ## Box 14.4 Women's role in horticulture: Chile and South Africa
>
> In Chile and South Africa, employment in fruit export production is contracted on a wage labour system by commercial farms (rather than plantations or smallholders which can be found elsewhere). In Chile these tends to be off-farm while in South Africa it continues to be on-farm black labour. As household subsistence has increasingly depended on market purchase, women's wages have become an important element in household survival. However, the insertion of women into paid employment has only been partial, possibly limiting change to underlying gender relations. During the season, women largely continue to take responsibility for domestic work and childcare, adding to their work burden, and are less likely than men to find out-of-season employment. Out of season, they return to a primarily reproductive role within the home.
>
> *Source:* Barrientos (1999).

employment, particularly of women, that provides these producers with a buffer against risk and allows them to minimize the cost of employment within this highly seasonal sector.

Agro-industries, such as fruit and vegetable exports, are sometimes seen by policy-makers to absorb dislocated labour from peasant agriculture and replace 'inefficient' peasant food production with cheaper imports (Razavi, 2002). However, both international factors and the competition in this sector, as well as household-level factors including the control over wages from agro-industry, will affect household food security with direct impacts on the situation of women and children.

In parts of Asia and Central America, there has been a huge expansion in aquaculture since the mid-1980s. Large tracts of land as well as mangrove forests in coastal Asia have been taken over for shrimp farms, which export to Europe and the US. The high costs of these operations for local populations and the environment are beginning to be documented (Wichterich, 2000). While poor and landless families may gain from waged labour on shrimp farms, land for local food production has been taken away, soil salinity has increased, food crop yields have declined and the availability of cheap fish for low-income consumers has declined since this is required as aquaculture feed.

In Africa, studies of women's involvement in cash crops over decades have shown that their time for food production and preparation is negatively affected. As Wichterich (2000, p72) puts it, 'The market is occupying the most fertile land, as subsistence production moves out to the margins... Less and less of agriculture serves to feed the local people themselves.' Iniquitous gender relations and women's lack of rights to land exclude them from participation in decision-making over land and natural resource use in many parts of the world. Yet, women continue to bear the major responsibility for household food security and management of natural resources. Their perspectives, although critical to planning for food security, are not reflected at the policy level.

BOX 14.5 WOMEN'S ROLE IN HOUSEHOLD FOOD SECURITY: ORISSA, INDIA

In the Indian state of Orissa, forest produce is an important component of seasonal food security for tribal communities as well as the poorest sections of non-tribal communities. Tribal women collect firewood, fruits, edible flowers and leaves, roots and shoots and, in times of scarcity, mango and tamarind seeds, which are the main sources of food and livelihood during at least four months of the year. The increasing commercial exploitation of these products has resulted in their declining availability for consumption. Deforestation and policy restrictions on free access to forests and forest produce have most affected tribal women, who were earlier able to tide their families over lean periods by living almost entirely on food collected from forests. Again, since marketing of the main commercial forest produce is monopolized by a few traders/companies, women are forced to sell their wares to these traders at unremunerative prices. In such a situation, practices such as short weighing, under-pricing and part payment are common and difficult for tribal women to challenge. The alternative is to sell their products clandestinely to middlemen and become victims of further exploitation.

The Public Distribution System for food has been unable to deal with this crisis. Fair price shops are inadequate in number and unevenly distributed and the commodities available do not match local dietary habits. First, none of the indigenous products that are regularly consumed is available in these shops. Orissa is a predominantly rice-eating area; the allocation of rice is only 13 kg per household, which is far short of the need. On the other hand, the allocation of wheat, which is consumed only in urban areas, is 20 kg per household. Consumers have to buy their quota of rations in one go, but as most poor women cannot put together the amount of money required, their entitlement is sold off to others.

Source: UNDP India (1999).

Market liberalization has tended to benefit larger farmers and widen inequalities between them and small, resource-poor farmers (Bryceson and Jamal, 1997). In many developing countries, the expansion of export-oriented agriculture has reduced land for food production, sometimes eroding women's traditional land use rights. Commercial farming tends to be chemical intensive with negative longer-term environmental consequences. The erosion of the natural resource base, reduction in the per capita availability of land and the increasing need for money to meet basic household needs, as well as new economic opportunities, have led to livelihood diversification, away from or alongside smallholder agriculture.

However, the precariousness and insecurity of many alternative livelihood sources, along with the frequently unregulated privatization and commercialization of critical natural resources such as land, water and forests, have negative implications for household food security and poverty reduction in the longer term. The implications of a decline in women's key role in rural, and even urban, agriculture to secure household food supply have not been given adequate policy attention.

Implications for Sustainable Livelihoods

The feminization of poverty

The 'feminization of poverty' is another term frequently used in discussions on the effects of changes in global economic policies on women. The concept of the 'feminization of poverty' in its initial usage was a relatively simple one: that women and female-headed households tend to be disproportionately represented among the world's poor. However, the feminization of poverty is not only a phenomenon of increasing numbers, but it can also be used to illustrate the links between the social and economic subordination of women (Menon-Sen, 2001).

The increase in women's employment does not necessarily lead to poverty reduction and increases in household welfare. In other words, the fact of women's entry into waged labour is not enough to draw conclusions about the impact on poverty, nor does it tell us about the changes in women's economic, social and political position in relation to men. These depend not only on the quantum of women's earnings, but the degree to which women control their own income and the manner in which it is spent.

It is now more widely accepted that household organization and gender relations are critical variables in livelihood systems. One aspect of this is the recognition that women's control of the income they generate is highly variable. In parts of the world, women have almost total control over their own income (for example, in parts of west Africa). In others, their income is handed over to men or to older women (parts of south Asia). The relationship between women's income and their bargaining power is complex, changing and mediated by processes outside as well as inside the household.

There is a considerable body of research that indicates that women and men have different spending priorities (Bruce, 1989; Kanji 1995, Narayan, 2000). Women tend to emphasize food and basic goods for household consumption, while men tend to prioritize items for personal use or investment, rather than household maintenance. In contexts where men hold the purse strings and do not necessarily prioritize basic household needs, this has resulted in deterioration in children's nutritional status (Evans, 1997). A multi-country study found that the resources (cash and food produce) under the mother's (rather than the father's) control constitute the most important factor in determining the nutritional status of children in low-income households (Blumberg, 1990).

Policy Concerns

The consequences of liberalization and women's increased participation in the waged labour force, in terms of gender equality and the material conditions of women's lives, have remained largely invisible to policy-makers.

An Increase in 'Women's Work'

Firstly, women's increased involvement in paid work has not significantly reduced poor women's share of unpaid work in caring for households. Women's gender-ascribed 'caring' roles, the costs of raising children, the existence of social support structures which women can depend on and mechanisms to protect vulnerable groups all affect the extent to which women can enter and participate in the labour market. Along with decreased social provisioning by the state, liberalization and privatization have shifted the costs of social reproduction from the paid to the unpaid economy, with evidence of negative consequences for women's health and well-being and for household welfare in successive generations (Elson, 1995; Kanji, 1995; Moser, 1996). When women work for meagre incomes, girls may be taken out of school to help with household work, decreasing their opportunity to acquire marketable skills and increasing their chances of being poor in the future.

A Crisis in Masculinity?

In an increasing number of contexts across the globe, men have reacted to the increased dependence on women's earnings and the resultant blurring of their gender-ascribed 'breadwinner' roles with increased levels of depression and suicide, violence and abandonment of their families. In richer countries, the declining achievement of boys at school has become a public policy concern, as has male violence, and alcohol and drug abuse. In poorer countries, there is not enough research into these problems or public resources to address them. In many contexts, there is a likelihood of a backlash in the form of demands to curtail women's entry into the workforce. The longer-term consequences of this 'crisis in masculinity' and the implications for women's situations, as well as for more healthy and equitable gender relations in the future are largely unexplored questions.

Women's Participation in Decision-Making

In many contexts, economic and political liberalization is taking place simultaneously and new opportunities are provided to previously excluded groups to participate in political and policy-making bodies. The global diffusion of information and communication technology, although uneven, has created new possibilities for networking, advocacy and lobbying for interest groups in civil society all over the world.

However, women's increased labour market participation has not necessarily made it easier to participate in public life. Even when women are formally employed, there are restrictions on workers' organizations which did not exist in the past. Perhaps just as important, increased material poverty makes it difficult for more marginalized groups to take up opportunities for participation even at a local level. Large numbers of women are still excluded from opportunities for

---

Box 14.6 'Adjusting to adjustment' in Delhi, India

A study of working class households in Delhi revealed how they were 'adjusting to adjustment'. Most of the households covered in the study were dependent on the labour market for survival, with very few assets and resources to fall back on. Working-class households were also dependent on employers and kin networks for loans.

The majority of households had reduced consumption levels to cope with price rises. These ranged from cuts in food to cuts in leisure and non-essentials. However, it is significant that more than a fifth of the households studied were already at minimum consumption levels. In most cases, households became food insecure if even one member was withdrawn from the labour market. Other adjustments included buying and cooking food in bulk and buying cheaper unprocessed food for processing at home. These adjustments led to an increase in women's workload. Other adjustments like eating less, eating fewer meals and cutting down on fruits and animal products, were compromising the health of women and children.

Families had restructured their everyday lives in order to cut down on expenditure, by reducing spending on clothes, leisure, travel and deferring big purchases. These adjustments also had implications for working women, in terms of reducing their mobility, socializing and opportunities to organize.

While there had been no formal cuts in public spending on health, women's access to health services was being limited. Medicine is no longer free in public hospitals and fewer workers are covered under the provisions of the Employees State Insurance health services.

Households had resorted to cuts in educational expenses. Many families had taken children out of school, or had moved them to government schools from private schools. Families had taken loans to meet school expenses.

Source: Chhachhi et al (1997).

---

public participation, in the face of increasing workloads as well as gender biases that exist in the structures and processes for participation.

What Action Can be Taken?

The language of gender equality and women's rights is today visible even in 'hard' sectors such as economic policy. However, if this rhetoric is to be translated into reality, current debates about economic liberalization and the restructuring of production processes have to integrate gender analyses and women's perspectives.

A critical aspect of this gendered approach would involve recognition of the role of the 'care' economy and women's roles in unpaid work at the household and community levels. Given the intensification of women's work as well as the changes in men's roles, there is a strong case for investing greater public resources in supporting women's unpaid work. Investments to enable access to affordable food (for example through public distribution systems), setting up childcare facilities and ensuring the availability of water, fuel and fodder at the local level can not only enable women to access paid work, but can have a multiplier effect in terms of enabling children, particularly girls, to go to school.

Equitable and sustainable policies require a better understanding of the links between women's household survival strategies, livelihoods and larger-scale economic, social, environmental and political processes. Policy formulation in key sectors such as agriculture, trade, health and education need to be better integrated. Household-level food security and local livelihood systems should be given priority in agricultural policy-making; resources should be directed to supporting traditional subsistence agriculture. Ensuring women's access to land, the primary productive resource for most poor women, is a critical policy requirement. Policy-makers also need to recognize that the natural resources that underpin local livelihoods cannot be sacrificed to commercial interests. Protecting the traditional rights of access of communities to common property resources is an urgent priority. As the post-WSSD action plan points out, this entails mainstreaming gender perspectives in all policies and strategies to promote full and equal access for women to productive resources, public services and institutions, in particular land, water, equal opportunities, credit, education and health (United Nations, 2002, para 6d).

Greater international commitment is necessary to promote public regulation of labour standards, adequate working conditions and support to workers' organizations. A key policy challenge is how to prevent individual countries from competing on the basis of cheap labour and lax labour standards. However, labour laws cannot be seen in isolation and the links between economic, social and environmental policy have to be better understood.

Finally, it is not enough to advocate a larger share of the market for women and equal access for women and men to the opportunities brought about by global economic liberalization and integration. The issues highlighted here indicate the need for a more transformative agenda and a more radical rethinking of current priorities. Women's organizations and NGOs in both the South and the North have been advocating and demonstrating viable alternative approaches. These initiatives need to be explored further to derive policy lessons and ensure that secure and sustainable livelihoods for less powerful groups, both women and men, who are in the majority, become a more central concern, along with the public regulation of the power and profits of the few.

References

Barrientos, SW (1999) 'Gender and Employment Relations in Global Horticulture: The Anomaly of Change in Chile and South Africa', Mimeo

Blumberg, RL (1990) 'Income under Female versus Male Control: Hypotheses from a Theory of Gender Stratification and Data from the Third World', in RL Blumberg (ed) *Gender, Family and Economy: the Triple Overlap*, Sage Publications, Thousand Oaks, California

Bruce, J (1989) 'Homes Divided', *World Development*, vol 17, no 7, pp979–991

Bryceson, DF and Jamal, V (eds) (1997) *Farewell to Farms: De-Agrarianisation and Employment in Africa*, Research Series 1997/10, African Studies Centre, Leiden

Chhachhi, A, Gandhi, N, Gothoskar, S and Shah, N (1997) 'Adjusting to Adjustment', paper presented at the National Seminar on Policies and Strategies for Women Workers in the Context of Industrial Restructuring, July, New Delhi, unpublished

Elson, D (1995) 'Male Bias in the Development Process: the Case of Structural Adjustment', in D Elson (ed) *Male Bias in the Development Process*, Manchester University Press, Manchester

Elson, D and Pearson, R (1981) 'Nimble fingers make Cheap Workers: An Analysis of Women's Employment in Third World Export Manufacturing', *Feminist Review*, vol 7, pp87–107

Evans, JE (1997) *Growth Prospects Study: Rapid Assessment of the Impact of Policy Changes on Rural Livelihoods in Malawi*, report prepared for the World Bank and financed by UNDP, World Bank, Washington, DC

Fontana, M, Joekes, S and Masika, R (1998) *Global Trade Expansion and Liberalisation: Gender Issues and Impacts*, a study prepared for DFID by BRIDGE, Institute for Development Studies, Brighton, UK

Illo, J (2001) 'Earning a Living: Globalization, Gender and Rural Livelihoods', paper presented at the Experts Group Meeting on the Situation of Rural Women in the Context of Globalization, Mongolia, June, unpublished

Kabeer, N (2000) *The Power to Choose: Bangladeshi Women and Labour Market Decisions in London and Dhaka*, Verso Press, London

Kanji, N (1995) 'Gender, Poverty and Economic Adjustment in Harare, Zimbabwe', *Environment and Urbanization*, vol 7, no 1, pp37–55

Lim, L (1990) 'Women's Work in Export Factories: The Politics of a Cause', in I Tinker (ed) *Persistent Inequalities: Women and World Development*, Oxford University Press, Oxford

Mehra, R and Gammaye, S (1999) 'Trends, Countertrends and Gaps in Women's Employment', *World Development*, vol 27, no 3, Special Section: Women Workers in a Globalizing Economy, pp533–550

Menon-Sen, K (2001) *Gender, Governance and the 'Feminisation of Poverty': the Indian Experience*, UNDP, India

Moser, C (1996) *Confronting Crisis: A Comparative Study of Household Responses to Poverty and Vulnerability in Four Poor Urban Communities*, ESD series, no 8, World Bank, New York

Narayan, D (2000) *Voices of the Poor: Can Anyone Hear Us?* Oxford University Press for the World Bank, New York

Pearson, R (1998) '"Nimble fingers" revisited: Reflections on Women and Third World Industrialisation in the Late 20th Century', in C Jackson and R Pearson (eds) *Feminist Visions of Development: Gender Analysis and Policy*, Routledge, London and New York

Pineda, M (2000) 'Presentation on Women's Participation in the Maquilas of the Dominican Republic', Institute for Development Studies, Brighton, UK, unpublished

Razavi, S (2002) 'Introduction: Gendered Pathways of Agrarian Change', in S Razavi (ed) *Shifting Burdens: Gender and Agrarian Change under Neoliberalism*, Kumarian Press, Bloomfield, CT

Standing, G (1999) 'Global Feminization through Flexible Labor: A Theme Revisited', *World Development*, vol 27, no 3, March, pp1077–1095

UNDP India (1999) 'Strengthening Natural Resource Management and Sustainable Livelihoods for Women in Tribal Orissa', Sub-Programe document under the Food Security Programme, UNDP India

United Nations (1999) *World Survey on the Role of Women in Development: Globalization, Gender and Work*, United Nations, DESA, New York

United Nations (2002) *World Summit on Sustainable Development Plan of Implementation*, UN doc. A/CONF.199/20*, 4 September 2002

Wichterich, C (2000) *The Globalized Woman: Reports from a Future of Inequality*, Zed Books, London

Environment and Human Health: Towards a Shared Agenda for Sustainable Development

Gordon McGranahan, IIED and Marianne Kjellén, SEI

Inter-sectoral collaboration is widely advocated, if rarely implemented. Sustainable development represents one of the most ambitious calls for inter-sectoral collaboration to date. This chapter focuses on an inter-sectoral relationship that could become central to the pursuit of sustainable development and deserves special attention – that between the environment and health sectors. The first section summarizes the case for a shared environment and health agenda, drawing on some simple generalizations about how economic status is currently related to environmental burdens and health impacts. The next two sections elaborate on these relationships, focusing first on the different spatial and temporal scales of environmental risks, and then on different health burdens associated with some of these risks. The final section explores some of the implications for sustainable development. From the start it must be recognized that the relationships being described are not laws of development. Indeed, a central challenge for sustainable development is to change these relationships in order to achieve a more equitable world, for both present and future generations.

The Case for More Complementary Environment and Health Agendas

Health and environmental improvement are complementary goals, both of which can legitimately claim to be central to sustainable development. However, while environment concerns – and particularly those affecting future generations – have been a defining feature of sustainable development from the start, health concerns remain implicit and often seem peripheral. This is doubly unfortunate. First, a stronger health focus in environmental debates and policy could help to ensure that the environmental needs of the poor receive the priority they deserve. Second, a stronger environmental focus in health debates and policy could help to avoid an over-emphasis on curative measures, and the neglect of the long-term health implications of environmental change.

Closer cooperation is also justified on the grounds that both health and environmental problems often arise through the combined 'side effects' of actions whose motivation has little to do with either health or the environment. Particularly for the environment, but also for health, a curative approach is insufficient at best. When people pursue their livelihoods, travel, produce or consume, the consequences of their actions for public health and the environment are rarely their primary concern. Yet these activities play a more important role in determining environment and health outcomes than medical treatment or environmental rehabilitation. Much the same applies to government sectors, where the goals of improved health and environment depend as much on the policies of ministries of transport and industry, for example, as on those of ministries of health and environment. In effect, health and environment may be sectorally defined, but require multi-sectoral strategies.

The health and environment sectors often describe almost identical goals in relation to the environmental dimension of sustainable development: addressing the threats to people's present or future well-being that result from human-induced damage to the environment. Traditionally, however, environmental health has concentrated on the more localized and immediate threats, while environmentalists have increasingly concentrated on dispersed, indirect and long-term threats.

Viewed from a sectoral perspective, this division is understandable. It reflects where each sector's expertise and institutional interests lie. Health experts have added little to our understanding of how, for example, land degradation affects food security. And the institutional base of most health professionals lies in curative rather than preventive care. Environmental experts, on the other hand, have added little to our understanding of how, for example, bad sanitation affects people's health. And the institutional base of most environmental professionals lies in preventing humans from damaging the environment rather than preventing the environment from damaging humans. Partly as a result, very different priorities often emerge from the health and environment sectors. In relation to DDT and malaria, for example, while environmentalists and health specialists may recognize the dangers of both DDT and malarial mosquitoes, health specialists tend to be far more positive about DDT as a means of combating malaria than environmentalists.

From a sustainable development perspective, this division is problematic. It can foster international environmental agendas that ignore many of the most serious, life-threatening environmental problems, implying that they are not really environmental issues. It can foster international health agendas that ignore the potential health impacts of ecological damage and global environmental change, implying that they are not really health issues.

For health to become more central to sustainable development, the health implications of ecological damage and global environmental change would have to be taken more seriously within the health sector. However, the focus of this chapter is on how a health perspective can help to situate environmental health problems on the environment and development agenda, and ensure that the environmental burdens currently contributing to the ill health of many of the world's poor are addressed more explicitly.

Poverty, Affluence and Shifting Environmental Burdens

Economic growth has long been associated with a shift towards more dispersed, delayed and indirect environmental burdens. The environmental burdens associated with poverty, particularly in low-income countries, tend to be localized: inadequate household sanitation, indoor air pollution, pressures on local resources and so on. In middle-income settings, and particularly industrializing and motorizing cities, many of the localized burdens tend to be less prevalent, while settlement-wide burdens, such as pollution of the ambient air and the waterways and regional resource depletion are often more severe. In many affluent settings, measures have successfully reduced burdens that fall in and around the settlement, but global burdens, such as carbon emissions and pressures on distant ecosystems, are high. These relationships, summarized in Figure 15.1, reflect an environmental transition that helps to explain some of the environment and health differences commonly observed between countries.

From a sustainable development perspective, all of the environmental burdens represented by the curves in Figure 15.1 must be addressed. The environmental burdens associated with poverty are not only caused (in a loose sense) by poverty, but are contributing to the persistence of poverty. Alternatively, the environmental burdens associated with affluence are not only caused by affluence, but both the burdens themselves and measures to address these burdens could close off development opportunities for poorer countries and people. The form which this transition has taken historically contributes to the fact that a far higher share of the burden of disease in low-income countries is due to environmental factors, while a far higher share of the environmental burdens originating in affluent countries is likely to fall beyond national boundaries and on future generations. More generally, the curves illustrate the tendency for the environmental burdens of poverty to fall on the poor themselves, while the environmental burdens of affluence fall on a far more spatially and temporally dispersed 'public'. In effect, the environmental burdens reinforce existing economic inequalities.

Economic Status and the Environmental Contribution to the Present Burden of Disease

Table 15.1 compares the burden of disease in 'developing' and 'developed' countries. The metric is disability adjusted life years (DALYs) lost as a result of

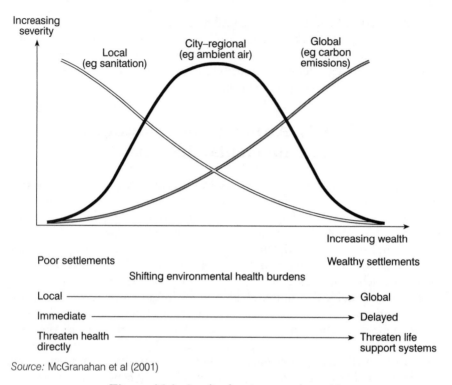

Source: McGranahan et al (2001)

Figure 15.1 *A stylized environmental transition*

the cited health problems – a measure developed in the 1990s as part of a major effort to improve the coherence and consistency of international health statistics. (More recent estimates of DALYs than those presented in this chapter are now available in the World Health Organization's *World Health Report 2002* (WHO, 2002), which focuses on reducing health risks.) The overall message: not only is the burden of disease higher in low-income countries but infectious diseases are far more important. In 1990, the top two disease burdens in the world, acute respiratory infections and diarrhoeal diseases, were infectious diseases that do not even appear in the top ten burdens of disease in 'developed' regions.

Figure 15.2 summarizes the results of a recent attempt to estimate the share of different disease groups that can be ascribed to the physical environment (as opposed to, for example, lifestyle choices or the social environment). It indicates that a large part of the environmental share in the burden of disease relates to diarrhoeal diseases, acute respiratory infections and malaria, all of which are far more prevalent in low-income settings.

Like many environmental problems, the environmental health problems that arise in poor and unserved neighbourhoods and settlements are often closely interconnected and pose public health risks, at least at the local level. Bad sanitation may lead to contaminated groundwater and faeces finding their way into solid waste, on to open land, into drainage ditches and generally into

Table 15.1 *Burden of disease, by cause and region (1990)*

World			Developing Regions			Developed Regions		
Disease or Injury	DALYs (000s)	% of total	Disease or Injury	DALYs (000s)	% of total	Disease or Injury	DALYs (000s)	% of total
Lower respiratory infections	112,898	8.2	Lower respiratory infections	110,506	9.1	Heart disease (ischaemic)	15,950	9.9
Diarrhoeal diseases	99,633	7.2	Diarrhoeal diseases	99,168	8.1	Unipolar major depression	9780	6.1
Perinatal conditions	92,313	6.7	Perinatal conditions	89,193	7.3	Cerebro-vascular disease (stroke)	9425	5.9
Unipolar major depression	50,810	3.7	Unipolar major depression	41,031	3.4	Road traffic accidents	7064	4.4
Heart disease (ischaemic)	46,699	3.4	Tuberculosis	37,930	3.1	Alcohol use	6446	4.0
Cerebro-vascular disease (stroke)	38,523	2.8	Measles	36,498	3.0	Osteoarthritis	4681	2.9
Tuberculosis	38,426	2.8	Malaria	31,749	2.5	Lung cancers, etc	4587	2.9
Measles	36,520	2.7	Heart disease (ischaemic)	30,749	2.5	Dementia, etc	3816	2.4
Road traffic accidents	34,317	2.5	Congenital anomalies	29,441	2.4	Self-inflicted injuries	3768	2.3
Congenital anomalies	32,921	2.4	Cerebro-vascular disease (stroke)	29,099	2.4	Congenital anomalies	3480	2.2
Malaria	31,706	2.3	Road traffic accidents	27,253	2.2	Chronic obstructive lung disease	3365	2.1

Source: Murray and Lopez (1996), Table 5.2
Note: DALYs = disability adjusted life years, a measure of the number of 'healthy years' that are lost due to premature death, disability and disease.

contact with people. Flies may breed in human and other waste, and contaminate food. Solid waste may find its way into drains, causing accumulations of water in which mosquitoes breed. Microbial food contamination makes thorough cooking important, but cooking with smoky fuels may expose women and children to hazardous pollutants. Mosquitoes may spread diseases such as malaria, while the mosquito coils and pesticides used to combat them may add

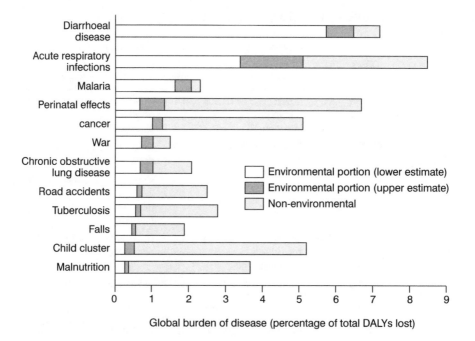

Global burden of disease (percentage of total DALYs lost)

Source: Kjellén (2001) after Smith et al (1999, Figure 3)

Figure 15.2 *Physical environmental contribution to the global burden of disease,*
by selected disease groups

to the air pollution and chemical hazards. Crowding and poor housing can exacerbate most of these problems.

The extent to which these environmental problems become a risk to health depends upon social, economic and cultural factors. For example, lead in dust becomes a major risk when children play in the dirt and ingest lead-rich soil. Infants are particularly prone to smoke exposure if they are carried on their mother's back. Faeces in solid waste become a particular problem if the waste is left in piles for collection, and people pick through it. Alternatively, appropriate behavioural changes are also context-dependent. More careful supervision of children, for example, may reduce their exposure to environmental hazards, but result in an income loss with even greater consequences for health. At the local level, environmental risks are so bound up with social and economic conditions that it can be difficult and even counterproductive to address them in isolation.

Poverty is also related to ill health through non-environmental routes. It can lead to malnutrition, increasing susceptibility to both environmental and non-environmental health risks. Violence is often an important health risk, particularly for the poor. Social exclusion can contribute to mental health problems. The spread of HIV/AIDS is closely related to poverty. And of course health care is typically more restricted and of lower quality in conditions of poverty.

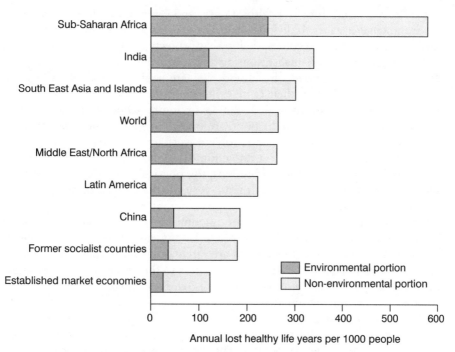

Source: Smith et al (1999, Figure 4), cited in Kjellén (2001)

Figure 15.3 *The environmental portion of the global burden of disease*

However, while those living in poverty also suffer more from non-environmental health problems, the share of the burden of disease arising from (physical) environmental hazards is greater in low-income settings. Thus, in the regional estimates provided in Figure 15.3, the environmental portion of the burden of disease is estimated to be highest in sub-Saharan Africa and lowest in established market economies.

Implications for Sustainable Development

This schematic presentation of environment and health, while ignoring a number of important environment and health issues, illustrates a central challenge for addressing the environmental dimensions of sustainable development. If sustainable development is about meeting the needs of the present generation without compromising the abilities of future generations to meet their needs, and if the environment is to be one of the basic pillars of sustainable development, then the approach to environmental issues must consider the needs of the present generation as well as those of future generations. This means taking the environmental health issues of the poor seriously.

One could argue that these are not really environmental issues. After all, income poverty alone is enough to ensure that poor groups suffer more than the affluent from the ill health, injury and premature death caused by environmental hazards. Individuals and households without adequate incomes are less able to afford accommodation that protects them from environmental risks: for example, good quality housing and adequate provision of piped water. In their struggle to secure a livelihood, they are liable to undertake work that exposes them (and often their families) to environmental hazards. They have the least resources to cope with illness or injury when they occur. Their governments are also likely to be poorly resourced to address these deprivations.

The local environmental health problems suffered by so many of the world's poor are not, however, simply a reflection of economic poverty. In common with larger-scale environmental burdens, the physical attributes of most local environmental burdens make them very difficult to address through conventional market mechanisms or government regulations. In economic terms, they involve a range of environmental externalities, public goods (or 'bads') and common property problems. In any case, formal regulations to address local environmental burdens are rarely designed to meet the needs of the poor. Many cannot even secure legal access to their homes, and work in the informal sector. Under these conditions it is hardly surprising that there is little formal support for the initiatives of poor groups to improve their living and working environments. Yet their capacity to pursue environmental improvements is not only influenced by local politics and governance, but also by national and even global politics. The international politics of privatization, for example, has helped to create a situation where urban water regimes often emerge from negotiations involving national governments, international agencies and multinational companies, with little or no representation from urban poor groups (who, it must be acknowledged, typically have very little influence over public utilities either). Neither environmental nor health perspectives can ensure that the needs of the poor receive the attention that they deserve, but they could at least contribute to a more balanced and equitable approach.

In theory, health could help to provide a unifying framework within which the range of different environmental burdens could be interpreted, assessed and acted upon. After all, local environmental hazards (such as poor sanitation) and global threats to life support systems (such as climate change) may be difficult to compare in physical terms, but both eventually threaten human health. Given the current state of knowledge about environmental risks and health, it is barely possible to estimate the DALYs associated with localized, short-term environmental hazards, let alone assign values to more indirect, dispersed and long-term risks (such as those associated with global deforestation, loss of biodiversity or carbon emissions). Alternatively, in a more qualitative assessment of the risks of different environmental burdens, a health perspective can complement residents' own perspectives on the one hand, and perspectives claiming to represent a broader public interest on the other.

Overall, a combined agenda encompassing health and environmental issues stands a far greater chance of ensuring that local initiatives for sustainable development enter the mainstream of local politics and policies. Increasingly, efforts to raise local awareness of global environmental issues in high-income countries are emphasizing the health consequences of, for example, global climate change. The health consequences of environmental problems are a more immediate concern in most low-income countries. Moreover, a health perspective could help to raise global awareness of local environmental issues in low-income countries.

References

Kjellén, M (2001) *Health and Environment*, Swedish International Development Cooperation Agency, Stockholm

McGranahan, G, Jacobi, P, Songsore, J, Surjadi, C and Kjellén, M (2001) *The Citizens at Risk: From Urban Sanitation to Sustainable Cities,* Earthscan, London

Murray CJL and Lopez, AD (eds) (1996) *The Global Burden of Disease*, Harvard School of Public Health, World Bank, World Health Organization, Washington, DC

Smith, R K, Corvalan, C F and Kjellström, T (1999) 'How Much Global Ill Health is Attributable to Environmental Factors?', *Epidemiology*, vol 10, no 5, pp573–584

WHO (2002) *World Health Report 2002*, World Health Organization, Geneva

Chapter 16

The Links between Migration, Globalization and Sustainable Development

Cecilia Tacoli, IIED

Increased migration is one of the most visible and significant aspects of globalization: growing numbers of people move within countries and across borders to look for better employment opportunities and better lifestyles. Although migration is usually seen as problematic, it contributes to sustainable development. For households in poor areas, remittances improve security and, with the support of appropriate policies, can contribute to local economic growth. In industrial countries with ageing populations, migrant workers are an increasingly important part of the labour force and support national welfare systems. National and international policies need to reflect the contribution of migration to sustainable development, and to explicitly protect the rights of migrants that are all too often ignored in attempts to curb their movement.

Migration, both cross-border and within a single country, is not usually seen as desirable. Migrants moving from rural settlements to urban centres are held responsible for the unmanageable growth of megacities in countries in the South, and many governments attempt to slow down or reverse migration from the countryside. International migrants are often thought to increase unemployment in industrialized countries by undercutting local wages, and to benefit from welfare systems to which they seldom contribute.

Despite increasingly stringent immigration controls and the difficulties of making a living in the cities of the South, people continue to move. In part, this is because they have always moved; migration has long been a strategy for reducing risk by diversifying income sources, and in many countries it is not unusual for family and kin to maintain strong affective and economic links sometimes across extreme distances. People also move in a variety of directions: between different rural areas, from towns to countryside, from one town to another. This chapter addresses only rural to urban and international migration, since these are the movements which, more than others, have attracted the attention of policy-makers.

International migration is difficult to quantify because of the often large number of undocumented migrants, and estimates of internal migration are even more problematic. However, the consensus is that movement has increased and intensified in the last two decades, and that 'new' groups of migrants are emerging, such as young, single women who move independently rather than for marriage and under the authority of older relatives and men (Bilsborrow, 1998).

Policies designed to curb international migration usually only make migrants' lives more difficult while benefiting illegal smugglers and employers who hire undocumented migrants to avoid complying with existing pay and working regulations. Policies which attempt to restrict internal migration, by making it difficult for migrants to gain access to urban housing and basic services, are also usually unsuccessful. More often than not, policy-makers simply ignore the fact that mobility is an important part of people's lives. This can have a negative impact on low-income households: for example, housing subsidies in South Africa can only be used in one location, either rural or urban, despite the fact that many households can be defined as multi-spatial, with some members living in urban centres and others in rural settlements (Smit, 1998). In Botswana, relief or aid measures for livestock owners are only designed for rural dwellers, but one-third of households in low-income neighbourhoods own cattle in their rural home areas as a safety net against uncertain livelihood prospects in the city (Kruger, 1998).

In the past two decades, there has been an unprecedented increase in the liberalization of the movement of capital, goods and services, but the same cannot be said of the movement of labour and people. While international migrants in the 19th and early 20th centuries were seen as a resource for both sending and receiving countries, nowadays they are more likely to be seen as a problem that calls for restrictive control policies, especially by the governments of rich receiving states (Sorensen et al, 2002). And while the most extreme form of control over internal movement, South Africa's apartheid regime, has been dismantled, a number of countries, including China and Vietnam, still attempt to control the movement of their citizens while, at the same time, opening up their economies (Dang, 2001). As migration is reduced to a question of international and internal policing and control, its role in contributing to sustainable development is widely overlooked. This is despite the increasingly fundamental role of remittances in the economies of low-income countries and in the livelihoods of many households in the South.

Three aspects of migration are especially important: first, the factors relating to global changes in production and trade, which influence migration; second, the wide variety of migration forms, including their composition (such as gender and age of migrants, and whether they move as family groups or individually), their direction and the intended duration (seasonal, temporary – short to medium term – or permanent); and third, the contribution of migrants to their home areas and to their host communities. A better understanding of these can lead to more effective policies for sustainable development.

International Migration and Globalization

It is estimated that, in 2000, between 150 and 185 million people lived outside their country of birth or citizenship, a figure roughly double that of the mid-1960s (IOM, 2000). Of these, between 80 and 97 million were migrant workers and their families (ILO, 2001) and between 12.1 and 14.5 million were refugees (UNHCR, 2001). In relative terms, migrants form around 2.5 per cent of the world population, a figure not much different from that for much of the last century. Perhaps what differentiates current migrants from most migrants in the 19th and early 20th centuries are the strong links that often remain between those who move and their relatives in home areas.

The annual amount sent by migrants to their home areas is a good indication of the strength of these links: in 2000, worldwide international remittances were estimated to exceed US$100 billion (including those sent through formal channels such as banks and those sent though informal channels), of which at least 60 per cent was thought to go to low-income countries. By comparison, the volume of international development assistance in the mid-1990s was only US$50 billion, net of debt repayment (Sorensen et al, 2002).

The global reorganization of labour markets has an important impact on migration. In high-income nations, demand is high for semi-skilled and unskilled workers, such as cleaners and housemaids, and for seasonal agricultural workers. The 'underground economy' or informal sector is the largest employer of undocumented international migrants. Much of it consists of small-scale enterprises in the textile/clothing and building/civil engineering industries, which act as subcontractors for larger firms which, increasingly, rely on outsourcing rather than on directly hiring employees. Outsourcing reflects the need for more flexibility and adjustment to irregular production patterns in certain industries. However, outsourcing firms are not usually responsible for the recruitment practices of their subcontractors, who tend to recruit undocumented migrants to minimize costs, especially those relating to welfare and taxation (Garson, 2000).

Undocumented migrants do not create informal labour markets in high-income countries, and illegal immigration benefits employers more than migrants. Moreover, migrants typically contribute more in taxation and tend to claim less in welfare benefits than non-migrants, and there is no evidence that migrant labour negatively affects wage and unemployment levels (Tapinos, 2000). But the perceived threat to local populations in host countries has fuelled discrimination and fear, and the introduction of increasingly restrictive policies which, rather than stemming migration, end up benefiting illegal smugglers and employers who seek to avoid taxation and labour regulations.

Another potential problem of restrictive immigration policies is that they tend to ignore seasonal labour requirements, which may also vary between different national sub-regions. This is often the case for agricultural work, which in many cases attracts temporary migrants from neighbouring nations who only stay for a few months and who invest their wages in their primary activity at home. Immigration policies tend to be highly centralized, as they are implemented primarily by law and order agencies, which makes it difficult to respond to seasonal and geographically limited labour requirements. In some European countries, local governments are demanding to play a more central role in managing the flows of migrants to fit labour requirements.

Rather than increasing restrictions, what is necessary is an increase in the flexibility of labour markets while maintaining and strengthening workers' rights and improving working conditions. This is a far more complex challenge, but one which has to be faced. Especially in Western Europe, immigration can contribute to moderating the negative impact of an ageing population, as the decline in fertility rates will result in a much lower ratio of people in employment to pensioners. Documented migrants, whose employers pay full non-wage contributions, are an asset in supporting pension and health systems, and policy-makers need to take this into account.

Internal Migration and Globalization

Other important aspects of globalization are the relocation of manufacturing to countries where labour is cheaper, and the increase in the number of international tourist resorts in low-income countries. In many cases, workers are migrants from the rural areas, often women. Globalization therefore has an impact on internal migration as well as on international movement. Moreover, it has a clear impact on who moves and who stays – and the number of young women in low-income nations migrating independently is unprecedented.

Although wages and working conditions in these sectors are often below international standards, they are nevertheless attractive to migrants. One major reason for this is the dearth of formal sector employment in non-agricultural sectors in many low-income countries, making the rare opportunities interesting enough that people are prepared to migrate.

The second reason is the increasing need for cash incomes in the rural areas, as user fees are now prevalent for most basic services, such as health and education. At the same time, economic reform has hardly benefited small farmers, whose incomes are often not sufficient to cover anything but the bare necessities, and sometimes not even those. Reliance on remittances from a migrant family member has increased in many low-income nations during the last decade, even as employment insecurity and the escalating costs of living in the cities have effectively reduced the amounts that migrants are able to send. In the recent past, young adult migrants were usually able to return to the family farm during the agricultural season, but the growing distance of destinations and the requirements of employers make these flexible arrangements increasingly difficult, and add to the constraints on family farming (Bah et al, 2003).

The third reason behind the increase in migration is often overlooked. Economic motives are by far the most important reason for voluntary movement (that is, excluding movement caused by conflict and environmental disasters), but other motives should not be underestimated. Improved access to information and exposure to different ways of living, even in remote settlements, combined with the emergence of previously unknown employment opportunities, cheaper transport costs and increasingly extensive migrant networks, mean that for many young men and women migration is seen primarily as a way of experiencing the wider world. Sometimes, this attitude is deeply entrenched in whole communities: in southeast Nigeria, young men who do not migrate are considered 'lazy', and are often derided by their communities for not being able to accumulate wealth.

At the same time, these same young men complain that the constant demand for free labour to undertake community works makes it impossible for them to 'make money'. Migration has the benefit of being a socially acceptable way of gaining independence – both personal and financial – from parents and community elders; even the migration of young, unmarried women is now considered acceptable in traditional communities, as long as they contribute to their household's income through remittances. This reflects significant social and cultural transformations that policy-makers cannot ignore.

The Contribution of Migrants to their Home Areas

Migrants' contributions to their families and communities of origin are significant. As noted earlier, the estimated global amount of remittances is higher than that of official aid flows, and transfers from internal migrants are likely to be equally important. For low-income households, remittances are often the only way to make ends meet. This is the case in many sub-Saharan nations, where credit recovery problems and parastatal institutions' mismanagement have severely restricted small-scale farmers' access to formal credit. However, most low-income households use migrant relatives' remittances for consumption purposes or to pay for health and education expenditures, leaving little for investment in farming. It is mainly better-off households which can invest to improve agricultural productivity, as well as in non-farm activities and housing.

But in many cases, migrants' remittances are not directed exclusively to their households, and recognition and support from central and local government can greatly increase the positive impact of these flows of money. For example, migrants to the US from the Mexican state of Zacatecas have created hometown clubs to collect contributions for projects in their home villages and towns. Under a 3:1 programme, Mexican federal and state governments provide three dollars for each dollar contributed by the US clubs for the development of hometowns. The programme helped a farming village of 2500 inhabitants to implement a US$1.2 million drinking water and drainage project with US$300,000 in club contributions (*Migration News*, 2002). In Swaziland, where agricultural labour shortages are related to high levels of male migration to South Africa's mines, remittances have enabled women to hire tractors. This has compensated for the lack of male labour, and has resulted in an increase in agricultural production and in the number of family fields under cultivation. The critical role of local government was the initial provision of second-hand tractors and a capital disbursement which would have been unaffordable for individual households

(Simelane, 1995). But such cases, where remittances are considered an important resource deserving support, are still rare and, in most instances, the potential role of remittances in promoting sustainable development is ignored by policy-makers. With decentralization processes under way in many nations, local governments will be best placed to identify needs and priorities and, provided they have sufficient capacity and access to resources, they can play a key role in linking up with migrant associations and other civil society actors.

But migrants are able to send widely varying amounts. Unskilled migrants tend to earn significantly less than those who are skilled or just literate. Education is thus an important element of successful migration. Moreover, young migrants, and especially young women, are subject to social pressure to look after their relatives. However, in many traditional societies, women have limited access to assets: where women have equal access to land and are entitled to inherit it, they are more likely to invest in their home area (Bah et al, 2003). Migrants may also contribute new skills and open up new areas of employment, for example non-farm jobs in rural settlements, if and when they return. But whether they do so depends on whether sufficient infrastructure exists in their home areas.

Conclusion

Migration has always been an important part of how individuals and households organize their livelihoods, and it is likely to increase because of the combination of emerging new opportunities and constraints on traditional livelihoods and social and cultural values. Policy-makers should recognize this state of affairs, and appreciate the potential and actual contribution of migrants to sustainable development and poverty reduction in host and home areas. Policies should therefore concentrate not on issues of control but, rather, on ensuring that migration is a choice and not the only available option. This means reducing the constraints which force people to migrate, ensuring that migrants' rights are respected in host areas, and recognizing and supporting migrants' contributions and their rights in home areas.

References

Bah, M, Cissé, Diyamett, B, Diallo, G, Lerise, F, Okali, D, Okpara, E, Olawoye, J and Tacoli, C (2003) 'Changing Rural–Urban Linkages in Mali, Nigeria and Tanzania', *Environment and Urbanization*, vol 15, no 1, pp13–23

Bilsborrow, R (ed) (1998) *Migration, Urbanization and Development: New Directions and Issues*, UNFPA and Kluwer Academic Publishers, New York and Norwell, MA

Dang, NA (2001) *Migration in Vietnam: Theoretical Approaches and Evidence from a Survey*, Transport Communication Publishing House, Hanoi

Garson, JP (2000) 'Where do Illegal Migrants Work?' *OECD Observer*, 24 February 2000

ILO (2001) 'The Asylum–Migration Nexus: Refugee Protection and Migration Perspectives from the ILO', paper presented at the UNHCR Global Consultations on International Protection, Geneva, June 2001, unpublished

IOM (2000) *World Migration Report 2000*, International Organization for Migration, Geneva

Kruger, F (1998) 'Taking Advantage of Rural Assets as a Coping Strategy for the Urban Poor', *Environment and Urbanization*, vol 10, no 1, pp119–134

Migration News (2002) 'Mexico: Hometown Clubs', vol 9, no 8, August, http://migration.ucdavis.edu/mn/more.php?id=2681_0_2_0

Simelane, SH (1995) 'Labour Migration and Rural Transformation in Post-Colonial Swaziland', *Journal of Contemporary African Studies*, vol 13, no 2, pp207–226

Smit, W (1998) 'The Rural Linkages of Urban Households in Durban', *Environment and Urbanization*, vol 10, no 1, pp77–88

Sorensen, NN, van Hear, N and Engberg-Pedersen, P (2002) *The Migration–Development Nexus Evidence and Policy Options – A State of the Art Overview*, Copenhagen

Tapinos, G (2000) 'Illegal Immigrants and the Labour Market', *OECD Observer*, 24 February 2000

UNHCR (2001) *The State of the World's Refugees: Fifty Years of Humanitarian Action*, Oxford University Press, Oxford

USCR (US Committee for Refugees) (2001) *World Refugee Survey 2001*, USCR, Washington, DC

Chapter 17

Research Partnerships for Sustainable Development

Steve Bass, IIED

Sustainable development (SD) is a continuing process, with the potential to lead to wealth creation and the eradication of poverty. It will take very different forms, depending upon local livelihoods, sectoral contexts, existing institutions and resources. Universal analyses and standard solutions for SD will rarely be applicable. Therefore SD needs to be information- and knowledge-intensive.

Local knowledge and research capacities – and their engagement with policy-makers, producers and consumers on a continuing basis – are central requirements for SD. But they are often neglected or weak, and are poorly coordinated. More emphasis is needed on partnerships between researchers, policy-makers, advocacy groups, businesses and community organizations. Such partnerships are especially needed to generate a movement of 'bottom-up' research that engages and rewards the disadvantaged and their own knowledge systems. They are also needed between countries, to address the failings and opportunities for SD presented by inter-governmental processes.

The Challenge to Integrate Research into SD Policy Processes

Research is an important and integral component of the SD process, but has been comparatively neglected. SD is a process of transition that proceeds through innovation, leadership and learning. Research can offer orderly mechanisms for achieving this. Effective research mechanisms are both embedded within policy processes and deeply rooted in understanding of local conditions, so that they are needs-driven and can deal with changing circumstances. This requires considerable investment and strong, acknowledged mandates. Yet research capacities are often weak, or are neglected by other stakeholders. This may be one reason why there has been less progress since Rio than we would have liked.

Although improved means for 'participation' in SD decision-making have been emphasized recently, research has been comparatively marginalized. There is not always a clear understanding among the government, private sector and civil society 'pillars' of SD about the role of research in multi-stakeholder efforts to achieve the transition to SD. Consequently research may have neither a central role nor a continuing one. It is common that research institutions are increasingly marginalized during the process of developing any new SD initiative. If research does remain part of the initiative, this marginalization can result in impossible research demands, where the scope of research plans becomes too narrow, too broad, too politicized or too responsive to policy-makers' 'fashions' rather than local needs.

Research institutions themselves may neglect their role in SD – of offering means for the SD partners to make informed decisions – and end up dictating solutions, often influenced by the demands of their funders. Research institutions and networks need help in becoming more 'bottom-up' and 'needs-driven'. All of this requires the building of research partnerships that enable stakeholders to identify and develop their own solutions.

Research efforts should place a priority on engaging with more stakeholders than the powerful patrons of research – especially the disadvantaged and those who can help wealth creation. There is a complex system of drivers of research on environmental conservation, poverty eradication and SD. This comprises policy-makers, advocacy groups and researchers – as well as the general public, who create a climate of concern about specific issues. All are as much in need of good research as 'decision-makers'. However, the more powerful research drivers (eg development banks and government agencies) can be very selective about research subjects, specific researchers and ways of conducting research. This can constrain the capacity of researchers to utilize and generate SD knowledge. Furthermore, such powerful groups are creating a trend for SD knowledge production to become globalized, with a worrying emphasis on standard analyses, standard solutions and the marginalization of local and indigenous knowledge and research capacity.

Poverty concerns are key, yet they often enter the research and policy processes too indirectly (eg through donor requirements) rather than through information and ideas from poor groups themselves. More engaged and equitable forms of research and communication are emerging from the many, albeit isolated, local cases of action research. Their legitimacy, effectiveness and efficiency need to be assessed and promoted among research drivers.

Economic growth concerns are equally key, and research needs to engage those who invest in, and develop, the key economic sectors that offer most potential for livelihood improvements.

There are many opportunities for researchers to build partnerships through multi-stakeholder policy initiatives. For example, national sustainable development strategies (NSDSs) offer an opportunity to involve researchers in the whole cycle of policy debate: from setting objectives, to experimentation, capacity development and investment, mainstreaming, review and implementation.

Current policy initiatives for SD will be far more successful if they integrate research tasks. Greater efforts are required to ensure that research is integral to initiatives that advance Agenda 21 and the outcomes of the World Summit on Sustainable Development (WSSD). Two existing mechanisms are especially in need of improved research:

SD strategies at national level, notably PRSPs, NSDSs and conventional action plans

There is an 'epidemic' of strategies for poverty alleviation and environmental conservation, most of them with strong external drivers. But SD is a declared objective for all of them, and a potential theme to integrate them. Poverty reduction strategy papers (PRSPs) are central to many World Bank and bilateral support programmes in heavily indebted poor countries (HIPC), yet some PRSPs have not so much unleashed local knowledge and enriched local policy processes for SD as imposed conditionalities and values, recycled old data and left assumptions unchallenged. More generally, there has been reluctance to cover the necessary transaction costs of participatory approaches to determining SD issues and solutions.

Most SD strategies declare that they will harness policy-makers and concerned stakeholders in a country-driven, continuing process of learning. This will work best if the right research institutions and local sources of knowledge are already in place and are mobilized by the strategy, or if the strategies themselves can be used to build them. Then a strategy will be in a position to proceed on the basis of the best existing research material, synthesizing it and developing research programmes to fill the key information/innovation gaps. Stronger emphasis could also be given to methodologies such as scenario development, which can bring researchers and stakeholders with disparate views together to develop common visions and approaches to issues such as 'food futures'.

Improving the effectiveness of MEAs

Multilateral environmental agreements (MEAs) offer a means for SD, but their effectiveness relies on abilities to understand their local implications, to negotiate them, to implement them and to monitor their impacts. These are lacking. SD criteria are needed to guide coherence both within and between MEAs, and with other developmental frameworks such as NSDSs/PRSPs at the national level and the World Trade Organization (WTO) at the international level. Again, these are lacking. All of this calls for engagement between research and policy-makers, for:

- developing SD criteria applicable to MEA processes and outcomes;
- applying SD criteria in impact assessments of the effectiveness of MEAs, individually and together;
- analysing the failures of the inter-governmental and national systems which compromise MEAs;

- assessing local capacities for implementing MEAs in ways which would bring about SD; and
- feeding the above into agenda setting for negotiations (gaps, overlaps and needs for [re]negotiation).

These linked policy and research tasks need to be discussed, mandated and planned at the Conferences of the Parties (COP). Research partnerships spanning North and South (that accept that not all Northern and Southern positions can be identical) would be ideal for making progress. They would also help with other initiatives to improve global governance. For example – and more ambitiously – we need to work out how the development of the United Nations can be both serviced and challenged by research for SD. There is a growing need to put an effective policy imperative and associated research network in place for this.

Research needs to be engaged more fully in developing key post-WSSD initiatives

Local knowledge and research capacities need to be employed at an early stage in the following:

- The UN Secretary-General has identified water, energy, health, agriculture and biodiversity as of critical importance (WEHAB). In each of these areas, it is essential to have a clearer understanding of what is needed – and what works – at local, national and global levels to increase security in the provision of these goods and services.
- One of the principal outcomes of the WSSD process is the agreement of 'Type 2' partnerships to further implementation of internationally agreed priorities. Their effectiveness will depend to a large extent on information and analysis being available to enable innovation and learning.
- The New Partnership for Africa's Development (NEPAD) promotes SD as a shared set of guiding principles for African countries. The NEPAD Commission on Science and Technology has prioritized the translation of these goals into a programme of action which draws on African research and expertise.

Key institutions and methodologies need to be in place to enable all stakeholders to contribute to, and benefit from, research for SD. Knowledge utilization and development is a flexible process, to which anyone should be able to contribute. In addition to the above, three issues stand out:

Issues of ownership of SD research/knowledge

These issues will need to be resolved, to improve the incentive to contribute knowledge to SD initiatives. For example, development banks and consultancy firms frequently use the knowledge generated by research institutions and local communities without returning anything directly to these sources of knowledge.

Communication is an inseparable part of research

Both research and communications communities can and should work together better, to improve services to other stakeholders. Key principles include the following:

- Minimize the information overloads which all stakeholders are facing, through better research peer review and coordination of communications.
- Ensure policy-relevance, producing options that enable the policy process to take place, but avoiding policy prescriptions.
- Ensure research communications are relevant to the context, are simple enough but not simplistic.
- Build communications back-up and follow-up in research processes: the 'report right at the end' often helps neither the researcher nor the recipient in achieving good knowledge sharing.
- Ensure attention to stakeholder empowerment in the process of 'disseminating a message'; it is not merely a question of choosing the right medium.
- Consolidate research/communications programmes as far as possible – with a few, clear strategic objectives – to achieve more impact than many 'scattergun' activities.

Open, transparent and participatory research partnerships are needed to prioritize SD issues and relate them to policy-making processes

Partnerships between researchers can enhance economies of scale, offering means to complement capacities for research, participation and communications, to share intellectual resources and information, and to attain a higher policy profile. But there are costs, too, and there is a clear need to establish the rationale in each case. It would be valuable to compare the utility of different models of research partnerships, especially those that have been designed to link closely with policy (notably various MEA models, including the Intergovernmental Panel on Climate Change and the Subsidiary Body on Scientific, Technical and Technological Advice to parties to the Convention on Biological Diversity), as well as those with a less direct link to policy (such as the World Conservation Union, IUCN; the Consultative Group on International Agricultural Research; and the Regional and International Networking Group, Ring).

All successful research partnerships are built on trust. This trust building takes time, and users of research should examine how such partnerships have evolved, or whether they are merely opportunistic. Research organizations that have proved to be of value to policy-makers and campaigners need to be identified and supported.

It is clear that SD also requires partnerships beyond just research institutions. Partnerships are also required with policy-makers, advocacy groups, businesses, non-governmental organizations and community-based organizations. With such stakeholders, the research community, while seeking means to improve demand-led SD research, cannot be purely passive and responsive. Research coalitions are needed for bottom-up research that engages and empowers the disadvantaged and draws upon and enhances their own knowledge systems. They are also needed between Northern and Southern countries to address the failings and opportunities for SD that are presented by inter-governmental structures. The research community needs to be prepared to react to inappropriate demands by clearly advocating better approaches. It needs to be fearless in disseminating insights into options for governance, policy and technology, but it must also recognize that it cannot dictate political and business decisions.

In short, the research community, with its stakeholders, needs to rethink both its objectives and its '4Rs' – its rights, responsibilities, rewards and relationships – so that it is increasingly fit to play its role in the transition to SD.

Part 4

Poverty Reduction and Natural Resource Management

Chapter 18

Poverty and Environment

*Damian Killeen, Poverty Alliance (Scotland) and
Shaheen Rafi Khan, SDPI*

Despite the linkage of poverty and environmental concerns at the level of
macro policy and locally, there is no consensus that the interests of the poor
and of the environment are mutually compatible. Ambivalence about this
relationship exists among those whose prime concern is environmental as well
as among those most concerned with poverty eradication. Without international
agreement on what should constitute the maximum and minimum levels of
sustainable living standards, it is difficult to see how this ambivalence can be
resolved.

The environment is the source of what every one of us needs to survive:
air, water and food. It is also the source of the materials we require to take our
lives from pure survival to subsistence and beyond: shelter, clothing, tools and
the infrastructure of collective human settlement. The absence or denial of
these basic necessities constitutes absolute poverty. Unequal access to basic
necessities and other environmental resources is the foundation of relative
poverty. In addition to being excluded from access to basic resources, the poor
are also most likely to be subjected to the degrading or polluting impacts of the
consumption patterns of others. In industrial and post-industrial societies this
may take the form of exposure to higher levels of toxicity in the air, water and
earth. Where local sustainable patterns of agriculture are diverted to
monoculture for the global market, the breaking of traditional fertility cycles is
associated with negative changes in social structures and economic relationships.
All of these are directly associated with worsening health profiles and earlier
morbidity among the poorer populations.

While the linkage between the social, economic, environmental and political
dimensions of sustainable development is clearly acknowledged in Agenda 21
and the need for poverty eradication is recognized, this is only rarely carried
forward into integrated development programmes. The European Commission,
for example, while promoting the production of national action plans for

combating social exclusion and poverty and also promoting a European approach to sustainable development, does not seek for these to be integrated in any meaningful way. Global efforts through the United Nations to reduce or cancel the indebtedness of 'developing' countries and to increase levels of aid are a significant contribution towards addressing current imbalances but do not address the root causes of these imbalances. These questions have been most positively addressed across the world through the Local Agenda 21 process but with a questionable impact on the major political and economic barriers to sustainable development.

Barriers also exist between those most concerned with these issues. Environmentalists are concerned that meeting the demands of poorer people for improved standards of living will contribute to increases in the unsustainable consumption that they are seeking to reverse. Poverty activists, both North and South, are concerned that universally applied demands for reduced energy consumption will serve only to further exclude the poor from the benefits that the wealthy have already achieved. Yet there are also many examples of good practice across the world – such as the promotion of localized food economies and improved domestic energy efficiency – that are simultaneously addressing poverty reduction and environmental degradation. There are lessons to be learnt and adapted for adoption and replication elsewhere, and a general need to monitor and evaluate how multilateral agreements and institutions relate to these initiatives.

Is Poverty to Blame for Environmental Degradation?

When people living in poverty are asked to identify their priorities, care for the environment or the need for sustainable development are rarely at the top of their lists. Housing, feeding and clothing the family, education for their children and care in their old age are much more significant concerns. Both production (or employment) and consumption patterns are determined more by these basic needs than by any consideration of their longer-term impact. The poorest people are sometimes seen as complicit with those forms of economic activity in which the environmental costs of production are displaced on to the public purse or into the future.

This ignores the extent to which people living in poverty are able to exercise choice in their productive or purchasing behaviour and the degree to which this is determined by more powerful players in the local and global markets. Where employment is at a premium any work is an advantage whatever the potential risks it poses to the planet (or to oneself); where a family has to be fed, the most filling food and the cheapest protein will be preferred whatever its means of production; where geographical isolation or a lack of transport infrastructure is an issue, people will use vehicles which are energy inefficient to access employment and low prices.

This is not to suggest that people living in poverty are content with these choices or that they are unaware of the differences between their own lifestyles and those of others who are more advantaged. While it is sometimes suggested that poorer people behave the way they do because they lack education or have lost basic skills, the evidence often shows that this is not the case. A major part of the experience of Local Agenda 21 and of more specific anti-poverty initiatives has been that the poorest people can be the most willing to explore and adopt new ideas and ways of organization and work. This is particularly the case if, by taking the risks of innovation, they are not at the same time disenfranchised from the means of meeting their basic needs. It is an irony of the sustainable development process that energy efficiency programmes or collective, self-help initiatives, such as food cooperatives (box schemes) and credit unions, which were initially developed in response to the needs of poorer communities, are increasingly being adopted by the more advantaged to enhance their own lifestyles.

Removing the Barriers

Poorer people are attracted to more environmentally sustainable activities when they see that adopting them will enable them to improve their standards of living through the use of their own, self-directed, labour and through improved cooperation with other members of their community. For many who have to make efficient use of whatever resources come to hand on a daily basis and who understand only too well the damage caused by money lenders, the idea of not mortgaging the future for today's consumption seems no more than common sense.

But there are real barriers to making this common sense a reality. By definition, poorer people lack capital in the form of land or investments and are excluded from many financial services; patterns of settlement, travel to work and the changing demographics of family and social life can make collective endeavour more difficult; systems of welfare and taxation, through the operation of 'poverty traps', can penalize initiative and undermine prospects for longer-term success. Each of these barriers is capable of being addressed. However, to do so requires significant changes to be made in the current distribution of resources and power, including gender relations in households and in the wider economy. The challenge to the promoters of sustainable development is whether or not they are prepared to take on board the vested interests that sustain the inequitable and unsustainable status quo.

Globalization and Poverty

It is a commonplace of much of the debate about sustainable development that these vested interests are now 'globalized' in a way that transcends the authority of individuals, local communities, national governments or international treaties. The concentration of global trading powers in the hands of a relatively small group of around 500 companies is associated with increasing poverty and inequalities in both the developed and developing worlds, as well as with major environmental degradations and the threatened exhaustion of irreplaceable natural resources. For some, the acquisition of power by ever-smaller numbers of these companies has replaced the conventional history of relationships between nation states as the dominant narrative of humankind's increasingly destructive presence on Planet Earth. The frustration of protestors at Seattle and Genoa is an expression of the powerlessness felt by many to reverse this process of the increasing concentration of economic and political power in the hands of the few.

However, there is nothing new or non-historical about globalization. Ever since merchants realized that personal and then political empires could be developed through the acquisition and exploitation of the natural resources and labour of 'foreign' peoples we have seen the lifestyle costs of the more powerful transferred to those less able to exercise individual and national choice. It is only the scale that has changed. It has also long been the case that economic power and political power have colluded nationally and internationally for mutual benefit to the exclusion of indigenous populations and of the poor. National governments are active partners in transferring powers from themselves to globalized companies through processes of regulation, deregulation, investment and subsidy; their hope in doing this is to achieve competitive advantage in the global market and to attract the benefits of economic growth. For many centuries these benefits have accrued to Northern and Western countries to the disadvantage of those in the East and in the South.

Free market capitalism is credited with being the dominant means of achieving economic growth worldwide, except that its successes do not always derive from market freedoms and those who contribute to creating success do not always equitably share the rewards it generates. While the free movement of investment capital across the world is actively encouraged, a corresponding free movement of labour is disparaged and legislated against as 'economic migration'. While the economies of developing countries are increasingly opened up to imports from developed countries, such as alcohol, tobacco, soft drinks and fast foods, those same countries are prevented from exporting their own produce through the 'competition' policies of the World Trade Organization.

Unable to develop their own economies without external investment, poorer countries find that this investment is tied to requirements to 'liberalize' with the consequence that traditional patterns of trade, exchange and barter are undermined. Debt repayment levels mean that US$1 loaned to a developing country will require that country to generate US$9 before the debt burden can be met. Unequal access to the information technology that is driving much of this economic development contributes significantly to the lack of a level playing field. The consequence of this 'unfree' global market capitalism is that the rewards increasingly go to the money managers and those, such as politicians, who ease their way, rather than to those who create wealth through their own labour and use of the resources that are natural to where they live. The resistance to the Jubilee 2000 international debt cancellation campaign by wealthy countries, despite the successes that the campaign has achieved, bears eloquent witness to the priorities of the major economies and the power that they feel entitled to exercise over those who are less advantaged.

Global capitalism, in its recent incarnation, is an expression of the view that market mechanisms underpin and supersede all moral and ethical considerations and that markets are, in some 'invisible' way, self-correcting to the benefit of everyone. The role of governments, therefore, should not, theoretically at least, include interference in the operations of the market. This view has not been borne out by the evidence of the increasing disparities between countries and the widening income inequalities that have developed between the rich and the poor in the developed world. The rising tide of economic growth has not lifted all boats and the trickle down from the successful entrepreneurs towards the less able has not occurred. This has become increasingly recognized by, among others, the International Monetary Fund and the World Bank together with the forgotten observation of Adam Smith that a free market requires a 'social foundation' of rules, incentives and values if it is to succeed. What these rules, incentives and values should be for the 21st century and beyond is crucial to the debate about sustainable development.

Globalization is not, of itself, a negative phenomenon if it enhances our potential to act on a global scale to eradicate poverty and hunger and to share and care for the resources of nature more equitably and sustainably. But, if globalization is to be a force for good, its 'social foundation' needs to be secured. While this is an issue for world summits and major international conventions, the social framework for global developments is also a matter for local communities, regions and nations. A measure of the negative impact of global capitalism to date is the extent to which the discussion of such issues has become devalued and, along with it, respect for and participation in political activity. The idea that the economic role of governments is, primarily, to provide the context in which markets can operate freely has become so engrained that the mark of good government now is to offer low taxation and low public spending whatever the distribution of wealth and the clearly apparent levels of need. This constitutes an abdication of leadership by politicians who are aware of the weaknesses and dangers of unfettered market capitalism in the long term but who are too closely associated with its current beneficiaries in the short term to confront the problems created by their behaviour. The challenge of leadership will be for politicians to articulate a global code of conduct for sustainable development, together with the measures for policing those situations when it is flouted.

Poverty and Environment in Pakistan: The National Dimension

The vicious spiral of poverty and degradation, referred to as the poverty–environment nexus, is rooted in the absence of sustainable human development (SHD). Simply, SHD means development which is efficient, equitable and sustainable in terms of resource use, resource access and resource resilience. 'Resources', used in the generic sense, refer to capital, human and environmental resources. In Pakistan, for example, low financial allocations for conservation and non-consultative and extractive management practices have led to increasing environmental degradation and pollution.

A cyclical, downward spiral defines the relationship between poverty and environmental degradation. In the first place, poverty increases the vulnerability of the poor to degradation. Second, by restricting choices and entitlements for the poor, it turns them into potential predators of natural resources. However, the converse of this is that limited choices also create an impetus for nurturing resources and using them in a sustainable manner. A credible construct, which contextualizes the poverty–degradation relationship is probably a blend of the two. In other words, poverty does not necessarily induce degradation but if it does this reflects unavoidable responses rather than deliberate acts.

SHD also has management implications. The advantages of responding to environmental problems through cooperation, rather than confrontation, are apparent. Cooperation converts a zero, indeed, negative sum game into a win–win situation, where all can share the benefits of resource conservation and reduced pollution. In terms of organizational responses, environmental management has a preventive, integrative and inter-generational aspect. It requires behavioural and organizational changes. Its professional ethos is 'husbandship': more respectful cultivation and protection of plants, animals and the land. It calls for partnerships between governments, non-governmental organizations (NGOs), the private sector and communities.

The term management is used here in its eclectic sense, embracing the entire range of laws, rules and regulations, as well as organization culture. The case of forestry below illustrates how stakeholder confrontations can give rise to adverse environmental and political consequences. Communities become environmental predators and, in extreme cases, outright conflicts can ensue.

Forestry management: The source of predation and conflict

The primary forests in the Northern Areas and the North West Frontier Province (NWFP) have many important economic uses and are a source of livelihoods for communities. In addition, many ecological and environmental benefits and imperatives are associated with them. The data shows a rapid decline in both coverage and the quality of forest stands. Such deforestation has led to a spate of onsite and downstream ravages, such as biodiversity loss, erosion, flooding and dam sedimentation.

The root cause of deforestation and degradation lies in forest management practices, which have focused more on economic than on environmental utility. Such practices also deny community subsistence needs. Colonial governments originally weakened community rights to the use of forest resources. Usufruct rights continued but were heavily proscribed. Further, community management traditions, already fragile, have eroded with new opportunities for employment and out-migration. Also, demographic and development pressures have forced communities out of their ancestral lands into marginal areas, where competition for resources is severe, resulting in further violations of indigenous property rights.

The management system has been unable to cope with these changes. The conflicting interests of commercial loggers, private developers, government and military agencies, hunters and impoverished communities have placed it under relentless strain. The forest department tends to choose the path of least resistance, coming down with a heavy hand on the disempowered communities and colluding for personal gain and profit with vested interests. Officials have become increasingly vulnerable to outside economic inducements, as opportunities for financial and professional betterment become hostage to fiscal insolvency. The situation contains the seeds of conflict, with communities forced to act as predators, rather than as guardians of the commons.

While there is little doubt that under the presently hostile management and tenure regimes, communities are showing a propensity to raid forest resources, their activities pale in comparison with the activities of the so-called 'timber mafia': commercial loggers willing to undertake illegal logging, driven by rising timber prices. The timber trade also demonstrates a distinct anti-community bias; while communities are entitled to a substantial share of revenues (royalties) from the logging in guzara (community) forests, active collusion between the mafia and the forest department results in appropriation of the bulk of these royalties. This has given rise to conflict situations in the remote Northern Areas and parts of the NWFP.

Dir-Kohistan in the Northern Areas is one such example. After independence its rich forests were declared state property and the communities were promised a 15 per cent royalty in the income from the forests. Commercial logging began on a large scale. Initially, this was done through contractors, who cut more trees than the legal limit, did not share the proceeds and went so far as to disallow communities their traditional subsistence rights. Discord began as early as the 1970s, erupting into outright violence when authorities resorted to force and shot dead a number of community leaders. This led to the abolition of the contractor system, which was replaced by the Forest Development Corporation (FDC). The community share of the royalties was increased to 60 per cent. This was an enormous windfall, provided the communities were given their due share. However, very little of this windfall filtered down to them.

Growing resentment against the government, the FDC and the contractors finally came to a head in the early 1990s. Village youths banded together to form the 'Kalkot Youth Welfare Society (KYWS)'. They set up a manned checkpoint to stop all movement of timber outside the valley, and both the written and spoken rhetoric became confrontational. The government attempted to diffuse the situation initially. It set up an Inquiry Committee in 1997 to investigate the community's grievances. The findings of the committee vindicated the community's stance and advised redress but the district administration failed to act upon its recommendations. Encouraged by its moral victory, the KYWS took its resistance to a new level. A smuggler was shot dead at the checkpoint by the community guards, new checkpoints were set up and the society organized peaceful marches and sit-ins, first locally in Shringal, Dir and Timergarah and eventually in the provincial capital, Peshawar. However, no resolution of the problem is in sight. The provincial and district governments have adopted a hostile stance, accusing the communities of taking the law in their own hands. An uneasy stalemate prevails at present, with a real risk that the situation will escalate into large-scale conflict.

Environmental Justice in the UK: The National Dimension[1]

One country can impose environmental injustices upon another by taking more environmental resources than they are proportionately entitled to and leaving other countries to get by on very little. Developing countries also suffer from the appropriation of environmental resources by richer countries. The UK is one of the richest 20 per cent of countries that use 80 per cent of global environmental resources.

These injustices are also evident within the UK. Even in rich countries, there are major environmental problems which have profound impacts on people. These impacts are borne disproportionately; the available evidence strongly suggests that poor people suffer from the worst environmental conditions (see Box 18.1).

Policies as well as impacts can be deeply unjust. Substantive injustices are caused, in part, by the way policies are developed. For example, waste disposal policies are not designed to hurt poorer communities, but can do so through the decision-making process if wealthier groups can affect decisions more easily and avoid any risk of harm. In 1998, residents of Greengairs, a relatively poor community of Scotland, found that a local landfill operator was accepting toxic waste from Hertfordshire in England, a much richer area. Dumping of this waste is illegal in England, but regulations are less strict in Scotland. Community campaigning brought an end to the dumping and also secured other environmental and safety improvements, but inadequate enforcement of regulations, derisory fines and poor identification of pollution levels are still major problems.

An analysis of current UK performance shows that a lot remains to be done. The UK has major environmental injustices; poorer people in the UK suffer worse environmental impacts and have less access to basic resources than their richer counterparts. Environmental injustice is a component of poverty and inequality in the UK. The UK is also imposing major environmental injustices on other countries and future generations.

The extent of environmental justice in the UK effectively demolishes the argument that the poor have less reason to care about the environment, because poorer people live in the worst environments and their quality of life is reduced as a direct result.

Our conception of environmental justice therefore brings together the need for global and inter-generational equity in resource consumption and ecological health with a priority to act with those who are the victims of that inequality in the present. No less than a decent environment for all, no more than our fair share of the Earth's resources (Scandrett et al, 2000).

BOX 18.1 EXAMPLES OF ENVIRONMENTAL INJUSTICE IN THE UK

Pollution

Factories emitting toxic pollutants are located with disproportionate frequency in poor communities. Research that compares the government's data on factories that pollute the environment with the income data for particular areas shows that:

- There are 662 factories in the UK in areas with an average household income of less than £15,000, and only five in postcode areas where the average household income is £30,000 or more.
- The more factories there are in an area, the lower the average income. In Teesside, one area has 17 large factories. The average income in the area is £6200, 64 per cent less than the national average.
- In London, more than 90 per cent of polluting factories are in areas with below average income, and in the northeast the figure is over 80 per cent.

Transport

A recent government inquiry into inequalities in health noted that 'The burden of air pollution tends to fall on people experiencing disadvantage, who do not enjoy the benefits of the private motorized transport which causes pollution' (Acheson et al, 1998). As with pollution, road accidents affect the poorest people worst. Children in social class 5 are five times more likely to be killed in road accidents than children in social class 1.

World Summit

The World Summit on Sustainable Development sought to promote an integrated approach to the social, economic and environmental dimensions of sustainable development. What is the relevance of this event to people suffering poverty and environmental degradation across the world? Since the Rio Summit in 1992 there has been much debate about how the values and principles expressed at this and subsequent summits should be realized; but the extent of environmental degradation and the gap between the poorest and the wealthiest have continued to increase. Is there a political will to confront the many conflicts of interest that undermine progress towards justice and equity?

One test of this willingness might be an effort by national governments to agree a range of practical policy mechanisms that would be supported globally and that would enable the poorest and the weakest to see that the world community is upholding their interests. This might be a prime focus for future sessions of the UN Commission on Sustainable Development and the newly created Regional Implementation Forums which will address action for sustainable development at UN regional levels.

At an Expert Meeting on the Social Dimension of Sustainable Development held in Sweden in 1998 (Ministry of Social Affairs and Health Finland, 1998) the participants identified some core values and principles and a framework for a 'global social policy system' that, together, could form the basis for a global agenda that produces real benefits. They proposed that:

- global responsibility is a necessity;
- poverty, inequality and exclusion are violations of human rights;
- respect for human diversity is a cornerstone of social development;
- social responsibility is everybody's responsibility;
- children first – distant future generations later.

They identified the goals of development as:

1   Enabling environments that include, for example:
    - economic opportunities including the enhancement of opportunities for women and people with disabilities;
    - focus on employment generation;
    - good governance, including development of democratic institutions; and
    - accessible and healthy built environments.
2   Improved human security, including access to basic social security and basic social services for all.
3   An inclusive society for all people.
4   Eradication of human poverty.
5   An 'inclusive world for all nations' through the strengthening of regional and global management arrangements.

Finally the experts proposed an outline 'global social policy' agenda which could enable these goals to become possible.

- active, new, human-security policy including the prevention of economic, social and ecological disturbances in addition to the present peacekeeping focus of the military dimension;
- a continuous forum for global social-sector policy dialogue which would keep social, economic and ecological issues on the same agenda;
- a universal human and social rights enforcement system with accessible (regional) institutional arrangements;
- management of global environmental issues;
- management of international trade and financial transactions;
- management of social and labour standards;
- management of global 'taxation' and redistribution of incomes;
- debt management and debt relief systems;
- development support (capacity building);
- last resort safety nets and humanitarian aid;
- civil society involvement arrangements;
- a mechanism to manage the inclusion of agreed-upon principles and measures into national legislation and their follow-up.

The specific measures proposed in this agenda are controversial but they are a constructive attempt to bring social, economic and environmental/ecological considerations together in a way that our global institutions seek. Across the world, local, regional and national governments are setting themselves targets that are consistent with this agenda but their efforts are undermined by the more damaging aspects of free trade and by a development culture based on continuous growth and international competition. The search for advantage between individuals, social groups and nations is at the root of poverty and pollution. As the human race begins to extend its ecological footprint to other areas of the solar system, will we spread waste, conflict and injustice or will our impact be a benign expression of the sustainable development that we are committed to achieving?

In the 11 years since Rio there has been an increasing appreciation that the implementation of Agenda 21 has focused on the delivery of 'environmental' outcomes to the relative exclusion of social development objectives. This was recognized by the UN at the Johannesburg Summit by the funding of a Global People's Forum attended by many thousands of grass-roots activists from around the world, including many representatives of civil society organizations from South Africa. Within the political summit, concern was also expressed that failures to fully appreciate the impact of sustainable development policies on the poorest peoples had contributed to a political disenchantment with global political processes and that greater inclusion of these peoples will be essential to long-term success.

Much of the concern expressed by community groups challenged the commitment of central and local governments and what were described as 'elite' NGOs to the empowerment of communities. These organizations were criticized for offering only 'instrumental' forms of participation that would involve communities in predetermined plans and programmes. Communities are not offered full participation in the analysis of needs and the design of responses to them. Participation is also perceived as a 'grass-roots' concern and not one that relates to wider political and social culture. The consequence of this approach for many people represented at the Global Forum was that the social dimension of sustainable development is treated only as an unwelcome and often avoidable cost of achieving other objectives. This approach to empowerment and participation was perceived by many at the Global Forum as undermining those aspects of sustainable development that require a wider sharing of power and the building of greater social solidarity.

The social dimension of sustainable development was the theme of a major workshop at the Johannesburg Summit hosted by the UK's Department for International Development (DFID). This workshop and the material that supported it (Department for International Development, 2002) sought to restructure the conventional 'three-legged' approach to the social, economic and environmental dimensions of sustainable development in a way that is more reflective of the implications of change on all aspects of the behaviour of people in society and which provides a basis for more sustainable social development. DFID's approach identifies four dimensions to development:

- **biophysical** ('natural' and manufactured goods and processes, human biology);
- **institutional** (formal and informal, social, political, educational and financial);
- **technical** (knowledge, tools, skills and practice);
- **ethical** (philosophical and attitudinal influences on policy and behaviour).

Within this framework and against a background of a commitment to human rights including economic, social and cultural rights, DFID proposes that socially sustainable development must attend to issues of social justice, solidarity, participation and security. Considered from this perspective, poverty and poverty eradication, with their links to human health and well-being, politics and power, empowerment and capacity building and the ethics of equity, become central concerns for sustainable development. A sustainable environment for the comfortable cannot be acquired at the expense of the further degradation of the poorest in the world.

Notes

1   This section draws on material from Seymour (2000).

References

Acheson, D (chairman) (1998) *Independent Inquiry into Inequalities in Health Report*, The Stationery Office, London
Department for International Development (2002) *Negotiating Social Sustainability*, DFID, London, September 2002
Ministry of Social Affairs and Health, Finland (1998) *Putting People at the Centre of Sustainable Development*, Ministry of Social Affairs and Health, Finland
Scandrett, E, McBride, G and Dunion K (2000) *The Campaign for Environmental Justice in Scotland*, Friends of the Earth Scotland, Edinburgh
Seymour, J (ed) (2000) *Poverty in Plenty: A Human Development Report for the UK*, Earthscan, London

Forest Policy and Practice since the UN Conference on Environment and Development

Steve Bass, James Mayers and Sonja Vermeulen, IIED

Forests in Sustainable Development: A Quick Report Card since Rio

Initiatives that treat forestry as a 'sector' seem to be increasingly prone to failure. Forests are resources that other sectors use, in many different and often competing ways, to produce both public and private goods and services. The results of this use can vary widely in their contribution to sustainable development, from forest asset liquidation (land clearance for agriculture and infrastructure), to direct productive uses (plantation and natural forest management), to protective uses (wildlife conservation and water supply).

The actual uses of the forest have tended to reflect the economic and political powers of particular forest stakeholders, and their support from government agencies and policies. They have also tended to reflect beliefs, policies and political intentions that express how society wants to organize itself, divide its wealth, consume the products of wealth and embark on what it believes are the best paths for development. Thus forests are also symbols of people's relations with nature. Today, there is often no clear or shared vision of this. Typically, unchanged forest policies reflect the desires of previous (possibly colonial) governments and clash with the values of more impetuous stakeholders.

Clashes tend not to be about forests as such, or about the various goods and services. Rather, they tend to be about what comes in between: *forest management*. It is the forest management regime that defines the boundary between the public functions of forests (notably environmental services) and private benefits (notably timber). This is why forest management is so contentious and why managers are often viewed with suspicion. There have been attempts in the 1990s to define sustainable forestry. However, many 'top-down' policy interventions (and especially the international initiatives that emerged before and after the 1992 Rio Earth Summit) have been discredited; it is now clear that, by and large, local specificities disallow global solutions.

If the forest problem is one of entrenched policy and institutional inequities which many recent well-meaning initiatives have not really been able to tackle, where can we point to real progress since Rio? What pressures are building up that need to be dealt with? And what ideas are emerging for the future?

Ten years and five (tentative) transitions

Sustainable development is a journey. We have not arrived. But we can look back to Rio and see how we have been doing:

Routine expectations of multi-stakeholder involvement

We have progressed beyond an earlier assumption (or faith) that leadership by (inter-)governmental bodies would bring about sustainability. The experiences of collaborative forest management, 'parks for people', and the increasing albeit faltering participation through the Inter-governmental Panel/Forum on Forests, etc, are establishing the expectation of multi-stakeholder involvement as a norm. 'Prior informed consent', a novelty in 1992, is becoming routine. We acknowledge that initiatives can and should be *with* people rather than *for* people, although we are struggling with the mechanics, costs and politics of 'full' participation.

Evolution of pragmatic national systems for continuous improvement

We no longer rely on neat, supply-driven, international precepts that are manifest in master plans/dreams such as the Tropical Forest Action Plan (TFAP), or the idea of a global forests convention. Instead, in the last decade, many countries have assembled a number of elements of good forest sector governance: legally recognized permanent forest estate with designated use categories for multiple goods and services; updated management plans; more fora for multi-stakeholder debate (such as the national certification working groups); and partnerships (including an extraordinary growth in company–community partnerships). The new understanding of national forest programmes (NFPs) is much more about systems of continuous improvement for understanding and coping with change, than of 'master' plans which grow ever more out of date – and, indeed, that NFPs can be quite eclectic and 'messy'.

Growing consensus on sustainable forest management (SFM)

We have progressed from routine confusion and argument among stakeholders (leading to imposed, stalled and parallel initiatives) to a somewhat clearer and more widely shared vision. The decade has seen the emergence of a range of initiatives to define principles, criteria and indicators (PC&I) of SFM which have both allowed a lingua franca to evolve and resulted in a 'distillation' of knowledge which can be interpreted in local policy and plans while remaining globally recognizable. We have also see the emergence of SFM fora internationally, building on the unique role of the International Tropical Timber Organization in the 1980s. The Forest Stewardship Council is a great example, being structured around sustainable development principles.

The emergence of consumer discrimination between production processes

Ten years ago, most consumers literally did not know what they were buying. Such 'wood-origin-blindness' certainly contributed to rampant asset stripping. Where government action had failed, consumer action is achieving results. It is now possible to know where a piece of wood or paper has been grown, and even how it has been grown. Certification has developed rapidly as a consumer-led approach to judicious buying (more properly this was retailer-led as the branding possibilities are good). While this has had the immediate effect of benefiting existing good producers rather than stopping asset stripping or helping weak but willing producers, it is all helping to increase transparency.

A significant environmental clean-up

We have progressed from environmental damage as a routine part of forest management (deforestation, waste, erosion and pollution), to routine environmental management at least in some big companies. In one decade, many companies moved from defensive attitudes, to promoting vanity projects and 'greenwash', to genuine business objectives for sustainability (spurred on by some market forces, cost savings, emerging legislation, and aided by tools such as environmental management systems (EMS) which were rapidly taken up). By 1995, the International Institute for Environment and Development (IIED) was able to reveal figures showing how a majority of international companies now adopt most of the environmental practices studied. For such companies, most environmental problems are largely a thing of the past (although their 'first-mover advantage' is partly also in defining 'good' environmental practice in ways that suit them). The challenge is now integrating social externalities.

If some of these areas of progress are still more evident in forest stakeholders' thoughts and words than in the forest, and if there is still a confusing 'policy inflation' resulting from piecemeal approaches to sustainability, we can at least recognize some strong trends. Yet most forests, particularly in the tropics, are in worse shape than in 1992. So also are many forest-dependent poor people, hundreds of whom are murdered every year trying to protect their forests. And crime pervades the tropical timber trade, a significant proportion of which is from illegal sources.

Five big trends that won't go away

Five trends accelerated in the 1990s, but were not really handled at Rio or by its immediate successors:

Globalizing economic power

The majority of traded forest products derive from fewer and fewer countries and companies. Almost half the annual wood harvest is processed by the top 50 forest products companies. Most products also derive from simpler forests that have 'weeded out' diversity through the technologies and scale economies of larger corporations. Corporate mergers and buyouts are on the increase. With all this comes increasing (foreign) consumer/retailer powers to set the local standards for forest management. This includes environmental and social standards, operating through today's discriminating markets. The question is whether, in the drive to ensure 'nice' globalization, we are making the mistake of assuming that 'nice' corporations alone can meet all livelihood and forest needs.

Globalizing advocacy and knowledge production for SFM

Inter-governmental discussions in the 1990s highlighted the need for shared obligations and called for action on 'all forests' and not just tropical forests. Whereas groups such as the World Wide Fund for Nature (WWF) and the World Bank used to fight their own corner, they are now forming powerful alliances; indeed, there is a World Bank/WWF alliance with bold targets for both production and protection of forests. Such influential players and their values and targets can easily come to dominate research and policy agendas and the definition of 'correct' knowledge. As with other forms of globalization, some groups will be marginalized. The question is whether such developments can help and not threaten local voices and knowledge systems.

Privatizing forest land, resources, management and services

It is significant that every one of the 23 countries recently studied by IIED showed this trend and none was nationalizing. Hence the growing concern for the public benefits of forests. The dilemma is whether this privatization is 'giving away' government or improving its effectiveness and efficiency. At present, there are still many a priori objections among forest stakeholders to market-based solutions: how much is this due to ignorance or mistrust of the new policies and institutions required to control the market?

Localizing decision-making and resource control

It is remarkable how many countries are in the midst of decentralization processes, some in order to 'downsize' governments, but others (as in parts of the Sahel) in response to new understanding of the potential of making local people effective forest managers. In addition, there is increasing advocacy for rights-based development, and the expectation is now of a balance between 'top-down' and 'bottom-up'. The question is: how much can localized control achieve in the face of entrenched inequities and the other trends above?

No stable financial basis for SFM

Not so much a trend as an enduring constraint to turning SFM dreams into realities, markets for SFM are immature, price discovery for sustainable 'commodities' is difficult, and in any case externalities are rarely included in prices. The financial basis for actual cases of SFM ranges from no profit to windfalls. Meanwhile, the terms of trade for primary products appear to decline and big business investment leads to boom–bust price cycles. Whereas many call for 'new and additional finance' for SFM from outside the forestry system, recognizing its public benefits, we might ask what we really know about finance flows within the forestry system, and where might the leverage points for SFM be?

Five challenges for the future

Think and act 'extra-sectoral'

Ghettoized forestry solutions to forest problems often fail because they deal with only the proximate cause of the problem, and not the underlying cause which may be extra-sectoral (and often international) policy, such as for trade, finance and land use. Forestry is an open system, not a closed one, and needs to be treated as such.

There is a huge need to engage with international processes in the World Trade Organization (WTO), and with follow-up to the UN Financing for Development (FfD), as well as to support those national and local processes that are set up for cross-sectoral integration of environmental and social concerns (national strategies for sustainable development and Local Agenda 21) and not to do so only through the World Bank, as so often at present. A poverty focus can help both to address these structural issues and to keep forestry's profile high.

Consider 'governance PC&I' to complement 'SFM PC&I'

The main bridge to be built between the neat SFM words and thoughts of the 1990s, and real-world action, must surely be one of improved forest governance stakeholders jointly forming the SFM 'meta-institution'. It is increasingly clear that there are limits to continued (inter-)governmental action without local involvement.

At *global* level, we must review the UN bodies involved in forestry, rationalize them and improve their accountability. At *national* level, NFPs have promise for integrating all the 'magic bullets' such as certification and forest fora into a system for continuous improvement. Since the 'magic bullets' have tended to make the good forest players better, and left the bad alone, a focus on stopping illegal activities may be desirable. But the principal need is to improve *local* governance for forest goods and services which itself is often the best tactic to forge demand for SFM and for integration 'at the top'.

Ensure markets for environmental services really work

Markets for environmental services (MES) will become increasingly sophisticated; the political and commercial drivers are ensuring this. The challenge must be to ensure they work not just for those with the scarcest commodity (currently information and contacts, which favours the 'brokers'), but also for forest-dependent people, and especially the poor.

The various environmental conventions require better coherence to do this, so that, for example, the Kyoto Protocol is better informed about forest biodiversity and does not just favour large tracts of plantations. There is also a need to clarify rights to the commodities, reduce the transaction costs for poorer groups, and find ways of achieving accountability.

Responsible forest business from a Southern perspective

The past decade has accumulated codes of practice and standards for 'good forestry' that are inevitably based on what big, well-resourced Northern companies practice. Good practice by small groups, in their own environments, has been much less visible.

There is now a need to focus on small/medium enterprises and especially their role in creating jobs. Opening IIED's 30th Anniversary Conference, Ashok Khosla noted the huge challenge for India in creating 15 million new jobs each year. Given that small-scale forestry plays complex roles in people's livelihood systems, and in environmental services, there is a need to encourage local visions and standards for forestry (that will also tackle the 'social standards' dilemma still being faced by bigger companies). The retailer incentives that dominated success in 'greening business' in the 1990s may need to be complemented by different forms of incentives, for example access to land and resources such as (micro-)finance, and insurance. There is also a need for a strong information drive, so that other countries understand what is right for Southern conditions. Model (partnership) forests may be a useful vehicle.

Information on how forest assets are really being used

The 1990s saw a sea change towards 'people-first' approaches to forestry. But these have often outstripped capacities for avoiding the risk that we are merely democratizing forest degradation. Although there is awareness of a multitude of stakeholders, goods and services in the SFM equation, we are still usually in the dark about who uses what forests and how well they are managed. A business that managed its assets (and stakeholder relations) in that way would be in trouble. True, we are collecting more and more data. Indeed, a forest manager can hardly get started without being required to do so today. But we are not really making good use of this data, especially in making decisions on social and environmental aspects. Such information will become increasingly important in a world of considerable uncertainty in economic, climatic and social systems.

It is surely time to broaden national assessment capacities and to make active use of them in policy and planning. This will require better links between existing sources of information (for example, all that detailed information from certified forests currently does nothing to build up a good national picture) and encouraging participatory monitoring to keep track of the values that really matter locally. Simple indicators of SFM progress and publicity for that progress will enable a more sure-footed approach along the path to SFM in the next decade. Resilience will elude us without it.

Finally, although we have made some useful transitions towards SFM, there is still a long way to go within the forestry profession. Some would say there is still a crisis among foresters. The above challenges need to be addressed as much through the education of foresters and those who use forests as through policy change and field programmes.

Power from the Trees: How Good Forest Governance Can Help to Reduce Poverty

Forestry is not a magic bullet for poverty eradication, any more than any other sector is on its own. But good forestry does offer some high-potential routes out of rural poverty. Forestry can contribute to food security, provide resource safety nets and sometimes enterprise opportunities where little else exists. Forests have also proved to be fertile ground for pioneering good local governance.

What is needed is for national and international governance frameworks to take a lead from local initiative and convert laudable intentions into some practical action. It is time to remove the barriers that prevent forests and trees from contributing to the livelihoods of poor people and to support emerging opportunities for sustainable local forestry enterprises.

Changing environment, new world order, same old poverty

While trade, technology, information systems and many human aspirations and concerns become more global, the world's forests are declining. Global climate changes are expected to have further drastic impacts on forests. Yet demands on forests and trees are increasing – roughly 1.6 billion people are estimated to rely on forest resources for at least part of their livelihoods. With economic inequity increasing, this reliance becomes more significant and poor people need safeguards more than ever.

Emerging opportunities for pro-poor forestry

The world's rapid pace of change means increased challenges for poor people, but can also provide new opportunities for improved livelihoods based on sustainable use of natural resources. Forest resources can usually only provide contributions, rather than whole livelihoods (Wunder, 2001). But they can also complement and strengthen other key components of livelihoods and poverty reduction: for example, through their use in food production, education and primary health care. Furthermore, if key actions are taken, many more poor

---

BOX 19.1 WHO RELIES ON TREES AND FORESTS?

60 million indigenous people living in the rainforests of Latin America, Southeast Asia and west Africa depend heavily on forests.

350 million people living in, or next to, dense forests rely on them for subsistence or income.

1.2 billion people in developing countries use trees on farms to generate food and cash (World Bank, 2001).

What do poor people get from trees and forests?

Subsistence goods such as fuelwood, medicines, wood for building, rope, bushmeat, fodder, mushrooms, honey, edible leaves, roots, fruits

Goods for sale: all of the above goods, arts and crafts, timber and other wood products

Indirect benefits such as land for other uses, social and spiritual sites, environmental services, including watershed protection and biodiversity conservation

---

forest producers, traders and workers can participate in local initiatives that offer commercial prospects. The challenge is to support specific changes that will lead to a greater role for forest and tree resources in the livelihoods of poor people. This challenge – primarily a local forest governance challenge – requires immediate action at two 'higher' levels of governance: national and international.

Forests for reducing poverty: Four national governance challenges

Strengthen rights, capabilities and local decision-making

Support poor people's own decision-making power Forests and trees, like other resources, can only contribute to reducing poverty when poor people are able to make decisions and put them into practice – to be in control. Poor people are rarely completely powerless, but their authority to manage their local environments, or indeed their own lives, often goes unacknowledged. On the other hand, initiatives with forests and trees appear to have a strong record in engendering preparedness, capability, social networks and local institutions. These are just the kinds of skills and capital that are needed for marginalized groups to become participants in policy processes and better advocates for their own rights and capacities.

Strengthened communities can take action to improve local livelihoods by improving access to infrastructure, education and health services. This feature of forest management activities among poor people – the improvement of local institutions and bargaining power – is a key reason why addressing poverty through a focus on forest resources makes sense.

BOX 19.2 BENEFITS TO LOCAL LIVELIHOODS FROM PRO-POOR FORESTRY

Rights to access, control and use of forest and tree resources

More say in decisions over use and management of forest resources

Reduced vulnerability, not only through secure forest resources but also through political empowerment

Income from forest goods and services

Improved governance through more effective local institutions

Partnership to enhance capacities

Direct benefits from environmental services

Increased powers of negotiation

Secure poor people's forest rights Many people stay poor because they have insufficient rights to manage their resources, including forests. Evidence increasingly shows that transferring or returning ownership of forest assets to poor people, and securing long-term access and control rights, are politically feasible and cost-effective strategies for poverty reduction (Arnold, 2001).

Clear tenure rights allow local people to protect forests from outside encroachment, to increase their local food and forest security, and to enter into business contracts. Proven new mechanisms for devolving forest rights to poor communities include: joint forest management agreements (India, Tanzania), ownership or control of village forest reserves by indigenous and rural communities (Ghana, Nicaragua), long-term concessions (Bolivia, Indonesia), household forest allocations (China, Vietnam), conditional handover of forest resources consonant with government policy (Nepal, Philippines), and complete transfer of forest resources (Mexico, The Gambia). These vary in the security they offer poor people, but all are valid under different circumstances and all can be stepping-stones to poverty reduction.

Back up rights with the capability to claim them Rights on their own are not enough; they must be supported by the capability to claim and defend them against more powerful actors. Clear constitutional guarantees, as well as specific supportive legislation and regulations are necessary, but are still not sufficient on their own. Poor people need to be aware of their rights and to be able to access effective routes to recourse.

Devolution of forest use and management rights requires effort to establish the effectiveness, legitimacy and accountability of local institutions (Shackleton et al, 2002). Management of budgets, costs and benefits should be devolved along with responsibilities. Local institutions need sufficient autonomy to act on, modify and enforce local rules. In addition, regional or national laws should define rules by which communities interact with outsiders, provide basic protection for individuals and disadvantaged groups against the abuse of local power, and set guidelines for the protection of legitimate public interests.

**BOX 19.3 ADVANTAGES TO GOVERNMENTS OF
PRO-POOR FORESTRY**

Reduced central government costs

Environmental benefits

Local conflict resolution

Natural resources for local development

Effective management through partnership

Recognize links between forestry and local governance Initiatives aimed at improving poor people's use and control of forest resources provide entry points to elements of good governance such as representation, transparency, accountability, equitable taxation and increased civil society roles. The forestry sector has quite a good record in initiating public sector reform, capacity building and improvement of rights to natural resources, and has recently focused its attention on practical means for the elimination of corruption and illegal trade. The forestry sector is becoming increasingly effective in generating lessons for other sectors, learning from other sectors and providing a springboard to broader action on governance (Brown et al, 2002).

Improved access to, and transparency of, information on forest resources is central to people-centred development and requires appropriate information technologies and communication channels to assist local decision-making. The inclusion of information in local planning improves freedom of choice for poor people.

Reduce poor people's vulnerability

Make safety nets not poverty traps In situations of persistent poverty, forest products can help people cope with hard times. For the very poor, access to forest resources provides a vital buffer, absorbing agricultural risk and reducing vulnerability. The very poor have less access to market opportunities or participatory forestry initiatives. They need, above all, measures that protect their access to resources in the face of privatization and trade liberalization, for example rights to move freely and glean on public land, which do not lock them into forest dependence.

Cut the regulatory burden on poor people The regulations that govern poor people's use of forests are often excessive and inconsistent: for example, imposing timber felling bans on community forests but not on commercial forests. Access of poor people to forest resources is over-regulated while the more powerful interests can defy control, which undermines the rule and legitimacy of law. When poor people have enough say in defining regulations, they will usually adapt these regulations effectively and support their enforcement.

BOX 19.4 REGULATIONS BENEFIT LIVELIHOODS AND FORESTS WHEN POOR PEOPLE HAVE RIGHTS AND CONTROL

In Niger, where rural fuelwood markets were established, villagers gained control of fuelwood harvesting and trading through a set of regulations developed with their involvement. These provide a fairer balance of rights, responsibilities and revenues to poor people and the government, and extra revenues to both through higher prices.

Regulation often vastly exceeds government capacity available for enforcement; US$5 billion per year is lost worldwide by governments unable to collect taxes from forest concessions, and a further US$10 billion is lost from illegal cutting of forests. Regulatory frameworks need to focus more on effectively curbing the excesses of the powerful rather than on limiting use by the poor.

BOX 19.5 THE CHALLENGE TO MAKING FORESTRY PROFITS LEGAL AND EQUITABLE

At the East Asian Ministerial Conference on Forest Law and Governance, in September 2001, an unprecedented international commitment was made to combat illegal logging and other forest crimes. At the same conference it was said that in Indonesia alone, an estimated US$600 million per year in royalties, reforestation funds and export tax payments does not reach the government. This represents four times the total government expenditure in the forestry sector, and about three-quarters of the annual budget for education.

Poor forest dwellers are also often expected to bear costs of forest management, rehabilitation and protection – costs way out of proportion to the benefits they derive. Regulatory frameworks can mean that despite their expected role as forest stewards, rural communities face major barriers in trying to acquire commercial rights to forest areas. States should simplify planning and monitoring requirements for small-scale forest managers. Effective planning, utilization and monitoring can be based on clear guidelines, without elaborate management plans.

BOX 19.6 WATER, FORESTS AND POVERTY REDUCTION

Global consumption of fresh water doubles every 20 years – twice the rate of population growth. Forest watersheds influence the local water cycle and improve water quality, but poor rural people's needs are increasingly challenged by external water demands. In India, many villages have active collectives to manage watersheds and negotiate with downstream users.

Box 19.7 Agriculture, forests and poverty reduction

Trees have many agricultural uses, such as food, fuel, fodder, fertilizer, shade, windbreaks, fencing, packaging, water regulation and erosion prevention. In Nepal, poor farmers – unable to purchase fertilizers – try to maintain a 3:1 ratio of forest to agricultural land, to sustain supplies of livestock fodder and hence manure to fertilize their crops.

Box 19.8 Health, forests and poverty reduction

Forests provide medicines and critical food supplements. One billion people depend on drugs derived from forest plants for their medicinal needs. People living beside rainforests in Ghana receive more protein from forest products than from crops or livestock. In arid environments, forests are crucial to food security in dry seasons and years.

Enable market opportunities to be seized by poor people

Remove the barriers to market entry Small-scale producers of timber and other forest products are frequently subjected to costly controls when harvesting, transporting and selling wood and other forest products, while state and large corporate producers are sometimes subsidized. States should provide enabling conditions for poor people in those markets where small producers would have a comparative advantage. A next step is to remove constraints to poor people's access to the more profitable and dynamic opportunities in forestry, such as secondary processing and forest support services (Mayers and Vermeulen, 2002).

Access to information on the value of forest resources in the marketplace is crucial. Emerging small-scale producers need support to analyse their markets and establish a competitive position, and to learn the financial and organizational viability of different business models and how to manage market risks.

Base land use decisions on the true value of forests In the predominant system of state and corporate tenure over forest land, forest resources remain undervalued. Current valuation methods for forest goods and services do not reflect real costs and benefits. In particular, they do not take into account the opportunity costs of renewing forest resources, or the role of rural people in producing and providing forest goods and services. The losers are the rural poor and the forests, which remain unattractive as a form of land use. Greater control over resources and more secure tenure rights for poor people would ensure that these real values of forest resources are reflected in the market. In addition, policy-makers need to recognize and include them in their decisions.

Secure individual or communal tenure allows attractive returns to poor people from forestry when the government and private sector work on providing the right conditions rather than on promotional campaigns. In India, for example, farm forestry was kick-started, but not sustained, by the government's programme of vigorous promotion of farm forestry and the private sector's out-grower schemes in the 1970s and 1980s. Today there is more commercial realism. Development of more competitive and accessible markets – and the concomitant removal of regulatory barriers, such as the permits needed for planting, cutting and transport of wood – has made farm forestry a profitable option even to poorer landowners who are able to plant trees only along field boundaries and contours (Saigal et al, 2002).

Ensure that markets for environmental services benefit poor people Market-based mechanisms to pay for environmental services, such as watershed protection, carbon storage and biodiversity conservation, already exist or look feasible in many countries (Landell-Mills and Porras, 2002). The central rationale is that those who benefit from the services that forests provide should pay those – often the rural poor – who maintain the forests. At the same time, these payments must benefit poor people in a cost-effective and equitable way. For environmental service markets to benefit poor people, their rights must be secured; payments should be treated as a supplement to, rather than substitute for, sustainable forest use; and systems for market transactions and compliance must be equitable, transparent and efficient.

Support associations and financing for local forest businesses Increased support is needed to improve the capacity of local forest businesses to access markets and match supply to demand (Scherr et al, 2002). Strengthened producer organizations, cooperatives, alliances and federations can reduce transaction costs, negotiate with buyers and provide economies of scale. Support measures are also needed to protect the rights of employees, particularly in contracted and outsourced sectors.

Financing local forest businesses requires innovation. Credit tends to benefit wealthier people who have individual land titles. Poor people will continue to rely on savings as the primary source to make investments. Many individual and group savings schemes have proved to be effective in forestry. Traders of forest products and conservation agencies need to support more local forest businesses, and venture capitalists may find that helping local enterprises to scale up their operations is a sound investment.

BOX 19.9 ENERGY, FORESTS AND POVERTY REDUCTION

Wood remains the main fuel for cooking and heating among poor people in Asia and Africa. Small-scale rural producers and traders can take advantage of the growing urban market for firewood and charcoal. In 1998, a small producers union in Burkina Faso negotiated a 30 per cent farm-gate price rise.

Box 19.10 Employment, forests and
poverty reduction

Up to 47 million people work in forestry industries globally. Forest investment can have high employment multipliers. In Guyana, forestry has benefited the national economy, expanding from 1 per cent of gross domestic product (GDP) in 1987 to 8 per cent in 1999, directly employs 19,000 people, and is the primary income source for the rural poor. Amerindian communities' timber sales are one of their main sources of income.

Work in partnership

Simplify policies and support participatory processes National forest policies, which have proliferated over the last few years, have created layer upon layer of new directives, while the capacity of over-structured and under-resourced forestry departments to implement them has decreased. One of the highest priorities in the forestry sector is to turn this around, by finding ways to simplify policies and share them more widely (Macqueen et al, 2001). This means that local forest producers must be able to actively participate in policy negotiation and prioritization. Agencies supporting poverty reduction need to adopt flexible, best-bet approaches, and offer regular exchange of information and experience inside the agency and with other stakeholders.

Promote inter-agency learning and action Single-sector solutions will not reduce poverty. An improved understanding of the various elements and dynamics of poverty suggests that multiple agencies need to be engaged (Wollenberg et al, 2001). At national level, insufficient intersectoral coordination and unnecessary duplication result in poorly targeted action, sometimes at the expense of the priorities of poor people. Reports and evaluations have been highlighting this problem for many years but it seems to recur time after time. Mechanisms for interagency collaboration often exist but require concerted effort to create real interchange, recognition of comparative advantage of different agencies, negotiation and a steady focus on knowledge generation with poverty reduction priorities.

Most countries are required – under various commitments and degrees of pressure – to produce national forest programmes (NFPs), poverty reduction strategy papers (PRSPs) and national sustainable development strategies (NSDSs). These approaches, and a range of other sectoral and cross-sectoral planning processes, require a concerted multi-stakeholder process as well as concrete content and product. Yet, they are generally pursued independently, instead of being used as opportunities for a broader understanding of poverty and the role of forests in reducing it. They should be treated as systems of continuous processes – of information flows, analysis, debate, experiments, monitoring and learning – rather than parallel-track master plans (Mayers and Bass, 1999).

BOX 19.11 LAND TITLES, FORESTS AND POVERTY REDUCTION

Titles to land need to be recognized, enforceable and tradable to benefit poor people. In Bolivia in 1998, the smallholder institution, the Central Intercomunal Campesina del Oriente de Lomerio (CICOL), developed vertically integrated forest enterprises, geared towards forest product certification, which allowed 25 Chiquitano communities to secure legal recognition of indigenous territorial claims.

Make the private sector and NGOs partners in poverty reduction Support is needed to increase capabilities and create partnerships among businesses and NGOs to spearhead the contribution of forestry in reducing poverty. Collaborative forest management remains a vital way forward and NGO roles, in particular, are crucial. The challenge is to reduce transaction costs while maintaining the drive for equitable local governance and sustainability. NGOs and the private sector can also provide specialized business services.

Partnerships between industry and local producers can enable industry to secure forest product supplies with competitive cost structures and prices, while providing credit, extension, markets and skills development to poorer producers, through contracts on tree production and trading and other forms of contract arrangements. A true partnership approach requires a long-term perspective, flexible contract terms and attention to reducing business risks. Cooperative arrangements and the bargaining position of small producers need to be strengthened, especially to enable them to gain a stake in the benefits of downstream processing and trade.

Forests for reducing poverty: Five international governance challenges

Forestry's protagonists, particularly at the international level, often bemoan their powerlessness in the face of the disinterest or intransigence of others responsible for trade, macroeconomic and non-forest sectoral policies, institutions or markets that constrain or prevent forestry from reaching its potential. But they should make new alliances and try harder. When the advocates of forestry's potential to reduce poverty collectively make their case and push for change they may surprise themselves to find that some forward steps are possible. Five challenges for effective international forest governance stand out:

Recognize the power of good forest governance to reduce poverty – but not through brute 'enforcement'

Forestry has advantages over many other sectors in offering high potential routes out of rural poverty. Forestry can provide resource safety nets and sometimes enterprise opportunities where little else exists. Sustainable rural livelihoods are often highly complicated and some elements of livelihoods can be helped by forestry while others cannot. Yet the governance required to allow forestry to contribute to improved livelihoods is not unattainable, as shown in the above sections of this chapter. The forest sector has pioneered approaches to pro-poor governance change (Byron and Arnold, 1999). Supporters of poverty reduction should take a longer look at these and integrate support for forest's potential to generate livelihood benefits into NFPs, NSDSs, PRSPs and other cross-sectoral approaches.

Governance is much more than just law enforcement; it involves fundamental rights, institutional roles, policy 'sticks and carrots', and systems by which decisions are actually put into action and monitored. The UN Forum on Forests' generally feeble ministerial message to the World Summit on Sustainable Development (WSSD) contains an important call for enforcement of forest and protected-area laws. This joins other significant efforts, such as the Southeast Asian and African Forest Law Enforcement and Governance initiatives, to combat illegal logging and the power of some forest industries to run amok. However, great care must be taken; enforcement of current laws is in some contexts irrelevant, or at worst highly detrimental, to poor people. Laws frequently prop up existing exploitation systems, denying the rights and blocking the potential of poor people at local level (Brunner et al, 1999). Enforcement without regard for human rights and livelihood opportunities must be prevented.

BOX 19.12 FOREST PRODUCT MARKETS, FORESTS AND POVERTY REDUCTION

Small-scale forest product enterprises are among the top three non-farm rural commercial activities in most countries. More than a quarter of Brazil's timber is produced by micro-enterprises. In South Africa, government policy has increased opportunities for poorer farmers to participate in timber markets, and large companies are pursuing out-grower schemes with considerable local benefits.

Stop marginalizing forest communities and start listening to poor people

The balance struck thus far at international level between conservation and development has done little for the rural poor. The potential of vast tracts of forest in tropical countries to contribute to sustainable livelihoods has been removed as they are turned into protected areas, without reference to their historical owners or users, to satisfy North American and western European preoccupations with global biodiversity, at minimum cost to themselves.

Meanwhile some sections of the forest industry are working hard to ensure that forestry production is widely perceived as a specialized business to be undertaken only by large corporations in subsidized plantations in high-productivity areas. Just as poor people are beginning to establish their rights and potential to develop their livelihoods through use of forest resources, they are in danger of being condemned to the margins as passive onlookers to commercial forest production and conservation (ILO, 2001).

It is time to listen to poor people's organizations involved with forest issues, to engage with their ideas on how to influence the governance agenda with respect to poverty and forests, and to commit to supporting them. Backing should be given to the organizations that poor people already have – such as *campesino* forestry organizations from Central America, forest user groups from Nepal, the National Council of Rubber Tappers from Brazil, people's natural resource management organizations from the Philippines – to get to meetings of relevant inter-governmental fora. Here they can be helped to build on what they are already doing, and to enable new partnerships. Multi-stakeholder poverty–forests learning processes should be fostered, and codes of conduct developed for supporters of pro-poor forestry and national forest programmes that integrate poverty reduction priorities.

Stop making international proposals and start implementing some

The last thing the world needs right now is more inter-governmental proposals for action on forests. The Inter-governmental Panel – then the Inter-governmental Forum – on Forests, set in train in Rio in 1992, has produced hundreds of them already. Some of these are just what we require. Now they need to be implemented. The UN Forum on Forests (UNFF) is supposed to oversee and facilitate this, but so far has been a major disappointment, as governments have refused to move on from negotiating and proposal making. While many civil society organizations and some governments will abandon ship, it is not too late to refocus the UNFF and a wide range of other pieces of the international forest policy process towards making some solid commitments, targets and indicators based on what is already agreed. International fora should be used to hook up demand for help with supply, and to share learning about the tactics for change.

BOX 19.13 BIODIVERSITY CONSERVATION, FORESTS AND POVERTY REDUCTION

Biodiversity of trees and crops in the managed forest/agricultural landscape can often be more important to poor people than those in protected areas. In Nigeria, carefully managed farmland provides a more varied and higher yielding source of fuelwood and fruits than local woodland. Global conservation efforts will be more constructive in helping poor people if they promote sustainable management of utilized biodiversity rather than focusing only on forest protection.

Demand responsible forest enterprise and fair trade

The huge effort that has gone into forest certification is beginning to pay off in terms of environmental performance, but is yet to represent an effective tool for pro-poor forestry (Bass et al, 2001). Bright international ideas such as the Global Reporting Initiative will also strengthen corporate responsibility commitments. But much of what is called corporate social responsibility is nothing more than cynical reputation management.

Furthermore, there is much concern that progress with social responsibility, like agreements on investment codes and protocols, will favour only large companies. Calls to greater accountability tend to bolster the positions of the biggest corporations, pushing out the more livelihoods-linked small- and medium-scale companies unable to make the grade, or worse still, pushing production into sectors that are not subject to scrutiny. Types of partners other than limited liability companies, such as cooperatives, should receive more attention and support: a shift of focus from 'corporate' responsibility to 'enterprise' responsibility.

International forestry fora should sharpen their powers to install the elements of good forestry governance and management into international trade rules and investment systems. Post-WSSD, for example, the UN Commission on Sustainable Development and other relevant bodies should support actions in other fora to mainstream social criteria in certification and fair trade protocols. A particular effort is needed at the WTO to bring an end to overt and disguised subsidies and dumping.

BOX 19.14 CARBON MANAGEMENT, FORESTS AND POVERTY REDUCTION

The possibility of managing forests for their carbon storage values represents a major opportunity for some poor people. In Costa Rica, groups of smallholders already receive payments from certified carbon offsets. Local land rights and equitable distribution of benefits must be secured in these schemes.

Get your own house in order: increase accountability of the 'lumbering giants'

The UN and international financial institutions presiding over the pieces of the global sustainable development jigsaw are insufficiently accountable and democratic. The 2.5 billion people in poverty today have no vote in the Bretton Woods and UN agencies, and hence do not wield the political power to demand change. These bodies operate in ways which are mysterious to those they are supposed to represent. Which of them could give a clear and credible answer to four basic questions of power: Who do you really represent? What is the extent of your power? How do you exercise it? How do we get rid of you? The legitimacy of these lumbering giants, and their ability to help forests play their part in poverty reduction, will depend on their future answers to such questions and their practical demonstration of effectiveness over time.

Commitments and clear steps for reform are needed – reform towards getting global governance right *for* local governance. Civil society scrutiny will need to play a large part. Much can be learnt from experience with local-level forest governance. Findings from local forest management in many parts of the world point to the great importance of process-led approaches, of building confidence among stakeholders, and taking time to ensure that everyone has the same level of information. Like these local processes, international bodies must show transparency, clarity of vision and effective communication to stand a chance of delivering for the disadvantaged as well as the powerful.

References

Arnold, JEM (2001) *Forests and People: 25 Years of Community Forestry*, Food and Agriculture Organisation of the United Nations, Rome

Bass, S, Thornber, K, Markopoulos, M, Roberts, S and Grieg-Gran, M (2001) *Certification's Impacts on Forests, Stakeholders and Supply Chains*, Instruments for Sustainable Private Sector Forestry series, International Institute for Environment and Development, London

Brown, D, Schreckenberg, K, Shepherd, G and Wells, A (2002) *Forestry as an Entry Point for Governance Reform*, ODI Forestry Briefing 1, Overseas Development Institute, London

Brunner, J, Seymour, F, Badenoch, N and Ratner, B (1999) 'Forest Problems and Law Enforcement in Southeast Asia: The Role of Local Communities', *Resources Policy Brief*, World Resources Institute, Washington, DC

Byron, N and Arnold, M (1999) 'What Futures for People of the Tropical Forests?' *World Development*, vol 27, pp789–805

ILO (2001) 'Globalization and Sustainability: The Forestry and Wood Industries on the Move', report prepared for the Tripartite Meeting on the Social and Labour Dimensions of the Forestry and Wood Industries on the Move, International Labour Organization, Geneva

Landell-Mills, N and Porras, I (2002) *Silver Bullet or Fool's Gold? A Global Review of Markets for Forest Environmental Services and their Impact on the Poor*, Instruments for Sustainable Private Sector Forestry series, International Institute for Environment and Development, London

Macqueen, D, Barrance, A and Holt, G (2001) 'Common Problems of Forest-Dependent Poor and Priority Research and Development Themes to Address them', *International Forestry Review*, vol 3, pp105–120

Mayers, J and Bass, S (1999) *Policy that Works for Forests and People: Series Overview*, International Institute for Environment and Development, London

Mayers, J and Vermeulen, S (2002) *Company–Community Forestry Partnerships: From Raw Deals to Mutual Gains*, Instruments for Sustainable Private Sector Forestry series, International Institute for Environment and Development, London

Saigal, S, Arora, H and Rizvi, SS (2002) *The New Foresters: The Role of Private Enterprise in the Indian Forest Sector*, Instruments for Sustainable Private Sector Forestry series, Ecotech Services, New Delhi, and International Institute for Environment and Development, London

Scherr, S, White, A and Kaimowitz, D (2002) *Making Forest Markets Work for Low-Income Producers*, Forest Trends, Washington, DC, and Center for International Forestry Research, Bogor, Indonesia

Shackleton, S, Campbell, B, Wollenberg, E and Edmunds, D (2002) *Devolution and Community-Based Natural Resource Management: Creating Space for Local People to Participate and Benefit*, Natural Resources Perspectives series number 76, Overseas Development Institute, London

Wollenberg, E, Edmunds, D and Anderson, J (eds) (2001) 'Accommodating Multiple Interests in Local Forest Management', special issue of *International Journal of Agricultural Resources, Governance and Ecology*, vol 1, nos 3/4

World Bank (2001) *A Revised Forest Strategy for the World Bank Group*, Draft 30 July 2001, World Bank, Washington, DC

Wunder, S (2001) 'Poverty Alleviation and Tropical Forests: What Scope for Synergies?', *World Development*, vol 29, pp1817–1834

Chapter 20

Poverty Reduction through Conservation and Sustainable Use of Biodiversity

Izabella Koziell, DFID and Charles McNeill, UNDP

Growing concern over the effects of biodiversity loss on progress towards sustainable development led to the establishment of the UN Convention on Biological Diversity (CBD) in 1992. To date, over 180 countries have ratified it, demonstrating a significant global commitment to the cause. The CBD presents a comprehensive series of pragmatic and innovative principles for action (Box 20.1), which have been further elaborated by six Conferences of the Parties. Yet there has been insufficient advancement in operational terms. This lack of progress should be taken very seriously as biodiversity loss, together with other forms of environmental degradation, has the potential to undermine progress towards the achievement of the Millennium Development Goals (MDGs, see www.undp.org/mdg and Box 20.3).

Fortunately, 2002 signalled a turning point for biodiversity and the MDGs on the international agenda. In April, the parties to the CBD established 2010 as the target year for significantly reducing the loss of biodiversity. In May, UN Secretary-General Kofi Annan set out five 'WEHAB' priorities (water, energy, health, agriculture, and biodiversity and ecosystem management) for the World Summit on Sustainable Development (WSSD). In July, the United Nations launched a comprehensive strategy on the MDGs based on four pillars, including an important analytical effort, the 'Millennium Project' (www.unmillenniumproject.org). In September, the Johannesburg Plan of Implementation endorsed the 2010 target for reducing biodiversity loss.

Although there is increasing understanding that the 'environment', including biodiversity, offers many interesting poverty reduction opportunities, in practice these are often overlooked, and may function outside the prevailing policy environment. Far more attention needs to be directed to the linkages between biodiversity and the MDGs.

Box 20.1 The UN Convention on Biological Diversity

The Convention on Biological Diversity's objectives are:

- the conservation of biological diversity;
- the sustainable use of its components; and
- the fair and equitable sharing of the benefits arising out of the utilization of genetic resources.

The CBD objectives provide much opportunity for building on the links between livelihoods development and the conservation and sustainable use of biodiversity. This is further supported by the convention's explicit recognition that 'economic and social development and poverty eradication are the first and overriding priorities of developing countries'. The problem is that there is little guidance, insufficient models, and a lack of effective tools and mechanisms which are needed to achieve conservation objectives, while at the same time positively enhancing poverty reduction processes.

For instance, it is unlikely that the first MDG – 'eradication of extreme poverty and hunger' through 'halving, between 1990 and 2015, the proportion of people whose income is under $1 day and in hunger' – can be achieved solely through the adoption of conventional economic approaches to poverty reduction. And, even if poverty is successfully halved, if approaches and technologies have not been sustainable, the associated pressures exerted on the world's biodiversity are likely to threaten the sustainability of the poverty eradication process itself. They are likely to push the *other half* remaining into even deeper poverty. Furthermore, while a significant proportion of poor people are keen to adopt similar lifestyles to those in industrialized countries, this does not apply to all poor people; some may choose to continue a lifestyle that maintains a close interaction with natural ecosystems, or biodiversity, and that does not focus singularly on material accumulation. The critical factor here is that poverty reduction processes should also offer people choice and security – and paying closer attention to the links between biodiversity, poverty reduction and the achievement of sustainable livelihoods can help achieve this.

The fourth and fifth MDGs, respectively, to 'reduce child mortality' and to 'improve maternal health' have clear linkages to biodiversity (see Boxes 20.2 and 20.3). The seventh MDG, 'ensuring environmental sustainability', attempts to recognize some of the above challenges and the following two indicators assess some aspects of biodiversity: 'the proportion of land area covered by forest' (indicator #25), and 'the ratio of area protected to maintain biological diversity to surface area' (indicator #26). Making progress on this last indicator will require serious and innovative thinking as pressures on existing protected areas are enormous, and will increase given the need to eliminate hunger. Fortunately, the Fifth World Parks Congress, in Durban, offers an important opportunity for such innovative thinking on options for meeting people's needs in and around protected areas.

BOX 20.2 BIODIVERSITY CONTRIBUTES TO POVERTY REDUCTION IN AT LEAST FIVE KEY AREAS

Food security: human society is highly dependent on genetic resources, including those from wild and semi-domesticated sources, for the productivity of its agriculture, livestock and fisheries. These resources also provide communities with an adaptation capacity so varieties can be created that best cope with changing local conditions. Biodiversity is also a source of alternative food products during periods of scarcity.

Health improvements: biodiversity is a source of the invaluable information and raw materials that underpin medicinal and health care systems, both for the 'informal' sector, which meets local health care needs of some 60 per cent of the world's people, and the 'formal' sector, which derives a majority of the world's modern drugs from biodiversity. Poor people also suffer most when water and air are scarce or polluted and from diseases associated with disrupted ecosystems. Further, a variety of sources of foods support better nutrition and therefore improved health.

Income generation: poor people tend to be the most directly dependent upon the utilization of biodiversity for their livelihoods, and are therefore the first to suffer when these resources are degraded or lost. Biodiversity also offers potential for marketing unique products, many of which are extremely valuable, but the benefits only infrequently accrue to the poor.

Reduced vulnerability: poor people are most often exposed to, and least prepared to cope with, unpredictable events such as fluctuations in access to food and other resources, and to environmental shocks and risks. Ecosystem degradation exacerbates the frequency and impact of droughts, floods, landslides, forest fires and other natural hazards, and can intensify competition and the potential for conflict over access to shared resources such as food and water.

Ecosystem services – forests, wetlands, coastal ecosystems, etc – provide essential services that contribute in numerous ways to the productive activities of rural and urban poor people, including the generation of water, cycling of nutrients, replenishment of soil fertility and prevention of erosion. These services are public goods, providing indirect values that are not traded in the marketplace but are vital to the livelihoods of all people.

Also within this seventh MDG, there is a third indicator: 'the proportion of population with sustainable access to an improved water source, urban and rural' that relates to the target 'to halve by 2015 the proportion of people without sustainable access to safe drinking water'. The achievement of this target is indirectly related to the quality of the ecosystems that biodiversity provides, as described in Box 20.2. Further thinking and analytical work is urgently needed on how biodiversity can positively contribute to the achievement of the MDGs.

There are several reasons why biodiversity has not yet made its full contribution to global poverty reduction efforts. First, biodiversity is an abstract concept: defined as the 'variability of all organisms from all sources ... and the ecological complexes of which they are part ... this includes diversity within species, between species and of ecosystems' (United Nations, 1992). This notion of diversity has not proved easy to convert into a tangible entity. Planners and

BOX 20.3 MILLENNIUM DEVELOPMENT GOALS AND TARGETS

Goal 1: Eradicate extreme poverty
   Target 1: Halve, between 1990 and 2015, the proportion of people whose income is less than one dollar a day
   Target 2: Halve, between 1990 and 2015, the proportion of people who suffer from hunger
Goal 2: Achieve universal primary education
   Target 3: Ensure that, by 2015, children everywhere, boys and girls alike, will be able to complete a full course of primary schooling
Goal 3: Promote gender equality
   Target 4: Eliminate gender disparity in primary and secondary education preferably by 2005 and empower women to all levels of education no later than 2015
Goal 4: Reduce child mortality
   Target 5: Reduce by two-thirds, between 1990 and 2015, the under-five mortality rate
Goal 5: Improve maternal health
   Target 6: Reduce by three-quarters, between 1990 and 2015, the maternal mortality ratio
Goal 6: Combat HIV/AIDS, malaria
   Target 7: Have halted by 2015, and begun to reverse, the spread of HIV/AIDS
   Target 8: Have halted by 2015, and begun to reverse, the incidence of malaria and other major diseases
Goal 7: Ensure environmental sustainability
   Target 9: Integrate the principles of sustainable development into country policies and programmes and reverse the loss of environmental resources
   Target 10: Halve, by 2015, the proportion of people without sustainable access to safe drinking water
   Target 11: By 2020, to have achieved a significant improvement in the lives of at least 100 million slum dwellers
Goal 8: Develop a global partnership
   Target 12: Develop further an open, rule-based, predictable, non-discriminatory trading and financial system. Includes a commitment to good governance, development and poverty reduction, both nationally and internationally
   Target 13: Address the special needs of the least developed countries (LDCs). Includes: tariff and quota free access for LDC exports; enhanced programme of debt relief for heavily indebted poor countries (HIPC) and cancellation of official bilateral debt; and more generous Official Development Assistance (ODA) for countries committed to poverty reduction
   Target 14: Address the special needs of landlocked countries and small island developing states (through Barbados Programme and 22nd General Assembly provisions)
   Target 15: Deal comprehensively with the debt problems of developing countries through national and international measures in order to make debt sustainable in the long term
   Target 16: In cooperation with developing countries, develop and implement strategies for decent and productive work for youth
   Target 17: In cooperation with pharmaceutical companies, provide access to affordable, essential drugs in developing countries
   Target 18: In cooperation with the private sector, make available the benefits of new technologies, especially information and communications

Source: www.undp.org/mdg

policy- and decision-makers have therefore often overlooked it. Local people and the general public, while they continually interact with it, are simply not aware of their enormous dependence nor do they recognize that their enjoyment of the natural world often derives from their interaction with unusual plants, animals or landscapes, none of which would exist if not for biodiversity. It is often only when biodiversity has disappeared, or becomes scarce, that a more direct and broader appreciation of its value develops. However, if we were to wait until an appreciation of biodiversity's value occurs due to scarcity on a global scale, then the consequences would be disastrous.

Why is Biodiversity Important?

There is often confusion about why biodiversity has become a focus of attention through the establishment of the Convention on Biological Diversity. Why not simply pay attention to natural resources – surely that is enough? But biodiversity is so much more – it encompasses all living natural resources, and harbours the processes and interactions within and between them, and the ecosystems within which they fall. Thus biodiversity forces a more holistic and more comprehensive thinking about natural and agricultural systems.

Biodiversity is also valuable for the range of resources it supports that provide people with choice. Biodiversity provides 'replacements' and alternatives, allowing resource users to switch from one resource to another, if the first becomes scarce, or if markets demand changes. Access to diverse species enables the diversification of livelihood sources through, for instance, planting multiple crops, staggering food production throughout the year, or engaging in alternative income-generating activities, such as collection of non-timber forest products. The availability of diverse resources also allows different genders, and cultural or age groups to engage and benefit from different activities. This is especially important as it can help to reduce competition or conflict that might otherwise occur if each group had to compete for the same resources – as is indeed the case in many parts of the world where diversity and the choices it supports have become scarce.

There are many other notable benefits that biodiversity offers. Some of these are very under-appreciated by the public as well as policy-makers, such as the ecosystem services that sustain society itself, and its research value. Biodiversity provides a medium for the study of phenomena and interactions that underpin much technological innovation (see Box 20.2, and the work of the Millennium Ecosystem Assessment at www.millenniumassessment.org for further information).

We are clearly all dependent on biodiversity, but we differ enormously from one another in the way we value it and use it. Where people have no alternative means of acquiring food and their other basic needs, such as clothing, building materials and medicines, or where they do not have the capacity to regulate the environment, such as through building dams or protecting themselves from floods, biodiversity's value is usually much greater.

Where we are concerned with producing vast quantities of one valuable product, such as wheat, and have access to artificial external inputs that can regulate the production environment, biodiversity's direct use value may be lower, as artificial inputs replace nature's services. This is not to undermine its value to all society, as urban consumers, for instance, depend heavily on the maintenance of genetic diversity for the enhanced production of food and other crops, but to point out that there are groups, like the poor, who are more directly and more critically dependent upon it than others.

The Challenge

Unfortunately, the habitats which harbour some of the world's most valuable biodiversity are being lost at ever-faster rates and over progressively wider areas (WWF, 2000). It so happens that many of these areas also coincide with severe income poverty, and social and political marginalization. This coincidence has led many to assume that financially poor and marginalized peoples are primarily responsible for biodiversity loss. While this may sometimes be the case, a deeper understanding is developing to counter this assumption. Where poor people are overexploiting local resources, this has arisen usually because they have been pushed to the margins of existence – as more powerful groups have appropriated lands or resources more successfully – forcing them to subsist from areas or resources too small and too unproductive to properly support a sustainable existence.

This pattern occurs at ever-increasing scales. Indeed, over-consumption by industrialized countries is more frequently singled out as a key driver of biodiversity loss and increased poverty. Recognizing key drivers might be a significant step forward, but identifying suitable countermeasures presents the poverty reduction, economic development and biodiversity communities with a most difficult challenge.

A key problem lies in the fact that conventional development pathways – as pursued by industrialized countries – value the generation and accumulation of private goods: food, clothing, buildings and other material goods that can be traded and exchanged. Maintaining public goods – biodiversity, the atmosphere, the oceans – does not (yet) yield direct economic gains. The fact that they sustain the continued production of valued goods is often overlooked, with potentially disastrous consequences. Development approaches pursued by industrial countries have had some demonstrable success, at least in economic terms. But there are many examples where short-term economic gains have occurred at enormous cost to local people, especially the great many that are dependent directly on natural resources.

Also of direct relevance to the MDGs is the fact that tropical countries are beset by a host of health and ecological challenges that are distinct and more severe than those encountered by temperate countries. A high burden of disease from pests and parasites, including malaria, is concentrated in the tropics, and other endemic diseases sharply shorten life spans. Tropical agricultural productivity, reduced by fragile soils and inappropriate technologies, is 30–50 per cent below temperate levels, leading to poor nutrition which further undermines health. Since past 'North to South' transfers of technological knowledge from temperate environments have often resulted in ineffective and unsustainable practices it appears that tropical nations and communities urgently need assistance in identifying, promoting and applying technologies appropriate to the tropical region itself.

It is now time to consider alternative approaches that are complementary to conventional methods to reduce poverty. Providing the poorest and most marginalized rural peoples with greater choice, involving them in decision-making, engaging with them in partnerships, assisting them in learning from each other, has real potential to provide pragmatic solutions.

The Opportunity

There is increasing evidence of financially poor, politically and socially marginalized peoples, who have managed to strengthen the security and sustainability of their livelihoods by realizing the value of their biodiversity asset in many diverse and pioneering ways. In fact, more than 400 such community initiatives throughout the world were identified through nominations for the 2002 Equator Initiative awards. Representatives of 27 communities received the 2002 Equator Prize during the Johannesburg World Summit on Sustainable Development where they had opportunities through workshops to share their experiences with each other and with other communities (www.equatorinitiative.org). The United Nations Development Programme (UNDP)/Global Environment Facility (GEF) Small Grants Programme has also identified hundreds of such local initiatives. Other examples are provided below:

- The Makuleke Land Claim in South Africa illustrates how the Makuleke community regained ownership of land 20 years after they were removed from it to make way for the Kruger National Park. After several years of negotiation, the various parties managed to resolve their differences and achieve a classic win–win for biodiversity conservation and for livelihoods improvement of the Makuleke community. The community was allowed back on to their lands on condition that they manage the land sustainably – engaging in livelihood activities that conserve or sustainably use the local biodiversity, such as ecotourism. The community found this an entirely acceptable offer and agreed to sign the joint management agreement, to both parties' benefit (Steenkamp and Uhr, 2000).
- A partnership initiative called AmazonLife generates sustainable economic development options for traditional populations in the Amazon which are compatible with their culture and which protect the biodiversity of their territories. Through the initiative, local indigenous and rubber tapper families in the Brazilian Amazon produce sheets of rubber vulcanized through an exclusive process to be used as a leather substitute to manufacture bags, knapsacks, briefcases, clothing, shoes and so on. Niche markets have been created outside Brazil and these products are in high

demand. Each family involved in the process of collecting the natural rubber and making the sheets of leather-like fabric is part of an informal network that is safeguarding over 100,000 hectares in the Amazon.

- Also in the Amazon, the Brazil Nut Programme of the Amazon Conservation Association has been working in partnership with *castaneros* (Brazil nut harvesters) to strengthen the role that Brazil nuts play in sustainable livelihoods. As the ecosystem that supports Brazil nut production is quite diverse, maintaining livelihoods dependent on these nuts creates the incentive to conserve this ecosystem, rather than converting it to other uses.
- Seed fairs are increasingly popular methods of promoting agro-biodiversity while strengthening food security. Farmers are keen to participate as they provide an opportunity to obtain crop varieties with interesting and valuable qualities and exchange ideas on seed sources. In Maragwa, Kenya, seed fairs have been held annually, having been originally initiated by an NGO in 1996.
- The decline in fish stocks in the Khong District of southern Lao People's Democratic Republic raised many local concerns. In response, the government in strong collaboration with the local communities established the Lao Community Fisheries and Dolphin Project, which has established co-management planning mechanisms and regulations to sustainably manage the inland aquatic resource. Villagers have reported that as a result of these monitoring activities over a number of years there have been increases in the stocks of 50 species (Baird, 2000).

Increasing awareness of the existence of these various initiatives, analysis of the factors underlying the success of each, and dissemination of positive impacts and lessons learnt to sectoral policy- and decision-makers must become a priority – especially those that have arisen in the absence of any donor or external support and are entirely self-driven and self-motivated. The more widespread uptake of successful initiatives has been hampered by unsupportive or non-existent policy, institutional and legislative frameworks, often reinforced by strict conditionalities around loans that dictate which policies highly indebted countries can pursue. Consequently, they have proved difficult to replicate. Hence the need to learn from successful initiatives and transpose this learning into policy development.

However, this does not mean that wider adoption of such activities is not possible.

There is a critical need now to build on these success stories by understanding which factors have contributed to their success in balancing biodiversity conservation with sustainable livelihoods, which factors constrain their wider adoption, and then to analyse how to create a more enabling environment – within policy, institutions and legislation – at local, national and international levels.

This opportunity must not be overlooked: the tropical zone continues to hold some of the world's most valuable biodiversity. The uniqueness of this asset and its value to all societies must offer comparative advantage through basing livelihood and economic development activities on maintaining a set of biodiverse assets, whether this means supporting corporate–community partnerships in ecotourism, the production of 'bird-friendly' coffee by smallholders, or direct payments to landholders from the marketing of environmental services (Landell-Mills and Porras, 2002).

This is not intended to argue for sweeping changes towards 'biodiversity-friendly' forms of development. Rather, it is about highlighting the fact that there might be alternative and complementary ways of achieving viable and sustainable poverty reduction, which build on the conservation of the existing valuable biodiversity asset. Such initiatives have the potential to manage the trade-offs and maximize the win–win opportunities between biodiversity conservation and poverty reduction more effectively.

What is being advocated is the need to explore the sort of incremental changes, within policy, institutions and legislation, that could help to provide the enabling environment for such activities to be tried, refined and expanded where appropriate. It is clear that there are many areas within the tropical region where conventional development has simply not worked for the majority and, if we are to be really serious about achieving the first Millennium Development Goal for all, then there is a real need to consider these alternative approaches.

Priority areas of work required to move this important new agenda forward include the following:

- Stimulate the flow of information on innovative and successful community practices integrating biodiversity and poverty by establishing a 'clearing house of good practices' along with a deeper analysis and understanding of the policy, legal and socio-political environment that would allow for their more widespread adoption, then test these various approaches.
- Generate a wider appreciation for the contribution that environmental goods and services make to production systems and markets, find ways to incorporate these in accounting procedures, and develop innovative payment systems to communities for provision of ecosystem services and other public goods.
- Expand worldwide demand and markets for goods produced in 'biodiversity-friendly' ways and establish certification systems for sustainably produced community goods and services that do not discriminate against small or marginal producers.
- Provide appropriate support to indigenous and other local peoples to address resource access and land ownership issues and facilitate processes that work towards bringing marginalized peoples into decision-making processes around land use (through capacity building, provision of information, applied 'socially' oriented research activities, etc).
- In support of the UN Millennium Project, undertake a systematic analysis of the MDGs to identify opportunities where activities related to biodiversity can and should make a contribution to the achievement of the MDGs (through a careful review of each goal, target and indicator), and address the need to define and formulate new indicators for the MDGs since the current ones only reflect a limited aspect of biodiversity.

BOX 20.4 ABOUT THE EQUATOR INITIATIVE

The Equator Initiative was created by UNDP in partnership with BrasilConnects, the Government of Canada, the International Development Research Centre (IDRC), IUCN (the World Conservation Union), Television Trust for the Environment (TVE), and the United Nations Foundation. The initiative aims to reduce poverty through the conservation and sustainable use of biodiversity in the equatorial belt by identifying and strengthening innovative community partnerships. It was designed recognizing that the world's greatest concentration of both human poverty and biological wealth is found in tropical developing countries, where the loss of biodiversity is accelerating as poverty is increasing. However, there are many creative and effective ways through which indigenous and other local communities are rising to these challenges. Whether for food, medicine, shelter or income generation, these groups are using their biological resources in a sustainable way to improve their livelihoods – yet their innovations remain largely unknown.

Current Equator Initiative partners:

- BrasilConnects (Brazil): www.brasilconnects.org
- Government of Canada: www.canada.gc.ca
- Government of Germany: eng.bundesregierung.de
- IDRC (Canada): www.idrc.ca
- IUCN, the World Conservation Union (Switzerland): www.iucn.org
- Television Trust for the Environment (TVE, UK): www.tve.org
- United Nations Foundation (UNF, USA): www.unfoundation.org

Contact details:
Equator Initiative
United Nations Development Programme
One UN Plaza, New York, NY 10017, USA
Tel: 1.212.906-6206 Fax: 1.212.906-6973
Email: EquatorInitiative@undp.org
website: www.equatorinitiative.org

The Equator Initiative seeks to promote a worldwide movement to address these challenges through a three-part programme to:

1   recognize local achievements through the 'Innovative Partnership Awards for Sustainable Development in Tropical Ecosystems';
2   foster South–South capacity building through community-to-community learning exchanges;
3   contribute to the generation and sharing of knowledge for policy impact through publications, radio, television and the Internet.

References

Baird, IG (2000) *Towards Co-Management of Mekong River Inland Aquatic Resources, Including Fisheries, in Southern Lao PDR*, Evaluating Eden Discussion Paper no 15, International Institute for Environment and Development, London

Landell-Mills, N and Porras, I (2002) *Silver Bullets or Fool's Gold? A Global Review of Markets for Forest Environmental Services and their Impact on the Poor*, International Institute for Environment and Development, London

Roe, D, Mayers, J, Grieg-Gran, M, Kothari, A, Fabricuis, C and Hughes, R (2000) *Exploring the Myths and Realities of Community-based Wildlife Management*, Evaluating Eden Series Overview no 8, International Institute for Environment and Development, London

Steenkamp, C and Uhr, J (2000) *The Makuleke Land Claim: Power Relations and Community-Based Natural Resource Management*, Evaluating Eden Discussion Paper no 18, International Institute for Environment and Development, London

United Nations (1992) *Convention on Biological Diversity*, United Nations, New York

WWF (2000) *Living Planet Report*, World Wide Fund for Nature Year 2000 'List of Threatened Species', available at www.redlist.org

Chapter 21

Reconciling Agriculture and Wildlife: Policy and Research Challenges of 'Ecoagriculture'

Sara J Scherr, Forest Trends and Jeffrey A McNeely, IUCN

Conventional wisdom holds that modern farming is largely incompatible with wildlife conservation. Thus policies to protect wildlife typically rely on land use segregation, establishing protected areas from which agriculture is officially excluded. Farmers are seen as problems by those promoting this view of wildlife conservation. This chapter argues, however, that enhancing the contribution of farming systems is an essential part of any biodiversity conservation strategy, and requires new technical and policy research.

Many studies have emphasized the importance and feasibility of establishing protected areas for wild biodiversity (Pimm et al, 2001). But recently published research demonstrates that strategies for wildlife conservation that ignore farmed areas are almost certain to fail. Population Action International recently overlaid global population data with maps delineating Conservation International's 'biodiversity hotspots' – areas holding 44 per cent of the world's vascular plant species and 35 per cent of its bird, mammals, reptiles and amphibians. Their analysis showed that 1.1 billion people live in the 25 biodiversity hotspots (Figure 21.1), most of which have higher population growth rates than the global average (Cincotta and Engelman, 2000). UN Food and Agriculture Organization (FAO) and other data on rates of malnutrition indicate that at least a fifth of all malnourished people live in these biodiversity hotspots (WFP, 2000). Farming is the principal livelihood of most of these people, and in low-income biodiversity-rich countries, it is a major engine of economic development (Pinstrup-Andersen et al, 1997). While protected areas are necessary in these biodiversity hotspots, and elsewhere, they are not sufficient. Additional approaches are needed.

Over a third of the global agricultural extent is in high-intensity systems that generally use high levels of agrochemicals for continuous cropping, and

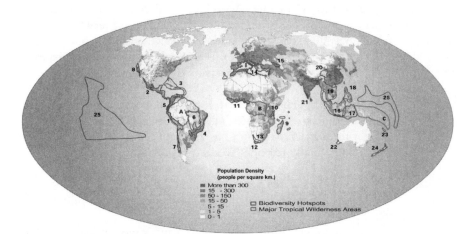

Humans and wild species share the same land in many areas where biodiversity is richest and most at risk. Agriculture is the biggest cause of species extinctions today. Ecoagriculture is one of the greatest hopes for preserving biodiversity for the future (Cincotta and Engelman, 2000). Courtesy of Population Action International

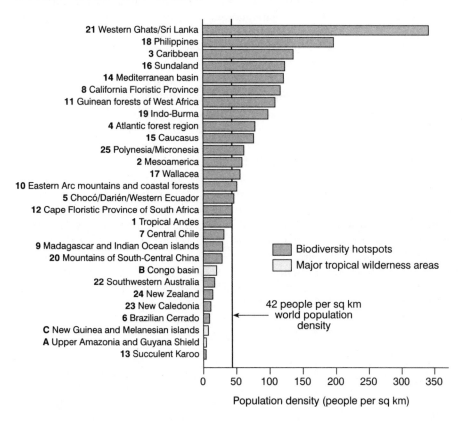

Figure 21.1 *Global biodiversity hotspots*

often reshape land and waterways (Wood et al, 2000).[1] The rest of the agricultural extent is under extensive farming systems that use far fewer inputs, but require relatively large expanses of land to produce relatively low crop and livestock yields. Agriculture is necessary to feed people, but both broad types of agriculture have had notable negative impacts on wild biodiversity:

- Nearly half of all temperate broadleaf forest and tropical and subtropical dry forest, and a third of temperate grass and shrubland, have been lost as wildlife habitat through conversion to agricultural use; conversion rates are especially high in Asia and Europe (Wood et al, 2000).
- Irrigation is practised on over 250 million hectares and uses over 70 per cent of all fresh water – 89 per cent in low-income countries – often diverting water resources needed by land-based and aquatic wildlife (Wood et al, 2000).
- Globally, over half of wetlands – among the planet's most valuable wildlife habitats – have been converted to agriculture (Frazier, 1999).
- Farming has led to significant soil degradation on 16 per cent of all crop, pasture and forestland worldwide, and half of all land within the agricultural extent, thereby affecting the diversity of soil micro-organisms (Scherr, 1999).
- Excessive use and poor management of crop nutrients, pesticides and penned livestock wastes are a major cause of habitat pollution that can kill wildlife directly or impair reproduction (Wood et al, 2000).

Can ways be found to reduce, or even reverse, the impacts of agriculture on wild biodiversity? Given present agricultural technologies and policies, most farmers can increase biodiversity significantly only by reducing production and livelihood security. Initiatives to promote more ecologically sensitive farming systems (called 'sustainable', 'regenerative' or 'organic' agriculture) are expanding, often with positive impacts on wild biodiversity, but they focus mainly on preserving 'useful' wild species, such as pollinators or beneficial soil microfauna.

Such evidence suggests a need to redouble efforts to establish protected areas 'off limits' to agriculture. But this is not enough. Of over 17,000 major sites already devoted to conserving wild biodiversity, 45 per cent (accounting for 20 per cent of total protected land area) have at least 30 per cent of their land used for agriculture (Figure 21.2). Most of the rest are islands within a 'sea' of agriculture (McNeely and Scherr, 2001). Some ecologists calculate that even if the existing protected areas do continue as wildlife habitat, 30–50 per cent of their species may still be lost because such isolated protected areas do not contain large enough populations, especially of large species with relatively low populations, to be viable (McNeely and Scherr, 2001).

FAO statistics still show that only 12 per cent of global land area is in agriculture, and previous remote sensing data were consistent with this, as they defined land units as 'agricultural' only if agriculture covered 60 per cent of the area. Our International Food Policy Research Institute (IFPRI)–World Resources Institute (WRI) re-analysis of the same data (Wood et al, 2000), which counts as 'agricultural' land units with at least 30 per cent of area under

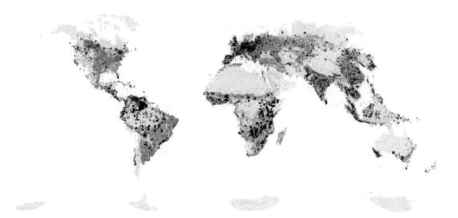

Agricultural share of protected area
(per cent)

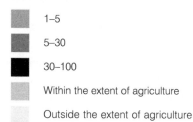

1–5

5–30

30–100

Within the extent of agriculture

Outside the extent of agriculture

Nearly half of the areas currently protected for biodiversity are themselves heavily used for agriculture, and many of them are located in regions where agriculture is a major land use. Neither fencing off wildlife nor restricting farming can save the world's threatened species from extinction (Wood et al, 2000).

Notes: The extent of agriculture estimate from Pilot Analysis of Global Ecosystems (PAGE) (Wood et al, 2000) includes areas with greater than 30 per cent agriculture, based on a reinterpretation of GLCCD, 1998 and USGS EDC, 1999. The protected areas within the extent of agriculture were derived from *Protected Areas Database* (WCMC, 1999). For protected areas represented only by points, a circular buffer was generated corresponding to the size of the protected area. The share of protected areas that is agricultural was calculated for each protected area using the PAGE agricultural extent.

Figure 21.2 *Geographic relation between protected areas and agricultural land*

agricultural use (a level at which significant ecological changes to the entire unit may be expected from agricultural use in a part), presents a very different picture. It shows that about 10 per cent of the area is under intensive agriculture use. Another 17 per cent is in more extensive agriculture or planted pasture. Another 40 per cent is in grasslands, of which much is used for grazing of domestic livestock. Thus the scale of agricultural impact is much greater than had previously been recognized. In many countries (such as the UK), as much as 70 per cent of land area is in agricultural use.

In Europe and North America, wealthy urban populations are able to transfer large financial payments to their small farming populations to take land out of (surplus) production to preserve as wildlife habitat or to provide financial incentives for conservation farming. But in poor countries with large rural populations, this approach is viable only in a few selected areas receiving generous foreign assistance, or where protected areas also provide highly valued environmental services (such as water and tourism) to urban populations. Elsewhere, environmental planners must rely upon local support for conservation efforts. While protected areas are still required, and need to be expanded, they ultimately will be successful only if environmental values are embedded *within* production systems that are economically competitive.

An essential strategy for conserving wild biodiversity, especially that found in highly populated, poor rural areas around the world, is to convert agriculture that is destructive of biodiversity into a new type of agriculture: 'ecoagriculture'. Ecoagriculture, which builds on the concept of 'ecosystem management', refers to land use systems that are managed both to produce food and to protect wildlife and other critical ecosystem services. For ecoagriculture, enhancing rural livelihoods through more productive and profitable farming systems becomes a core strategy for both agricultural development and conservation of biodiversity.

Ecoagriculture encompasses two sets of strategies for land and resource management. First, it increases wildlife habitat in non-farmed patches in agricultural landscapes, creating mosaics of wild and cultivated land uses, by:

* creating new protected areas that also directly benefit local farming communities (by increasing the flow of wild or cultivated products, enhancing locally valued environmental services or increasing agricultural sustainability);
* establishing habitat networks and corridors in 'in-between' spaces that are compatible with farming (such as hedgerows or windbreaks); and
* raising the productivity of existing farmland to prevent or reverse conversion of wild lands (where that is possible, given tenure, labour and price conditions; efforts to protect or restore the biodiversity value of uncultivated lands are also undertaken).

Second, ecoagriculture enhances the habitat quality of productive farmlands, by:

* reducing agricultural pollution through new methods of nutrient and pest management, and farm and waterway filters;
* modifying the management of soil, water and natural vegetation to enhance habitat quality; and
* modifying the mix and configuration of agricultural species to mimic the structure and function of natural vegetation.

At least 36 examples of ecoagriculture, from diverse regions of the world and types of farming systems, have been documented to have significant positive impacts on wildlife populations, farm yields and farmer income. A quarter of these are already being practised on millions of hectares (including wild lands re-established as a result of crop intensification on a smaller area; integrated pest management and organic production to reduce pesticide pollution;

minimum tillage in mechanized cropping; trees grown in pastures; and species-rich agroforests). The rest are being used on a smaller or pilot scale.

To have a meaningful impact on biodiversity conservation at global or regional scales, ecoagriculture must be developed and promoted for many more systems, on far larger areas. Agricultural and environmental policies need to be modified to encourage these new approaches. In some cases, ecoagriculture systems can be developed by using available components and information from scientific and local knowledge, and by improving these through trial and error to design landscapes that address both local livelihood and conservation objectives. But in most cases major scientific initiatives will also be required, using sophisticated methods and tools from various disciplines. Indeed, ecoagriculture is feasible now in large part because of our greater capacity to find synergies through scientific management. Advances in conservation biology, agricultural ecology, plant breeding, ecosystem monitoring systems and modelling are revolutionizing our ability to understand and manipulate wildlife–habitat–agriculture interactions. For example, recent research on cotton, maize and tobacco has demonstrated the potential for farmers to assist plants in manipulating predator–prey interactions through allelochemicals that activate plant defence genes that attract the predators of their insect pests. Completely new, low-cost and environmentally benign pest control systems could be developed based on this basic research.

New technologies, supported by needed policy changes, are enabling the design of farming systems and landscapes supporting ecoagriculture. For example:

- Using new methods to monitor wildlife and analyse patterns of 'countryside biogeography', conservation biologists have been able to determine spatial and temporal movement patterns and territorial requirements for wildlife. These are enabling the design and placement of corridors and habitat patches in farmlands, and spatial configuration of wild and domesticated plant species within farms, for cost-effective wildlife conservation. Local farmers can organize themselves effectively to play a lead role in designing landscape and farm interventions.[2]
- The use of analytical spectrometry with remote sensing has enabled scientists to identify sources of nitrogen- and phosphorus-rich agricultural sediments in Lake Victoria that feed water hyacinth (an invasive alien species) and cause turbidity and loss of native aquatic biodiversity. These data are being used by public agencies and farmer groups to target revegetation and conservation programmes.
- Scientists working in west Africa developed a natural biocide, from a strain of an environmentally friendly fungus (*Metarhizium anisopliae*), which was successful in controlling grasshopper and desert locust pests that were devastating grain crops in west Africa, and greatly reduced the need for insecticides that had been threatening stork and songbird populations. Field-based research and monitoring programmes are essential elements for success of such efforts.

- Veterinary research to develop a livestock vaccine against rinderpest, a viral disease, has not only greatly protected domestic cattle in east Africa, but also protected millions of wild buffalo, eland, kudu, wildebeest, giraffe and warthog that share rangelands and reserves, and that are also susceptible to the disease (Woodford, 2000). New park zoning and use regulations, as well as communications systems with local herders, are needed for successful co-management.
- Crop breeders in the US are developing native perennial grains (such as bundleflower, leymus, eastern gamagrass, Maximilian sunflower) that can be grown more sustainably with much less environmental damage in dryland farming regions. The systems are not yet economically competitive, but yields have reached 70 per cent of annual wheat varieties, while production costs are lower; habitat value for wildlife is many times higher than in conventional wheat fields (Pimm, 2000). Promoting these species will require changes in agricultural subsidy policies.
- In the humid tropics, research has demonstrated the benefits for both sustainability of production and biodiversity conservation of farming systems that 'mimic' the structure of the natural forest ecosystems. Millions of hectares of multi-strata 'agroforests' in Indonesia produce commercial rubber, fruits, spices and timber, often in a mosaic with rice fields and rice fallows (Leakey, 1999). The number of wild plant and animal species in these agroforests are often nearly as high as in natural forests. Maintaining these systems involves policy reforms to strengthen farmers' tenure claims and level the playing field with subsidized rice production.
- In Central America, researchers are developing modified systems of shaded coffee with domesticated native shade tree species, which maintain coffee yields while also diversifying income sources and conserving wild biodiversity (Lacher et al, 1999; Beer et al, 2000). Farmer adoption of these systems has been promoted through changes in public coffee policy to favour shade systems, technical assistance and, in some cases, price premiums in international markets for certified 'biodiversity-friendly' coffee.

An ambitious policy and research agenda is needed to develop and promote the adoption of farming systems that increase production, wildlife and also farm incomes in areas of high biodiversity value. Such research will require a full partnership of ecological/wildlife sciences and the agricultural sciences, generally working in association with operational-scale conservation and agricultural development programmes. Priority areas for such efforts include regions of high biodiversity value threatened by agricultural development; regions where agricultural productivity growth depends on restoring environmental services critical for agriculture; and regions where biodiversity conservation will benefit the poor directly through ecosystem restoration and income opportunities.

How can resources for such an agenda be mobilized on a globally significant scale? First, private R&D by large-scale commercial food producers and agro-processors could play an important role in areas where they dominate land use and production. Private food-processing companies that obtain a large share of their raw material from smallholder farmers located near protected areas may be motivated to encourage ecoagriculture (eg current trends to reduce agrochemical use in cocoa production). Private agricultural service companies might, for example, sell pest control services to farmers rather than simply selling them products. Private tourism industry that benefits from wild biodiversity may be willing to help support ecoagriculture. Public and civic conservation groups can encourage this work, and monitor wildlife impacts of farming systems.

But public sector institutions and civic organizations will have to play a leading role in ecoagriculture development, simply because so much of the necessary research is in support of providing 'public goods'. In many parts of the world, wildlife conservation organizations will need to take the lead in developing ecoagriculture strategies, and contracting for targeted research to support those strategies, as is already being done in many US organizations (for example, the support given by Ducks Unlimited to research on winter rice flooding in California; or the Nature Conservancy support to conservation ranching in the western US). The Consultative Group on International Agricultural Research, the Global Environment Facility, the United Nations Foundation and other international donors can lead in funding ecoagriculture research and development in and around globally important protected areas, such as World Heritage Sites and Biosphere Reserves; such an effort is already under development in Kenya.

However, this new challenge emerges just at a time when public resources for agriculture are declining. International aid for developing country agriculture has declined by almost 50 per cent in real terms between 1986 and 1996. In relation to their agricultural production, developing countries spend, on average, only a fifth as much as more developed countries on agricultural research and development. The Future Harvest Centres – a network of 16 international agricultural and environment research institutions supported by a consortium of public and private donors, the Consultative Group for International Agricultural Research – have faced declining resources even as their mandate has expanded to address agricultural sustainability and biodiversity conservation.

Developing the scientific basis and policy framework for ecoagriculture is an exciting challenge that should attract the best minds from numerous disciplines. It is essential to increase resources for both agricultural and environmental research, to improve the integration between them, and to integrate agriculture fully into ecosystem management, to ensure both sustainability and wildlife conservation. To accelerate ecoagriculture development in 'hotspots' for both biodiversity and rural poverty, several important steps are needed:

- Develop and fund (from sources not already being used for agricultural research or biodiversity conservation), a Global Programme for Ecoagriculture Research and Development, in selected biodiversity hotspots. These could focus on collaborative efforts by the Future Harvest Centres, public agricultural institutions, conservation organizations and

farmer organizations to develop operational systems, backed by socio-economic analysis and supportive policy interventions (US$50 million per year over 5 years).
- Establish a budget line item in the US National Science Foundation and counterpart organizations in Europe and Japan to fund basic research in biodiversity hotspots, on interactions between agricultural systems and wildlife habitat and species, and landscape ecology, agricultural ecology, wildlife behaviour and so on (US$15 million per year over 5 years).
- Undertake international and national policy research to determine cost-effective market, legislative and institutional interventions to promote ecoagriculture on a large scale (US$10 million per year over 5 years).
- Develop networks of researchers and farm leaders who work in particular habitat types, from both agricultural production and wildlife perspectives, and link them through websites, e-workshops and field tours in biodiversity hotspots of mutual interest (US$5 million per year over 5 years).
- Develop programmes to educate farmers, agricultural researchers and policy-makers in key elements of ecosystem management, and to educate wildlife biologists, ecologists and conservation policy-makers in key elements of agricultural resource management (US$10 million per year over 5 years).

In a recent essay (Janzen, 1998), the conservationist Daniel Janzen argued that we must re-conceptualize wildlife protection as 'gardenification'. In a world where the human population may reach 9 billion by mid-century, it is not enough to 'leave wildlife alone'; 'wild lands' must be actively managed as we already do our agricultural lands. This point can be taken a step further: agriculture itself needs to be re-conceptualized as a producer of both food and key ecosystem services, such as biodiversity conservation. With such compelling evidence on the vulnerability of wildlife to agricultural expansion and intensification, and the dependence of much of the world's poor on agricultural development, ecoagriculture has become a pressing policy and research priority.

Notes

1 'Agricultural extent' was defined in the Pilot Analysis of Global Ecosystems (PAGE) study to include land units (rather than areas) with greater than 30 per cent agriculture.
2 Promising examples include LandCare groups in Australia, farmer federations in the Philippines and forest user groups in Nepal.

References

Beer, J, Ibrahim, M and Schlonvoigt, A (2000) 'Timber Production in Tropical Agroforestry Systems of Latin America', in Krishnapillay, B, Soepadmo, E, Lotfy Arshad, N, Wong, A, Appanah, S, Wan Chik, S, Manokaran, N, Lay Tong, H and

Kean Choon, K (eds) *XXI IUFRO World Congress, 7–12 August, 2000, Kuala Lumpur, Malaysia*, Sub-Plenary Sessions, vol I, IUFRO, Kuala Lumpur

Cincotta, RP and Engelman, R (2000) *Nature's Place: Human Population and the Future of Biological Diversity*, Population Action International, Washington, DC

Frazier, S (1999) *Ramsar Sites Overview: A Synopsis of the World's Wetlands of International Importance*, Wetlands International, Wageningen, The Netherlands

Global Land Cover Characteristics Database (GLCCD) (1998) Version 1.2. Loveland, TR, Reed, BC, Brown, JF, Ohlen, DO, L Yang, Z Zhu and Merchant, JW (2000) 'Development of a Global Land Cover Characteristics Database and IGBP DISCover from 1km AVHRR Data', *International Journal of Remote Sensing*, vol 21, nos 6/7, pp1303–1330), available at http://edcdaac.usgs.gov/glcc/glcc.html

Janzen, D (1998) 'Gardenification of Wildland Nature and the Human Footprint', *Science*, vol 279, pp1312–1313

Lacher, T, Slack, R, Coburn, L and Goldstein, M (1999) 'The Role of Agroecosystems in Wild Biodiversity', in WW Collins and CO Qualset (eds) *Biodiversity in Agroecosystems*, CRC Press, New York

Leakey, RRB (1999) 'Agroforestry for Biodiversity in Farming Systems', in WW Collins and CO Qualset (eds) *Biodiversity in Agroecosystems*, CRC Press, New York

McNeely, JA and Scherr, SJ (2001) *Common Ground, Common Future: How Ecoagriculture can Help Feed the World and Save Wild Biodiversity*, IUCN, Future Harvest, Washington, DC

Pimm, S (2000) 'In Search of Perennial Solutions', *Nature*, vol 389, pp126–127

Pimm, S L et al (2001) 'Can We Defy Nature's End?', *Science*, vol 293, p2207; for full list of 32 authors see: www.zoo.cam.ac.uk/zoostaff/balmford.htm

Pinstrup-Andersen, P, Pandya-Lorch, R and Rosegrant, M (1997) 'The World Food Situation: Recent Developments, Emerging Issues and Long-Term Prospects', *2020 Vision Food Policy Report*, International Food Policy Research Institute, Washington, DC

Scherr, SJ (1999) *Soil Degradation: A Threat to Developing Country Food Security by 2020?* IFPRI Food, Agriculture and the Environment Discussion Paper 27, International Food Policy Research Institute, Washington, DC

USGS EDC (1999) United States Geological Surveys Earth Resources Observation Systems (EROS) Data Center, *Carbon in Live Vegetation Map*, Sioux Falls, SD, USGS EDC, unpublished data

Wood, S, Sebastian, K and Scherr, SJ (2000) *Pilot Analysis of Global Ecosystems: Agroecosystems*, International Food Policy Research Institute and World Resources Institute, Washington, DC

Woodford, M H (2000) 'Rinderpest or Cattle Plague', Briefing Note to Future Harvest, unpublished

World Conservation Monitoring Centre (WCMC) (1999) *Protected Areas Database*, Cambridge, WCMC, unpublished data

WFP (World Food Programme) (2000) *Map of World Hunger*, WFP, Rome

Chapter 22

Improving Access to Water and Sanitation: Rethinking the Way Forward in Light of the Millennium Development Goals

Gordon McGranahan and David Satterthwaite, IIED

Most of the world's governments and international agencies have committed themselves to the Millennium Development Goals, one of which is to achieve environmental sustainability (see www.un.org/millenniumgoals/). A water target set in relation to 'environmental sustainability' is:

> *To halve, by 2015, the proportion of people without sustainable access to safe drinking water.*

The World Summit on Sustainable Development, in 2002, added a sanitation target:

> *To halve, by the year 2015, the proportion of people who do not have access to basic sanitation.*

If these targets are achieved, it will make a significant contribution to the goal of eliminating poverty. The most recent Global Water Supply and Sanitation Assessment estimated that as of 2000 'one-sixth (1.1 billion people) lacked access to improved water supply and two-fifths (2.4 billion people) lacked access to improved sanitation' (WHO/UNICEF, 2000, p1). A significant share of the 'improved' water supplies and sanitation facilities are still likely to be inadequate, at least in urban areas (UN-HABITAT, 2003). Inadequate water, sanitation and hygiene is one of the most important global causes of ill health, and in *The World Health Report 2002* was estimated to account for 1.7 million deaths each year and 3.7 per cent of the overall global burden of disease (WHO, 2002).

There are serious doubts about the quality of the statistics underlying most of these estimates, and the focus on 'drinking water' in the targets is questionable (gaining access to sufficient water for washing can be just as important). But there can be no doubt that halving the share of people without reasonable access to adequate water and sanitation to meet their basic health needs would improve the lives of many of the world's low-income residents, including especially the women and children.

During the 1990s, the two 'new' policy agendas in the water and sanitation sector that received the most attention were private sector participation in water and sanitation utilities, and integrated water resource management. These agendas were not driven by the desire to improve water and sanitation provision in deprived areas. The push for private sector participation was part of a broader neo-liberal agenda that was actually more pronounced in other utility sectors, such as telecommunications, power and transport. Water resource management was part of an environmental agenda primarily concerned with preventing environmental resources from being abused, and only secondarily with improving access for those currently without. In the process of promoting these agendas, however, many over-ambitious claims were made concerning the role that increased private sector participation and integrated water resource management could and should play in addressing the water and sanitation problems of those groups that currently lack adequate access.

The recent international water and sanitation targets provide an important opportunity to correct these claims, and develop a strategy more responsive to local needs and priorities, and more supportive of good local governance. Water sector reforms are clearly needed, but the role of the private sector and of water resource management should emerge from, not drive, local water sector reforms.

This chapter first examines the emergence of the private sector participation and water resource management agendas. It proceeds with a critical assessment of why these agendas do not provide the basis for meeting the water and sanitation targets. And it concludes that the appropriate role of international development agencies in achieving the water and sanitation targets is not to decide how these targets should be pursued globally, but to support those strategies that have the best chance of succeeding locally.

New International Water and Sanitation Agendas in the 1990s

There was a time when publicly owned and operated utilities seemed to many to be the ideal route for achieving universal access to adequate water and sanitation. The challenge for the idealized public utility was, simply put, to plan the best way to pipe the clean water in and drain the dirty water out; and then to implement the plan. Good planning included choosing the appropriate technologies (especially challenging in rural areas), finding the requisite finance (especially challenging in low-income countries), preventing pollution (especially challenging in densely populated areas), and avoiding excessive leakage and over-consumption (especially challenging in dry regions). But once the public sector had helped to achieve near-universal coverage in most high-income countries, this also seemed the obvious way to go in other parts of the world.

In many situations, however, public provisioning did not live up to its ideals, and in the 1990s it came in for sustained criticism. The International Drinking Water Supply and Sanitation Decade had just ended, and universal provision seemed nearly as far away as ever (WHO, 1992). Environmental issues were beginning to be taken more seriously, and environmentalists were talking of a global water crisis, driven by increasing water demand in the face of limited supplies (Hinrichsen et al, 1998). Central planning was in disrepute, and market economists were debating how rapidly to privatize the state enterprises in formerly planned economies (Stiglitz, 2002). From both environmental and free market perspectives, public utilities came to be seen as part of the water and sanitation problem rather than part of its solution.

The two agendas that responded to these emerging concerns were those of improving water resource management (from the environmental perspective) and increasing private sector participation (from the free market perspective) (Finger & Allouche, 2002). Terms like integrated water resource management (IWRM), demand-side management (DSM), private sector participation (PSP) and public–private partnership (PPP) began to appear with increasing frequency in international policy documents (see, for example, the publications of the Global Water Partnership and the World Water Council, set up in the 1990s to address international water issues). Relatively little has actually been invested in improving water resource management, and private sector participation remains contentious. In terms of the number of customers they serve, public utilities still dominate. However, the combined effect of these agendas has been to undermine the favoured position of public utilities, particularly when water sector reforms are being considered.

Proponents of both water resource management and private sector participation have also made ambitious claims for how well their agendas coincide with the goal of reducing the share of the world's population without reasonable access to adequate water and sanitation. In the literature arguing for improved water resource management, existing deficiencies in provision are often presented as part of a global water crisis, and symptomatic of water resource scarcity and mismanagement. Alternatively, in the literature arguing for more private sector participation, existing deficiencies are often presented as part of a crisis in central planning, and symptomatic of public sector failures that private sector participation could overcome.

In both cases, such claims should be treated with scepticism. When new policy agendas are being promoted, their benefits tend to be exaggerated. Benefits to groups considered deserving, but not directly represented in the policy arena, are especially prone to exaggeration. Neither water resource management nor private sector participation derives its core support from the desire to extend water and sanitation services. The fact that so many people in regions with plentiful water resources lack reasonable access to adequate water and sanitation does not sit well with the claim that water resource scarcity is at the root of their access problems. Public sector failures may well help to explain existing deficiencies, but there is little evidence to suggest that bringing in the private sector will cure these failings, and improve access to adequate water and sanitation for those currently without.

Misinterpreting the Global Water Crisis

The need to take an integrated approach to water management is central to many of the new tools and approaches being discussed at international water conferences. IWRM is intended to overcome the many problems that can arise as a result of the uncoordinated use of increasingly scarce water resources. The integration of water resource management should ideally take place across a number of different dimensions. Upstream management should be integrated with downstream management in order to ensure that downstream needs are considered when taking upstream decisions. Meeting one demand for water should be balanced against the opportunity costs of not meeting others in order to ensure that water is allocated efficiently and equitably. The use of water to bear away wastes should be balanced against the impacts this may have on its capacity to meet other human and environmental demands. Managing supplies should be integrated with managing demands in order to ensure that costly additions to supply are not undertaken when there are less costly opportunities to reduce demands. Environmental demands for water and the relations between water and land use should be considered alongside human water withdrawals in order to ensure ecological sustainability.

In institutional terms, IWRM attempts to address the numerous boundary problems that water systems pose. From an economic perspective, water involves extensive externalities: water users (and others) often affect the water systems to the detriment of other users, without having to bear the costs. From a planning perspective, the water-related decisions of one ministry (eg agriculture) often have consequences for users outside that ministry's traditional concerns. Similarly, the water-related decisions in one planning district (or country) often have consequences for people living in other districts (or countries).

The goals of IWRM may be laudable, and most of the insights upon which it is based may be very sound, but the reasons why so many low-income households fail to gain reasonable access to adequate water and sanitation have little to do with the growing global scarcity of water resources. Better management of upstream water resources can be important to achieving sustainable water systems, but will only rarely improve access to adequate water or sanitation among currently deprived downstream residents, or result in the sort of health improvements that better water and sanitation provision allows. Similarly, avoiding water waste is important, but if water policies focus narrowly on saving water, the water that is saved is unlikely to find its way to the residents who need it most. Worse still, misguided attempts to protect water resources can actually impede efforts to improve water and sanitation conditions in deprived areas.

It is of particular concern that the international promotion of IWRM has been grounded in a misleading narrative of a global water crisis, driven by increasing water demand in the face of limited supplies. The basic message of this narrative is that the world is running out of water, that the consequences of this increasing scarcity are increasingly evident, and that only by giving water resource management higher priority (and adopting IWRM) can this emerging crisis be averted (McGranahan, 2002). In this crisis narrative, current water problems are just a foreshadowing of the problems to come if the appropriate messages are not taken to heart.

Numerous attempts have been made to measure this growing water resource scarcity. The term water stress has been coined to describe a region or watershed where there is 'insufficient water of satisfactory quality and quantity to meet human and environmental needs', and the indication that such conditions are present is most often taken to be that there are less than 1700 cubic metres of freshwater resources per capita (termed the Falkenmark indicator). On the basis of this indicator, it has been estimated that some 25 per cent of the world's population live in regions facing water stress, and that by 2025 this share will increase to 35 per cent (Hinrichsen et al, 1998). While the measures and interpretations of water stress are becoming more sophisticated, the presumption that water resource scarcity is at the root of people's problems in getting reasonable access to water adequate to meet their daily needs is still an integral part of the global water crisis narrative.

If water stress were a major cause of the difficulties so many households face in getting reasonable access to adequate water and sanitation, one would expect to find a negative relationship between water stress and the share of households with access to 'improved' or adequate water supplies. Figure 22.1 summarizes the water access statistics for about 100 countries with data on water stress, gross domestic product (GDP) per capita and the share of the population with access to improved water supplies (countries with GDP per capita over US$10,000 were excluded since they almost all have 100 per cent coverage regardless of the level of water stress). For both water-stressed and non-water-stressed countries, the average share of the population estimated to have reasonable access to improved water supplies increases with per capita income. However, at each of the three income levels, the average share among countries facing water stress is actually higher than among those countries not facing water stress.

This result is hard to reconcile with recent literature on water resource management and scarcity. It is often presumed that those without reasonable access to adequate water supplies are facing these difficulties because of water stress. Statistics on household access to water are routinely cited alongside those on national and river basin water stress, as if their interconnection were self-evident. The fact that those people identified as lacking reasonable access to improved water sources are actually less likely than most to live in water-stressed conditions undermines a key premise of the global water crisis narrative.

The only evident reason why a higher share of the population in water-stressed countries might have reasonable access to improved water sources is that water stress can drive people and their governments to improve their water

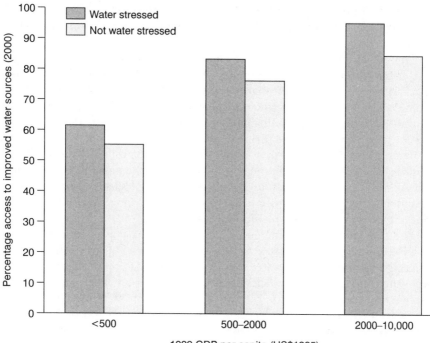

Note: The shares presented weight the shares for each country equally regardless of population. Countries are defined as water stressed if their internal renewable water resources per capita are less than 1700 cubic metres.

Source: The estimates are based on data drawn from the Data Compendium of the United Nations Environment Programme (2002). The original data sources are the World Bank (GDP), WHO (access to improved water supplies) and the FAO (freshwater resources per capita).

Figure 22.1 *National share of households with access to improved water sources by GDP per capita and presence or absence of water stress*

supplies. This could imply that the statistics on access to 'improved' water sources are misleading, since they may obscure the possibility that unimproved sources in areas without water stress may be adequate, while even improved sources may not be adequate where water stress is severe.

Nonetheless, these results are very damaging to the claim that better water resource management at the water basin level is going to enable the water and sanitation targets to be met. Instead, they support the view that water resource scarcity is neither necessary nor sufficient for there to be serious water supply problems at the household level. It is not necessary because political, economic and institutional factors can and often do lead to water deprivation even where overall water resources are plentiful. It is not sufficient because human settlement with plentiful water resources may be located in regions facing water stress, and in any case the quantities of water required to meet household water needs are small relative to total water withdrawals. This even applies at the global level: supplying 3 billion people with an additional 50 litres a day would still require less than 2 per cent of the total amount of fresh water withdrawn for human use, estimated at over 3000 cubic kilometres a year (Shiklomanov, 2000).

Thus, if IWRM is to take the water and sanitation targets seriously, it cannot treat water scarcity as the pre-eminent concern. It must also address those aspects of water management that prevent a significant part of humanity from gaining access to water even when it is plentiful. As described below, using the example of demand-side management (DSM), the tools of IWRM can be relevant to settlements where people do not have adequate access to water and sanitation. However, somewhat ironically, from the perspective of those without adequate access to water and sanitation, these tools have come to be associated with an approach to water resource management that focuses too narrowly on preventing water resources from being misused and ignores other challenges to achieving better water and sanitation provision.

The concept of DSM emerged along with IWRM as part of a critique of the tendency to respond to growing demand by investing in large infrastructure projects to tap more distant water supplies and ignoring opportunities for using local water resources more efficiently. It was originally an expert-led approach, emphasizing the need to promote water conservation measures. It has since been expanded to encompass 'economic' water pricing, an approach intended to be more 'demand-responsive', while still preventing water from being wasted or polluted.

The need to move away from a narrow supply-fix approach can be just as compelling when the priority is to extend provision to more people, and improve the services water can provide. Indeed, on the more expert-led side, health specialists often argue that the supply-fix approach of most water utilities neglects the importance of hygiene education and sanitation, and their potential role in helping people get the most out of their water supplies. Alternatively, on the demand-responsive side, local activists often argue that the supply-fix approach often fails because it ignores the importance of local organization.

Table 22.1 summarizes these different perspectives on DSM, each of which has somewhat different implications for the way in which DSM is undertaken. Demand-side strategies should ideally be able to accommodate multiple goals and recognize when each of these arguments is pertinent.

The local context should be critical to demand-side management. Some, mostly affluent, cities urgently need to conserve water, but have few water-related health problems. Some, mostly low-income, cities have severe water-related health problems, including inadequate provision for sanitation, but abundant freshwater resources. In some cities the most critical demand-side improvements could be achieved through getting water markets and prices right, while in others the key is to help low-income communities organize to address their own water and sanitation problems or make appropriate demands of water and sanitation utilities. But most urban centres face a variety of water and sanitation problems, and their demand-side strategies need to reflect this. The institutional settings of different cities also vary, further complicating demand-side strategies.

Table 22.1 *A more integrated perspective on demand-side water management*

	The conservation argument	*The hygiene argument*	*The marginal cost pricing argument*	*The community-action argument*
Guiding concern	Water stress is a growing problem in most parts of the world, due to excessive water consumption	Water- and sanitation-related diseases still constitute a large share of the global burden of disease	Water is a scarce commodity, with an economic value in numerous alternative uses	Adequate water and sanitation is a basic need, without which people cannot live healthy and fulfilling lives
Key insight	There are many unexploited opportunities for saving water without reducing the services water provides	Achieving health depends on how water and sanitation facilities are used as well their quality and quantity	Public water providers typically price water well below its (marginal) economic cost	Low income communities have more possibilities for addressing their water and sanitation needs and negotiating with outsiders when they are well organized
Contributory factors	Householders using piped water often cannot tell how much of their water is going to which purposes, are not aware when they are wasting water, and do not have the means of judging water conserving technologies	Householders often cannot discern the consequences of their water and sanitation practices on their own health, and rely on social norms which may be inappropriate	Even commercial providers rarely bear the full (marginal) costs of water withdrawal, and in any case do not operate in a competitive market	Tenure disputes and political repression can compound the difficulties of poorly organized communities
Demand-side consequences	Users are unaware and unconcerned about water-conservation, and waste water unnecessarily	Users often fail to adopt safe water and sanitation practices, and do not achieve the potential health benefits even when they receive piped water	Consumers overuse water, leading to resource problems and/or depriving others of valuable water	Residents receive inappropriate or inadequate water and sanitation services, or must rely on informal and often costly and inadequate water sources
Suggested response	Conservation education and promotion should become an integral part of piped water provision	Hygiene education and promotion should become an integral part of water provision	Piped water pricing should be based on long-run marginal costs, giving users the incentive to manage their own demand efficiently	Poor communities should mobilize (or be mobilized) around local water and sanitation issues; providers should respond to community as well as individual demands

Source: McGranahan (2002)

From the perspective of the water and sanitation targets, the tendency to emphasize the conservation and economic pricing perspectives is a problem (McGranahan, 2002), and DSM must pay more attention to the following:

Securing better access to water for the poor

Demand-side management in high-income countries focuses on wasteful and excessive consumption of water. Waste and excess also occur in low- and middle-income countries, but under-consumption is usually a more critical problem in deprived areas. Many households do not consume sufficient water to meet their basic needs for health. It is important not only to prevent conservation-oriented measures from further reducing the water consumption of deprived households, but also to implement demand-side measures that improve access to water, even if (and in some cases especially if) this increases their consumption.

Promoting sanitation and the hygienic use of water

Especially in conditions of poverty, it is important that demand-side management take account of needs for improved sanitation and hygiene behaviour, and access to sanitation facilities. Health is one of the major benefits that water and sanitation facilities can help to provide, but depends upon how the water is used and whether adequate sanitary facilities are also available and used. Users often lack a relevant knowledge of hygiene, and experts in DSM are often ignorant of both hygiene issues and local conditions in low-income settlements. From a health perspective, better sanitary improvements can also be critical, but will be ignored if DSM focuses exclusively on water deficiencies. Taking health issues seriously will require a major shift in the approach to DSM, but can be seen as an extension of IWRM.

Empowering deprived groups

One of the goals of demand-side management in low-income areas should also be to give more influence to those currently deprived of water and sanitation. The 'supply-fix' approach has often favoured affluent consumers over both future generations and the poor. Orthodox DSM attempts to address the concerns that are particularly relevant to future generations. Future generations cannot take an active part in designing and implementing demand management. Those currently lacking adequate water and sanitation can. To assist the currently deprived, DSM cannot simply rely on finding better means to manipulate the demand for water, but must help ensure that those most likely to be deprived (including especially women in low-income households) gain more influence over water and sanitation provision and use.

Overselling private sector participation

The case for private sector participation relies heavily on the failures of public utilities. Supporters of PSP typically claim that public utilities are inclined to be inefficient, overstaffed, manipulated by politicians to serve short-term political ends, unresponsive to consumer demands, and, particularly in low-income settings, inclined to provide subsidized services to the urban middle class and leave the urban and rural poor unserved. In many instances, there is at least some truth to these claims. Indeed, such problems were noted long before PSP became the order of the day.

In the 1990s, as indicated above, PSP was promoted as the fresh new alternative to the public utilities. Private companies would bring sorely needed private finance to the sector. They would depoliticize water and sanitation provision, introduce efficiency improvements and reduce costs. They would recognize the economic value of water, and ensure that it was distributed to its most valuable uses. Independent regulation, along with competition for concessions and other contracts, would prevent the abuse of monopoly powers. If necessary, targeted subsidies would be used to assist those households who could not afford to pay the real cost of adequate water and sanitation. But new research indicated that even the poor were usually willing to pay at least for water, and indeed were often already paying more than their more affluent neighbours, who tended to be better connected in both senses of the term (Serageldin, 1994).

There are at least three types of problem associated with most promotional accounts of how privately operated utilities can address the world's worst water and sanitation problems. First, there is little in the history of private sector water and sanitation provision to suggest that increasing PSP will, in itself, help meet the water and sanitation targets. Second, contemporary evidence does not support the claims that are often made on behalf of PSP: for example that it will attract large amounts of private finance, depoliticize water and sanitation provision, and ensure that the efficiency of the utilities increases. Third, debating the relative merits of publicly and privately operated utilities detracts attention from the many problems that can arise regardless of whether utilities are privately or publicly operated, as well as focusing attention on water over sanitation. These issues are discussed below in turn.

PSP's long history

Private sector participation and public–private partnerships are not actually new. Even 'innovations' such as public–private partnerships and competitive bidding for water concessions, have existed in various forms for well over a century, and these past experiences do not inspire a great deal of confidence.

At the turn of the 19th century, for example, New York City faced the classic dilemma: public sentiment favoured a city-owned supply, but the city's financial resources were considered insufficient (Koeppel, 2000). In an attempt to overcome this dilemma, a proposal was put forward for a 'public-spirited private enterprise' to be owned in equal shares by 2000 citizens. But this proposal was considered over-ambitious. A few years later, the city opted for a less constrained private enterprise: the Manhattan Company. Even this company turned out to be a public–private partnership of sorts. Unfortunately, the partnership seemed to involve using the water company's charter to provide banking services for the politicians who helped to get this charter through the state legislature, rather than to develop a water system suitable for New York City. The banking operations eventually evolved into Chase Manhattan Bank, while the water operations served primarily to convince New Yorkers of the merits of public waterworks; once the city managed to rid itself of the Manhattan Company (which had also been granted extensive water rights) it never again opted for a private utility.

More generally, attempts during the late 20th and early 21st centuries to justify a shift towards privately operated utilities on the basis of the failures of public utilities should be viewed with scepticism, given that in the late 19th and early 20th century the failures of private water companies were used to justify a shift towards public utilities. Looking at recent claims made for PSP would also seem to justify such scepticism.

Exaggerated claims for PSP

In the 1990s, proponents of PSP claimed that the private sector could solve three of the most critical problems facing many public utilities: insufficient financing, inefficiency and political manipulation. This could be achieved because PSP would attract private finance, introduce commercial incentives and remove the day-to-day decisions on water and sanitation provision from the public sphere. In practice, the level of private finance has been disappointing, commercial incentives have also been successfully applied to a number of public operators, and ill-conceived PSP has actually heightened the politics of water and sanitation provision.

The private sector will provide the needed finance

Investments in water and sanitation PSP projects grew rapidly in the 1990s, peaking in 1997. Similar trends, but with far higher overall investment levels and a sharper peak in 1997/1998, are evident in telecommunications, electricity and transport (Izaguirre and Rao, 2000).

The initially rapid growth might seem to support the claim that PSP attracts private finance and could play an important role in financing the increased investment that would be needed to meet the water and sanitation targets for the year 2015. However, the overall investment in PSP projects in water and sanitation between 1990 and 1998 only amounted to about US$26 billion (Izaguirre and Rao, 2000). Moreover, the public sector and international development banks have invested heavily in PSP projects. Foreign direct investment in water and waste infrastructure in low- and middle-income countries in this period amounted to less than US$2 billion (Sader, 1999). By way of contrast, overall water and sanitation investments are currently estimated at about US$16 billion a year and, according to World Bank estimates, this would have to increase to about US$23 billion in order to meet the water targets (World Bank, 2002).

Generally, there is little evidence of private companies or lenders wishing to invest in projects providing water and sanitation to the economically depressed villages, towns and squatter settlements where most households without adequate water and sanitation actually live. Understandably, there seems to be a strong preference for large cities, preferably with a substantial middle class. PSP investment has been concentrated in other ways as well. Of the estimated US$25 billion invested in PSP water and sanitation projects between 1990 and 1997, over two-thirds were concentrated in four countries (Argentina, the Philippines, Malaysia and Turkey) and an even greater fraction involved at least one of the four companies most active at the time (Ondeo, Vivendi, Thames Water and Aguas de Barcelona) (Silva et al, 1998).

The private sector will remove unwanted politics

The claim that PSP depoliticizes water and sanitation provision might superficially seem far-fetched, given the political conflicts that have accompanied some of the more contentious private sector initiatives. To be fair, however, the sort of politics that proponents of privatization claimed it would help avoid was the politics of patronage not that of civil dissent. Many public utilities have ended up providing subsidized services to the middle classes, while leaving the poor unconnected. This may in part reflect the greater political influence of the more affluent residents and their ability to wield it more selectively. Thus, the population at large may be able to rally around issues such as water prices, but it takes a different sort of political leverage to lobby for extending the water pipes and sewers to a specific neighbourhood. It is quite possible that in many instances low-income residents would be better off if they were at least offered water and sanitation services at their true cost, rather than subjecting those costs to political and economic manipulation.

Only the most extreme private sector advocates argue that decisions on pricing and network extension should be left to private water and sanitation operators (Brook Cowen and Cowen, 1998) since private network operators with the right to set prices would have a strong incentive to use their monopoly positions to overprice water. Indeed, except in England and Wales, there are very few cases where water or sewerage networks have actually been transferred to private ownership, and even where ownership is transferred the need for regulation is generally recognized. In most cases, PSP involves public–private collaboration, and leaves the public sector with major responsibilities (Johnstone et al, 2001). Unless the public sector creates a regulatory environment that actively prevents patronage politics from interfering with water and sanitation provision, there is no reason to expect PSP to make a positive contribution. Indeed, in countries where corruption is rife, public–private collaboration can provide many opportunities for patronage politics. Moreover, many of the urban residents without adequate access to water and sanitation live in settlements where tenure is disputed, and private companies are unlikely to want to invest in water pipes or sanitation infrastructure without unambiguous government endorsement (Lyonnaise des Eaux, 1998). Such politics are even evident where low-income settlements have received water and sanitation services, as a recent case study of four barrios in Buenos Aires clearly documents (Schusterman et al, 2002).

Moreover, internationally as well as locally, the vested interests in PSP politics can cause serious problems. When international development agencies promote PSP, or require PSP as a condition for loans, this can itself be interpreted politically. The fact that services, potentially including water and sanitation, are emerging as an important issue in international trade negotiations (through the General Agreement on Trade in Services) is likely to heighten the international politics of PSP.

The private sector will bring the necessary efficiency

Perhaps the strongest claim for private operators is that they are more efficient than public sector operators; but even these claims are highly misleading. With a poorly designed contract or an inappropriate regulatory environment, there may be no incentive for a private utility operator to strive to reduce costs and increase efficiency. Indeed, under a poorly regulated cost-plus contract, a private operator faces pretty much the same efficiency incentives as the stereotypical public utility operator. On the other hand, it is perfectly possible to set up a public utility to face the commercial pressures that are held to drive private sector efficiency. Also, the fact that a handful of transnational companies dominate the sector is not only politically controversial, but economically disquieting.

PSP as a diversion

Debating the relative merits of public and private provision also detracts attention from the many reasons why people fail to gain access to water and sanitation, which have nothing to do with whether utility operators are public or private. Where extending networked systems is the key to improving access to water and sanitation, many of the same challenges need to be addressed regardless of who is operating the utility. If tenure problems can inhibit public utilities from extending provision to low-income communities, they can also inhibit privately operated utilities. If pervasive corruption can subvert public utilities, it can also subvert privately operated utilities. Conversely, if a sound regulatory environment is needed to prevent profit-seeking private utility operators from ignoring the water and sanitation needs of the economically and politically deprived, good regulation is also needed to curb similar tendencies among public utility operators.

For a large share of those without adequate water and sanitation, improvements are unlikely to come from conventional water and sanitation utilities in any case. Sewerage systems and piped water networks are ill suited to the dispersed rural settlements where most of them live. Piped networks are generally the least-cost means of transporting water around a city, but even in urban centres water-borne sewerage systems are not always the least-cost means of disposing of human waste safely. If investment funds are channelled into the networked utilities at the expense of more cost-effective and decentralized options, then, again regardless of the ownership and operation of large utilities, this will not only favour those who are already relatively well served, but will also favour water over sanitation improvements (indeed, this may help explain why sanitation improvements lag behind water improvements).

Of course PSP need not be limited to large companies capable of operating network utilities. For many of the more deprived urban dwellers, the most relevant private operators are informal water sellers delivering water on foot or by truck (or in some cases through pipes), vendors of water pumps and latrine components, and private latrine and water kiosk operators. The participation of these private operators is not being promoted internationally with the same vigour, however.

Refocusing on the Water and Sanitation Targets and Supporting Good Governance

The water and sanitation targets define outcomes that international development assistance should help to achieve, but do not specify how they are to be achieved. This is just as well. Water and sanitation targets cannot be met simply by giving public utilities more finance to invest in water pipes and sewers. Nor, however, will the water and sanitation targets be met by identifying other generic solutions, such as water resource management and private sector participation. If they are to be met, it will be through local strategies, responding to the needs and desires of those inhabitants who still do not have access to adequate water and sanitation.

In the long run, better water resource management may be critical to achieving sustainable improvements in urban water and sanitation provision. However, policies designed only with a view to conserving and managing water resources can also make it unnecessarily difficult to extend adequate water and sanitation provision to those currently deprived.

In the right circumstances, water markets and PSP may be able to help improve efficiency and increase the financial resources available for improving water and sanitation services. However, attempts to increase private sector participation can also create new regulatory and corruption problems, direct finance to urban centres and neighbourhoods that are already comparatively well served, and further polarize the politics of water and sanitation provision.

Ultimately, it is in the public sector that the most critical decisions must be taken, and it is when these decisions are based on good local governance that the targets are most likely to be met.

References

Brook Cowen, P and Cowen, T (1998) 'Deregulated Private Water Supply: A Policy Option for Developing Countries', *The Cato Journal*, vol 18, no 1, pp21–41

Finger, M and Allouche, J (2002) *Water Privatisation: Trans-National Corporations and the Re-Regulation of the Water Industry,* Spon Press, London

Hinrichsen, D, Robey, B and Upadhyay, UD (1998) *Solutions for a Water-Short World,* Johns Hopkins University School of Public Health, Baltimore

Izaguirre, AK and Rao, G (2000) 'Private Infrastructure: Private Activity Fell by 30 Percent in 1999', Private Sector Viewpoint Note 215, Public Policy for the Private Sector series, World Bank, Washington DC.

Johnstone, N, Hearne, R and Wood, L (2001) 'Regulation of Social and Environmental Concerns with Increased Private Sector Participation in the Provision of Water and Sanitation', in N Johnstone and L Wood (eds) *Private Firms and Public Water*, Edward Elgar, Cheltenham, UK

Koeppel, GT (2000) *Water for Gotham: A History*, Princeton University Press, Princeton, New Jersey

Lyonnaise des Eaux (1998) *Alternative Solutions for Water Supply and Sanitation in Areas with Limited Financial Resources*, Suez-Lyonnaise des Eaux, Nanterre, France

McGranahan, G (2002) *Demand-Side Water Strategies and the Urban Poor*, International Institute for Environment and Development, London

Sader, F (1999) *Attracting Foreign Direct Investment into Infrastructure: Why Is It So Difficult*, World Bank, Washington, DC

Schusterman, R, Almansi, F, Hardoy, A, McGranahan, G, Oliverio, I, Rozenszteijn, R and Urquiza, G (2002) *Experiences with Water Provision in Four Low-Income Barrios in Buenos Aires*, WEDC, University of Loughborough, Loughborough, UK

Serageldin, I (1994) *Water Supply, Sanitation, and Environmental Sustainability: The Financing Challenge*, World Bank, Washington, DC

Shiklomanov, I A (2000) 'Appraisal and Assessment of World Water Resources', *Water International*, vol 25, no 1, pp11–32

Silva, G, Tynan, N and Yilmaz, Y (1998) 'Private Participation in the Water and Sanitation Sector – Recent Trends', Private Sector Viewpoint Note 147, Public Policy for the Private Sector series, World Bank, Washington, DC

Stiglitz, J E (2002) *Globalization and its Discontents*, Norton, New York

UNEP (2002) *Global Environment Outlook 3*, UNEP and Earthscan, London

UN-HABITAT (2003) *Water and Sanitation in the World's Cities: Local Action for Global Goals*, Earthscan, London

WHO (1992) *The International Drinking Water Supply and Sanitation Decade: End of Decade Review (as at December 1990)*, World Health Organization, Geneva

WHO (2002) *The World Health Report 2002: Reducing Risks, Promoting Healthy Life*, World Health Organization, Geneva

WHO/UNICEF (2000) *Global Water Supply and Sanitation Assessment 2000 Report*, World Health Organization, Geneva and United Nations Children's Fund, New York

World Bank (2002) 'Water – The Essence of Life', DevNews Media Center, Feature Story, 17 May 2002, available at www.worldbank.org/

Part 5

Markets and Sustainable Development

Chapter 23

Do the Poor Count?

Roberto Bissio, Third World Institute

In 1995 world leaders committed themselves to eradicating poverty in the world.[1] Every year since then Social Watch has asked governments what they have done to implement this commitment ... and every year, we have reported on what has and has not been achieved.

These commitments have been reaffirmed and they have evolved. In 2000, heads of state and government gathered at the UN Millennium Assembly and promised: 'We will spare no effort to free our fellow men, women and children from the abject and dehumanizing conditions of extreme poverty' (United Nations, 2000, para 11). And poverty was as much at the heart of the discussions of corporate and government leaders meeting at the World Economic Forum in New York in February 2002 as it was at the alternative World Social Forum of civil society organizations in Porto Alegre:

> *No other cause or campaign has ever enjoyed such strong moral support ... and so few actual results.*

More than half of humanity lives in poverty. A disproportionate majority of the poor are women and children. The struggle ahead seems overwhelming. It has rightfully been compared to the 19th century campaign to abolish slavery.

The task of 'freeing the entire human race from want' would be no minor accomplishment. Yet it is an achievable one, which can be done with the wealth and knowledge that is available now. To feed and educate every girl and boy adequately and to provide health services to every mother would require only a minor percentage of the personal fortunes of a handful of the richest men (there are few women on that list) on this planet. Doing it therefore becomes 'an ethical, social, political and economic imperative of humankind' (United Nations, 1995). This is not just an expression of the highest hopes of well-meaning but naive compassion. It is what over a hundred presidents and prime ministers from around the world committed themselves to do – and by doing so they established a benchmark against which their actions are to be judged.

Yet the different UN conferences have failed to provide a common definition of 'poverty', making it difficult to judge progress or to compare the performance of different countries. To measure the satisfaction of basic needs requires fairly sophisticated statistical tools and costly surveys that are not yet available in many countries. Thus, to make comparisons possible, the World Bank, a multilateral institution that lends more than US$30 billion a year to developing countries, started to publish estimates of how many people live with less than one or two dollars a day ('purchasing power parity' dollars and not 'nominal exchange rate' dollars). With less than the local equivalent of one dollar a day people are not supposed to be able to satisfy their minimum food requirements, whereas two dollars should suffice to meet these and other essential needs.

Based on those estimates by the World Bank, the media widely disseminated in 2000 a figure of 1.3 billion people (roughly one out of five of the world's inhabitants) living in extreme poverty. The UN General Assembly's Millennium Declaration of September 2000 set as a target:

> *to halve, by the year 2015, the proportion of the world's people whose income is less than one dollar a day and the proportion of people who suffer from hunger and, by the same date, to halve the proportion of people who are unable to reach or to afford safe drinking water.*

And, in an optimistic tone that was also widely publicized, the leaders of the eight most powerful countries announced in July 2000 that 'the percentage of poor in developing countries declined from 29 per cent in 1990 to 24 per cent in 1998' (G8, 2000).

The world leaders are to be commended for having transformed the 1995 commitment to eradicate poverty into measurable and time-bound goals. Citizen groups such as the Social Watch network, with active members in over 50 countries, can now hold them accountable. Yet the perception of the Social Watch national coalitions in more than 50 countries, and that of an overwhelming majority of the NGOs that work with the poor is not that poverty is declining. Most will actually state the contrary.

Based on the assumption that people on both sides of the debate are honest, Ravi Kanbur, who led the team that prepared the World Bank's report on poverty (and resigned shortly before its publication) attempted to explain the difference in perception by pointing out that a decline in the proportion of poor people might happen without their actual number being reduced (because population is increasing as fast or faster than the reduction). Both would be right: the proportion of people living in poverty is decreasing, as the World Bank claims; but the number of people queuing for assistance at the overloaded social services stays the same. In fact, the perception that poverty is decreasing might even lead to a decrease in the proportion of budget allocation in services to the poor.[2]

In Latin America, some political leaders have entered this debate by arguing the existence of a 'psychological factor'. Even when poverty is actually decreasing, increased inequities make people feel poorer because their distance to the rich has also increased.

More recently, a study by Columbia University researchers Sanjay G Reddy and Thomas W Pogge concluded that it is not true that both sides are right.[3] The World Bank measurements of poverty are 'misleading and inaccurate' and therefore result in 'a large understatement of the extent of global income poverty and to a false appearance of its decline'. Even assuming that at the base year of 1985 one PPP (purchasing power parity) dollar was enough to pay for a basic food basket and assuming also that the statistical adjustment of the line was accurate (a rather difficult task), the cost of food to the poor usually increases more steeply than the cost of all goods for the general public on which PPP is based. And empirical evidence shows that the prices actually paid by the poor for basic food are higher than the average national prices for those same products. Both factors lead to undercounting the poor, in some cases by half.

As a result of his own critique of the Bank's methodology, UNDP expert Jan Vandemoortele concludes that:

> *monitoring progress toward the international development target of reducing income poverty does not require an international poverty line. Global progress is best monitored on the basis of national poverty lines. This may not yield a quantitative estimate for global income poverty, nor will it produce internationally comparable poverty data. But global poverty estimates are seldom robust and the quest for comparable poverty data is elusive'* (Vandemoortele, 2001).

And, on top of that, 'income poverty' is essentially a flawed concept. The Millennium Declaration itself, in spite of its unhappy reference to the $1 a day line, refers in the same paragraph to food and water as at least as important as money when it comes to 'making the right to development a reality for everyone and to freeing the entire human race from want'. For Nobel prize-winning economist Amartya Sen, 'poverty must be seen as the deprivation of basic capabilities rather than merely as lowness of incomes' (Sen, 1999). By such a measure, if the people of a country are healthier, better educated and have access to public services without discrimination, that country is making progress in reducing poverty.

More and more experts and countries want 'a rights-based approach to development'. Under international law, human rights are not limited to civil and political liberties (such as freedom of expression or the right not be jailed without due process). They also include social, economic and cultural rights, all of which have been defined as 'indivisible' by a summit of world leaders in Vienna in 1996. In social sciences, these rights are called 'basic needs' and many countries assess their progress towards reducing poverty by counting the number of people who lack satisfaction of three or more basic needs, such as access to safe water, primary education, decent housing or enough food. A 'poverty line' thus defined is useful in identifying who the poor are and where they live, and therefore makes it easier to decide on social policies and to assess their effectiveness. At the same time, the definition of some basic needs – including what constitutes a decent house, or the quality of the primary education – varies from country to country.

Mary Robinson, former Irish president and UN High Commissioner on Human Rights stated: 'extreme poverty is a denial of human rights'. Deepa Narayan, senior World Bank official and main author of the three-volume World Bank study, *Voices of the Poor*, makes the human rights–poverty connection with the statement: 'with surprising coincidence the poor from all regions feel powerless and voiceless'.

A growing number of legal experts agree on the need to define poverty as a denial of rights, capabilities and access to resources. This is consistent with poverty measures based on satisfaction of basic needs and with internationally agreed targets on, for example, malnutrition, infant mortality, access to education and safe water. Some poverty situations are critical and worse than others, but since a rights-based approach is about participation and empowerment, no one is 'too poor', or 'not poor enough' to be excluded from human rights protection.

If this is the case, why is it relevant to count the poor properly? Isn't the very obvious situation of misery enough to mobilize compassion and solidarity, independently of whether the number of persons living in abject misery is one billion or double that figure?

The answer is that wrong measurements lead to wrong policies. In the words of Vandemoortele:

> the widespread use of the $1-per-day norm has led the world community to internalize two incorrect lessons regarding poverty reduction, namely that: (i) gradual progress is being made globally towards the poverty target for 2015, and that (ii) aggregate growth is the principal avenue for reducing poverty further. Without downplaying the importance of growth, one must question whether aggregate growth is a priori good for the poor.[4] The fact that the poor do not gain from stagnation and recession does – unfortunately – not prove that the opposite will be true. More nuanced positions and conclusions are warranted, given the many complexities that govern the relationship between growth and poverty.

We are being told again and again that 'globalization' is the key to solving the poverty problem. If only all restrictions on international trade and the flow of capital were lifted, greater riches could be created and their circulation would be like water in connecting vases, lifting all to the level of those who were lucky (or clever) enough to have started earlier.

This is not what is actually happening. In the last decade, many barriers to capital have been lifted, regulations have been abandoned, corporate taxes have been lowered. And as a result wealth and power is more concentrated now than ever before. Joseph Stiglitz, winner of the Nobel Prize for Economics in 2001, concluded: 'We do not see Adam Smith's "invisible hand", because it doesn't exist'.[5] For the market to operate as an efficient distribution mechanism, all participants should concur to it with the same information, something that never happens in practice. Unconstrained, the 'market forces' (a euphemism for the force of a handful of corporations to 'beat the market') are not the tide that lifts all boats, but a tidal wave, a tsunami creating havoc on the weak economies and the livelihoods of the weak.

Human rights laws, both international and national, conflict increasingly with the rules of the globalizing world economy. When the defence of human rights conflicts with economic interests the outcome is uncertain. The issue of anti-AIDS medication provides a dramatic example. AIDS is having a devastating impact in many poor countries, particularly in Africa. Cheap anti-AIDS medications could be produced in Brazil or India and eventually sold to African patients at one-tenth the price of the same medicine produced by pharmaceutical corporations. But this production has been challenged at the World Trade Organization (WTO) as a violation of international trade rules (including the WTO's agreement on Trade-Related Intellectual Property Rights, TRIPs). While the severity of the issue has been acknowledged, and shifts to allow countries to manufacture these drugs for their own populations have occurred, a satisfactory solution to the broader problem has yet to be found.

Which shall prevail: the right to life of HIV-positive persons in poor countries, or the intellectual property rights (IPRs) of transnational corporations? Both laws are of equal status, but violation of trade rules results in heavy economic sanctions, while human rights violations invoke no comparable enforcement measures.

The Uruguay Round of trade negotiations and over one thousand bilateral investment agreements concluded in the last decade created new rights for transnational corporations – from IPRs to the right to sue national governments in ad hoc international tribunals – without any balancing obligations.

The Sub-Commission on the Promotion and Protection of Human Rights of the UN Economic and Social Council (ECOSOC) stated in its resolution 2000/7 (August 2000): 'there are apparent conflicts between the intellectual property rights regime embodied in the TRIPS Agreement, on the one hand, and international human rights law, on the other'. In 1998, the Sub-Commission on Prevention of Discrimination (since renamed the Sub-Commission on Promotion and Protection of Human Rights) warned members of the Organisation for Economic Co-operation and Development (OECD) about the possible conflict between their human rights obligations and rules being proposed under the Multilateral Agreement on Investment (MAI).

In a report submitted on 25 January 2001, the Human Rights High Commissioner's special rapporteur on the right to adequate housing, Miloon Kothari, concluded that 'decisions regarding liberalization, deregulation and privatization have constrained the exercise of monetary and fiscal policy options for social purposes', thus affecting the right to adequate housing. Blame was not placed on macroeconomic adjustment and debt service alone. 'There is also a need to ascertain whether the prescriptions of "good governance" (by the World Bank and the UNDP) and "poverty reduction" (by the Bank and the IMF) are compatible with housing rights principles and State obligations', the special rapporteur said.

In another report to the Human Rights Sub-commission at its meeting in August 2000, on 'globalization and its impact on full enjoyment of human rights', two special rapporteurs, Joseph Oloka-Onyango from Nigeria and Deepika Udagama from Sri Lanka, said that there is a need for 'critical reconceptualization of policies and instruments of international trade, investment and finance'. The two jurists said that instead of being treated as peripheral, human rights should be brought directly into the debate and policy considerations of those formulating policies and operating the WTO, the World Bank and the IMF.

There is thus a growing volume of analysis and concerns expressed over conflicts between international trade and financial rules and human rights obligations on issues of poverty and poverty eradication. The heads of state at the 1995 Social Summit drew the same conclusion:

> *We know that poverty, lack of productive employment and social disintegration are an offence to human dignity. We also know that they are negatively reinforcing and represent a waste of human resources and a manifestation of ineffectiveness in the functioning of markets and economic and social institutions and processes* (United Nations, 1995, para 23).

Therefore,

> *public policies are necessary to correct market failures, to complement market mechanisms, to maintain social stability and to create a national and international economic environment that promotes sustainable growth on a global scale* (United Nations, 1995, para 6).

The ingredients of such an 'enabling environment' at the national level are human rights, progressive taxation, social security and fair access to resources and public services. At the international level the list is also well known: a solution to the debt burden, market access for developing country products, controls over the disruptive flows of speculative capital and, last but not least, more, higher quality development aid that effectively reaches the poor. Some of the measures aimed at securing a *global public good*, like the proposed currency transaction tax to tame financial speculation, may at the same time generate the resources needed to eradicate poverty. In the case of the carbon tax, cleaning the air we breathe could curb unsustainable consumption and production patterns and at the same time finance education, access to safe water and basic health services for all.

Yet it is obvious that those proposals have been blocked and resisted by the powerful few in such a way that even studying them further has been declared an international taboo. 'Coherence' in policy-making aimed at achieving sustainable development was one of the catchwords repeated again and again at the UN International Conference on Financing for Development in March 2002 in Monterrey. Yet the very policies that the Millennium Declaration, the Social Summit and Agenda 21 request from governments in order to protect the environment and eradicate poverty are being declared illegal by the trade rules imposed by the World Trade Organization or the macroeconomic policies demanded from developing countries by the Bretton Woods institutions.

We must put an end to the double standards and hypocrisy of an international system that moves capital freely around the world but does not grant workers the same right, that requires poor countries to open their markets but does not require the same of rich countries, that forces developing countries to tighten their belts in times of recession but allows rich governments to intervene when they face similar crises.

Double standards beget cynicism, apathy, corruption and deterioration of democratic life and the very social fabric that holds communities together. Double standards also motivate people to raise their voices, organize, demand transparency and advocate for change. Therein lies our hope. After all, the presidents, prime ministers and kings who were gathered in Copenhagen, who have the power to introduce reforms, wrote: 'We can continue to hold the trust of the people of the world only if we make their needs our priority' (United Nations, 1995, para 23).

Notes

1   This commitment was made at the World Summit for Social Development, held in Copenhagen, Denmark, which was attended by 115 heads of state and government, an attendance record surpassed only by the Millennium Summit of the United Nations General Assembly in 2000.
2   See Kabur's comments in www.people.cornell.edu/pages/sk145/papers/Disagreements.pdf.
3   'How NOT to count the poor' is available at www.socialanalysis.org.
4   The rate of economic growth for a country is an average indicator that hides enormous differences among families, including changes in opposite directions. It is not unlikely that the distribution of growth within the country will be strongly influenced by the pattern of distribution of human, physical, financial and social capital. Hence, an average growth rate of 5 per cent does not guarantee that the poor will see their income rise by a similar rate, if at all.
5   From notes taken by the author at Joseph Stiglitz's conference at the Central Bank in Montevideo, November 2001.

References

G8 (2000) *Communiqué Okinawa 2000*, Okinawa, 23 July 2000, available at: www.mofa.go.jp/policy/economy/summit/2000/documents/communique.htm, accessed 3 September 2003
Sen, A (1999) *Development as Freedom*, Knopf, New York
United Nations (1995) *World Summit for Social Development: Copenhagen Declaration*, March 1995, United Nations, New York
United Nations (2000) *Millennium Declaration*, September 2000, United Nations, New York
Vandemoortele, J (2001) 'Questioning some Norms, Facts and Findings Related to Growth and Poverty', paper presented at the *WIDER Development Conference on Growth and Poverty, 25–26 May 2001, Helsinki*, UNDP Bureau for Development Policy, New York

Chapter 24

The Chains of Agriculture: Sustainability and the Restructuring of Agrifood Markets

Bill Vorley, IIED

In the nine years since the UN Conference on Environment and Development (UNCED) at Rio, global agriculture has been a success in production terms, keeping pace with population. But by other measures of sustainability – ecologically sound land management, vibrant and resilient rural and regional economies, social equity and public legitimacy – the achievement of sustainable agriculture and rural livelihoods (SARL) in many countries is still a distant prospect.

A process of rural differentiation is under way, between what Reimer (1996) and Davila Villers (in Rounds, 1998) have classified as **Rural Worlds 1, 2** and **3** (Box 24.1). The negative aspects of these changes can be exaggerated, and the process of diversification under way in the peasant and smallholder economy can be misunderstood (eg Rigg and Nattapoolwat, 2001). But the continued marginalization of small and mid-size peasantry and family farming in both developing and developed countries, and the continued land degradation and externalities from poor or imbalanced land use, are affronts to the expectations of UNCED and the World Food Summit.

Full implementation of Chapter 14 of Agenda 21 would be a big step towards resolving the root causes of major environmental and social crises, from the 'Dead Zone' in the Gulf of Mexico,[1] to air pollution and haze in Southeast Asia, and rural unrest in China. The 2002 World Summit on Sustainable Development (WSSD) provided an opportunity for us to ask whether the gap between expectations and reality which has opened up during the decade of rapid political and economic change since UNCED can be attributed to a shortfall in scope and vision, as well as a failure of implementation.

BOX 24.1 DIVERGING RURAL WORLDS

The farmers and entrepreneurs of **Rural World 1** are a globally competitive minority (in Canada, for example, Rural World 1 comprises 5–10 per cent of the rural population) connected into the global agrifood economy. Through contracts with a rapidly consolidating agricultural handling and processing industry and even directly with retailers, these farmers are becoming an extension of agribusiness. State resources, especially subsidies and credit programmes, have benefited Rural World 1, in accordance with the political influence and economic power of large modern enterprises. Commodity supply management and price stabilization institutions have been converted into agencies with the purpose of transferring resources to this powerful lobby (Binswanger and Deininger, 1997).

Rural World 2 comprises the family farmers and landed peasantry who have traditionally constituted the bedrock of the rural economy, from India to the American prairies. But low levels of capitalization and poor integration with downstream food businesses leaves this sector exposed when governments withdraw from agriculture and liberalize agricultural trade, or when agribusiness concentrates market power (and hence profits) off the farm. Rural World 2 faces declining returns and increased risks from agricultural commodity production. Off-farm work is now the norm. This is an ageing farm population whose children are unlikely to succeed them. Niche marketing, such as agritourism, organics and local markets, has provided viable alternatives to a minority of Rural World 2, mainly in industrialized countries.

The livelihoods of **Rural World 3** focus mainly on survival. It is characterized by fragile entitlements, self-exploitation and unwaged family labour income, and depleted human and natural resources. Livelihoods are fractured into diverse mixtures of off-farm work, temporary migration and subsistence agriculture. Rural World 3 is globally redundant relative to food and fibre production. Indigenous groups are over-represented in Rural World 3. They are generally excluded from policy-making, despite the rhetoric of 'pro-poor' development strategies. The global economy of Rural World 1 and the economy of Rural World 3 appear to be completely separate, but they do paradoxically come face to face in the apple orchards of Washington State and the strawberry fields of California. There, migrants from rural Mexico and Central America constitute the bulk of the labour force for major agro-industries.

Source: Bill Reimer (1996) and R Davila Villers (in Rounds, 1998).

What Was Agreed at Rio?

Agenda 21[2] is premised on overcoming the constraints to smallholder agriculture by improving access to resources and improving local governance, with the state as the primary agent of change.

The chapter in Agenda 21 on 'promoting sustainable agriculture and rural development' (Chapter 14) is first and foremost a call to governments, with the support of international organizations, to implement SARL. There are in this chapter around 125 calls for governments to initiate or strengthen programmes of research, extension and land tenure, primarily aimed at sustaining production through conservation and management of natural resources and germplasm.

What's Missing?

The Rio agreements in general and Chapter 14 of Agenda 21 in particular *overstated* the ability of the state to respond to the challenges facing Rural Worlds 2 and 3, in the face of government withdrawal from agriculture. It also *understated* two of the key constraints facing smallholder and family agriculture: access to markets and pricing, related to the terms of trade between farming and the rest of the agrifood chain.

The agricultural sectors in many countries have been liberalized through privatization and deregulation, often as a result of structural adjustment policies, donor conditionalities and compliance with trade agreements. The state has withdrawn from interference in production activities and the functioning of markets. Structures such as marketing boards have been broken up. Many agrifood markets have experienced a rapid transition to world prices.

Small farmers North and South are encouraged to deal with the withdrawal of government from the business of agricultural support and commodity trading by exploiting their comparative advantage and forging direct relations with the market.

In a perfect world, the increased risk from exposure to market fluctuations and removal of safety nets[3] would be countered by improved market information and reduced information asymmetries, efficient scales of production and marketing, contract farming, and improved liquidity. Problems of quality, efficiency and competitiveness on smaller farms could be overcome through social organization. Producer organizations[4] and social capital[5] – as social mechanisms to adapt to the market economy – are the means by which Rural Worlds 2 and 3 are supposed to defend themselves from being bypassed and marginalized by liberalization and globalization.

World markets are however distorted by the dumping of exports at prices below the cost of production, especially from the EU and US.[6] Liberalization of trade means that international markets set price and quality standards in domestic markets. Agriculture which is oriented towards both the export sector and internal markets must then turn out products at a similar cost and quality as those that can be bought on the world market. Access to new market opportunities in an open economy is thus predicated on an end to distortions caused by dumping.

But there are two other limitations, linked to the management of risk and dealings with markets, which introduce a strong bias within the process of liberalization in favour of Rural World 1.

First, the state has also withdrawn from investment in extension, public research, rural infrastructure and credit provision under the same fiscal constraints and donor influence that brought about economic liberalization. This limits access to technology, information and markets, even for strong local peasant organizations.

Second – and the theme of this chapter – is the *restructuring of markets*. Many markets are undergoing rapid change, with *closed supply chains* rapidly replacing traditional arm's-length or spot markets. The restructuring of markets and power relations beyond the farm gate has been under-reported in the debate about sustainable agriculture and rural poverty, both North and South. The trends were considered to be typical of industrialized country agriculture rather than peasant systems. Agenda 21 reflects this: the private sector and the market hardly figure. Chapter 14 makes *no* demands of the private sector and little mention of markets. The chapter on 'strengthening the role of business and industry' (Chapter 30) focuses mainly on product stewardship and technology transfer. The section on 'strengthening the role of farmers' (Chapter 32) contains two calls for involving farmers in policy formulation and for the support of farmers' organizations.

Liberalization of agricultural markets relocates risk from the state on to the individual (McDonald, 1999), and also elevates the importance of the private sector and off-farm capital as arbiters of sustainability. As governments – especially in the South – withdraw from heavy involvement in agriculture, to be replaced by direct dealings between farmers and agribusiness, the gap of private sector policy must be addressed.

The Chains of Agriculture

Buyer-driven (as opposed to producer-driven) supply chains or value chains,[7] have sophisticated forms of coordination and integration, and rules of participation. The implications for smallholder agriculture of these new forms of agrifood governance can be overstated. But as we shall see later, the rules of participation in vertically coordinated supply chains with privatized standards, and the rise of contracts and specialized intermediaries, are proving to be powerful drivers of divergence and marginalization within farm communities. It is by understanding supply chains and their role in concentrating capital in the agrifood system that we get a clear understanding of agricultural markets and the future sustainability of farming.

The analysis of commodity chains has its theoretical roots in *demand* orientations informed by neoclassical economics and the notion of the sovereign consumer, as compared with the *supply* orientation of political economy (Wilkinson, 2000). A traditional political economy approach to the agrifood chain would propose that capital is accumulated by controlling the tangible means of agricultural production: land, labour, nutrients and chemicals, water, genetics and seeds, feed, equipment and capital. Combining supply chain analysis and political economy reveals, however, that it is ownership and control of *intangible* assets, especially information, brands and patents, rather than control of the *tangible* means of production, that raises sufficient barriers to competition to allow the concentration of capital from a supply chain and the conversion of that capital into mobile financial capital (Pritchard, 2000). In other words, the governance of supply chains hinges on controlling the means of coordination rather than the means of production.

Management and control of information is a feature of industrial size and concentration, rather than monopoly.

Size confers logistical control, reduced transaction costs, economies of scale, improved market and meteorological intelligence, and access to and control of the most valuable intellectual property and the most comprehensive distribution network. Size confers 'absolute cost advantage': the ability to outbid smaller farmers or companies for resources and ideas, to invest more heavily in research and development and patent protection (for instance, to obtain critical mass in genomics), to set predatory prices, to externalize risk, to raise external capital, and to mount lavish promotional campaigns. Size also confers access to information related to the workings of government that selectively benefit the company, and the ability to remould the social and political environment to an individual's or company's own benefit.[8]

Size can be achieved through acquisition or through strategic alliance, which is a common feature of buyer-driven chains. Global clusters and strategic alliances in agrifood industries (eg Heffernan,1999) are examples of corporate convergence, which is becoming the global norm. Under these conditions of 'cooperative capitalism' (Grieder, 1997), transactions become based on industrial relationships rather than on open markets. These networks transcend national and transnational (eg EU) regulation.

Size and Concentration in Agrifood Industries

The years since Rio have seen an astonishing process of concentration in upstream and downstream global agrifood industries.

In retailing

In both the EU and US, it is retailers who determine what food processors want from farmers. Retailers are the point of contact between the majority of Organisation for Economic Co-operation and Development (OECD) citizens and the rural economy. The supermarket sector is most concentrated in the EU, but is also rapidly consolidating in the US. In the nine years since Rio, US food retailing chains have concentrated dramatically (Hendrickson et al, 2001); the five leading chains have moved from 19 per cent control of grocery sales to at least 42 per cent (Harl, 2001). Since 1992, global retail has consolidated enormously and three retailers – Carrefour, Ahold and Wal-Mart – have become truly global in their reach. In 2000, these three companies alone had sales (food and non-food) of US$300 billion and profits of US$8 billion, and employed 1.9 million people. It is predicted that there will be only 10 major global retailers by 2010.

In processing

Partly out of necessity to exercise countervailing economic power to retailers, processing industries are also rapidly consolidating their economic and market power. The economic power of the top eight food multinationals has been compared to that of half of Africa. In 2000, US$87 billion in food industry deals were announced; Nestlé, Philip Morris and Unilever emerged as the 'Big Three' of global food makers. The justification for such massive accumulation

---

BOX 24.2 PROCESSING TOMATOES AS A STRATEGIC AGRICULTURAL COMMODITY

The globalization of the Mediterranean, Mexican and Creole diets has been accompanied by a marked rise in the market for processing tomatoes. The industry is bifurcating into scale processors for the industrial paste market, such as Morning Star in California which buys 1 million tons of tomatoes each year, and the smaller branded producers. Some processing companies such as Heinz have been able to extract greater value from the industry by controlling the seed market, thus forming an agribusiness 'sandwich' with the grower in the middle. Heinz has 30 per cent of the global processing tomato seed market, and this figure grows to 70 per cent in Australia. By linking grower contracts with their proprietary seeds and germplasm, Heinz could price their elite seeds at over AU$2000/kg (1990 figures), compared with an average tomato seed price of AU$70/kg. Grower influence over the value of their crop in Australia has been further diminished by state deregulation of bargaining arrangements; collective bargaining has been replaced with confidential individual contracts. Revealing contract prices is now illegal (as a 'collusive behaviour') under the Trade Practices Act.

Source: Pritchard (2000) and personal communication.

---

of market power is 'to have more clout in the consolidating retailing environment'.[9] We are likely to see a growth in networks and cross-ownership between food processing and the seed sector, in which the farmer is contractually sandwiched, just a step away from the farmer as renter rather than owner of contracted crops or livestock (see Box 24.2).

In farm inputs

Concentration in the input sector proceeded at breakneck speed in the 1990s. Only six companies now control 80 per cent of pesticide sales, down from 12 in 1994 (Dinham, 2000, 2001). There were US$15 billion of amalgamations in the US seed industry in the period 1995–2000. From a value chain perspective, input manufacturers – as suppliers to the least profitable sector of the agrifood system, namely farming – are in a strategically weak position. The level of concentration in the business is in part a desperate drive to maintain profitability against declining strategic value of chemicals, seeds and biotechnology. Value chain thinking rather than technical hubris is key to the sustainability of these industries. Survival will depend on strategic alliances with processors and retailers around food quality, safety and health.

What Does This Mean for SARL?

We have seen that highly concentrated food processing, retail and food service industries, as key agents within buyer-driven chains, are able to consolidate their supply base and demand increasingly stringent levels of quality, compliance with standards and codes of conduct (including proof of 'sustainable agriculture' production techniques), and post-production service from their suppliers.

If valuable agricultural markets are subsumed into relatively closed supply chains governed by downstream private actors, what does this mean for SARL and the opportunities for agriculturally led development?

Participation in buyer-driven supply chains can link small farmers to the modern economy, with lower market risk and greater new markets, to inputs, and to financing. Contract agriculture, as one means of making this connection, does not (as painted by some critics) have to 'turn farmers into wage labour on their own farms'. Small producers South and North can be global actors rather than perpetual victims of imposed models and global forces (eg Bebbington and Batterbury, 2001; Eaton and Shepherd, 2001).

But the control of supply chains in agrifood by clusters of powerful downstream industries has profound impacts on agriculture, especially in weakening the link between farm prices and food prices.

High levels of concentration in downstream processing and retailing industries mean lower levels of value-added going to local communities; 78–85 per cent of value added in the agrifood chain in the US and UK, for example, is *not* done by farms.[10] The farmers' slice of the retail cost of a basket of foods sold in grocery stores shrinks further once they have paid for seeds, fertilizers, feed and machinery, finance, labour and land rental costs; again from a very concentrated sector in the case of seeds and chemicals. The size of the food market also shrinks as intense retail competition and concentrated retail buying power is translated into consumer surplus. Farmers have to produce more, but get less.

During the 1990s, the average annual median return on equity for the US food manufacturing industry was 17.2 per cent, and 18 per cent for food retail. Over the same period, return on equity for US farming averaged 4.5 per cent (Taylor, 1999). Benbrook's rough estimates for the performance of US agriculture puts return on assets in the late 1990s at only 0.4 per cent, compared with nearly 4 per cent for life sciences,[11] 9 per cent for food processing, 10.6 per cent for retail and 16 per cent for food service (Benbrook, 1999).

Market access to supply chains for producers does not have much to do with classical notions of 'efficiency'. Rather, market access is a feature of the ability to exploit marketing advantage, meet large processor and supermarket demands for consistency of supply (reliable quality), speed of response, compliance with standards and payment of fees.[12] Coordination by supermarkets of their supply chains raises the requirements for farms and firms to stay in the market. For instance, the example of grape production in Brazil, for which Collins (2000) notes that although production costs are lower and quality higher among small-scale producers, marketing advantage accrues to large-scale producers through their better access to post-harvest cold storage and refrigerated transport services. In Latin America as well as Europe and North America, there is a growing tendency for supermarkets and processors to use this form of coordination to source sub-regionally or regionally, and occasionally extra-regionally (Reardon and Berdegué, 2000), rather than locally or nationally.

As buyer power increases, so barriers to entry for smallholders to markets other than for basic commodities become more daunting. Small farmers of

Rural Worlds 2 and 3 – in both South and North – often lack the strong and direct relationship with the market enjoyed by large-scale producers, such as contracts with processors or supermarkets. Buyers preferentially contract with larger farms and firms that can meet these demands, because they deliver lower transaction costs and risk. Smaller farmers with little land and capital see little benefit from the investments needed to achieve the quality and efficiency required to meet the expectations of an agribusiness processor, even in the unlikely event that they can raise the capital (McDonald, 1999). Smaller farmers also present higher per unit costs for contractors, and have greater problems meeting stringent quality and safety requirements (Reardon and Barrett, 2000). Rural Worlds 2 and 3 have experienced declining returns from agriculture, stuck in commodity activities with low barriers to entry (Kaplinsky, 2000).

Only Rural World 1 has integrated itself economically and politically with downstream actors, using its capitalization, infrastructure, technical expertise and market information to meet the requirements of shippers, processors and retailers, and the political influence to direct state resources in support of their interests. Yet even for this highly capitalized group it is very difficult to prevent bargaining power (and therefore profitability) from being eroded as downstream agribusiness becomes ever more concentrated. The contracts that Rural World 1 negotiates with downstream agribusiness are often low risk and low return.

Captive supply[13] of livestock under contract to the large integrators, for example, is drying up markets in many countries for non-contracted animals and forcing down wholesale prices. Farmers are left with 'take it or leave it' deals with a few integrators. Captive supplies of beef cattle and swine in the US are now such a large part of the livestock industry that there is no competitive market where prices can be discovered. The spread of closed contract production systems into the grain sector does not bode well for price and farm income.

Buyer-driven chains, while appearing very remote from agriculture in developing countries, are in fact making rapid inroads into areas considered to be entirely dominated by spot markets. Consider that 20–35 per cent of the rural retail sector in Central America is already controlled by supermarkets, and that a single firm controls 60 per cent of chicken purchases in Central America. Growth is particularly rapid in emerging economies of Latin America and eastern Europe. In Chile, 14 of 15 main food products are now sold through contracts between farmers and supermarkets and processors, rather than through spot markets. Thousands of small dairy operations have failed in Chile, Argentina and Brazil in the 1990s; cooperatives of small farmers and processors have gone bankrupt or suffered membership declines. In the 1990s, the share of the retail sector controlled by supermarkets in Argentina increased from 20 per cent to 80 per cent (Reardon and Berdegué, 2000).

Price pressure is forcing farmers into unsustainable practices in order to sustain family income from a fixed land base. Overstocking and neglect of practices which favour biodiversity (Nowicki, 2000) or soil quality are typical features of farming areas under price pressure.

How 'Sustainability' Can Drive Consolidation and Marginalization

What happens when requirements for 'sustainable agriculture' are introduced into established supply chains, perhaps in response to pressure from NGOs or state regulators? Standards for 'sustainability', such as conditions for farmworkers or techniques for soil and pest management, are part of a trend from performance to process standards. Another characteristic is that these are private rather than public standards. Private process standards are features of buyer-driven chains, marked by

> a shift in [the] centre of gravity from technical norms to reduce transaction costs in broad homogenous commodity markets, to strategic instruments of product differentiation, agrifood chain coordination, market creation and share growth (Reardon et al, 2001).

'Sustainability' as a set of process standards can provide leverage for large enterprises to control markets and raise barriers to competition. When a processor or retailer develops a strategy for sourcing more 'sustainable' products, they can – as governors of the supply chain – push all compliance costs and risks down to suppliers. Standards and codes of practice thus favour well-capitalized farms (not necessarily always 'large' farms). 'Sustainability' is understood by farmers as another new set of outsiders deciding what goes on inside the farm gate – as with policies of importing countries such as 'due diligence' and phytosanitary standards – and as a cost of contracting with vastly more powerful market players. Standards are seen as another example of the North 'pulling up the ladder of development' on Rural Worlds 2 and 3.

Northern environmentalism has thus been a blessing and a curse. It is an important and unwitting driver in the consolidation of Rural World 1, and may hold back smallholder farmers from building equitable (and therefore economically sustainable) trading relationships with downstream actors. The proponents of sustainability, in catalysing a public–private response which packages 'sustainability' into technical, regulatory and managerial frameworks, have seen the supply chains respond with another force of marginalization of small farmers and peasants.

These issues add to smaller farmers' growing problems of market access within rapidly concentrating supply chains.

How Can Markets be Re-governed?

Governments are faced with the challenges of achieving local rural development in a period of globalization in the agrifood system, liberalization of markets, reduced state intervention, and a reconsideration of the role of agriculture in rural employment and livelihoods.

Despite the rhetoric of poverty reduction through access to resources (for instance, via land reform) and more inclusive governance, especially participation of rural people in policy processes, it is becoming clear that improving governance in public policy-making is not enough to reduce poverty (Bebbington, 2001). The livelihoods frameworks provided by rural sociology, with their household and community perspective, are also inadequate tools for understanding the workings and influence of supply chains.

Control of and influence over markets is key to the circulation rather than extraction of economic assets, either within agrifood markets or through non-farm activity such as tourism where control over markets is easier.

How can public *and* private sector policy be reformed to achieve this re-governance of the agrifood system, so market liberalization is an inclusive process rather a driver of rural differentiation? Public regulation is not geared up to deal with supply chain structures. And within the supermarket- or processor-driven supply chains, where standards and prices are dictated by distant actors, there are few opportunities for smallholders and family farmers to influence the market or exert democratic influence over agrifood futures. With growing distance between point of decision over production methods/technologies and production itself, there is a need for global governance over supply chains.

We first need to recognize the political nature of the rules and frameworks that compose market structures, understanding that markets and political authorities (and hence economic interests) are parts of the same ensemble of governance, rather than contrasting principles of social organization (Underhill, cited in Nowicki, 2000).

Following from this recognition, there are seven ingredients for advancing the interests of equitable and sustainable rural development, outlined below:

1 *Producer organizations*

Organization of smallholders is widely seen as an antidote to smallholders' problems of dealing with buyer-driven chains. Developing organizational capacity among small farmers can allow extraction of more benefits and less risk from contract farming, as demonstrated by small rice-potato farmers in northern Thailand (Box 24.3). Governments and international cooperation can assist these organizations, by recognizing them as partners in decentralization and providing a legal framework covering oversight of contracts and provision of bank credit, which enables smallholders to access lucrative value-added markets without losing out to intermediaries.

2 *Industrial policy*

Policies that protect markets are as important to sustainable development as policies that protect land and water. Industrial policy is a valid instrument in agricultural and rural development, in penalizing collusion and preventing undue concentrations of economic power. Vigorous competition (antitrust) policy must address buyer concentration (oligopsony) and its effects on supplier

---

BOX 24.3 SMALLHOLDERS AND AGRIBUSINESS: CONTRACT POTATO PRODUCTION IN NORTHERN THAILAND

In the San Sei district of northern Thailand, small (averaging 1 ha) farmers have developed a sustainable rice-potato production system, on which they have built outstanding marketing arrangements. National legislation in 1987 and 1995 emphasized the promotion of high quality value-added products for exports, through cooperation between industrial firms, farmers and financial institutions. Efforts of local officers in coordinating contracts between firms and farmers have made initial establishment possible, and supported the progress of the whole industry by building the right conditions of trust between firms and farmers. Farmers have found that growing both processing potatoes under contract with processing companies and cooking potatoes for the domestic market can spread risk and avoid over-dependence on one partner, diversifying their enterprises between contract and open market arrangements. Organization by farmers has allowed them to effectively pull down service and resources from government authorities and local politicians. Farmer organization in the form of a Potato Growers Cooperative has been effective in managing supply and therefore the price of cooking potatoes. Contract farming has helped to promote the production of a quality product and assured quantity. However, the development of the modern formal contract is a long process; in northern Thailand, it took at least 30 years.

Source: Gypmantasiri et al (2001)

---

welfare and the distribution of profits as well as profit levels along the agrifood chain. Other tools are a legal environment which allows agricultural bargaining as a form of countervailing power, and legislation or ombudsmen to protect producers and uphold principles of fairness, full information and equity in supply chains (Boehlje and Doering, 1999; Harl, 2001).

3 *State support for building small producers' capacity*

Governments can help players to develop new competences for participation in supply chains, especially in meeting quality standards. There is also a spin-off of raising production standards for the domestic market. There is a key role for the state in informing farmers about the market to overcome information asymmetries that disadvantage remote farmers in market transactions. State support can be very beneficial in providing alternative structures to supply chains, such as school meals programmes, poor-to-poor markets and local farmers' markets.

4 *Corporate ethics and private sector policy*

A clear commitment by industry to move beyond its eco-efficiency positions laid out at UNCED is essential. While issues of corporate accountability and corporate social responsibility were addressed in vague terms at WSSD (United Nations, 2002, para 18), there is a long way to go before these translate into applicable guidelines which could influence the food industry. Food retailer and processor policies affect livelihoods and environmental health right across the supply chains, way beyond the points of production and sale. Accountability of global food processors and retailers, as drivers of agrifood markets, must extend beyond their consumers, to include national objectives for sustainable development. For instance, South Africa's goal of developing rural economies around smallholder land reform beneficiaries should be supported by global agrifood corporations in their sourcing policies. Standards and codes of conduct should be accompanied by training and capacity building to ensure inclusion rather than exclusion of Rural Worlds 2 and 3 in the chain. A commitment to sharing the cost of compliance would be a small but valuable gesture.

5 *Civil society scrutiny*

Increased size and concentration in agrifood industries has advantages for sustainability, in that they become sensitive to scrutiny by civil society groups ('stakeholder value'; see Koechlin and Wittke, 1998), in order to defend brand equity and shareholder value. Civil society benchmarking is another pillar of improving the governance of agrifood chains. It raises public expectations for private sector support for sustainable agriculture, draws consumer and investor attention to best practices, and can be a tremendous educational opportunity.

6 *Strengthening the farmer's voice in the process of setting standards and codes of conduct*

Standards and codes of conduct, including those for sustainability, should be undertaken as a partnership with producers rather than enforced from a distance. Standards can then take into consideration local realities and aspirations.

7 *Removing market distortions: Ending overt and disguised dumping of agricultural produce*

Trade liberalization exposes third countries to highly subsidized models, potentially undermining more sustainable, less intensive local models of agriculture. If one country's 'sustainability' is achieved at the expense of another's (especially by putting up fences, and by throwing surplus production over that fence), then that is not 'sustainability' at all (Vorley, 2001). Regions or countries should not build agricultural and rural policy based on a presupposition of large agricultural exports, if clear markets for those goods do not exist and/or if their status as major exporters requires large quantities of non-renewable inputs (Einarsson, 2000). Post-WSSD there is a clear role for governments to specifically support actions in other fora such as the WTO to bring an end to overt and disguised dumping of agricultural produce.

What Happened at Johannesburg?

How much did WSSD address the marginalization of small and family-based farming, South and North?

The final policy declaration included a commitment to 'making globalization equitable and inclusive' in part through the active promotion of corporate accountability.[14] The summit succeeded in getting the issue of distorting agricultural subsidies higher on the political agenda. And the 'polarization of agribusiness and small-scale farming cultures of agriculture' was highlighted by MS Swaminathan in the WSSD plenary session on 'Partnerships in Agriculture'.

'Partnerships' featured in the title of the session because partnerships – especially between public and private sectors – were one of the major outcomes of the World Summit. But the opportunity of addressing the restructuring of agrifood chains as key drivers of rural marginalization was unquestionably missed. The paper *A Framework for Action on Agriculture* commissioned by WSSD Secretary-General Nitin Desai called for 'cooperative actions on the part of governments, business, civil society, international organizations and other relevant stakeholders to address the challenges' of resource-poor farmers. The CEOs of 11 major private sector agricultural companies[15] signed a 'Declaration of Corporate Support', as a contribution to the Millennium Development Goals and WSSD. The declaration was said to 'make a tangible contribution to the notion of public–private partnerships'. But the agreement focuses entirely on research and development, continuing the tradition of productivist interpretations of the crisis in smallholder agriculture.

The contribution of the food and drink industry, outlined in their report *Continued Improvement Towards Sustainability* for the WSSD, also missed the mark, hardly venturing beyond corporate commercial imperatives (provide employment, satisfy consumer needs, comply with legal norms) as their part in achieving 'sustainability'. The growing concentration in the processing and retail sector and the challenge of improving the equity and fairness of trading relations received almost no mention.

A meeting of minds was not helped by the continued perception among NGO delegations that business is bad for sustainability. Intellectual inbreeding was encouraged further by a summit structure which pushed the NGO delegation 30 km from the government negotiations.

Conclusions: A Post-WSSD Agenda

Massive changes are taking place in the geography of agricultural production in response to the creation of buyer-driven supply chains, governed by non-agricultural sectors and driven by global sourcing and advances in processing and transportation technologies. At the same time, we are witnessing a divergence between and within agriculturally dependent rural economies, North and South. The simultaneous integration and exclusion of communities with respect to agrifood systems mirrors the emergence of the dual economy across the farming world. A global division of labour separates a core – the Rural World 1 – from a majority of flexible and casualized smallholders, family farmers and farmworkers.

Markets are undergoing rapid change, with closed commodity chains rapidly replacing wholesale or spot markets. Highly concentrated food processing, retail and food service industries at the end of these chains are having an increasingly important impact on decisions made on the farm. Downstream processors and retailers are demanding stringent levels of quality, compliance with standards and codes of conduct and post-production service from their suppliers. Whether an apple grower in Kent, or a coffee producer in Peru, the major supermarket chains control access to consumers.

The transition of sections of the agrifood system towards coordinated supply is proving to be a powerful driver of divergence within farm communities, and of alienation of producers from the value of their product. Primary economic benefits are increasingly found in areas outside production. The less money that is available to farming, the less opportunities there are to invest in diversified, sustainable systems.

The sustainable agriculture movement has been slow to appreciate these developments, and this is reflected in the production focus and public sector focus of Agenda 21 and the lack of progress achieved at WSSD. Being realistic about sustainability requires an appreciation of where control lies in the agrifood chain, and the rapid shift in balance of power from the state to the firm.

Small farmers are defending their interests under these systems. The right conditions of government policy, information technology, farmer organization and corporate responsibility can support fair trade between agribusiness and small farmers, and additionally improve quality and consistency of product. The survival of rural areas at the margins, in the competition for a global pool of capital, depends on the creation of those conditions without delay.

Notes

1   A hypoxic area at the mouth of the Mississippi, fuelled by fertilizer runoff, which has reached a record size 2001 (8000 km^2).
2   Available at www.un.org/esa/sustdev/agenda21text.htm.
3   Such as tariff barriers, supply management, price supports, production subsidies and access to credit.
4   Cooperatives and other economic organizations to negotiate with the market, replacing the peasant unions and other political structures by which rural people negotiated with the state.
5   A broad term encompassing the norms and networks facilitating collective action for mutual benefit.
6   Agriculture in the US and EU is over-stimulated by direct and indirect production subsidies amounting in 1999 to nearly US$170 billion. Producer support estimates (value of gross transfers from domestic consumers and taxpayers to support agricultural producers) according to the OECD amounted to US$54 billion in the US and US$114.5 billion in the EU.
7   A value chain is an integrated customer-oriented chain controlling the supply chain from product concept to consumer purchases, continually measured for profitability and customer relationships.
8   Agribusiness has a long history of influence over supra-national trade policy, from Cargill's role as one of the principal architects of the US proposal presented to the General Agreement on Tariffs and Trade (GATT) agricultural negotiations in 1987 to industry dominance of the Intellectual Property Committee that drafted the

GATT TRIPs (Trade-Related Intellectual Property Rights) Agreement and the Codex Alimentarius, an international food standard body authorized under the GATT to set international food safety standards. The *New York Times* has written of a 'symbiotic relationship' between the US Department of Agriculture (USDA) and 'some of the politically influential companies it regulates'.

9   Merrill Lynch analyst Len Teitelbaum quoted in the *Agribusiness Examiner* vol 101, 11 January 2001, commenting on the announcement in early 2001 that Tyson was to buy IBP to create a giant US$23 billion meat producer that will control 30 per cent of the US beef market, 33 per cent of the chicken market, and 18 per cent of the pork market. Available at www.eal.com/CARP/.

10 Recent figures from the UK show farmers and primary producers accounting for £8.2 billion (15 per cent) of the gross value added of £56 billion in the UK food chain (see Elitzak, 1998; MAFF, 1999).

11 Companies which have a business platform based on complementary pharmaceutical, chemical and biotechnological technologies.

12 Retailers govern access to consumers, and can demand payments from their suppliers of 'hello' or 'street' money, 'slotting fees', 'pay to stay' fees, in-store advertising and promotional allowances, volume discounts or rebates, coupons and guaranteed sales, all valued at between US$930 million and US$9 billion in the US alone, or up to 50–75 per cent of the total net profit for large retailers (Hendrickson et al, 2001).

13 Animals contracted by packers (livestock processors) and integrators for future delivery in order to have a predictable source of raw materials for their plants.

14 'We commit ourselves to making globalization equitable and inclusive. To this end, we will take concrete measures to create an enabling environment, promote good governance at all levels, including democratic values and the rule of law, and encourage corporate accountability and enhance international cooperation' article 7 of WSSD Political Declaration.

15 BASF, Bayer CropScience, Cargill, Dow AgroSciences, DuPont, Emergent Genetics LLC, Monsanto, Mahyco, Merial, Seminis and Syngenta. The declaration is online at www.cgiar.org/pdf/pscdeclarationaug2002.pdf. accessed on 3 September 2003.

References

Bebbington, AJ (2001) 'Globalized Andes? Landscapes and Livelihoods in the Andes', *Ecumene*, vol 8, no 4, pp414–436

Bebbington, AJ and Batterbury, SPJ (2001) 'Transnational Livelihoods and Landscapes: Political Ecologies of Globalization', *Ecumene*, vol 8, no 4, pp369–380

Benbrook, C M (1999) 'World Food System Challenges and Opportunities: GMOs, Biodiversity, and Lessons from America's Heartland', paper presented as part of the University of Illinois World Food and Sustainable Agriculture Program, 27 January 1999, available at www.aces.uiuc.edu/~ILwfood/

Binswanger, H P and Deininger, K (1997) 'Explaining Agricultural and Agrarian Policies in Developing Countries', *Journal of Economic Literature*, vol 35, pp1958–2005, available at www1.worldbank.org/wbiep/povertyandgrowth/econgro_useful_references.html

Boehlje, M and Doering, O (1999) 'Market Performance and Price Discovery Issues in an Industrialized Agriculture', paper presented at a National Symposium on the Future of American Agriculture, University of Georgia, Athens, Georgia, 25–27 August 1999, available at www.agecon.uga.edu/FAA/boehlje.htm

Collins, JL (2000) 'Tracing Social Relations in Commodity Chains: The Case of Grapes in Brazil', in A Haugerud, MP Stone and PD Little (eds) *Commodities and Globalization: Anthropological Perspectives*, Rowman and Littlefield, New York

Dinham, B (2000) 'Merger Mania in World Agrochemicals Market', *Pesticides News*, vol 49, pp10–11

Dinham, B (2001) 'Corporate Change', *Pesticides News*, vol 53, pp12–13

Dolan, C, Humphrey, J and Harris-Pascal, C (1999?) 'Horticulture Commodity Chains: The Impact of the UK Market on the African Fresh Vegetable Industry', IDS Working Paper no 96, Institute of Development Studies, Sussex, UK, available at www.ids.ac.uk/ids/index.html

Eaton, C and Shepherd, AW (2001) *Contract Farming – Partnerships for Growth*, AGS Bulletin no 145, FAO, Rome, available at www.fao.org/ag/ags/agsm/contract.htm

Einarsson, P (2000) *Agricultural Trade Policy – As if Food Security and Ecological Sustainability Mattered*, Church of Sweden Aid and The Swedish Society for Nature Conservation, available at www.forumsyd.se/globala.htm

Elitzak, H (1998) 'Marketing Bill Rose, while Farm Value Declined in 1997', *FoodReview*, September–December 1998, pp21–24

Grieder, W (1997) *One World, Ready or Not: The Manic Logic of Global Capitalism*, Touchstone, New York

Gypmantasiri, P, Sriboonchitta, S and Wiboonpongse, A (2001) *Policies for Agricultural Sustainability in Northern Thailand*, International Institute for Environment and Development, London

Harl, N (2001) 'The Structural Transformation of the Agricultural Sector', paper presented at the conference *Fixing the Farm Bill*, National Press Club, Washington, DC, 27 March 2001

Harris-Pascal, C, Humphrey, J and Dolan, C (1998) *Value Chains and Upgrading: The Impact of UK Retailers on the Fresh Fruit and Vegetables Industry in Africa*, Institute of Development Studies, Sussex, UK, available at www.ids.ac.uk/ids/index.html

Heffernan, W (1999) 'Consolidation in the Food and Agriculture System', report to the National Farmers Union, 5 February 1999, available at www.nfu.org/

Hendrickson, M, Heffernan, W D, Howard, P H and Heffernan, J B (2001) *Consolidation in Food Retailing and Dairy: Implications for Farmers and Consumers in a Global Food System*, report prepared for the [US] National Farmers Union, 8 January 2001, available at www.nfu.org/

Kaplinsky, R (2000) *Spreading the Gains from Globalisation: What can be Learned from Value Chain Analysis?* IDS Working Paper no 110, Institute of Development Studies, Sussex, UK, available at www.ids.ac.uk/ids/index.html

Koechlin, D and Wittke, A (1998) 'Sustainable Business and the Pesticide Business: A Comparison', in W Vorley and D Keeney (eds) *Bugs in System: Reinventing the Pesticide Industry for Sustainable Agriculture*, Earthscan, London, pp107–135

Lewontin, R C (1998) 'The Maturing of Capitalist Agriculture: Farmer as Proletarian', *Monthly Review*, vol 50, no 3, July/August, pp72-84

MAFF (1999) *Working Together for the Food Chain: Views from the Food Chain Group*, available at www.maff.gov.uk

McDonald, J (1999) 'The Neoliberal Project and Governmentality in Rural Mexico: Emergent Farmer Organisation in the Michoacan Highlands', *Human Organization*, vol 58, no 3, pp274–284

Nowicki, P (2000) *Agriculture and Biodiversity: Vertical Integration within the Agricultural Sector – The European Dimension*, report for the IUCN European Regional Office, unpublished

Pritchard, B (2000) 'The Tangible and Intangible Spaces of Agro-Food Capital', paper presented at the 10th International Rural Sociology Association World Congress, Rio de Janeiro, Brazil, July 2000

Reardon, T and Barrett, C B (2000) 'Agroindustrialization, Globalization and Institutional Development: An Overview of Issues, Patterns, and Determinants', *Agricultural Economics*, vol 23, no 3, pp195–205

Reardon, T and Berdegué, J A (2000) 'Concentration in the Processing and Retail Segments of the Agrifood System in Latin America, and its Effects on the Rural Poor,' report of the International Workshop, Santiago, Chile, 27–28 November 2000, Red Internacional de Metodología de Investigación de Sistemas de Producción (RIMISP), Chile

Reardon, T, Codron, J-M, Busch, L, Bingen, J and Harris, C (2001) 'Global Change in Agrifood Grades and Standards: Agribusiness Strategic Responses in Developing Countries', *International Food and Agribusiness Management Review*, vol 2, no 3

Reimer, B (1996) *A Whole Rural Policy for Canada*, submission to the Canadian House of Commons Standing Committee on Natural Resources for its Study on Natural Resources and Rural Economic Development by the Canadian Rural Restructuring Foundation, 28 May 1996, available at artsci-ccwin.concordia.ca/socanth/CRRF/whole.html

Rigg, J and Nattapoolwat, S (2001) 'Embracing the Global in Thailand: Activism and Pragmatism in an Era of Deagrarianization', *World Development*, vol 29, no 6, pp945–960

Rounds, RC (ed) (1998) *NAFTA and the New Rural Economy: International Perspectives*, CRRF Working Paper Series no 10, Canadian Rural Restructuring Foundation c/o The Rural Development Institute, Brandon University, Manitoba

Stone, MP, Haugerud, A and Little, PD (2000) 'Commodities and Globalization: Anthropological Perspectives', in A Haugerud, MP Stone and PD Little (eds) *Commodities and Globalization: Anthropological Perspectives*, Rowman and Littlefield, New York, pp1–25

Taylor, CR (1999) *Economic Concentration in Agribusiness*, testimony to the US Senate Committee on Agriculture, Nutrition and Forestry, 22 January 1999

United Nations (2002) 'World Summit on Sustainable Development Plan of Implementation', UN doc A/CONF.199/20*, 4 September 2002

Vorley, W (2001) 'Farming That Works: Reforms for Sustainable Agriculture and Rural Development in the EU and US', background paper for the NTA Multi-Dialogue Workshop, *Sharing Responsibility for Promoting Sustainable Agriculture and Rural Development: The Role of EU and US Stakeholders,* Lisbon, 24–26 January 2001

Wilkinson, J (2000) 'From the Dictatorship of Supply to the Democracy of Demand?: Transgenics, Organics and the Dynamics of Demand in the Agrofood System', paper presented at the 10th International Rural Sociology Association World Congress, Rio de Janeiro, Brazil, July 2000

Chapter 25

Pro-poor Tourism: Harnessing the World's Largest Industry for the World's Poor; Turning the Rhetoric into Action for Sustainable Development and Poverty Reduction

Dilys Roe, IIED and Penny Urquhart, Khanya, South Africa

Countless texts on tourism begin with the phrase 'tourism is one of the world's largest industries...' What does this mean for the potential of tourism to contribute to sustainable development and poverty reduction? Proponents of the travel and tourism industry claim that it is well placed to contribute to sustainable development on the grounds that it:

- has less impact on the environment than many other industries;
- is based on an enjoyment of the natural and cultural environment and so is motivated to protect them;
- can play a positive role in awareness raising and consumer education through its vast distribution channels;
- provides an economic incentive to protect habitat which might otherwise be converted to less environmentally friendly land uses.

Furthermore, the tourism industry is one of the world's largest employers (an estimated 200 million people worldwide work in the sector) and is one of the few options for economic development in many areas. Tourism contributes to foreign exchange earnings (the World Tourism Organization – WTO – estimates that it is the main source of foreign exchange for 38 per cent of countries), government revenues (eg through taxes, visas, levies etc) and to the informal

---

BOX 25.1 TOURISM FACTS AND FIGURES

International tourism accounts for:

- 36 per cent of trade in commercial services in advanced economies and 66 per cent in developing economies;
- 3–10 per cent of gross domestic product (GDP) in advanced economies and up to 40 per cent in developing economies;
- US$476 billion in tourism receipts in 2000.

Tourism is one of the top five exports for 83 per cent of countries and the main source of foreign currency for at least 38 per cent of countries.

Ten countries, of which six are European account for 67 per cent of all international tourists.

Source: World Tourism Organization

---

economy (eg through stimulation of small and medium-sized enterprises, SMEs, etc). The UN Centre for Trade and Development (UNCTAD) (Diaz Benavides and Perez-Ducy, 2001) notes that tourism is the leading service export sector in 24 of the 40 least developed countries (LDCs). Tourism developments often bring with them infrastructure such as piped water, roads, electricity and so on.

Sceptics argue that, driven by private sector interests, tourism is at odds with sustainable development and poverty reduction. Local people are rarely involved in planning and decision-making while national governments desperate for foreign exchange are keen to incentivize investment, not to put up barriers, including planning controls, which address community concerns. Furthermore, the asymmetry in bargaining power between large operators in tourist originating countries and local suppliers means that local people are unable to dictate the terms and conditions under which tourism occurs. The costs and benefits of tourism are not distributed equally either geographically (both between and within countries) or socially. Tourism is noted for high levels of revenue 'leakage' and, of the revenue that is retained in the destination country, much is captured by rich or middle-income groups, not those that necessarily bear the costs. Tourism is also a volatile industry, extremely susceptible to events which are difficult to control: political unrest, exchange rate fluctuations, natural disasters. The impacts of the terrorist attacks in the US on 11 September 2001 on the global industry are a prime example of this.

Research on **pro-poor tourism** (Ashley et al, 2001), however, noted that these problems are common to many types of economic development in a globalizing world, while tourism appears to have certain characteristics that have greater pro-poor potential than other industries:

- It is a diverse industry. This increases the scope for wide participation, including the participation of the informal sector.
- The customer comes to the product, providing considerable opportunities for linkages (eg souvenir selling).

- Tourism is highly dependent upon natural capital (eg wildlife, scenery) and culture. These are assets that some of the poor have, even if they have no financial resources.
- Tourism can be more labour intensive than manufacturing (though less labour intensive than agriculture).
- Compared with other modern sectors, a higher proportion of tourism benefits (jobs, petty trade opportunities) go to women (though it is not known whether these are necessarily the poorest women).

Considerable progress has been made in addressing the negative impacts of tourism over the past 20 years. While it cannot be claimed that all tourism is now sustainable, progress is marked, particularly within the hotel sector in terms of resource use, waste reduction and so on. However, the major – but not exclusive – emphasis has been on environmental sustainability. For example, the 1996 WTO/World Travel and Tourism Council (WTTC)/Earth Council document, *Agenda 21 for the Travel and Tourism Industry: Towards Environmentally Sustainable Tourism*, refers to the interdependence of development and environmental protection, but its main thrust is on environmental sustainability. Socio-economic and poverty reduction criteria, while often featuring in guidelines, codes of conduct and so on, are usually at the bottom of the list. Furthermore, the focus of sustainable tourism initiatives has been mainly location- or product-based rather than integrated into broad-based national or local sustainable development or poverty reduction strategies.

This approach to 'sustainable tourism' fails to take into account the links between poverty, environment and development. In a world of growing inequality, there can be no doubt that attacking poverty is a critical component of sustainable development. Global stability depends upon this recognition. Significantly, the seventh meeting of the UN Commission for Sustainable Development in 1999 urged governments to: 'maximize the potential of tourism for eradicating poverty by developing appropriate strategies in cooperation with all major groups, indigenous and local communities' and a work programme for sustainable tourism has been developed. The UN has also, for the first time in 2001, included sustainable tourism in its Programme of Action for the Least Developed Countries.

Achieving sustainable development and poverty reduction through tourism requires action at all levels and by all stakeholders – not just the industry. National and local governments need to develop the appropriate policy and regulatory frameworks that encourage responsible tourism, and ensure that it is mainstreamed into sectoral policies, plans and strategies. Donors, too, have an important role to play in supporting sustainable development and poverty reduction through tourism. Despite the clear significance of tourism to developing countries and to poor people, while many donors are involved in tourism activities, few see it as a key development sector and it is not considered as a significant engine for poverty alleviation compared with agriculture, primary health and education, although no cost–benefit analysis has been undertaken to test this assumption. While the industry itself from airlines to individual hotels should take a lead in responsible behaviour, tourists too have a role to play. The

---

BOX 25.2 PRO-POOR TOURISM

Macroeconomic benefits aside, tourism can be made more pro-poor at the local level and contribute to sustainable livelihoods through a number of strategies:

- **strategies that increase economic benefits** (expanding business and employment opportunities for the poor, providing training so they are in a position to take up these opportunities and spreading income beyond individual earners to the wider community);
- **strategies to enhance other livelihood** (non-cash) benefits and mitigate costs (such as lost access to land, coastal areas and other resources; social and cultural disruption or exploitation, access to infrastructure and services, capacity building and training); and
- **strategies focused on policy and process reform** (by creating a policy and planning framework that removes some of the barriers to the poor, by promoting participation of the poor in planning and decision-making processes surrounding tourism, by encouraging partnerships between the private sector and poor people in developing new tourism products, and increasing access to information and communications).

Source: Pro-poor Tourism website: www.propoortourism.org.uk

---

key requirements from international initiatives to actions for individual consumers are highlighted below:

International Level

- A systemic change in the way the industry operates to redress the balance of power between the big operators in the tourist originating countries and the smaller enterprises in the receiving countries and to maximize the benefits from tourism retained in the host country. This requires the establishment of a framework for action by industry accompanied by monitoring, reporting and information sharing.
- Increased awareness of the need for more sustainable tourism among donors, governments, industry and tourists coupled with practical assistance on how to implement or operationalize sustainable tourism in order to move beyond the rhetoric.
- Introduction and more widespread use of environmentally sound technologies and management practices including mechanisms for technology transfer in the tourism sector (eg paralleled with the Clean Development Mechanism of the Kyoto Protocol for energy-related issues). In particular attention needs to be paid to emissions reductions from air transport and to waste management.
- Regional cooperation, particularly between small states, to share resources for tourism promotion, assist diversification and address transboundary environmental issues, such as marine pollution from shipping.
- Networks for research, dissemination and technology transfer.

- Attention to international agreements (eg the General Agreement on Trade in Services, GATS) to ensure that they do not undermine the domestic tourism industry.

National Level

- Development of national tourism strategies and master plans which reflect socio-economic as well as environmental concerns and are integrated with national sustainable development strategies. This includes ensuring that tourism is integrated into a diverse economic base to avoid over-dependency on a volatile industry.
- Establishment of a supportive legislative framework that establishes standards for tourism development including environmental impact assessment (EIA) requirements, core labour standards and incentives for investment.
- Participation of all stakeholders (national and local, public, private and civil society) in tourism planning development and management at both national and local levels.
- Provision to SMEs of access to financing, training and marketing, alongside measures to improve sustainability as well as the quality and diversity of their tourism products.

Destination Level

- Integration of tourism planning with planning for all sectors and development objectives to ensure that the needs of all areas are addressed and that tourism is well integrated with other local economic activities. Plans should create and share employment opportunities with local communities and contain guidelines for the sustainable use of natural resources, with special priority given to environmentally sensitive areas.
- Involvement of all stakeholders in tourism planning development and management.
- Development of locally applicable standards, regulations and indicators in response to specific local circumstances, while maintaining consistency with national and regional objectives and minimum standards.
- Introduction of measures to control and monitor tour operators, tourism facilities and tourists in any area.
- Exploration of a range of alternative forms of tourism to avoid over-dependency on big, overseas operators.
- Mechanisms to ensure that negative economic impacts on local communities are minimized; preferably there will be substantial economic benefits to local communities. This implies linkages with the informal sector, use of planning gain to ensure local employment, support to SMEs, equity partnerships, requirements to ensure contributions to the development/ maintenance of local community infrastructure and so on.

Product Level

- Implementation of comprehensive EIAs (which include an assessment of social impacts) for all tourism developments and ensuring that project proposals respond to regional development plans and guidelines for sustainable development.
- Investigation and use of alternative forms of energy, recycling, minimization of water use, waste reduction and effective waste disposal.
- Supply chain analysis to investigate the sustainability of materials and supplies (recyclable and recycled materials, locally produced, certified timber products, etc).
- Local ownership, or at least a share in ownership; for example, through company–community partnerships.
- Non-exploitative labour arrangements and industrial relations procedures which conform to local laws and international labour standards (whichever are higher).
- Priority to local employment coupled with staff training (including in environmental, social and cultural management).

Consumer Level

- Respect for local social and cultural traditions and practices, including those of minorities and indigenous peoples.
- Respect for human rights.
- Adherence to limitations or constraints on activities especially when these are exercised in particularly sensitive areas.

BOX 25.3 TEN SUSTAINABILITY NEEDS

Many of the requirements of sustainable tourism are necessary at all levels of operation, and the above can be distilled into ten core sustainability needs:

1 Industry responsibility and accountability   International
2 Principles, criteria and indicators for sustainable tourism
3 Increased use of environmentally sound technologies
4 Networks for research, dissemination and technology transfer
5 Understanding of the implications of international trade agreements
6 Development of national and local tourism strategies integrated with broader development strategies backed by a supportive legislative framework
7 Participation of all stakeholders in tourism policy and planning
8 Local benefits (financial and non-financial)
9 Management at the destination level
10 Increased consumer awareness   Consumer

BOX 25.4 SIGNIFICANCE OF TOURISM TO SOUTH AFRICA

While South Africa is considered a medium-income country, the inequality levels are among the highest in the world, and levels of poverty are high (11.5 per cent living below $1/day in 1993). In 1998 the tourism economy contributed 8.2 per cent of South Africa's GDP and 7 per cent of total employment. While this was up from a GDP contribution of no more than 2 per cent in 1994, it is still lower than the world average of over 10 per cent. Tourism is a major export (accounting for 13 per cent of total exports in 1998); inbound visitors bring foreign exchange directly into the economy. The growing international tourism market is balanced by a strong domestic market, making South Africa different from many other developing countries. It is critical to harness tourism's potential for job creation for a country where the increasing outward orientation of the economy has seen a net loss of jobs to date.

- Support for traditional cultural products, crafts and folklore rather than standardized versions of these.

The Significance of Tourism in Poor Countries

Tourism data does not provide the full picture of its economic significance. Statistics cover the contribution of international tourism to national GDP. They hide the significance of domestic tourism (and may underestimate regional tourists travelling by land) and the importance of tourism to a local economy. For example, tourism accounts for approximately 2.5 per cent of GDP in India, but it has been estimated that tourism (domestic and international) accounts for approximately half of economic activity in the hill region of Uttar Pradesh, popular for pilgrim trails.

Overlap Between Tourism and High Incidence of Poverty

Tourism is clearly of great significance to developing countries. But is it important in those countries with the highest proportion of poor people? The small island economies which are most dependent on tourism tend to be middle income and contain few of the world's poor. Nevertheless, analysis of tourism data shows that in most countries with high levels of poverty, tourism is significant or growing (Table 25.1). Tourism is therefore a fact of life for many of the world's poor.

Tourism and Poverty Reduction

International targets aim to halve the number of people living in poverty (defined as living on less than $1 per day) by 2015. Poverty reduction requires strategies on a variety of complementary fronts and scales, but a prerequisite of

Table 25.1 *Significance of international tourism to poor countries*

Country	Population below US$1 a day[a] (%)	Contribution of tourism industry (economy) to GDP[b] (%)	Growth in demand, in 2000[b] (%)
Mali	73	na	9.0
Nigeria	70	0.5 (2.0)	13.5
Central African Republic	66	1.2 (2.3)	10.8
Zambia	64	3.9 (11.0)	3.4
Madagascar	63	3.8 (8.0)	3.4
Niger	61	1.9 (3.6)	7.5
Burkina Faso	61	2.2 (4.8)	3.0
Sierra Leone	57	1.8 (2.7)	15.9
The Gambia	54	5.6 (11.0)	3.5
India	44	2.5 (5.2)	9.7
Lesotho	43	2.0 (10.4)	na
Honduras	41	4.4 (10.6)	4.3
Ghana	39	5.5 (8.4)	34.0
Mozambique	38	na	na
Nepal	38	4.5 (7.7)	6.3

a World Bank 2001 World Development Indicators
b WTTC Year 2001 Country League Tables
na = not available

significant progress is **pro-poor growth** – growth which benefits the poor. As an industry that is clearly important in many poor countries, can tourism be one source of such growth?

Sceptics argue that, because tourism is often driven by foreign, private sector interests, it has limited potential to contribute much to poverty elimination in developing countries. It is noted for high levels of revenue 'leakage' and, of the revenue that is retained in the destination country, much is captured by rich or middle-income groups – not the poor. Tourism is also a volatile industry. The recent foot-and-mouth outbreak in the UK is an obvious example of the speed and severity with which a national tourism industry can be affected by events outside its control. In poor countries, tourism can have a particular effect on the poor themselves, causing displacement, increased local costs, loss of access to resources, and social and cultural disruption.

However, many of the supposed disadvantages of tourism are in fact common to many types of economic development in a globalizing world, while many of the advantages appear to have greater pro-poor potential.

These potential opportunities need to be located within the context of several tempering factors: tourism is a demanding and highly competitive global industry, with the potential for much greater social impacts inherent in the fact that the customer comes to the product. The reliance of tourism upon natural and cultural capital highlights the importance of protecting the resource base on which the industry depends.

Given that tourism is already a fact of life for many of the world's poor, whether or not it is more or less pro-poor than other sectors is perhaps

---

BOX 25.5 TACKLING POVERTY THROUGH TOURISM IN SOUTH AFRICA

South Africa has identified tourism as a priority sector in terms of boosting the economy, job creation, foreign exchange generation, rural development and poverty alleviation, and black economic empowerment. Since the transition to democracy in 1994, greater resources have been allocated towards creating a supportive environment for tourism development. Given that attacking poverty and redressing past inequities of the apartheid system are overriding national priorities, promoting a kind of tourism that meets these goals is critical. South Africa's role as hosts of the 2002 World Summit provided an opportunity to demonstrate progress in these areas.

---

irrelevant. The challenge is to enhance the many positive impacts it can have and reduce the costs it can place on the poor. **Pro-poor tourism** (tourism that generates net benefits for the poor) attempts to do this.

Tourism and Sustainable Development: The Evolving Debate

There is already debate about how to make tourism more sustainable and/or responsible. The World Tourism Organization defined **sustainable tourism** as early as 1988 as:

> *leading to the management of all resources in such a way that economic, social and aesthetic needs can be fulfilled while maintaining cultural integrity, essential ecological processes, biological diversity and life support systems.*

In 1992 the Earth Summit in Rio established the triple bottom line of environmental, economic and social sustainability. Since then however, the major – but not exclusive – emphasis of the tourism industry has been on 'greening'. For example, *Agenda 21 for the Travel and Tourism Industry: Towards Environmentally Sustainable Tourism* refers to the interdependence of development and environmental protection, but the main thrust of the document is on environmental sustainability.

Coincidental with this has been the emergence of **ecotourism** (variously defined but generally agreed upon as tourism that is nature oriented, but that incorporates a desire to minimize negative social and environmental impacts), particularly in response to debates about the viability of top-down approaches to conservation in and around protected areas. This in turn spawned a broader interest in **community-based tourism**, often as a component of community-based natural resource management (CBNRM) strategies. Obligations of donors and governments under the Convention on Biological Diversity (CBD) with its emphasis on sustainable use and benefit sharing have served to reinforce this trend. Ecotourism remains an important focus for many, but disillusion with the

---

BOX 25.6 THE ROAD TO JOHANNESBURG

1980	Manila Declaration on World Tourism
1989	The Hague Declaration on Tourism
1996	Agenda 21 for the Travel and Tourism Industry
1997	Malé Declaration on Sustainable Tourism Development
	Berlin Declaration on Biological Diversity and Tourism
	Manila Declaration on the Social Impact of Tourism
1999	CSD 7 Tourism and Sustainable Development
2002	World Summit on Ecotourism

---

term is spreading and there is an increasingly acrimonious debate over the declaration by the UN of 2002 as the International Year of Ecotourism.

Within the tourism industry a number of initiatives have been established more recently in a move towards **responsible tourism**, including the VISTA (Vision for Industry in Sustainable Tourism Action) initiative of the Association of British Travel Agents, the Tour Operators Initiative backed by the World Tourism Organization/United Nations Environment Programme (UNEP)/ United Nations Educational, Scientific and Cultural Organization (UNESCO), the International Hotels Environment Initiative (IHEI) and Responsible Tourism Guidelines adopted by the UK Association of Independent Tour Operators.

In addition, tourism has continued on the international UN agenda since the Earth Summit. A Global Code of Ethics has been developed by WTO and Principles for the Implementation of Sustainable Tourism by UNEP.

However, while many of the above initiatives incorporate pro-poor elements, poverty reduction has not been seen as a priority on the sustainable tourism agenda of Northern countries. Significantly though, in 1999 explicit reference to pro-poor tourism was made at the seventh meeting of the Commission for Sustainable Development which urged governments to: 'maximize the potential of tourism for eradicating poverty by developing appropriate strategies in cooperation with all major groups, indigenous and local communities'.

However, at the 2002 World Summit on Sustainable Development in Johannesburg, the emphasis in the text agreed by governments was on 'sustainable tourism' and ecotourism more than on pro-poor tourism (United Nations, 2002, para 43). There is much that still needs to be done to make the case for the pro-poor approach to tourism and to encourage the key players in the industry to engage more fully in realizing change.

Making Sustainable Tourism More Pro-poor

Moving the sustainable tourism agenda to tackle poverty alleviation requires action on a number of fronts:

BOX 25.7 RESPONSIBLE TOURISM IN SOUTH AFRICA

South Africa has taken a slightly different approach in its conception of responsible tourism, which is stated as:

> *tourism that promotes responsibility to the environment through its sustainable use; responsibility to involve local communities in the tourism industry; responsibility for the safety and security of visitors and responsible government, employees, employers, unions and local communities.*

The transformation of the tourism industry towards a greater degree of ownership on the part of previously disadvantaged people is currently seen as critical for the implementation of responsible tourism policy principles. This transformation includes two main elements: black economic empowerment programmes aimed at emerging entrepreneurs, and policies and strategies to promote greater involvement in and benefit from tourism by poor rural communities.

Transformation is necessary to improve the structural inequalities of the tourism sector. While this is being tackled nationally in South Africa, the question of how to achieve transformation globally, in a highly vertically integrated industry, is a thorny one. It requires approaches that examine relationships at every step of the tourism supply chain from a perspective of social equity.

- Expanding the focus of mainstream tourism initiatives beyond mainstream destinations, to destinations where many of the world's poor live and/or recognizing that many of the world's poor live alongside mainstream destinations and their voices need to be heard.
- Putting the poor and poverty (including the environmental dimensions of poverty) at the centre of the sustainability debate, rather than *just* the environment.
- Moving beyond a community tourism focus to developing mechanisms that unlock opportunities for the poor at all levels and scales of operation.

The key distinctive feature of pro-poor tourism is that it puts poor people and poverty at the centre. Starting from there, it sees tourism as one component of the household, local and national economies and environment that affects them. The current sustainable tourism debate starts with mainstream destinations as a priority and targets environmental concerns with social issues towards the periphery. Poor people of the South are thus at the edge of the picture. The current approach to 'sustainable tourism' fails to take into account the links between poverty, environment and development. In a world of growing inequality, there can be no doubt that attacking poverty is a critical component of sustainable development. Global stability depends upon this recognition.

Strategies for Pro-poor Tourism

Pro-poor tourism (PPT) is defined as **tourism that generates net benefits for the poor**. Benefits may be economic, but they may also be social, environmental or cultural. Pro-poor tourism is not a specific product or sector of tourism, but an approach to the industry. Strategies for making tourism pro-poor focus specifically on unlocking opportunities for the poor within tourism, rather than expanding the overall size of the sector. Three core areas of focus include: increased economic benefits, enhancing non-economic impacts and policy/process reform. In each area, three distinct (but often overlapping) strategies can be identified.[1]

Strategies focused on economic benefits

1   **Expanding business opportunities for the poor:** small enterprises, particularly in the informal sector, often provide the greatest opportunities for the poor.
2   **Expanding employment opportunities for the poor:** unskilled jobs may be limited and low-paid by international standards, but are much sought after by the poor.
3   **Enhancing collective benefits:** collective community income from tourism can be a new source of income, and can spread benefits well beyond the direct earners.

Strategies focused on non-economic impacts

1   **Capacity building, training and empowerment:** the poor often lack the skills and knowledge to take advantage of opportunities in tourism.
2   **Mitigating the environmental impact of tourism on the poor:** tourism can lead to displacement of the poor from their land and/or degradation of the natural resources on which the poor depend.
3   **Addressing social and cultural impacts of tourism:** tourists' behaviour, such as photography and Western habits, is often regarded as cultural intrusion. Sex tourism exploits women. Tourism can affect many other social issues, such as health care.

Strategies focused on policy/process reform

1   **Building a more supportive policy and planning framework:** many governments see tourism as a means to generate foreign exchange rather than to address poverty. The policy framework can inhibit progress in PPT; reform is often needed.
2   **Promoting participation:** the poor are often excluded from decision-making processes and institutions, making it very unlikely that their priorities will be reflected in decisions.
3   **Bringing the private sector into pro-poor partnerships:** locally driven tourism enterprises may require input to develop skills, marketing links and commercial expertise.

Experience in Pro-Poor Tourism

PPT is relatively untried and untested, and there is no blueprint. Nevertheless, early experience reveals a number of common lessons:[2]

- PPT needs a diversity of actions, from micro to macro level, including product development, marketing, planning, policy and investment. It goes well beyond community tourism, requiring an integrated and holistic approach to the entire tourism system (see Box 25.8 on the Addo Elephant National Park).
- A driving force for PPT is useful, but other stakeholders, with broader mandates, are essential. PPT can be incorporated into tourism development strategies of government or business (with or without explicit pro-poor language). Broader policy frameworks and initiatives outside tourism, such as on land tenure, small enterprise and representative government, are also key.
- Location matters: PPT works best where the wider destination is developing well, and where effective networks can be developed between community and mainstream tourism elements.
- The poverty impact may be greater in remote areas, though tourism itself may be on a limited scale.
- PPT strategies often involve the development of new products, particularly based on local culture. But these should be integrated with mainstream products if they are to find markets.
- Ensuring commercial viability is a priority. This requires close attention to demand, product quality, marketing, investment in business skills and inclusion of the private sector.
- Economic measures should expand both regular jobs and casual earning opportunities, while tackling both demand (eg markets) and supply (eg products of the poor).
- Non-financial benefits (eg increased participation, access to assets) can reduce vulnerability; more could be done to address these.
- PPT is a long-term investment. Expectations must be managed and short-term benefits developed in the interim.
- External funding may be required and justified to cover the substantial transaction costs of establishing partnerships, developing skills and revising policies (not generally for direct subsidies to enterprises).
- While poverty eradication is the central component of PPT, environmental sustainability concerns need to be integrated into planning and operations as well for long-term success.

BOX 25.8 PRO-POOR TOURISM AROUND SOUTH AFRICA'S ADDO ELEPHANT NATIONAL PARK

A recent study centred on a participatory analysis of the tourism trading system in the area around the Addo Elephant National Park (AENP) in South Africa's Eastern Cape province. A key aim was to promote the integration of emerging community tourism initiatives with 'mainstream' tourism, specifically as an anti-poverty strategy. This required an exploration of how to maximize the linkages between the different components in the tourism system, which included government service providers, a range of existing tourism businesses, the South African National Parks Board (SANP), tourism marketing organizations and poor communities living around the borders of the park. Through a multi-stakeholder dialogue process, it became clear that community tourism projects, such as the drama groups, choral groups and arts and crafts groups in the Addo area, have the potential to add value to the tourism system through diversification of the mainly wildlife-related tourism product. And the role of the private sector in tourism partnerships is key for effective marketing and business skills development. The process of dialogue may ultimately lead to local standard setting and a locally developed sustainable tourism brand, with a strong anti-poverty focus.

Implications for Governments, Donors and Civil Society

Extending lessons from early experience across the industry would be a challenge – with considerable potential return – involving different constituencies. Government, the private sector, non-governmental organizations (NGOs), community organizations and the poor themselves all have critical and very different roles to play in PPT. The private sector can be directly involved in pro-poor partnerships. At a minimum, private operators should participate in product and market development to ensure commercial realism. There is much that only governments can do, so a leading role for government in PPT is a great advantage. At a minimum, there needs to be a policy environment that facilitates PPT. The poor themselves are critical to PPT, but they often also need to be organized at the community level in order to engage effectively in tourism. It is often invaluable to have a fourth party to catalyse and support PPT efforts of others; this is often, though not always, a role for a non-governmental organization. Donors, through their role in supporting tourism plans and the 'sustainable tourism' agenda, can also promote PPT.

- Those involved in tourism – policy-makers, planners, businesses, consultants – should incorporate pro-poor concerns at all levels.
- Those involved in the wider field of poverty reduction or rural development should explore and exploit the comparative potential of tourism where they are working.
- PPT can make good business sense, especially if it gives consumers more choice. Corporate engagement should be based on commercial opportunity not just ethical appeal.

- The 'sustainable tourism' agenda should be harnessed for poverty reduction. This requires a shift in focus from environment to poverty and from Northern to Southern destinations. As guidance or standards on social issues are often weak with sustainable tourism initiatives, practical lessons from PPT should be incorporated.

Does Pro-poor Tourism Work?

Early experience shows that PPT strategies do appear able to 'tilt' the industry at the margin, to expand opportunities for the poor and have potentially wide application across the industry. Poverty reduction through PPT can therefore be significant at a local or district level. National impacts would require a shift across the sector, and will vary with location and the relative size of tourism. This would be a challenge indeed, but surely a challenge worth rising to?

Sustainable Development and Poverty Reduction through Tourism: A 10-Point Multi-stakeholder Action Plan

Actions for the tourism industry:

- Maximize use of local suppliers and local staff and encourage supply chain partners to do the same.
- Provide technical advice to local tourism enterprises and help market them.
- Establish business partnerships with residents (eg though equity shares, concession arrangements and so on).
- Allow local people access to health care, communications and other services provided for tourists.
- Respect and promote local guidelines and norms.
- Provide commercial advice to NGO/government sustainable tourism initiatives.
- Build socio-economic considerations into existing checks and balances (eg health and safety procedures).
- Provide advice to customers and suppliers on sustainable tourism and pro-poor tourism.
- Engage in dialogue with local stakeholders to develop a shared vision of sustainable tourism.
- Encourage tourists to donate to community projects and to support local enterprises.

Actions for national and local government:

- Develop national tourism strategies and master plans which reflect socio-economic as well as environmental concerns and are integrated with national sustainable development and poverty reduction strategies

- Establish a supportive legislative framework that provides security of tenure for poor people and establishes standards for tourism development including EIA requirements, core labour standards and incentives for investment.
- Encourage local participation in tourism planning and decision-making.
- Use planning controls and investment incentives to realize poverty reduction and sustainable development objectives.
- Encourage dispersal of tourism to poorer areas as part of an integrated approach to rural/urban development.
- Ensure good policy is followed up with implementation, through linking policy to budgeting cycles and building sufficient implementation capacity at the appropriate levels of government, as well as devolution of resources.
- Provide support to local enterprises through access to credit, training, marketing through national tourism boards and so on.
- Revise regulations that impede the poor in employment or small business.
- Develop locally applicable standards, regulations and indicators.
- Explore a range of alternative forms of tourism to avoid over-dependency on big, overseas operators.

Actions for civil society (tourists, NGOs, media):

- Increase awareness of the sustainability issues associated with tourism and its poverty reduction potential.
- Lobby the tourism industry for greater responsibility and accountability.
- Lobby for the inclusion of sustainable development and poverty reduction objectives within multilateral trade agreements.
- Help local people to ensure their voice is heard at the international level.
- Support campaigns that aim to enhance the sustainable development and poverty reduction objectives of tourism.
- Respect local norms and traditions.
- Adhere to restrictions on activities, particularly in sensitive areas.
- Support local enterprises and avoid tourism products such as 'all-inclusive' resorts that provide limited, if any, benefits to the local area.
- Support local initiatives based on traditional practices or local products rather than 'imported' burger bars and fizzy drinks.
- Ask for locally grown produce in hotels – and don't expect it to look or taste the same as it does at home!

Actions for donors:

- Treat tourism on the same terms as any other industry when exploring poverty reduction interventions.
- Request an assessment of poverty reduction and sustainable development objectives when supporting tourism development.
- Ensure tourism consultants are aware of poverty and sustainable development and have to address them, given their considerable influence in tourism national plans.

- When supporting growth or anti-poverty strategies in specific areas where tourism exists, ensure that the pro-poor potential of tourism is assessed.
- Promote pro-poor tourism within the international agenda, with other governments and the industry, particularly by emphasizing a pro-poor and Southern focus within sustainable tourism.
- Support networks for research, dissemination and technology transfer.
- Promote and support regional cooperation, particularly between small states.
- Investigate international agreements (eg GATS) to ensure that they do not undermine the domestic tourism industry.
- Provide support to governments seeking to develop supportive policy and regulatory frameworks.
- Investigate mechanisms for providing micro-finance to small enterprises.

Notes

1   The distinctions are not rigid. Generating collective income often has non-economic implications since some collective benefits may be non-financial or spent on 'social' investments. Conversely, capacity building is listed here as a non-economic strategy but often enhances economic opportunities and participation.
2   See work by the International Institute for Environment and Development (IIED), Overseas Development Institute (ODI) and the Centre for Responsible Tourism (CRT) at www.propoortourism.org.uk/.

References

Ashley, C, Roe, D and Goodwin, H (2001) *Pro-poor Tourism Strategies: Making Tourism Work for the Poor*, ODI, IIED and International Centre for Responsible Tourism, London, available at www.propoortourism.org.uk

Diaz Benavides, D and Perez-Ducy, E (2001) *Tourism in the Least Developed Countries*, WTO and UNCTAD, Madrid

United Nations (2002) *World Summit on Sustainable Development Plan of Implementation*, UN doc A/CONF.199/20*, 4 September 2002, United Nations, New York

Chapter 26

Mining and Minerals: Breaking New Ground

Luke Danielson, IIED

A Clash of Beliefs

Nothing enrages many mining advocates more than the failure of some members of society to acknowledge their dependence on the products of the mining industry: 'Earth First: We'll mine the other planets later', has been a popular slogan at anti-mining conventions.

Nothing enrages some members of society more than mining. Much of the popular image of the industry truly is terrible: foreign capital in alliance with bloody dictators robbing the poorest countries of their mineral patrimony; violent seizures of the lands of indigenous or aboriginal peoples in a blind search for gold; black lung; silicosis; terrifying cave-ins; brutal suppression of violent strikes; tailings; dams collapsing and burying neighbours; air pollution from smelters, mercury and cyanide – all leaving in the end ravaged landscapes dotted with ghost towns, usually among the poorest regions in any country.

This image is hardly fair to some: not everything mining has done throughout history was wrong. The history of minerals use is inextricably interwoven with the history of civilization itself: from the Stone Age and the Copper Age to the Bronze Age and Iron Age to the age of coal and steel and perhaps the age of silicon. It is hard to say that mining has been a mistake without saying that civilization has been a mistake.

But the terrible image of mining is there in the minds of many. The best actors in the industry have improved their performance considerably, though the progress is often less than uniform even within individual companies. But the image sticks. It sticks because it was earned the hard way: through many years of bad performance. It sticks because many projects now in operation were planned and designed several decades ago, and reflect lower expectations of performance. It sticks because not everyone today is an industry leader, and we hardly have to look to history for bad examples. And it sticks because it works, and works well, for the industry's critics: 'Stop the threat of mining in X' is virtually guaranteed to attract attention, support, and contributions, without requiring much effort be exerted in trying to define just what the industry *should* be doing.

Meanwhile, far from the pollution and poverty, those in the richest economies are surrounded by goods, and usually have little or no idea where they came from or how they were made. Virtually all of these goods were made out of minerals, made using tools made of minerals, were conveyed to market in transport made out of minerals or made with energy that comes from minerals, often transmitted through pipes or wires made from minerals. But the 'disconnect' between production and consumption is so great that this reality is rarely appreciated. And where it is glimpsed, there is often denial: denial that *our* consumption could possibly be linked to *that* production, or that we really do use such immense quantities of minerals, or that we can't make everything we need with wood or hemp.

The greatest challenge to our powers of observation may be to see – really see – familiar objects that are right in front of us. Specialists in minerals see cities made of bricks and concrete, full of people who move around in steel buses or autos, using computers that may contain dozens of mineral products, powered by coal-generated electricity coming over copper wires, to transmit messages condemning the entire system of minerals production. They drink out of porcelain cups or glasses made from sand while calling for worldwide moratoria on mining projects. They fly in aluminium aeroplanes to meetings where they demand that organizations such as the World Bank cease all support for any mining activity. Minerals producers are sometimes enraged by this seeming contradiction. It causes some in industry to reject dialogue with their critics, call them ignorant, or to see ulterior motives.[1]

While the argument that minerals, as non-renewable resources, have no part in a sustainable future is profoundly wrong, so is the argument that we are doing all we can to reduce the impacts of primary production by ensuring optimal efficiency of use and recycling or recovery. Miners typically regard these as none of their business, ignoring the growing constituency of those deeply concerned not only about waste of minerals but by the adverse effects of metals in the environment or the impacts of profligate burning of coal.

The more that many in the global South look at the chain of minerals refining, fabrication and use, the more it looks to them like a rigged game. Developing countries receive many of the negative externalities of mining at the front end of the value chain. Primary production is not very profitable, and the profit margins and the development spin-offs look much more attractive further along the chain. But there are all kinds of hands, visible and invisible, that seem to hold back attempts by developing countries to make more complex and valuable products from the minerals they produce (IIED, 2002, box 8-1, p181). Dealing with these barriers should be a priority issue for the Doha Round of trade negotiations.

Over 100 countries, in a movement heavily promoted by the World Bank, have 'reformed' their mining codes to become more attractive to mining investors. Yet the elements of these codes – streamlined permitting processes, quicker and more 'automatic' approvals, less opportunity for objection – may well be limiting the ability to strike a balance between mining and other interests, such as indigenous communities on whose territory projects may be developed, or national parks and protected areas. And these other interests hardly feel this is promoting sustainable development.

These foregoing are just a few of the constituencies that are impatient with the way the minerals industries work today. The global coalition of forces against 'business as usual' in the mining sector is passionate, vocal and asking some penetrating questions about the industry's record. It hammers home a very unflattering view of the industry. The following might be typical:

[M]ining and mineral processing:

- *have disproportionately great impacts on indigenous peoples and poor, rural communities, whose lands are often forcibly seized for mining with little or no compensation, and enjoy few of the benefits of mineral extraction;*
- *are among the greatest threats to biological diversity worldwide, along with industrial logging and land conversion for agriculture;*
- *create extraordinary amounts of waste, much of it contaminated, and often create environmental problems – such as water pollution – that can endure for centuries – often yield little, if any, long-term net benefits for host countries and regions (as is becoming increasingly evident, the long-term clean-up costs of many mines may well exceed what the host countries gain while the mines are open);*
- *are a major contributor to climate change, with smelters and mines alone accounting for up to 10 per cent of world commercial energy use each year;*
- *are often closely linked with human rights abuses, bolster despotic regimes and can otherwise be antithetical to democracy, sustainability and inter-generational justice.*[2]

The minerals sector and sustainable development

The question of the role of the minerals sector in sustainable development is thus highly polarizing and deeply controversial. In some quarters it is seen as the only avenue open for economic progress in poor countries which have little prospect of attracting or generating other forms of development. Or it is viewed as a provider of most of the absolutely essential material basis on which the rest of the economy is run.

The minerals sector had little if any profile at the Rio Summit. And it was very unclear what role any of the participants in the sector – developing countries with important mining sectors, poor people and communities who depend on mining, companies who do mining, or NGOs that serve as watchdogs or critics of the industry – was to have in Johannesburg. There was also a wide variety of views as to how the World Summit on Sustainable Development (WSSD) should view this sector, and what role if any it should be assigned in an overall strategy for sustainable development.

Against this background, in late 1999, the International Institute for Environment and Development (IIED) began an innovative project designed to do what was possible to identify the key issues facing the sector and develop an agenda for moving towards sustainable development with the engagement of the principal actors. Given the deep conflict and distrust around the industry, this was a tremendous, perhaps insuperable challenge. From the beginning, it was clear that there were those on all sides who did not want to work towards a shared vision or common agenda, and that even those who did had a very long way to go before they were likely to agree on much.

The project therefore was carefully defined to avoid talk of 'consensus' or agreement, but rather described its work in terms of seeking dialogue and 'convergence' of views. IIED undertook this role, well aware that the evident distrust and differences made any progress questionable; any dramatic breakthroughs improbable; a demonstrable change in sector performance within two years impossible; and solutions to all of the major challenges facing the sector by September 2002 laughable. Despite these difficulties, IIED, the World Business Council for Sustainable Development (WBCSD) and the principal sponsors of the initiative (from the mining industry and from governments) believed that the exercise was necessary and potentially extremely important.

Even if the 'no man's land' between all of these deeply dug-in and distrustful adversaries is an uncomfortable place, it needs to be explored if there is to be any progress towards more effective models of development in the sector. If change is uncomfortable, so too is the status quo.

The Mining, Minerals and Sustainable Development project

IIED's Mining, Minerals and Sustainable Development project (MMSD) entered the field with a mandate to involve the points of view of all those who were interested in dialogue, in ways acceptable to them, to deepen understanding through research on key problems, to identify ways forward, and to report in time to inform the Johannesburg Summit. MMSD was therefore several things:

- It was an attempt at a global (worldwide) public policy process, whose results will need to be evaluated a year or two into the future when they are clearer.
- It was an enormous effort of synthesis that tried to bring together a vast amount of information from various disciplines in order to reach a much broader understanding than had previously existed of the problems of the sector.
- It was an attempt to attack head-on the question of implementation: how to move from lists of ideas about what should be done to developing concrete mechanisms and institutions to get them done.
- It was a major exercise in communication of ideas and dissemination of knowledge.

Each of these elements is worth a few words, both in the broader picture of the state of the sector and the narrower context of MMSD.

The dynamics of dialogue

The minerals sector comprises very different constituencies. Some hardly see themselves as identifiable groups or interests. Many are riven by internal differences.

These 'stakeholders' vary in the extent of their connection to the minerals sector. Some necessarily define themselves as central parts of it. (These would include among others mining ministries, minerals companies, metals fabricators, residents of communities dependent on mines or where mines are proposed, NGOs devoted solely to mining issues, or unions of workers in minerals industries.) Others, such as communities that are only indirectly impacted, banks that have the choice of lending to mining projects or other activities, finance ministries, or NGOs that campaign on a variety of issues, may be more or less involved depending on the issue. (One way of classifying stakeholders is depicted in IIED, 2002, p58.)

Different stakeholders vary considerably in their organization and ability to engage effectively on policy issues at the global level. The mine labour unions are clearly among the best equipped for this kind of engagement, with a global organization managed by elected leaders with real legitimacy and a clear mandate to speak for members who can remove them if they are dissatisfied (for example, the International Federation of Chemical, Energy, Mine and General Workers' Unions (ICEM); www.icem.org/).

But some key constituencies are very far indeed from this level of accountability. Communities impacted by mining may have a national level voice in Peru,[3] but none in Indonesia or the Philippines; artisanal and small-scale miners may have national level syndicates in some African countries, while others are jailed for their efforts to secure a livelihood. But there is no constituent-selected, democratically managed world leadership that is the advocate for these or other sets of interests in relation to the mining industry.

At the global level, do individual leaders or self-proclaimed spokesmen represent anything more legitimate or democratic than the foundation that writes them a cheque? The energy they devote to tearing down other potential spokesmen or limiting attendees at meetings to those with the 'correct' perspective is the best evidence of their own very tenuous standing. And when we enter – as just one of many examples – something like the 'on behalf of' world of non-indigenous London- or New York-based advocates for Southern indigenous interests, there are enormous issues over whether direct engagement with indigenous peoples is possible. The image that springs to mind is of the Wizard of Oz: an imposing voice coming from behind a curtain, while the reality is rather less impressive.

Yet the underlying interest groups out there are very important, even where they lack legitimate spokespersons. The necessities of sustainable development will require that these constituencies' interests are somehow considered. It will also require that their capacity to engage through legitimate leaders, selected in transparent processes, be increased. While this growth in capacity can be supported by other actors, the impetus must come from within the group.

In addition, every one of these major constituencies has a vocal faction that opposes engagement with other interests – at least on any terms those other interests are likely to accept. The *internal* work of getting these broad constituencies to any shared view of what it is they want from others is often much more daunting than the *external* work of negotiating with other stakeholders, even if it is much less visible outside the group.

Naivety over issues of representation is near universal in the minerals sector. Industry representatives sometimes assume that all of mine labour, or all of the human rights movement, can smoothly come into monolithic agreement on a platform – even though industry itself is unable to do this. Environmental groups who make sparks fly as they struggle to come to a shared agenda sometimes assume that all mining companies in the world or all mines ministries are in lock step pursuing a common strategy.

There was no chance that in a two-year MMSD process, all of these historical problems of capacity, legitimacy and democracy were going to be overcome on a global level. The principles of the project were therefore to treat all with whom it dealt with respect according to agreed rules (MMSD's Principles of Engagement are reproduced in IIED, 2002, p417), to build for the future, not just for the project, make progress where possible, and to do no harm in the process. It did rather well in working with many stakeholder groups; it was reviled by some organizations; some companies would not participate; some stakeholders set preconditions; a few environmental organizations said they would not participate in any dialogue with industry until someone – it was never clear who – declared a moratorium on all new mining projects in Africa, Asia and Latin America.[4] MMSD kept the door open to everyone, even the most critical, throughout its existence.

As a result of WSSD, partly as a result of the dynamics of a globalizing economy, partly because of acts of leadership, and perhaps partly because of the MMSD project, there has been some acceleration of the pace at which the stakeholders are organizing themselves to engage on a global level. The larger multinational minerals companies have gathered together to form the International Council on Mining and Metals to be their voice for sustainable development.[5] As time goes on we are gradually seeing that organization lose the laggards as the leaders show the way. Some 70 campaigning NGOs have formed the Global Mining Campaign.[6] The world's mines ministers are continuing to build both a global organization, the World Mines Ministries Forum, and regional organizations such as CAMMA in the western hemisphere, the APEC ministers' organization in Asia and the Pacific, and the nascent African ministers' organization.[7]

The idea of the opposition bonding together in worldwide organizations may seem menacing to some. This may seem absurd to the insiders in these organizations, who know of the internal conflicts, compromises and the fragile glue that holds such coalitions together. To others, particularly traditional adversaries, it may seem to herald stronger and more effective enemies.

But it also makes dialogue and negotiation possible. There is someone to talk to, someone to speak on behalf of a constituency with legitimacy, and someone capable of making the compromises necessary to get something done.

The more cohesive the bonds within the group, and the more democratically the leadership is selected, the more hard decisions can be made to stick. In the long run we need these international platforms if we are to avoid the free-riders and the potential of a rush to the bottom. Doing it right but alone is only possible for as long as the best are also the most efficient; when the rest catch up in productivity terms we are collectively no further forwards on social and environmental issues.

An international dialogue also makes it possible to have platforms and agendas, and see where the agreement and the differences lie. There is now an industry platform,[8] an NGO platform (Young and Septoff, 2002), and a number of regional mines ministers' platforms, among others. There is also a post-MMSD platform, shared to varying degrees by these constituencies, based on the idea of convergence and forward progress (IIED, 2002, ch16).

The process of creating a shared agenda within an interest group is a critical one; it is important among other things for the very necessary process of beginning to separate the good performers on all sides from the not-so-good performers. Companies that see a business case for sustainable development are no longer happy to be associated with the companies that expect governments to use armies to force unwilling local communities to accept projects. And the time may be here when NGOs looking for the way forward are no longer content to be held back by those who are incapable of internal democracy or uncomfortable with freedom of speech. Some governments that would like to see effective policies for channelling mining investment towards sustainable development are already frustrated by those who think that they can win the competition to attract investment by sacrificing their national environment. It seems this kind of 'sorting out' may be happening among several of the major constituencies in the sector.

It is critical to keep in focus that sustainable development requires action on multiple levels: not every issue is a global issue. Rather the presumption should be the reverse: issues should be dealt with at the lowest level at which all of those necessary to make the needed changes can be assembled.

MMSD therefore proceeded by decentralizing. It promoted the organization of autonomous regional projects in several of the principal mineral producing and consuming areas of the world. While it would have been useful to have more such efforts, lack of staff resources made it hard to progress further in the available time. And under the principle of 'do no harm', efforts in Southeast Asia, specifically Indonesia, were abandoned when it became clear that the level of distrust and conflict were so great that no honest multi-stakeholder platform could be constructed without a great deal of time.[9] The potential for eventual success in such an effort would have been jeopardized by trying to force the pace to meet MMSD's 2002 deadline.

The four regional processes that were organized were: South America;[10] Southern Africa;[11] Australia;[12] and North America.[13,14,15,16] Some of these regional processes in turn organized national-level projects of research and consultation.[17] In principle, an effort of this nature should have driven its consultation down to the national level in the countries where these industries are most important, and to the community level if not in every community, at least in a carefully selected sample. That was not done by MMSD; it has rarely been done anywhere. It was not as if we did not see the need for it but the budget and the capacity to organize it was wanting.

Principal issues from research and synthesis

Through what is probably the broadest process of consultation ever undertaken in the minerals industries, MMSD attempted to identify the key issues central to the sector's role in sustainable development.

This in itself was a major challenge. It had certainly never been done before on such a scale. And a major objection to sustainable development on the part of some government agencies and companies was the perception of an infinite or ever-lengthening agenda. From this perspective, progress in better management of environmental issues often took second place in our attempts to deal with the new community and social issues. But as fast as people began to address these, the issue shifted to the 'Dutch disease' (ie, the problems associated with the sudden development of a large natural resource sector) or human rights abuse or something else. Indeed, some environmental groups predicted this dilution of focus and expressed concern over a sustainable development focus for fear their issues would be lost in the broader mix.[18]

Issue definition started with the original scoping study on which the MMSD project was based in 1999, which included careful consultation with some 123 people and organizations known to be active in relevant issues in the minerals sector. When the project started, one of its first activities was a Strategic Planning Workshop in London, which helped to ensure wide involvement in defining key issues at an early stage.[19] The project website also had a prominent request that anyone who felt that any specific issue or theme needed to be examined should raise it. Many such comments were received.

Based on the Strategic Planning Workshop, the Scoping Report, and many individual comments and suggestions from stakeholders, MMSD prepared a 'Conceptual Framework and Topics for Analysis'.[20] The several thousand people in the project database were sent periodic bulletins; Bulletin 3 called attention to the availability of this document and invited comments.[21]

After receiving and synthesizing all of this response, MMSD published in early October 2000 a Proposed Outline for MMSD Draft Report[22] which indicated the results to date of identification of critical themes, and again asked for comment. This process was repeated several times in the course of the project. This cycle of publication of more advanced drafts, comment by the public, experts, and the Project Assurance Group, continued until the draft of the entire report was subject to public comment in early 2002.

This was accompanied by a series of over 20 in-depth workshops on subjects such as minerals and armed conflict, management of large volume wastes, the indigenous experience with mining, and mining in protected areas.[23] The process was detailed, time-consuming and exhaustive: issues emerged and became more clearly focused. If we can be criticized for this process it is most probably because we assumed that the capacity was there to respond to the deluge of consultative papers we sent out. It was not. The plain fact is all too few could comment fully while a minority were clearly never going to!

Despite this, the good news is that the issues now seem fairly clear. The emphasis changes in different parts of the world; there are local issues of importance; and there are very different views about what to do about the issues. But at the global level there is now a known and broadly accepted list of what the problems are in pursuing a more effective minerals sector contribution to sustainable development. The agenda has been circumnavigated. It may not be simple, but it is finite and its shape is known. MMSD divides it into nine parts, each of which receives a chapter in *Breaking New Ground* (IIED, 2002, Chapters 6–14).

Comparing this list of issues with the concerns of NGOs, or industry, or governments in various statements and pronouncements does seem to indicate some convergence. While different constituencies have very different emphases, priorities and solutions, a common definition of the problems does seem to be emerging.

MMSD approached this set of research problems with over 100 commissioned research projects. The results of these are available on the compact disk in the back cover of its report, *Breaking New Ground.*[24]

The challenge of implementation

The most difficult part of the process of change towards sustainable development is to agree concrete ways to implement the changes that are needed.

It is surprising how much agreement there is, at least at the level of principle, on desired objectives: there should be earlier and more effective consultation with communities when it is proposed to develop a project; there should be effective planning for closure from the outset; companies should respect the rights of workers to form unions of their choosing; practices such as disposing of mine wastes in rivers should be avoided. The list of broadly shared objectives is a long one.

The challenge comes in moving beyond the *should*. The *should* is in many cases simply a hope that someone, somewhere will somehow, some day make things happen. It is surprising how ready many of the actors in the sector are to adopt 'statements of should', and how utterly unready they are to respond to the most basic questions of *who* should or *how* should. Many of the grand normative declarations seem directed therefore as prayers at some vague paternalistic deity who, once we have decided what we want, is supposed to figure out some way to give it to us.[25]

If our lists of desired objectives are to be any more meaningful than children's lists in letters to Santa Claus, we need to spend at least as much time on the *who*, the *how*, and the *when* as on the *what*.

Getting seriously into the *how* at the global level is obviously very difficult. We are dealing – at least in a large part of the industry – with global markets in which companies, countries and groups of workers are competing for capital, and competing to sell products. There are very real limits on what individual governments can require unless other governments also require them. And there is a real limit on the willingness of governments to cooperate.

The difficulty starts with the fact that what is needed at the global level is very like what we want and expect from government generally, or at least good government:

- Broad minimum *standards* of performance…
- …developed through a fair process, open to all interests, so the results have real *legitimacy*.
- A meaningful system of positive *rewards* or negative *sanctions* that will encourage compliance with the legitimately adopted standards.

Developing this kind of framework is essential, both for better performance in the sector and for movement towards sustainable development. Since companies are competing in global markets, minimum standards really need to be universally applicable. The same applies to states; they compete at some level too. We have to face the facts: we have the potential rush to the corporate and the governmental bottom! There are obviously some major obstacles to be overcome to prevent that outcome.

One obstacle is the lobby of the 'poor performers': companies that have no capacity to deal more effectively with communities or environmental management, governments which have yet to develop more effective ways to manage mineral revenues than to steal them, NGOs that lack the vision for more than endless carbon copies of the last 'stop the mine' campaign, or United Nations agencies that try to block progress unless they benefit from the results.

Another is a set of very legitimate issues that must be accommodated. These include:

- a perception on the part of governments *and many others* in developing countries that any kind of global system will be overwhelmed and dominated by the better-resourced interests from the Organisation for Economic Co-operation and Development (OECD) countries, becoming just another system for benefiting the rich;
- unwillingness of governments to surrender sovereignty to anyone, especially if only developing countries are asked to cede any sovereignty;
- fears of constituencies that are not sufficiently organized to engage on a global level that their interests will be either submerged by the better organized, or 'represented' by spokesmen they did not choose and do not acknowledge.

In the run-up to Johannesburg there was serious discussion of whether the experience of global sectoral certification systems, such as the Forest Stewardship Council or Marine Stewardship Council, could provide insights to the minerals industries. A further possibility was the creation of an ongoing body capable of continuing exploration of a workable system of implementation in the minerals industries.[26]

WSSD did result in the announcement of one initiative that may respond to this need for a minimum framework of global standards: a Global Dialogue on sustainable development in the minerals and metals sector.[27] This is the first time that governments have agreed to discuss, at the global level, environmental, social and economic issues relevant to the minerals and metals sector, though it is not clear how many governments will participate and the level of resources they will commit. It certainly merits support and attention. Given the extent of the sustainability challenge for the industry, it is a modest step in the right direction – and it is sad that suspicion of motives among governments leads to a division among the leaders that in turn results in diplomatic stalemate. Hopefully this state of affairs can be broken.

Communication

One of the shortcomings of both the minerals sector as a whole and WSSD's contribution to resolving outstanding issues was the lack of shared communication among different stakeholder groups. There are very few means for companies and governments, or NGOs and labour, or other combinations of stakeholders, to share information and concerns on an ongoing basis.

In this sense, unless the Global Dialogue grows quickly to fill this void, WSSD will prove to have been a missed opportunity in the minerals sector. The mutually suspicious tribes met among themselves; the opportunities for interchange between divergent interests were rare indeed.

Conclusions and Results of the MMSD Project

The body of information brought together in the MMSD Project generated many conclusions about the challenges to be met in orienting the minerals sector towards sustainable development. Just three are mentioned here: the clear relationship between global-level controversies over projects and the lack of global governance; a hypothesis for why the economics of much of the industry are so poor; and the disproportionate focus on a very limited part of the industry.

Lack of global governance is a key part of the problem

Interestingly, the part of the mining industry that is at the centre of the white-hot international controversy over environment and development is not the biggest part of the industry, but a smaller subset. While the majority of the industry may have its disputes and problems, they do not reach the desks of senior United Nations or World Bank officials, but seem to be resolved elsewhere. This may well point us to something critical about what is wrong.

MMSD concluded that there are basically three groups of mineral commodities:

1   those sold in global markets (eg copper, gold, diamonds);
2   those sold in broad regional markets (eg many grades of coal, limestone); and
3   those that because of transportation costs are sold mainly in local markets (eg sand, construction stone, gravel).

Interestingly, in terms of key indicators such as the volumes of commodities produced and the number of people employed, the first of these groups is a *minority* of the industry. However, it is clearly where the *majority* of the 'global level' disputes arise. When was the last international campaign against a proposed limestone or gravel quarry or clay pit? When was the last major gold mine or nickel project that *didn't* generate a high profile NGO or community campaign? Why is this?

The conclusion may well be that for commodities sold locally, national government is still an effective mechanism for setting policy and resolving disputes. It is where industry operates in a globalized economy without globalized governance mechanisms that the most intractable problems occur.

A hypothesis for why industry economics are poor: exit barriers and subsidized production

One of the principal obstacles to progress towards sustainable development in the minerals sector is that the economic results, at least at the front end of the value chain – mining – have been poor. Companies see themselves as trapped selling fungible commodities in competition with competitors who achieve lower and lower costs of production. Burgeoning supplies of most mineral commodities have led to inexorably sinking prices.

This means that there is less economic rent for developing country governments to capture. And it means that these governments increasingly see themselves in competition to provide fiscal and policy environments that are conducive to lowering production costs – competition which the World Bank has been at some pains to foster. Falling prices also mean less for workers, less for communities and less for shareholders.

While phenomena this complex almost always have multiple causes, and there are difficulties generalizing about the markets for 92 very different mineral commodities, MMSD's work does suggest a new set of ideas that may help to explain this critical problem.

There are two points in the typical project life cycle where there is potential for great economic, environmental and social change in communities impacted by mining. One is at the outset when the project is being developed. The other is at the end of life when projects close.

The hypothesis is that typical projects give rise to very significant social, environmental and economic costs at closure. Because these costs are not fully acknowledged at the outset, and often ignored or poorly managed during the project life, neither the company nor government (nor anyone else) makes provision to pay them.

When – perhaps due to competition with newer projects employing more advanced technology – a mine is no longer competitive, and would in classic economic analysis therefore close, the mine owner, the government, the community, mine workers and other interests find that closure would impose on them costs they are unable or unwilling to pay. It can be cheaper for the project to stay open, even on the basis of subsidies, than to close. The subsidies can come from government, from internal cross-subsidization within companies, from labour or community 'give-backs', or some combination of them.

If in fact this is part of the problem – an industry with few barriers to entry but substantial barriers to exit – then the solution seems clear: developing projects that anticipate and internalize these costs; that progress in ways that ensure there is some kind of alternative local economy to turn to at closure; and no great set of environmental costs to be funded post-closure.

The broader industry and the potential for sustainable development

The great clashing of sword on shield that has taken centre stage in the minerals sector is focused almost entirely on the activities of multinational companies who are producing gold or a limited number of base metals. In fact, these activities are a small slice of the overall minerals sector.

If the focus is corporate social responsibility, or limiting the control of multinationals over the world economy, well and good. But if the focus is sustainable development, then the sustainable development potential of the rest of the sector – the majority of what is going on – needs to be assessed. Some examples:

Artisanal and small-scale mining (ASM)

The majority of direct livelihoods in the mining industry are in the small-scale and artisanal segment. Perhaps 15 million people are directly employed in this activity, supporting a total of 80–100 million family members. ASM is increasing in some countries. Many governments, environmental organizations and others have regarded this sector as a destructive anachronism that should be phased out; it is illegal in some countries. The resources and attention which have flowed in its direction have been small in comparison to the large projects of multinationals. Perhaps there are new and additional means to improve the quality of life and economic circumstances of the tens of millions of people involved, and ameliorate the environmental and labour abuses that are sometimes present. The Johannesburg Plan of Implementation regards this sector as a potential positive contributor to sustainable development, and calls for financial and technical support for 'safe and sustainable livelihood opportunities in small-scale mining ventures'.[28]

State-owned enterprises

State-owned enterprises are still quite important in the mining sector. The largest coal producer in the world is a state-owned company in India. The world's largest copper producer is CODELCO, a company owned by the government of Chile, which has played an important role in Chile's economic success. Do we accept without question the neo-liberal conclusion that all state-owned enterprises should quickly disappear, or that the only policy concern should be to help them close or privatize? Or do state-owned enterprises have a positive role in the future of the sector? If so, what is it?

Moving further along the minerals chain

A high priority for many developing countries is to move beyond mining and smelting into activities such as refining and fabrication of products, which would allow capture of more of the value added in final products and more of the livelihoods in the minerals chain. Yet many countries have failed to make much progress in this direction. The reasons include a world trade regime that places both tariff and non-tariff barriers on the entry of value-added products into the rich consumer countries. Is there room for an initiative to support development of value-added industries based on mineral wealth in developing countries? The Johannesburg Plan of Implementation contains a call to 'improve value-added processing'.[29]

Local production for local use

As indicated above, mineral products can usefully be classified by whether they are sold in local, intermediate or global markets. The heavy preponderance of effort by international institutions such as the World Bank has been on supporting development in the third of these three categories, the global or export sector. But what would be the development benefits of an increased emphasis on supporting more local minerals industries such as clay for bricks, gravel for building or limestone for concrete? Would building these industries where they are weak bring long-term economic benefits? Or should international institutions continue to focus nearly exclusively on strengthening the export sector?

Results of the Johannesburg Summit

In its official pronouncements, WSSD took a 'middle of the road' view. It recognized some of the very real economic, social and environmental problems of the industry, but rejected the ideas that sustainable development requires phasing the industry out, or that mining is inherently and always unacceptably destructive of communities, national development aspirations and the natural environment.[30] Its role in African development is specifically acknowledged.[31]

So the industry escaped the pariah status which some would assign it. But accepting that it may have a positive role in development while working to ameliorate the undeniable problems requires some sort of forward planning. While some positive steps were announced, they fall rather short of a brave new world. Three advances stand out from WSSD:

Artisanal and small-scale mining

WSSD may mark something of a watershed for ASM. After years of policies that seek to eradicate small-scale mining because of unsafe working conditions and serious environmental impacts, or informal, non-taxed status, there seems to be a realization that eradicating ASM is neither easy nor morally justifiable until and unless there is some alternative economic activity that offers hope to those whose livelihoods would be eliminated. Most countries now seem to recognize that driving the activity underground simply compounds the problems of child labour, environmental damage and occupational hazards. These problems are very real and cry out for action. But a cooperative and supportive approach by the authorities is likely to get much further than punitive measures. The Plan of Implementation explicitly recognizes ASM as a potential source of sustainable livelihoods.[32]

Mining and biodiversity

Specific and concrete results of WSSD included the announcement of a dialogue between the newly formed International Council on Mining and Metals (ICMM) and the World Conservation Union (IUCN) on mining that may impact protected areas.[33] This is a very useful step; there are a number of extremely difficult but important issues to deal with. They range from the problem of 'paper parks' – protected areas that may exist on paper but where the resources available to manage them are so inadequate to the task that resources are being rapidly degraded – to the question of the propriety of boundaries of many protected areas where it is now known that the most important resources in conservation terms are outside existing boundaries; to the question of what kinds of mineral exploitation are – and are not – consistent with the purposes for which protected areas were created. This dialogue appears set to proceed despite various attempts to derail it.[34]

A sustainable development support facility

Clearly a vision is emerging in which sustainable development requires cooperative action between different interests in the sector. Together, communities, governments, labour, NGOs and companies can do much for development that none of them can do on its own. But some of these participants lack the resources and the capacity to advance their own interests or hold up their end of partnerships. MMSD proposed the creation of a facility to serve as an independent capacity building resource for communities and governments in areas impacted by mining development. This would be a stand-alone facility perhaps sponsored by or supported by the World Bank. It would supply capacity building help to national and local government and communities, among other things giving them support to be effective participants in developing the Community Sustainable Development Plans that MMSD sees as a principal institutional improvement.

The World Bank has announced its support for MMSD's proposal. There was hope of its further elaboration and the development of concrete steps to its creation at WSSD. While the idea is still moving forward, there was no dramatic announcement of progress on this front at the summit.

For the time being, the Global Dialogue described above is the principal – in fact the only – ongoing institutional home for continuing discussion and work towards further progress in the minerals sector's contribution to sustainable development.

Notes

1   There has been, for example, no shortage of allegations that Oxfam International is acting from sinister motives, or trying to revive the SenderoLuminoso guerrilla movement in Peru, as a result of its questioning of the proposed Tambo Grande mining project in Peru.

2   Position paper of Friends of the Earth International, www.foei.org/mining/mssd.html.

3   CONACAMI; see www.conacamiperu.org/.

4   For example Mining Watch Canada, and other signatories of the 'London Declaration'; www.minesandcommunities.org/Charter/londondec.htm.

5   www.icmm.com.

6   www.globalminingcampaign.org.

7   www.wmmf.org; www.camma.org.

8   See ICMM Toronto Declaration, www.icmm.com/uploads/1~FinalJuly2.pdf, and the ICMM Charter, www.icmm.com/html/charter_intro.php.

9   The murder of Jafar Siddiq Hamzah, an NGO activist who had been advising MMSD, in August 2000 was another factor in this decision.

10 Centro de Investigacion y Planificacion del Medio Ambiente (CIPMA) and the Mining Policy Research Initiative (MPRI) of the International Development Research Centre (IDRC) (2002) *Mineria, Minerales y Desarrollo Sustentable en America del Sur.*

11 University of the Witswatersrand (2002) *Mining, Minerals and Sustainable Development in Southern Africa.*

12 Australian Minerals and Energy Environment Foundation (2002) *Facing the Future.*

13 International Institute for Sustainable Development (IISD) (2002) *Towards Change: The Work and Results of MMSD – North America.*

14 International Institute for Sustainable Development (IISD) (2002) *Seven Questions to Sustainability: How to Assess the Contribution of Mining and Minerals Activities.*

15 International Institute for Sustainable Development (IISD) (2002) *Learning from the Future, Alternative Scenarios for the North American Mining and Minerals Industry.*

16 International Institute for Sustainable Development (IISD) (2002) *Learning from the Future, A Profile of the North American Mining Sector.*

17 See for example the South American work reported in *Mineria, Minerales y Desarrollo Sustentable en America del Sur*, note 10 above, which included national-level consultative processes in Brazil, Chile, Peru, Bolivia and Ecuador.

18 Even so, a full analysis of the budget shows that we devoted more than half the total to what would be considered as mainstream environment issues.

19 See Final Notes from the Strategic Planning Workshop, www.iied.org/mmsd/mmsd_pdfs/final_notes_4_6_may.pdf. As seen from the list of attendees beginning on page 19, this was a very diverse group in terms of national origin, personal experience and attitudes towards the mining industry; it included a number of respected and notable critics of the industry.

20 See the website at www.iied.org/pdf/45_Consultation_doc.pdf.

21 www.iied.org/pdf/49_Bulletin_3.pdf.

22 See www.iied.org/pdf/64_Prop_Outline_Draft_Rep.pdf.

23 A list of these workshops appears on page 417 of *Breaking New Ground*; the proceedings and attendance lists for all of them are available on the CD in the back of *Breaking New Ground*, and on the IIED website, www.iied.org/mmsd.

24 Many of these background studies will ultimately appear as separate books or other publications. Two that have already appeared are Zillman et al (2002) and Tilton (2003).
25 A classic of this genre is the call of Mining Watch Canada and some other organizations for a world moratorium on new mining projects, to be proclaimed by some authority the existence of which has yet to be detected.
26 See IIED (2002, pp409–10). See also www.mining.wits.ac.za/PROPOSAL% 20FOR%20A%20GLOBAL%20AGREEMENT%20ON%20%20MMSD.doc.
27 www.nrcan.gc.ca/media/newsreleases/2002/2002102_e.htm.
28 Paragraph 10 d. See www.johannesburgsummit.org/html/documents/summit_docs/ 131302_wssd_report_reissued.pdf.
29 op cit para 46 c.
30 op cit para 46.
31 op cit para 58 g.
32 op cit para 10 d.
33 See www.iucn.org/info_and_news/press/miningicmm.pdf; www.iucn.org/info_ and_news/press/miningdoc.pdf; and www.icmm.com.
34 See for example Burton (1999).

References

Burton, B (1999) 'IUCN Softens Parks Policy to Appease ICME', *Mining Monitor*, vol 4, no 3, Mineral Policy Institute, New South Wales, Australia, p3

IIED (2002) *Breaking New Ground*, Earthscan, London

Tilton, John E (2003) *On Borrowed Time? Assessing the Threat of Mineral Depletion,* Resources For the Future.

Young, J and Septoff, A (eds) (2002) *Digging for Change: Towards a Responsible Minerals Future. An NGO and Community Perspective,* Global Mining Campaign, Washington, DC, available at www.rosiamontana.org/documents/pdf/diggingforchange.pdf

Zillman, Donald M, Lucas, Alastair and Pring, George (eds) (2002) *Human Rights in Natural Resource Development – Public Participation in the Sustainable Development of Mining and Energy Resources*, Oxford University Press, Oxford

Chapter 27

Corporate Citizenship: Revisiting the Relationship between Business, Good Governance and Sustainable Development

Halina Ward, IIED, Nicola Borregaard, RIDES and Paul Kapelus, African Institute of Corporate Citizenship

In plenary session at the 1992 Rio Earth Summit, Stefan Schmidheiny, chairman of the Business Council for Sustainable Development called for a bold new partnership between business and governments. 'Business must move beyond the traditional approach of back-door lobbying: governments must move beyond traditional over-reliance on command-and-control regulations' (Timberlake, 1992).

Agenda 21, the non-binding policy document adopted at Rio, stressed the need for cleaner production and responsible entrepreneurship. The notion of eco-efficiency – producing more while using less – was hailed as the way forward for businesses that wanted to link environment and development.

By the time of the 2002 World Summit on Sustainable Development in Johannesburg (WSSD), it was apparent that Agenda 21 had not aged well. The early 21st century agenda on business and sustainable development is both broader and deeper than that of the early 1990s. Eco-efficiency is still there, but 'corporate responsibility', 'corporate social responsibility' (CSR) and 'corporate citizenship' have all become mainstream terms in sustainable development thinking. Specialist corporate citizenship organizations have blossomed, new management and accounting tools have been developed, and issues have emerged within the business and sustainable development agenda that were not there at the time of Rio: business and conflict, business and human rights, business and sustainable livelihoods. And a powerful but divided 'corporate accountability' agenda has also emerged to challenge the widely held notion that corporate citizenship is all about voluntary business action to go beyond the 'baseline' of compliance with the laws of the countries in which businesses operate.

No sector or business model has a monopoly on responsible corporate citizenship. Good practice can be found in the indigenous businesses of the world's poorer countries as much as in the rich North. Yet many of the drivers for change in today's international corporate citizenship agenda lie with the concerns of Northern consumers, multinational corporations, financial institutions and international non-governmental organizations (NGOs).

The basis for many of the ideas in this paper is a bulletin board discussion that was hosted on the website of the Regional and International Networking Group between 18 February and 5 March 2002. The context was the run-up to WSSD. A majority of the participants reflected perspectives that drew on their experiences working with non-governmental organizations, communities and businesses in middle-income countries like South Africa, Chile and Pakistan. We have drawn on the bulletin board participants' insights in this chapter, with the aim of highlighting key elements of an agenda for business and sustainable development in the South.

The Challenge of Defining Corporate Social Responsibility

What is valued and defined as corporate social responsibility or corporate citizenship differs from one region or country to the next. The location of a particular operation and the socio-political circumstances should always be taken into account in arriving at locally appropriate definitions. How companies engage in the social responsibility agenda is very much dependent on how they choose to define social responsibility. For example, many people argue that a business case must be made for corporate social responsibility, and that issues of regulation and compliance with law should not be considered part of the agenda:

> *Corporate social responsibility is the concept that an enterprise is accountable for its impact on all relevant stakeholders. It is the continuing commitment by business to behave fairly and responsibly and contribute to economic development while improving the quality of life of the workforce and their families as well as of the local community and society at large* (Khurram Naayab, bulletin board participant).

From the business side, engagement with the corporate social responsibility agenda typically progresses through a number of stages (though not necessarily in a linear way). A first stage might be pure philanthropy (sometimes equated with the term 'corporate social investment' in South Africa), when businesses support community-based activities through donations of money or 'in-kind' contributions to charities or civil society based groups. Among managers in Latin America, opposition to the term philanthropy and its association with charity has been reported: 'Charity is OK, but it is something that belongs to the private behaviour of each individual. That is not part of the company's objectives, which are mainly the making of profits.' And often, the term is associated with unwelcome paternalism as distinct from a more 'partnership-based' approach to engagement between companies and organizations that might otherwise be viewed simply as beneficiaries of philanthropy.

Beyond philanthropy – in a stage described as 'corporate social responsibility' by bulletin board participants from Chile and South Africa – companies may approach engagement with community development as a business activity that needs to be managed, for example by establishing a corporate foundation. Activities are then developed in a systematic way, and companies may begin to take on board principles of sustainable development and seek to secure partnerships with government agencies, NGOs and other civil society organizations. Monitoring and evaluation methodologies are integrated into community development programmes and consideration is given to the long-term sustainability of projects once company support has ended. These efforts however remain within a framework of 'donor style' support to communities, without reference to the way the business itself is undertaken.

Beyond corporate social responsibility (terminology that has itself now been rejected by some business people who stress the one-way implications of the word 'responsibility') lies corporate citizenship. The practice of corporate citizenship involves recognition and strategic management of the full range of business functions with social or environmental dimensions. Making these links remains a challenge in many countries, and in many businesses, North and South:

> It seems that the whole discussion about impacts on the community is environmentally-technically biased, leaving the 'fuzzy' social issues to voluntary initiatives (Darinka Czischke, bulletin board participant).

There is still a strong perception among many stakeholders that companies invest resources in the corporate citizenship agenda simply to influence public perceptions without really changing the way that they do business. The structural problems of power inequalities in the relationship between companies and their external stakeholders threaten genuine progress, as does the 'mistrust created by the appalling actions of a number of free-riders'. Mistrust in turn fuels a growing demand that companies should be more accountable to stakeholders, both internal and external, for their actions. How to achieve that accountability – whether through national or international law, company reporting on impacts, participatory management or methods such as social auditing – is still a subject of hot debate:

> corporate social responsibility is not an alternative to profitability – or even necessarily in conflict with it. It is a WAY of doing business by which business managers 'internalize' externalities. When done well, this process generates greater profits – in the short term through innovation, in the medium term through reputation and in the longer term by creating new markets and anticipating new regulations (Faisal Shaheen, bulletin board participant).

CSR Drivers

Understanding what drives corporate citizenship in different contexts is critically important to the future evolution of the agenda. Significant challenges remain in getting the right balance of incentives for business practice that make the best possible contribution to sustainable development.

Many advocates of corporate citizenship stress the need to make a business case for responsible behaviour, since businesses are likely to respond most quickly to incentives that sustain or enhance business success. Lack of clarity over the extent of the case for business success through corporate citizenship – or indeed its relevance to the agenda – is a significant threat to progress:

> *there cannot be corporate responsibility without profit. We cannot negate the basis of a company's motivations. Its first responsibility is profits to its owners meaning most of the time shareholders and from there it can use corporate responsibility as another business tool. Corporate responsibility is related to profits as without them it cannot dedicate itself to corporate responsibility* (Ricardo Katz, bulletin board participant).

> *...various South African communities are very cynical about the 'do-good' announcements of companies whose primary goal is profit for their shareholders. For these rural (mining) and urban communities, the issue is about corporate accountability, in which these corporations must account to their workers and neighbouring communities for their actions – by providing access to information, access to justice, improved performance, and compensation for damages caused* (Chris Albertyn, bulletin board participant).

Table 27.1 highlights some of the other drivers that were addressed during the bulletin board discussion.

Risks and challenges

The practice of corporate citizenship has the potential to make a major contribution to sustainable development. But it also carries risks, some of which are particularly pronounced in developing countries. Others are common to the overall agenda and reflect the fact that it is still evolving.

Perhaps principal among the risks of the current corporate citizenship agenda is a failure to engage equitably with Southern stakeholders. Very often, environment and sustainable development policies have been introduced to the South by multinational companies. When the take-up of these policies in developing country subsidiaries is nourished by head offices, biases towards home country, global or national concerns can result – at the expense of approaches that build directly on local considerations and priorities. The advocacy of international NGOs in international fora where local organizations are often missing has at times exacerbated these biases. Many stakeholders in the South feel

Table 27.1 *Drivers of corporate social responsibility*

CSR driver	Significance to developing contexts
Personal ethics of individual entrepreneurs	In a number of instances it is the personal ethics of a CEO or another individual that drive the CSR agenda within a company. This alone cannot secure a sustainable organizational commitment to CSR since it depends on individual engagement.
Supply chain pressures from Northern trading partners	There is a greater move to adoption by companies of voluntary codes of conduct, driven by international financing requirements and head office reputation assurance. But there is yet to be a significant drive from Southern companies to adoption of voluntary codes of conduct beyond a reaction to supply chain pressures from Northern trading partners.
Laws and regulations	Effectively enforced, law can be a significant driver of responsible behaviour. But although legal frameworks for environmental responsibility have been developed in much of the world, legal frameworks that require management of the social impact of business activities are comparatively undeveloped. In many developing countries, perceptions are strong that any kind of new regulation, standards or enforcement simply discourage foreign direct investment.
Public relations and reputation assurance	Public relations considerations and reputation management are among the strongest drivers for businesses engaging in CSR. On the one hand, CSR is viewed by companies as a strategic tool for promotion of reputation and brand value. On the other hand, its potential to generate spin at the expense of real change is criticized.
Shareholder activism and investor relations	There is little experience of shareholder activism in the developing world. In the North, portfolio investors such as pension funds have traditionally been largely ignorant of environmental and social issues. Investors in the North are increasingly beginning to ask questions about the environmental and social practices of the companies that they invest in. Even so, even 'responsible' investors are still too reliant on limited voluntary company reporting and questionnaires filled in by companies themselves.
Social licence to operate	The notion that businesses need to secure a 'social licence to operate' from their stakeholders is widely touted as a significant driver for CSR. Increased time and expenditure in opening a new mine, demonstrable commitment to social advancement, and communication and cooperation with local stakeholders are among the requirements for businesses operating in the developing world.
Sustaining key aspects of the business	Enclave industries such as mining, tourism, plantations and agriculture often view certain social investments as critical to the success of their businesses. Building clinics to treat workers, spraying to prevent malaria outbreaks, providing education and treating water are some of the social development projects that businesses undertake. Companies that undertake these activities may create 'islands of development'. But history has demonstrated that in many cases these islands are fundamentally unsustainable because they rest on the continued profitability and investment of the businesses that fund them.

Table 27.1 *continued*

CSR driver	Significance to developing contexts
Cooperation in development	There are increasing examples of cooperation, partnerships and legislation that promote opportunities for social development such as public–private partnerships, decentralization and related policies such as Economic and Social Councils in Chile. It is becoming evident that so-called 'tri-sector partnerships' between businesses, NGOs and public institutions can promote more effective risk management and cost sharing while contributing to CSR.
Improving the business as a whole	A recognition that adoption of CSR practices has the potential to add value to businesses operating in the South is critical. The business imperative to manage social issues in society such as HIV and AIDS needs to be recognized.

that Northern NGOs have claimed and taken a leadership role for themselves, dictating terms without appropriate Southern involvement. The engagement of developing country stakeholders in the development of the existing body of guidelines for responsible business behaviour has been limited.

Further challenges arise from the fact that the corporate citizenship agenda is itself uncertain. For example, little is still known about the real impacts of CSR practices on the ground. Development and dissemination of monitoring and measurement tools to accompany the contemporary corporate citizenship agenda remains an important challenge. Furthermore, the extent to which measurement tools such as social audits are useful is still unclear. Critically for advocates of voluntary approaches to corporate citizenship, the lack of measurement tools also holds back growth in support for voluntary approaches among NGOs and local communities:

> *I believe that the greatest challenge to the corporate responsibility movement is that it has not agreed on any methodology for evaluating success or failure* (Elliot Schrage, bulletin board participant).

If a large body of guidelines for 'responsible' business behaviour have been developed, few have acquired prominence in the markets that they seek to influence. In countries where adoption of systematic corporate citizenship practices is recent, companies are often not used to evaluating social and environmental aspects of their behaviour, and independent studies are few and far between.

A second risk related to the inherent uncertainties of an immature agenda is more worrying. At the heart of the corporate citizenship agenda lies the task of defining and continuously redefining the role of companies as social actors. The corporate citizenship agenda draws attention to unclear definitions of the role of business in society, and particularly the challenge of drawing boundaries around expectations of business engagement in civil society, government and industry:

If we recognise the fact that governments and businesses are different types of institutions with different competencies and roles in society, I believe it would be a lot … easier to define the boundaries (Mokhethi Moshoeshoe, bulletin board participant).

In most industrialized countries, business activity takes place in the context of institutional and social networks that are, to a greater or lesser extent, well defined. Businesses are able to develop corporate citizenship practices within a well-defined social framework. In contrast, in many parts of the developing world, businesses in general face weak public institutions and public policy frameworks, and a lack of financial resources. Poverty, limited training possibilities and social organizations that are weak or very specific to their local context are common. Guidelines on corporate citizenship that are elaborated in industrialized country contexts cannot simply be transferred to these contexts.

Businesses need to arrive at a delicate balance between contributing to delivery of public goods and strengthening public institutions on the one hand, and taking over public functions on the other. Lack of strong local government structures and regulatory frameworks carry the risk that the corporate citizenship programmes of individual companies could drive out or become a substitute for public programmes to tackle social, environmental or economic issues. There is a risk too that public agencies in developing countries may view the privately financed construction of local health care facilities and corporate support for education and training as a substitute for public spending.

When companies interact with civil society-based organizations, social responsibility has to be balanced carefully against the risks of civil society dependence on companies. Getting the right balance is only possible if all social actors are adequately empowered to participate independently in definition of local priorities and allocation of resources. In developing countries, communities very often lack the level of organization needed to have an impact on business practices. Support is required both to set up community organizations and to strengthen their voices as stakeholders. In this context it becomes absolutely essential for companies to build long-term relations with local stakeholders. This is one part of a broader development challenge for businesses: to move beyond strategic approaches that create small 'islands' of engagement to sustain broader contributions to developmental processes in society.

Power imbalances between companies and communities have to be tackled through public sector policies that, over time, foster the development of strong civil society. The Venezuelan corporate citizenship practitioner, Yolanda de Venanzi, puts it very clearly: 'Corporate citizenship initiatives should stress the promotion of programmes that fit the goals of enhancing productive social values and the participation of local stakeholders in social development' (de Venanzi, 2002).

In many countries of the world, corporate citizenship has been pushed by non-profit organizations that have been set up by industry. While these organizations have certainly contributed to promoting responsible business behaviour, it is important to differentiate them from the civil society-based NGOs whose participation is vital for the monitoring and evaluation of CSR activities.

Business leadership is certainly important in promoting the uptake of corporate citizenship practices in areas where they are not established. But an exaggerated emphasis on leaders bears the risk of creating a two-class business environment: businesses that practice corporate citizenship and those that do not. The percentage of overall economic output from small and medium-sized companies is extremely large in developing countries. Significant challenges remain to analyse what corporate citizenship means for small and medium-sized companies in developing countries and to begin to apply the concept more systematically in this context. Corporate citizenship must not become restricted to business elites; it must not become an agenda that favours the interests of large corporations over smaller businesses that operate at the level of the 'human economy'.

Reorienting the Agenda

A corporate citizenship agenda that was shaped more by the insights and views of organizations in the South might look radically different. Creating the space for such a shift to take place will mean building the rights and the capacity of civil society, and especially community-based organizations, to engage more effectively with companies of all sectors and sizes even in the face of economic power imbalances. It will mean viewing poor people not as objects of corporate citizenship, but as key partners in its realization. It means designing monitoring systems for the local community, not only for shareholders or international investment groups. It might mean rejecting the tendency to seek harmonization in standards for responsible business behaviour beyond a minimum baseline below which no company anywhere in the world should be allowed to fall. Instead, the corporate citizenship agenda of the future could mean celebrating diversity in values and in regional distinctions in business practice.

There is a recognition too that fostering 'social entrepreneurs' and 'civic entrepreneurship' is important to the overall health and well-being of societies. Social entrepreneurship can build shared values, rooted locally, that can in turn inform the business world, generating new models for sustainable entrepreneurship that reflect more directly the values of the communities in which they are based.

The economic globalization agenda and its critics have themselves been major drivers of the contemporary corporate citizenship agenda. Economic liberalization punishes uncompetitive 'sick' firms and sectors without placing any inherent value on indigenous entrepreneurial activity. Critics of economic liberalism argue that enhancing the health of the domestic sector, rather than feeding the labour resource needs of foreign investors, should be a priority. For many stakeholders based in developing countries, these kinds of considerations – the architecture of economic liberalism – deserve to be centre stage. But the connections between the arguments of economic globalization critics and the corporate citizenship agenda are often not made. The rhetoric of corporate citizenship is principally about encouraging best practice. Censuring bad practice is too often considered taboo.

Corporate citizenship – under the umbrella of sustainable development – has an environmental, a social and an economic dimension. The 'fourth pillar' of sustainable development – governance – underpins all of these. But so far the economic dimension of corporate citizenship has not received nearly so much attention as it deserves:

> *...What we also need to ... demand of TNCs [transnational corporations] is that they display that they are knowledgeable and sensitive to the indigenous needs of the market through their market penetration and development strategies. Otherwise, loan pushing and the project implementation of white elephant projects will continue* (Faisal Shaheen, bulletin board participant).

The brand value that generates so much of the 'business case' for corporate citizenship often rests on the intermediaries in rich countries. Marketing and branding professionals in the North and the value added that their activities generate help to sustain the business case for responsible behaviour. Full recognition of the economic dimension of corporate citizenship might call for redistribution of financial rewards along the production chain.

When we gathered our thoughts from the bulletin board discussion in May 2002, we saw the World Summit on Sustainable Development as an opportunity to take stock. Partnerships were shaping up to be a key feature, with WSSD offering a home for so-called 'Type 2' partnership-based commitments to implement core WSSD themes. Over 220 were announced in advance of the summit, and 60 during the summit itself. The partnership theme was an interesting innovation in tune with a network governance theme that can only gather importance as the 21st century goes on. But in practice the partnerships announced at WSSD are likely to prove of limited value to progress in the CSR agenda. Relatively few attracted substantive business engagement; few involved public agencies in developing countries; and there is no clear follow-up mechanism agreed at international level to ensure that the partnerships announced around WSSD stay on track.

It was clear in the run-up to WSSD that a key test of credibility would be a capacity to consider voluntary approaches to corporate citizenship and more contentious issues of corporate accountability and 'worst practice' in a balanced way. Both are critically important elements in efforts to orient business activity towards sustainable development. In the event, a balance was struck in the political messages that came out of WSSD ... just.

The WSSD Plan of Implementation includes references to a number of emergent themes in development aspects of the corporate citizenship agenda: access to services; elimination of child labour; promotion of small and medium-sized enterprises (SMEs); community-based partnerships linking urban and rural people and enterprises as a contribution to food availability and affordability. The sustainable production and consumption agenda, too little tied to corporate citizenship, is there, expressly linked to a paragraph on voluntary corporate responsibility and accountability. Paragraph 17 reflects key features of the mainstream corporate citizenship agenda: multi-stakeholder dialogue, work-based partnerships, codes of conduct, public reporting on environmental and social issues. Its principal weakness is that it does not underscore a need for equity in the development and implementation of these private initiatives, for example so that they do not unfairly discriminate against producers in developing countries, or take account of local perspectives in countries of production:

> *Globalization should be fully inclusive and equitable, and there is a strong need for policies and measures at the national and international levels, formulated and implemented with the full and effective participation of developing countries and countries with economies in transition, to help them to respond effectively to those challenges and opportunities. This will require urgent action at all levels to...*

> *Actively promote corporate responsibility and accountability, based on the Rio Principles, including through the full development and effective implementation of inter-governmental agreements and measures, international initiatives and public–private partnerships, and appropriate national regulations, and support continuous improvement in corporate practices in all countries* (United Nations, 2002).

A separate key paragraph focuses on corporate accountability. The closely negotiated text of paragraph 49 forms part of a chapter on sustainable development in a globalizing world, which includes in its preamble a recognition of a need for globalization to be 'fully inclusive and equitable'. Some countries were concerned that the reference in the paragraph to inter-governmental agreements and measures might subsequently provide a measure of support for NGO-led efforts to promote new inter-governmental mechanisms for corporate accountability. Indeed, after efforts to secure an express statement to this effect were blocked, the US lodged an explanatory note which sets out its understanding that paragraph 49 'refers to existing inter-governmental agreements and international initiatives'.

WSSD was probably never going to be the right process to deliver a blueprint for what is needed: a new deal that moves discussion on the corporate citizenship agenda and its links to economic globalization to the South. Neither, thankfully, does it stand in the way.

References

de Venanzi, (2002) 'Special Issue on International Perspectives of Corporate Citizenship', *The Journal of Corporate Citizenship*, vol 5, Spring

Timberlake, L (1992) 'Changing Business Attitudes', in IIED *Earth Summit '92*, Regency Press Corporation, London

United Nations (2002) *World Summit on Sustainable Development Plan of Implementation*, UN doc A/CONF.199/20*, paras 47 and 49

Index

Page references in *italics* refer to tables, figures and boxes

DATE DUE

AUG 2 5 2008		
DEC 1 9 2008		
MAY 1 5 2009		
MAR 2 3 REC'D		
GAYLORD		PRINTED IN U.S.A.